NNUAL EDITIONS

ild Growth and Development 11/12

teenth Edition

TORS

en N. Junn
fornia State University, Fresno

en Junn is a professor of psychology and associate provost at California State University, sno. She received her BS with distinction in psychology and with high honors from the Univer- y of Michigan and her MA and PhD in cognitive and developmental psychology from Princeton niversity. Dr. Junn's areas of research include college teaching effectiveness, educational equity, culty development, and public policy as it affects children and families.

hris J. Boyatzis
Bucknell University

Chris Boyatzis is professor of psychology at Bucknell University and instructor at the Danish Institute for Study Abroad in Copenhagen, Denmark. He received a BA with distinction in psychology from Boston University and his MA and PhD in developmental psychology from Brandeis University. His primary interests are religious and spiritual development and cultural influences on child development. He is Associate Editor of the APA journal, *Psychology of Religion and Spirituality,* and is on the editorial board of four other journals.

Mc Graw Hill

Connect
Learn
Succeed™

The McGraw-Hill Companies

Mc Graw Hill

Connect
Learn
Succeed™

ANNUAL EDITIONS: CHILD GROWTH AND DEVELOPMENT, EIGHTEENTH EDITION

Published by McGraw-Hill, a business unit of The McGraw-Hill Companies, Inc., 1221 Avenue
of the Americas, New York, NY 10020. Copyright © 2011 by The McGraw-Hill Companies, Inc.
All rights reserved. Previous editions © 2010, 2009, and 2008. No part of this publication may be
reproduced or distributed in any form or by any means, or stored in a database or retrieval system,
without the prior written consent of The McGraw-Hill Companies, Inc., including, but not limited
to, in any network or other electronic storage or transmission, or broadcast for distance learning.

Some ancillaries, including electronic and print components, may not be available to customers
outside the United States.

Annual Editions® is a registered trademark of The McGraw-Hill Companies, Inc.

Annual Editions is published by the **Contemporary Learning Series** group within
the McGraw-Hill Higher Education division.

1 2 3 4 5 6 7 8 9 0 QDB/QDB 1 0 9 8 7 6 5 4 3 2 1 0

ISBN 978–0–07–805075–6
MHID 0–07–805075–8
ISSN 1075–5217

Managing Editor: *Larry Loeppke*
Developmental Editor: *Dave Welsh*
Permissions Coordinator: *DeAnna Dausener*
Senior Marketing Communications Specialist: *Mary Klein*
Project Manager: *Robin A. Reed*
Design Coordinator: *Margarite Reynolds*
Buyer: *Sandy Ludovissy*
Media Project Manager: *Sridevi Palani*

Compositor: Laserwords Private Limited
Cover: © BananaStock/PunchStock (inset); The McGraw-Hill Companies, Inc./John Flournoy,
photographer (background)

Library in Congress Cataloging-in-Publication Data
Main entry under title: Annual Editions: Child Growth and Development. 2011/2012.
  1. Child Growth and Development—Periodicals. I. Junn, Ellen N., *comp.* II. Title: Child Growth
and Development.
658'.05

www.mhhe.com

Editors/Academic Advisory Board

Members of the Academic Advisory Board are instrumental in the final selection of articles for each edition of ANNUAL EDITIONS. Their review of articles for content, level, and appropriateness provides critical direction to the editors and staff. We think that you will find their careful consideration well reflected in this volume.

ANNUAL EDITIONS: Child Growth and Development 11/12
18th Edition

EDITORS

Ellen N. Junn
California State University, Fresno

Chris J. Boyatzis
Bucknell University

ACADEMIC ADVISORY BOARD MEMBERS

Editors/Academic Advisory Board continued

Preface

In publishing ANNUAL EDITIONS we recognize the enormous role played by magazines, newspapers, and journals of the public press in providing current, first-rate educational information in a broad spectrum of interest areas. Many of these articles are appropriate for students, researchers, and professionals seeking accurate, current material to help bridge the gap between principles and theories and the real world. These articles, however, become more useful for study when those of lasting value are carefully collected, organized, indexed, and reproduced in a low-cost format, which provides easy and permanent access when the material is needed. That is the role played by ANNUAL EDITIONS.

We are delighted to welcome you to this eighteenth edition of *Annual Editions: Child Growth and Development 11/12*. The amazing sequence of events of prenatal development that lead to the birth of a baby is an awe-inspiring process. Perhaps more intriguing is the question of what the future may hold for this newly arrived baby. For instance, will this child become a doctor, a lawyer, an artist, a beggar, or a thief? Although philosophers and prominent thinkers such as Charles Darwin and Sigmund Freud have long speculated about the importance of infancy on subsequent development, not until the 1960s did the scientific study of infants and young children flourish.

Since then, research and theory in infancy and childhood have exploded, resulting in a wealth of new knowledge about child development. Past accounts of infants and young children as passive, homogeneous organisms have been replaced with investigations aimed at studying infants and young children at a "microlevel"—as active individuals with many inborn competencies who are capable of shaping their own environment—as well as at a "macrolevel"—by considering the larger context surrounding the child. In short, children are not "blank slates," and development does not take place in a vacuum; children arrive with many skills and grow up in a complex web of social, historical, political, economic, and cultural spheres.

As was the case for previous editions, we hope to achieve at least four major goals with this volume. First, we hope to present you with the latest research and thinking to help you better appreciate the complex interactions that characterize human development in infancy and childhood. Second, in light of the feedback we received on previous editions, we have placed greater emphasis on important contemporary issues and challenges, exploring topics such as understanding development in the context of current societal and cultural influences. Third, attention is given to articles that also discuss effective, practical

applications. Finally, we hope that this anthology will serve as a catalyst to help students become more effective future professionals and parents.

To achieve these objectives, we carefully selected articles from a variety of sources, including scholarly research journals and texts as well as semiprofessional journals and popular publications. Every selection was scrutinized for readability, interest level, relevance, and currency. In addition, we listened to the valuable input and advice from members of our board, consisting of faculty from a range of institutions of higher education, including community and liberal arts colleges as well as research and teaching universities. We are most grateful to the advisory board as well as to the excellent editorial staff of McGraw-Hill/Contemporary Learning Series.

Annual Editions: Child Growth and Development is organized into five major units. Unit 1 includes articles regarding some advances in trying to prevent and help premature babies, as well as how genetic and prenatal stress can affect development. Unit 2 presents information regarding brain development, perception, memory, and language in infants and young children, as well as information on schooling. Unit 3 focuses on social and emotional development, including peers, gender socialization and play, bullying and antisocial behavior, as well as issues of institutional deprivation, antisocial behavior, and resiliency. Unit 4 is devoted to parenting and family issues such as infant attachment, discipline, effects of divorce, sibling interactions, cultural differences in parental control and gay and lesbian parents. Finally, Unit 5 focuses on larger cultural and societal influences such as media and marketing, and on special challenges (e.g., obesity, autism, and traumatic situations such as coping with terrorism, war, or natural disasters).

Instructors for large lecture courses may wish to adopt this anthology as a supplement to a basic text, whereas instructors for smaller sections might also find the readings effective for promoting student presentations or for stimulating discussions and applications. Whatever format is utilized, it is our hope that the instructor and the students will find the readings interesting, illuminating, and provocative.

As the title indicates, *Annual Editions: Child Growth and Development* is by definition a volume that undergoes continual review and revision. Thus, we welcome and encourage your comments and suggestions for future editions of this volume. Simply fill out and return the *article rating form* found at the end of this book. Best wishes, and we look forward to hearing from you!

Ellen N. Junn
Editor

Chris J. Boyatzis
Editor

Contents

UNIT 1
Conception to Birth

UNIT 2
Cognition, Language, and Learning

The concepts in bold italics are developed in the article. For further expansion, please refer to the Topic Guide.

The concepts in bold italics are developed in the article. For further expansion, please refer to the Topic Guide.

UNIT 3
Social and Emotional Development

The concepts in bold italics are developed in the article. For further expansion, please refer to the Topic Guide.

UNIT 4
Parenting and Family Issues

The concepts in bold italics are developed in the article. For further expansion, please refer to the Topic Guide.

The concepts in bold italics are developed in the article. For further expansion, please refer to the Topic Guide.

UNIT 5
Cultural and Societal Influences

The concepts in bold italics are developed in the article. For further expansion, please refer to the Topic Guide.

The concepts in bold italics are developed in the article. For further expansion, please refer to the Topic Guide.

Correlation Guide

The *Annual Editions* series provides students with convenient, inexpensive access to current, carefully selected articles from the public press. **Annual Editions: Child Growth and Development 11/12** an easy-to-use reader that presents articles on important topics such as *fertility technology, prenatal development, brain development,* and many more. For more information on *Annual Editions* and other *McGraw-Hill Contemporary Learning Series* titles, visit www.mhhe.com/cls.

This convenient guide matches the units in **Annual Editions: Child Growth and Development 11/12** with the corresponding chapters in three of our best-selling McGraw-Hill Child Development textbooks by Santrock and Papalia et al.

Annual Editions: Child Growth and Development 11/12	Children, 11/e by Santrock	Child Development: An Introduction, 13/e by Santrock	A Child's World: Infancy through Adolescence, 12/e by Papalia et al.
Unit 1: Conception to Birth	**Chapter 2:** Biological Beginnings **Chapter 4:** Birth	**Chapter 2:** Biological Beginnings **Chapter 3:** Prenatal Development and Birth	**Chapter 3:** Forming a New Life: Conception, Heredity, and Environment **Chapter 4:** Pregnancy and Prenatal Development **Chapter 5:** Birth and the Newborn Baby
Unit 2: Cognition, Language, and Learning	**Chapter 6:** Cognitive Development in Infancy **Chapter 9:** Cognitive Development in Early Childhood **Chapter 12:** Cognitive Development in Middle and Late Childhood **Chapter 15:** Cognitive Development in Adolescence	**Chapter 6:** Cognitive Developmental Approaches **Chapter 7:** Information Processing **Chapter 8:** Intelligence **Chapter 9:** Language Development	**Chapter 7:** Cognitive Development during the First Three Years **Chapter 10:** Cognitive Development in Early Childhood **Chapter 13:** Cognitive Development in Middle Childhood **Chapter 16:** Cognitive Development in Adolescence
Unit 3: Social and Emotional Development	**Chapter 7:** Socioemotional Development in Infancy **Chapter 10:** Socioemotional Development in Early Childhood **Chapter 13:** Socioemotional Development in Middle and Late Childhood **Chapter 16:** Socioemotional Development in Adolescence	**Chapter 10:** Emotional Development **Chapter 11:** The Self and Identity **Chapter 12:** Gender **Chapter 13:** Moral Development	**Chapter 8:** Psychosocial Development during the First Three Years **Chapter 11:** Psychosocial Development in Early Childhood **Chapter 14:** Psychosocial Development in Middle Childhood **Chapter 17:** Psychosocial Development in Adolescence
Unit 4: Parenting and Family Issues	**Chapter 3:** Prenatal Development **Chapter 7:** Socioemotional Development in Infancy **Chapter 10:** Socioemotional Development in Early Childhood **Chapter 13:** Socioemotional Development in Middle and Late Childhood **Chapter 16:** Socioemotional Development in Adolescence	**Chapter 10:** Emotional Development **Chapter 13:** Moral Development **Chapter 14:** Families	
Unit 5: Cultural and Societal Influences	**Chapter 9:** Cognitive Development in Early Childhood **Chapter 10:** Socioemotional Development in Early Childhood **Chapter 13:** Socioemotional Development in Middle and Late Childhood **Chapter 16:** Socioemotional Development in Adolescence	**Chapter 9:** Language Development **Chapter 11:** The Self and Identity **Chapter 13:** Moral Development **Chapter 15:** Peers **Chapter 16:** Schools and Achievement **Chapter 17:** Culture and Diversity	

Topic Guide

This topic guide suggests how the selections in this book relate to the subjects covered in your course. You may want to use the topics listed on these pages to search the Web more easily.

On the following pages a number of websites have been gathered specifically for this book. They are arranged to reflect the units of this Annual Editions reader. You can link to these sites by going to www.mhhe.com/cls.

All the articles that relate to each topic are listed below the bold-faced term.

Aggression
22. A Profile of Bullying at School
25. The Role of Neurobiological Deficits in Childhood Antisocial Behavior

Antisocial behavior
28. Parental Divorce and Children's Adjustment
36. Childhood's End

Attachment
6. New Advances in Understanding Sensitive Periods in Brain Development
17. A Neurobiological Perspective on Early Human Deprivation
26. Children of Lesbian and Gay Parents
27. Evidence of Infants' Internal Working Models of Attachment

Autism
39. The Positives of Caregiving: Mothers' Experiences Caregiving for a Child with Autism
40. Three Reasons Not to Believe in an Autism Epidemic

Birth and birth defects
1. New Calculator Factors Chances for Very Premature Infants
2. Genes in Context: Gene–Environment Interplay and the Origins of Individual Differences in Behavior
3. Effects of Prenatal Social Stress on Offspring Development: Pathology or Adaptation?

Brain development
6. New Advances in Understanding Sensitive Periods in Brain Development
17. A Neurobiological Perspective on Early Human Deprivation
25. The Role of Neurobiological Deficits in Childhood Antisocial Behavior

Child abuse
17. A Neurobiological Perspective on Early Human Deprivation
35. Trials for Parents Who Chose Faith over Medicine
38. The Epidemic That Wasn't

Classroom management
14. When Should a Kid Start Kindergarten?
37. How to Win the Weight Battle

Cognitive development
4. Infants' Differential Processing of Female and Male Faces
5. The Other-Race Effect Develops during Infancy: Evidence of Perceptual Narrowing
6. New Advances in Understanding Sensitive Periods in Brain Development
7. Contributions of Neuroscience to Our Understanding of Cognitive Development
9. Language and Children's Understanding of Mental States
12. Future Thinking in Young Children
21. Children's Social and Moral Reasoning about Exclusion
27. Evidence of Infants' Internal Working Models of Attachment
24. Playtime in Peril

Cross-cultural issues
5. The Other-Race Effect Develops during Infancy: Evidence of Perceptual Narrowing
24. Playtime in Peril

Culture
8. It's Fun, but Does It Make You Smarter?
26. Children of Lesbian and Gay Parents
34. Goodbye to Girlhood
37. How to Win the Weight Battle
41. Getting Back to the Great Outdoors

Development
1. New Calculator Factors Chances for Very Premature Infants
6. New Advances in Understanding Sensitive Periods in Brain Development
14. When Should a Kid Start Kindergarten?
21. Children's Social and Moral Reasoning about Exclusion
26. Children of Lesbian and Gay Parents
27. Evidence of Infants' Internal Working Models of Attachment
24. Playtime in Peril
33. Siblings Play Formative, Influential Role as 'Agents of Socialization'

Developmental disabilities
17. A Neurobiological Perspective on Early Human Deprivation
41. Getting Back to the Great Outdoors

Discipline
29. Within-Family Differences in Parent–Child Relations across the Life Course

Drug use/abuse
38. The Epidemic That Wasn't

Economic issues
24. Playtime in Peril

Education
8. It's Fun, but Does It Make You Smarter?
14. When Should a Kid Start Kindergarten?
24. Playtime in Peril
37. How to Win the Weight Battle
41. Getting Back to the Great Outdoors

Emotional development
7. Contributions of Neuroscience to Our Understanding of Cognitive Development
9. Language and Children's Understanding of Mental States
17. A Neurobiological Perspective on Early Human Deprivation
26. Children of Lesbian and Gay Parents
27. Evidence of Infants' Internal Working Models of Attachment
34. Goodbye to Girlhood

Evolution
4. Infants' Differential Processing of Female and Male Faces

Internet References

The following Internet sites have been selected to support the articles found in this reader. These sites were available at the time of publication. However, because websites often change their structure and content, the information listed may no longer be available. We invite you to visit www.mhhe.com/cls for easy access to these sites.

Annual Editions: Child Growth and Development 11/12

General Sources

American Academy of Pediatrics
www.aap.org

This organization provides data for optimal physical, mental, and social health for all children.

CYFERNet
www.cyfernet.mes.umn.edu

The Children, Youth, and Families Education Research Network is sponsored by the Cooperative Extension Service and USDA's Cooperative State Research Education and Extension Service. This site provides practical research-based information in areas including health, childcare, family strengths, science, and technology.

KidsHealth
http://kidshealth.org

This site was developed to help parents find reliable children's health information. Enter the Parents site to find such topics as General Health, Nutrition and Fitness, First Aid and Safety, Growth and Development, Positive Parenting, and more.

National Institute of Child Health and Human Development
www.nichd.nih.gov

The NICHD conducts and supports research on the reproductive, neurobiological, developmental, and behavioral processes that determine and maintain the health of children, adults, families, and populations.

UNIT 1: Conception to Birth

Babyworld
www.babyworld.com

Extensive information on caring for infants can be found at this site. There are also links to numerous other related sites.

Children's Nutrition Research Center (CNRC)
www.bcm.tmc.edu/cnrc

CNRC, one of six USDA/ARS (Agricultural Research Service) facilities, is dedicated to defining the nutrient needs of healthy children, from conception through adolescence, and pregnant and nursing mothers. The *Nutrition and Your Child* newsletter is of general interest and can be accessed from this site.

Zero to Three: National Center for Infants, Toddlers, and Families
www.zerotothree.org

This national organization is dedicated solely to infants, toddlers, and their families. It is headed by recognized experts in the field and provides technical assistance to communities, states, and the federal government. The site provides information that the organization gathers and disseminates through its publications.

UNIT 2: Cognition, Language, and Learning

Educational Resources Information Center (ERIC)
www.ed.gov/about/pubs/intro/pubdb.html

This website is sponsored by the U.S. Department of Education and will lead to numerous documents related to elementary and early childhood education, as well as other curriculum topics and issues.

National Association for the Education of Young Children (NAEYC)
www.naeyc.org

The National Association for the Education of Young Children provides a useful link from its home page to a site that provides resources for "Parents."

Parent's Action for Children
http://store.parentsactionstore.org/prostores/servlet/StoreFront

Information regarding early childhood development is provided on the video series, *I Am Your Child,* that's available on this site. Resources for parents and caregivers are available.

Project Zero
http://pzweb.harvard.edu

Harvard Project Zero, a research group at the Harvard Graduate School of Education, has investigated the development of learning processes in children and adults for 30 years. Today, Project Zero is building on this research to help create communities of reflective, independent learners, to enhance deep understanding within disciplines, and to promote critical and creative thinking. Project Zero's mission is to understand and enhance learning, thinking, and creativity in the arts and other disciplines for individuals and institutions.

Vandergrift's Children's Literature Page
www.scils.rutgers.edu/special/kay/sharelit.html

This site provides information about children's literature and links to a variety of resources related to literacy for children.

UNIT 3: Social and Emotional Development

Max Planck Institute for Psychological Research
www.mpg.de/english/institutesProjectsFacilities/instituteChoice/psychologische_forschung

Results from several behavioral and cognitive development research projects are available on this site.

National Child Care Information Center (NCCIC)
www.nccic.org

Information about a variety of topics related to childcare and development is available on this site. Links to the *Child Care Bulletin,* which can be read online, and to the ERIC database of online and library-based resources are available.

Internet References

Serendip

http://serendip.brynmawr.edu/serendip

Organized into five subject areas (brain and behavior, complex systems, genes and behavior, science and culture, and science education), Serendip contains interactive exhibits, articles, links to other resources, and a forum area for comments and discussion.

UNIT 4: Parenting and Family Issues

The National Association for Child Development (NACD)

www.nacd.org

This international organization is dedicated to helping children and adults reach their full potential. Its home page presents links to various programs, research, and resources in topics related to the family and society.

National Council on Family Relations

www.ncfr.com

This NCFR home page will lead you to articles, research, and a lot of other resources on important issues in family relations, such as stepfamilies, couples, and divorce.

Parenting and Families

www.cyfc.umn.edu

The University of Minnesota's Children, Youth, and Family Consortium site will lead you to many organizations and other resources related to divorce, single parenting, and stepfamilies, as well as information about other topics of interest in the study of children's development and the family.

Parentsplace.com: Single Parenting

www.parentsplace.com/family/archive/0,10693,239458,00.html

This resource focuses on issues concerning single parents and their children. Although the articles range from parenting children from infancy through adolescence, most of the articles deal with middle childhood.

National Stepfamily Resource Center

www.stepfam.org

This website is dedicated to educating and supporting stepfamilies and to creating a positive family image.

UNIT 5: Cultural and Societal Influences

Association to Benefit Children (ABC)

www.a-b-c.org

ABC presents a network of programs that includes child advocacy, education for disabled children, care for HIV-positive children, employment, housing, foster care, and daycare.

Children's Defense Fund

www.childrensdefense.org

CDF is a national proponent and advocate of policies and programs that safeguard children's needs in the areas of amelioration of poverty, protection from abuse and neglect, and increased access to healthcare and quality education.

Children Now

www.childrennow.org

Children Now uses research and mass communications to make the well-being of children a top priority across the nation. Current articles include information on the influence of media on children, working families, and health.

Council for Exceptional Children

www.cec.sped.org

This is the home page for the Council for Exceptional Children, a large professional organization that is dedicated to improving education for children with exceptionalities, students with disabilities, and/or the gifted child. It leads to the ERIC Clearinghouse on disabilities and gifted education and the National Clearinghouse for Professions in Special Education.

Prevent Child Abuse America

www.preventchildabuse.org

Dedicated to their child abuse prevention efforts, PCAA's site provides fact sheets and reports that include statistics, a public opinion poll, a 50-state survey, and other resource materials.

UNIT 1

Conception to Birth

Unit Selections

1. **New Calculator Factors Chances for Very Premature Infants,** Denise Grady
2. **Genes in Context: Gene–Environment Interplay and the Origins of Individual Differences in Behavior,** Francis A. Champagne and Rahia Mashoodh
3. **Effects of Prenatal Social Stress on Offspring Development: Pathology or Adaptation?,** Sylvia Kaiser and Norbert Sachser

Key Points to Consider

- Think about a relative, friend, or acquaintance who had a premature baby. What factors may have contributed to this premature birth—maternal age, health, stress, diet, family history of premature deliveries? If you want to minimize the risks of a premature delivery, what steps might you and your partner take? If you have a friend who gives birth to a premature baby, what suggestions or precautions might you give your friend in caring for their premature baby?

- Find a classmate and debate each other on whether you think genes or the environment are more influential during prenatal development. Cite data or evidence from the articles in this Unit 1 to support your arguments or refute those of your classmate. Explain why maternal stress might be adaptive or potentially beneficial to a fetus during prenatal development. Why might prenatal maternal stress be deleterious?

Student Website
www.mhhe.com/cls

Internet References

Babyworld
www.babyworld.com

Children's Nutrition Research Center (CNRC)
www.bcm.tmc.edu/cnrc

Zero to Three: National Center for Infants, Toddlers, and Families
www.zerotothree.org

Carefree ideas of starting a family as exemplified by the nursery rhyme, *"First comes love. Then comes marriage. Then comes baby in a baby carriage,"* do not always hold true across the United States. It may come as a surprise that the United States has a higher infant mortality rate among some ethnic groups than that found in most industrialized nations. In spite of the recent explosion of knowledge about prenatal development, knowledge about how to sustain and promote development in fetuses who are born prematurely still lags behind. If they survive, babies born prematurely or very prematurely face crushing challenges once outside of the protection and nurturance of the mother's womb. The author of "New Calculator Factors Chances for Very Premature Infants" discusses a new method of statistically assessing the chances of a very premature baby's survival and likelihood of disabilities available online with the National Institute of Child Health and Human Development. The vast majority of very premature babies will die, and of those who do survive, roughly half will sustain permanent and debilitating disabilities necessitating significant hospital and ongoing future medical costs that continue well beyond the intensive care provided by hospitals. This online calculator helps physicians and parents understand the odds when making difficult life decisions regarding their premature baby.

Parents often wonder how their children can be so remarkably different from one another even as infants. How influential are genes over environment or visa versa? This question of nature versus nurture is addressed by the authors of "Genes in Context: Gene–Environment Interplay and the Origins of Individual Differences in Behavior" who explain how the environment can determine which genes become activated or remain silent early in development, leading to individual differences. Similarly, in "Effects of Prenatal Social Stress on Offspring Development: Pathology or Adaptation?" the authors cite new research showing that prolonged prenatal stress can result in hormonal changes that may affect the masculinization of the baby.

All of these articles highlight the powerful and enduring effects of the prenatal environment in shaping and supporting the genetic foundations of a given infant, and underscore the critical importance of optimal prenatal development.

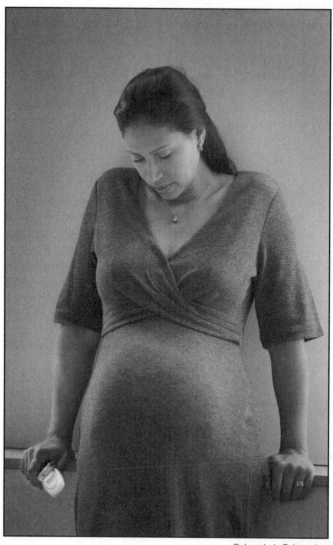

© Jose Luis Pelaez, Inc.

New Calculator Factors Chances for Very Premature Infants

DENISE GRADY

Researchers are reporting that they have developed a new way to help doctors and parents make some of the most agonizing decisions in medicine, about how much treatment to give tiny, extremely premature infants.

These are infants at the edge of viability, weighing less than 2.2 pounds and born after 22 to 25 weeks of pregnancy, far ahead of the normal 40 weeks. About 40,000 babies a year are born at this very early stage in the United States.

The new method uses an online calculator developed for such cases factoring in traits like birth weight and sex and generating statistics on chances of the baby's survival and the likelihood of disabilities (www.nichd.nih.gov/neonatalestimates).

The statistics are not a personal prediction. They estimate risk based on data from similar infants in a large study being published on Thursday in *The New England Journal of Medicine*.

Certain factors gave babies an advantage. At any given gestational age, they were more likely to survive and escape serious disability if they weighed more than others, if they were singletons rather than twins or multiples or if their mothers had been given steroids before birth to help the fetal lungs to mature.

Girls also fared better than boys of the same age, a factor doctors have known a long time without being able to explain.

Any of those factors was about as good as being a week older, which makes an enormous difference in development from 22 to 25 weeks' pregnancy, the researchers said. The finding means that a girl at 23 weeks could be as strong as a boy at 24.

"If you could take what the girls have and give it to the boys, we'd be one step ahead of the game," said Dr. Rosemary D. Higgins, an author of the study and a program scientist at the Neonatal Research Network of the National Institute of Child Health and Human Development.

Although some extremely premature infants do well, many die, sometimes after weeks or months of painful invasive procedures in the intensive care unit. Survivors often suffer brain damage, behavior problems, vision and hearing loss and other disabilities.

Outcomes are nearly impossible to predict at birth. Doctors and parents struggle to decide when aggressive treatment seems reasonable—and when death or severe disability seems so likely, even with treatment, that it would be kinder to avoid painful procedures and provide just "comfort care," letting nature take its course and letting the child die.

These decisions, made every day in hospitals around the country, are "heart wrenching and passionate," Dr. Higgins said. "No one ever thinks they're going to be in this situation, and it's difficult, for families and also for physicians."

Dr. Higgins said the study and the calculator were part of an effort to give doctors and parents more solid evidence to make decisions. She said people might be misled by occasional reports of tiny "miracle babies" who beat the odds and wrongly imagined high rates of survival and good health.

Dr. Higgins said she had no idea what overall effect the study and calculator might have on medical practice or whether they would lead to more or less treatment of extremely premature infants. Two families in the exact same situation could easily make opposite decisions about whether to pursue treatment.

Currently, decisions about using respirators, intravenous feeding and other forms of intensive care are mostly based on estimates of a baby's gestational age—how far along the pregnancy was. Intensive care is often given to infants born in the 25th week, but not the 22nd. The hardest judgment calls are for babies in the 23rd and 24th weeks.

Plugging numbers into the calculator shows that two infants with the same gestational age, the usual criterion to decide treatment, can have quite different odds of survival and disability.

For instance, a 24-week-old two-pound male twin whose mother did not receive steroids has survival odds of 69 percent and a 50 percent chance of having a severe impairment. A female twin the same age and weight has survival odds of 86 percent and a 23 percent chance of severe impairment.

In theory, at least, the calculator would seem to favor treating girls, because, all else being equal, their odds for survival are better.

The study included 4,446 infants born at 22 to 25 weeks at 19 hospitals in the Neonatal Research Network; 744, generally the smallest and most premature, did not receive intensive care, and all died. The babies were assessed at birth, and the survivors were examined again shortly before turning 2.

Over all, half the infants died, half the survivors had neurological impairments, and half the impairments were severe.

Many survivors spent months in the hospital, at a typical cost of $3,400 a day. The researchers estimated that if all babies born at 22 to 23 weeks received intensive care, for every 100 infants treated there would be 1,749 extra hospital days and zero to nine additional survivors, with zero to three having no impairment.

Dr. Eric C. Eichenwald, medical director of the newborn center at Texas Children's Hospital in Houston, said that the study was important and that its most striking finding was how large the benefits of the various factors could be.

Dr. Eichenwald said the calculator was "a way in which we can provide more accurate information to the process of counseling parents as to what the burdens of intensive care might be." Dr. Nehal A. Parikh, another author of the study, from the University of Texas Medical School at Houston, said he thought the statistics would help doctors in advising families.

"We lay out the facts, rather than our own opinions," Dr. Parikh said, "because we're not the ones taking these babies home."

Genes in Context

Gene–Environment Interplay and the Origins of Individual Differences in Behavior

Frances A. Champagne and Rahia Mashoodh

Historically, the question of the origins of individual differences in personality, aptitudes, and even physical features has led to debates over nature *versus* nurture. However, it is becoming increasingly clear that creating a division between genes and environment limits our understanding of the complex biological processes through which individual differences are achieved. The reality that the interaction between genes and environment is a critical feature of development is emerging as a central theme in laboratory studies and longitudinal analyses in human populations. However, appreciating the existence of this interaction is simply the first step in broadening our theoretical approach to the study of behavior. To move forward, we must ask "What do genes do?" and "How do genes and environments interact?" Recent studies combining molecular biology with the study of behavior may provide insight into these issues and perhaps even call into question our current understanding of mechanisms involved in the transmission of traits across generations. Here we will highlight these new findings and illustrate the importance of putting genes in context.

Laboratory and Longitudinal Approaches to Gene–Environment Interactions

Though recent advances in our ability to detect genetic variations have led to rapid progress in the study of gene-by-environment (G × E) effects, clues that G × E was critical in considering the origins of behavior have been available for a long time. In 1958, Cooper and Zubek published a report in which rats selectively bred to be either "maze-dull" or "maze-bright" were reared after weaning in either "enriched" environments containing increased sensory stimuli or "impoverished" environments containing limited sensory stimuli (Cooper & Zubek, 1958). In the rats reared under standard conditions, stable and heritable group differences in cognitive ability were observed in adulthood. However, maze-dull animals reared in an enriched environment showed a significant improvement in learning ability, and mazebright animals reared under impoverished conditions showed a significant decline in performance. This study provides evidence that, even when considering a genetically derived characteristic, our prediction of behavior must incorporate knowledge of the environmental context of development.

A more recent example of G × E comes from the Dunedin longitudinal study (Caspi et al., 2003), which explored the roles of variation in a gene that alters serotonin levels and exposure to stressful life events across a 20-year period in determining risk of depression. Levels of serotonin within neural circuits are altered by the number of serotonin transporter proteins, and in humans there are genetic variations that lead to either high or low levels of the serotonin transporter. The serotonin system has been implicated in variations in mood, and this system is the target of most pharmacological interventions in the treatment of depression. Among individuals within the Dunedin study, risk of depression was predicted by the interaction of serotonin transporter genotype and the number of stressful life events experienced. Thus, no differences in risk of depression emerged as a function of genotype when the number of stressful life events was low. However, when an individual had experienced a high frequency of stressful events, genotype effects were observed, with individuals possessing the low-serotonin-transporter-level gene variant being at greater risk of depression. Though certain genetic variations can lead to risk or resilience to psychological disorder (see Kim-Cohen & Gold, 2009, this issue), this "potential" may not be observed unless variation in the environment is considered.

Contextual Determinants of Gene Function

Empirical findings from G × E studies raise an important question: "If the effects of genetic variation can vary depending on characteristics of the environment, then what are environments doing to genes to alter their impact?" To address this question, we must first address the following question: "What do genes do?" Historically, *gene* was a term used to describe a unit of heritable material. Since the discovery of DNA, the study of genetics has come to mean the study of DNA, with *gene* defined as a particular sequence of DNA. Due to the complex nature of DNA, it is perhaps easier to employ an analogy that conveys the basic notions of gene function. Think of an individual's DNA as books in a library that have been ordered and arranged very precisely by a meticulous librarian. These books contain a wealth of knowledge and the potential to inspire whoever should choose to read them. Asking what DNA does is like asking what a book in this library does. Books sit on a shelf waiting to be read. Once read, the information in those books can have limitless consequences. Likewise, DNA sits in our cells and waits to be read by an enzyme called RNA polymerase, leading to the production of messenger RNA (mRNA)—a process referred to as *transcription* (Figure 1a). The mRNA transcript is a copy of the DNA sequence that can further be "translated" into protein. The reading, or *expression,* of DNA can, like the books in our library, have limitless consequences. However, without the active process that triggers such expression, this potential may never be realized. Importantly, it is the environment around the DNA that contains those critical factors that make it possible to read the DNA (Figure 1b; also see Cole, 2009, for extended discussion of the regulation of gene expression).

The control of gene expression is ultimately determined by how accessible the sequence of DNA is to factors within the cell that are involved in transcription. Influences that determine the expression of DNA without altering the sequence of DNA are referred to as epigenetic, meaning "in addition to genetic." One particular epigenetic mechanism that may have consequences for long-term changes in gene activity is DNA methylation (Figure 1c). DNA can become modified through the addition of a methyl chemical group to particular sites within the gene sequence. DNA methylation typically reduces the accessibility of DNA and can lead to "silencing" of the gene (Razin, 1998). In the library analogy, one can think of multiple factors that will influence the likelihood a book will or will not be read. Even books containing very valuable information may sit undisturbed and unread, gradually collecting dust. This may be particularly true if the book is hard to get to. It may be located on a shelf that is particularly difficult to reach or blocked by some piece of furniture. DNA methylation reduces the likelihood of transcription much in the same way that shifting furniture in a library can reduce the likelihood that a book will be read. The gene is there, but sits unread, collecting dust.

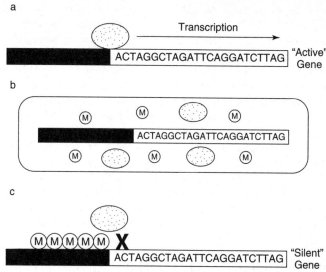

Figure 1 Illustration of the epigenetic control of gene expression and the environmental context of DNA. As shown in the top panel (a), genes consist of a sequence of DNA consisting of "C," "T," "A," and "G" nucleotides preceded by a promotor region of DNA (the black bar). The promoter region responds to factors that control the likelihood of transcription (reading of the DNA). In order for transcription to occur, enzymes that "read" the DNA (the gray oval) must bind to the promotor region of the gene. When this occurs, the gene is "active" and can alter the function of the cell. The environmental context of the gene, shown in the middle panel (b), includes factors that increase gene activity (i.e., enzymes that read the DNA, shown as gray ovals) and factors that decrease gene activity (i.e., methyl groups, illustrated as circles labeled "M"); these factors will determine the likelihood that a gene will be expressed. When a methyl chemical group attaches to the promotor region, as shown in the bottom panel (c), the enzymes that transcribe DNA are blocked and the gene becomes "silent"; this is referred to as DNA methylation.

Environmental Influences on Gene Activity

A recent breakthrough in our understanding of gene–environment interplay comes from studies exploring the epigenetic processes that are altered by an individual's experiences during development. Based primarily on studies in rodents, these paradigms address the question raised by G × E research: "What are environments doing to genes to alter their impact?" In rodents, variations in maternal care lead to individual differences in the expression of genes that alter the stress response. Low levels of glucocorticoid receptors (GR) within the hippocampus, a brain region critical for learning and memory, result in a prolonged response to stress. Analysis of DNA methylation within the regulatory region of the *GR* gene indicates that low levels of maternal care are associated with elevated levels of DNA methylation, which epigenetically silence this gene (Weaver et al., 2004). Moreover, the epigenetic status of the *GR* gene can be targeted pharmacologically in adulthood. Treatment with a drug that promotes increases in accessibility of DNA results in decreased *GR* methylation and a dramatic shift in the phenotype of adult offspring who received low levels of maternal care (Weaver et al., 2004). Conversely, when adult offspring

who experienced high levels of care are treated with a drug that increases the availability of methyl groups within the brain, they become indistinguishable from offspring who received low levels of maternal care (Weaver et al., 2005). These dynamic alterations in DNA methylation in adulthood have also been observed in studies of learning and memory (Miller & Sweatt, 2007). The experience of learning is associated with rapid changes in methylation of genes within the hippocampus, and if DNA methylation is inhibited there will be impairment in memory for the experience. These studies illustrate the role of epigenetic mechanisms in shaping the activity of the genome in response to environmental cues and demonstrate the plasticity that is possible through shifts in DNA methylation.

The prenatal period is characterized by rapid changes in brain development and is thus a sensitive time during which the quality of the environment can exert sustained effects on functioning. In rodents, exposure to chronic variable stress during the first trimester is associated with increased methylation of the regulatory region of the *GR* gene (Mueller & Bale, 2008). This effect could potentially be mediated by (a) stress-induced decreases in postnatal maternal behavior (Champagne & Meaney, 2006), (b) alterations to gene expression in the placenta (Mueller & Bale, 2008) that may restrict access of the fetus to maternal resources, or

(c) a direct influence of maternal stress hormone on fetal gene expression. Modification to the fetal "epigenome" can also be achieved through variations in maternal diet during pregnancy. A striking example of this phenomenon comes from work with a mouse model in which a mutation of the *Agouti* gene leads to alterations in coat color and metabolism. The severity of the effects of this mutation depends on the level of DNA methylation of the *Agouti* gene; high levels of DNA methylation will epigenetically silence this mutation and induce a "pseudoagouti" mouse that is comparable in phenotype to a mouse without the mutation. When pregnant female mice with the *Agouti* mutation are placed on a diet that is rich in methyl groups, the methylation status of this gene is altered such that offspring develop a pseudoagouti phenotype (Dolinoy, 2008). Thus, experience-dependent change in the epigenetic status of genes is not limited to the postnatal period.

Implications of Gene–Environment Interplay for Psychological Functioning

The molecular processes described in laboratory studies may also be critical in understanding the origins of individual differences in humans. Analyses of DNA methylation in cells extracted from fetal cord blood suggest that antenatal maternal depression and anxiety during the third trimester can lead to increased levels of DNA methylation of the GR gene promotor region, having consequences for the stress response of infants at 3 years of age (Oberlander et al., 2008). These effects emerge even in the absence of depression-induced decreases in postnatal mother–infant interactions. The stability of DNA methylation also permits analysis of the epigenetic status of genes in postmortem brain tissue, which can be correlated to life experiences and psychological functioning. In a recent study, DNA methylation of ribosomal genes in hippocampal tissue of suicide victims with a history of abuse and neglect was compared to that of controls. Elevated levels of methylation were detected in ribosomal RNA genes among suicide victims (McGowan et al., 2008), and this effect was found to be specific to the hippocampus. Ribosomes are critical for the production of proteins and thus serve as a critical link between the expression of genes and the level of protein created.

Studies of monozygotic (MZ) twins also provide important insights into epigenetic effects in humans. Comparison of the gene expression of 3-year-old and 50-year-old MZ twins indicates a higher level of discordance in patterns of gene expression among older twins that is associated with increasing differences in DNA methylation in older compared to younger twins (Fraga et al., 2005). Though it is unknown whether concordance in young twins is due to germ-line (the cells that transmit genetic material across generations) or prenatal factors and whether the emerging discordance is random or driven by specific environmental events, there is evidence that epigenetic variation in MZ twins may account for differential risk of mental illness. Analysis of methylation patterns within the catechol-O-methyltransferase *(COMT)* gene in tissue samples from 5-year-old MZ twins indicates varying degrees of discordance, with some MZ twin pairs showing a high degree of discordance and others being very similar in epigenetic status (Mill et al., 2006). *COMT* is an enzyme involved in the inactivation of neurotransmitters such as dopamine and norepinephrine, and disruptions in these neurotransmitter systems have been implicated in many forms of psychopathology. The divergence in methylation of the *COMT* gene within these twin pairs may predict differential risk of neurodevelopmental disorder in later life. Incorporating epigenetic analysis into twin studies represents a novel approach to the study of the origins of individual differences.

Transmission of Traits across Generations: Rethinking Inheritance

In addition to shaping developmental trajectories within an individual's life span, DNA methylation may also have implications for the transmission of traits from one generation to the next. There are two distinct pathways through which this transmission can occur: (a) the behavioral transmission of traits through experience-dependent changes in the methylation of genes, and (b) environmental effects that change DNA methylation in germ cells and are thus transmitted through the germ line of subsequent generations. An example of the first pathway comes from studies of the transmission of maternal care across generations. Variations in maternal care in rodents have been demonstrated to alter the epigenetic status of hypothalamic estrogen receptors of female offspring (Champagne et al., 2006). These receptors are critical in regulating maternal behavior and coordinate the sensitivity of females to hormonal cues. Experience of low levels of maternal care in infancy is associated with increased estrogen receptor promotor methylation, decreased receptor expression, and subsequent decreases in the adult maternal behavior of these offspring. Thus, there is a behavioral transmission of individual differences in maternal care across generations. Interestingly, the quality of environmental conditions experienced by these females at later periods in development can alter this transgenerational inheritance. Prolonged social isolation from peers and prenatal stress can lead to reductions in maternal care that are passed on to subsequent generations (Champagne & Meaney, 2006, 2007). These studies, which are conducted in rodents that have limited genetic variability, suggest that similarities in traits between parental and offspring generations involve far more than the inheritance of genes.

Though epigenetic characteristics of DNA are dynamic in response to environmental cues, these modifications are also stable and heritable. Thus, both genetic and epigenetic factors are transmitted down cell lineages with consequences for the activity of genes within these lineages. However, when considering the question of inheritance at the level of an individual, we must know whether epigenetic patterns within the germ line are correlated to those patterns found within the developing organism. In rodents, prenatal exposure to endocrine disruptors leads to abnormal methylation patterns in sperm cells that are observed several generations beyond the point of initial exposure (Anway, Cupp, Uzumcu, & Skinner, 2005). This germ-line epigenetic inheritance of environmentally induced effects provides further support for the notion that the transmission of traits across generations is not limited in scope to the inheritance of DNA.

Conclusion

Just as a library is more than a collection of books, the genome is more than just DNA. The challenge for the field of epigenetics is to determine the origins of the "uniqueness" of each individual's library by exploring the relationship between genetic and epigenetic variation. Though there are many basic questions to be addressed regarding the pathways whereby specific experiences target particular genes, this field of research certainly has promise in uncovering the nature of experience-dependent changes in development both within and across generations. Advances in tools available to study these effects in humans will be critically important in further exploring the role of epigenetics within the broad field of psychological science.

Recommended Readings

Champagne, F.A. (2008). Epigenetic mechanisms and the transgenerational effects of maternal care. *Frontiers of Neuroendocrinology, 29,* 386–397. Provides a thorough review of the potential role of epigenetic factors in mediating the effects of maternal care within and across generations.

Jirtle, R.L., & Skinner, M.K. (2007). Environmental epigenomics and disease susceptibility. *Nature Reviews Genetics, 8,* 253–262. A review of our current understanding of environmentally induced epigenetic changes and the influence of these processes on individual risk of disease.

Maher, B. (2008). Personal genomes: The case of the missing heritability. *Nature, 456,* 18–21. An interesting commentary on the relationship between heritability estimates and the biological processes that determine the relationship between genes and behavior.

Meaney, M.J. (2001). Maternal care, gene expression, and the transmission of individual differences in stress reactivity across generations. *Annual Review of Neuroscience, 24,* 1161–1192. A review of the profound influence of maternal care on gene expression and behavior of offspring.

References

Anway, M.D., Cupp, A.S., Uzumcu, M., & Skinner, M.K. (2005). Epigenetic transgenerational actions of endocrine disruptors and male fertility. *Science, 308,* 1466–1469.

Caspi, A., Sugden, K., Moffitt, T.E., Taylor, A., Craig, I.W., Harrington, H., et al. (2003). Influence of life stress on depression: Moderation by a polymorphism in the 5-HTT gene. *Science, 301,* 386–389.

Champagne, F.A., & Meaney, M.J. (2006). Stress during gestation alters postpartum maternal care and the development of the offspring in a rodent model. *Biological Psychiatry, 59,* 1227–1235.

Champagne, F.A., & Meaney, M.J. (2007). Transgenerational effects of social environment on variations in maternal care and behavioral response to novelty. *Behavioral Neuroscience, 121,* 1353–1363.

Champagne, F.A., Weaver, I.C., Diorio, J., Dymov, S., Szyf, M., & Meaney, M.J. (2006). Maternal care associated with methylation of the estrogen receptor-alpha1b promoter and estrogen receptor

alpha expression in the medial preoptic area of female offspring. *Endocrinology, 147,* 2909–2915.

Cole, S.W. (2009). Social regulation of human gene expression. *Current Directions in Psychological Science, 18,* 132–137.

Cooper, R.M., & Zubek, J.P. (1958). Effects of enriched and restricted early environments on the learning ability of bright and dull rats. *Canadian Journal of Psychology, 12,* 159–164.

Dolinoy, D.C. (2008). The Agouti mouse model: An epigenetic biosensor for nutritional and environmental alterations on the fetal epigenome. *Nutrition Reviews, 66*(Suppl 1), S7–S11.

Fraga, M.F., Ballestar, E., Paz, M.F., Ropero, S., Setien, F., Ballestar, M.L., et al. (2005). Epigenetic differences arise during the lifetime of monozygotic twins. *Proceedings of the National Academy of Sciences, USA, 102,* 10604–10609.

Kim-Cohen, J., & Gold, A.L. (2009). Measured gene–environment interactions and mechanisms promoting resilient development. *Current Directions in Psychological Science, 18,* 138–142.

McGowan, P.O., Sasaki, A., Huang, T.C., Unterberger, A., Suderman, M., Ernst, C., et al. (2008). Promoter-wide hypermethylation of the ribosomal RNA gene promoter in the suicide brain. *PLoS ONE, 3,* e2085.

Mill, J., Dempster, E., Caspi, A., Williams, B., Moffitt, T., & Craig, I. (2006). Evidence for monozygotic twin (MZ) discordance in methylation level at two CpG sites in the promoter region of the catechol-O-methyltransferase (COMT) gene. *American Journal of Medical Genetics B: Neuropsychiatric Genetics, 141,* B421–B425.

Miller, C.A., & Sweatt, J.D. (2007). Covalent modification of DNA regulates memory formation. *Neuron, 53,* 857–869.

Mueller, B.R., & Bale, T.L. (2008). Sex-specific programming of offspring emotionality after stress early in pregnancy. *Journal of Neuroscience, 28,* 9055–9065.

Oberlander, T.F., Weinberg, J., Papsdorf, M., Grunau, R., Misri, S., & Devlin, A.M. (2008). Prenatal exposure to maternal depression, neonatal methylation of human glucocorticoid receptor gene (NR3C1) and infant cortisol stress responses. *Epigenetics, 3,* 97–106.

Razin, A. (1998). CpG methylation, chromatin structure and gene silencing-a three-way connection. *EMBO Journal, 17,* 4905–4908.

Weaver, I.C., Cervoni, N., Champagne, F.A., D'Alessio, A.C., Sharma, S., Seckl, J.R., et al. (2004). Epigenetic programming by maternal behavior. *Nature Neuroscience, 7,* 847–854.

Weaver, I.C., Champagne, F.A., Brown, S.E., Dymov, S., Sharma, S., Meaney, M.J., et al. (2005). Reversal of maternal programming of stress responses in adult offspring through methyl supplementation: Altering epigenetic marking later in life. *Journal of Neuroscience, 25,* 11045–11054.

Address correspondence to **FRANCES A. CHAMPAGNE**, Columbia University, Department of Psychology, 406 Schermerhorn Hall, 1190 Amsterdam Avenue, New York, NY 10027; e-mail: fac2105@columbia.edu.

Effects of Prenatal Social Stress on Offspring Development
Pathology or Adaptation?

SYLVIA KAISER AND NORBERT SACHSER

Ontogeny is the development of an individual from the moment the egg is fertilized until death. Most research on *behavioral* ontogeny has focused on the early postnatal phase, probably because socialization and learning processes are thought to play their most important role during this time. However, there is growing evidence that environmental influences before birth also have impact on the individual's development later in life (de Weerth, Buitelaar, & Mulder, 2005). In particular, stressors acting on the mother during pregnancy can have distinct and long-term effects on behavior, reproductive functions, and the immune, neuro-endocrine and autonomic systems of her offspring (de Kloet, Sibug, Helmerhorst, & Schmidt, 2005).

In most experimental studies on the effects of prenatal stress, pregnant female animals have been subjected to non-social stressors (e.g., bright light, restraint). Interpretation of these studies is difficult, because such artifical stressors typically do not occur in those animals' natural environments (Kaiser & Sachser, 2005). In their natural habitats, animals have to cope with a variety of stressors that depend on their ecological niche. They have to adjust to the physical environment (e.g., weather) and to the biotic world that surrounds them (e.g., predators, food shortage). A major part of an individual's biotic environment consists of other members of the same species, which can be defined as that individual's "social world." In fact, a majority of human and animal daily expectations, motivations, and behaviors are directed toward encounters with conspecifics. On the one hand, this social world can support welfare and health (e.g., through the effects of social support). On the other hand, it can result in severe stress, eventually leading to disease and even death (e.g., in the case of social defeat, social instability, or crowding; von Holst, 1998). Thus, the social environment represents a very influential stressor, which, during pregnancy, can be crucial for the development of the offspring (Kaiser & Sachser, 2005).

Effects of the Prenatal Social Environment on Offspring Development and Behavior
Animal Studies

The most comprehensive insights from studies of nonhuman animals regarding prenatal social influences on offspring development have been derived from studies in guinea pigs (Kaiser & Sachser, 2005). For example, when compared to daughters whose mothers had lived in a stable social environment during pregnancy (that is, group composition was kept constant, with one male and five females), female guinea pigs whose mothers had lived in an unstable social environment (every third day, two females from different groups were exchanged) showed conspicuous behavioral masculinization (e.g., displaying high levels of male-typical courtship behavior) later in life, increased testosterone concentrations, and a male-typical distribution pattern of androgen receptors in parts of the limbic system (Kaiser, Kruijver, Swaab, & Sachser, 2003). Compared to male guinea pigs whose mothers had lived in a stable social environment, those whose mothers had lived in an unstable social environment during pregnancy showed behavioral infantilization (e.g., displaying behavioral patterns usually shown only by very young male guinea pigs, such as sitting in close bodily contact), delayed development of the adrenocortical system, and down-regulation of androgen receptor expression in the limbic system (Kaiser, Kruijver, Straub, Sachser, & Swaab, 2003).

Studies of prenatal social influences on offspring development have been conducted only in a few other species (e.g., mice, rats, squirrel monkeys). Although a variety of different social stressors have been applied in these experiments (e.g., crowding, social confrontation, changing group membership), a common characteristic of all approaches is the induction of social instability. In general, under such conditions, the number of interactions with conspecifics increases and the predictability and controllability of social encounters dramatically decline. Interestingly, modern stress research shows that, in animals as well as in humans, situations of uncertainty or unpredictability are a major source of stress responses (von Holst, 1998).

When all experimental studies on prenatal social stress are compared, some general conclusions can be drawn: Female offspring show a masculinization of behavior, endocrine state, and brain development. Male offspring show a less pronounced expression of male-typical traits (e.g., demasculinization, feminization) and/or a delay in development. In addition, there are some indications that both sexes might have a more or less severe impairment of reproductive functions (cf., Kaiser & Sachser, 2005).

Human Studies

The long-lasting effects of prenatal stress on offspring are also well known in humans: Children of mothers who were stressed during pregnancy develop higher risk of different diseases (including cardiovascular illness and diabetes) and may experience physical and cognitive developmental delays (e.g., Huizink, Mulder, & Buitelaar, 2004; Wadhwa, 2005). However, only limited data concerning the effects of *social* stressors during pregnancy on human offspring later in life are available. Those few studies, however, point to distinct effects on behavioral and physiological development. For instance, family discord during pregnancy leads to behavioral disturbances in children, and such children are more likely to develop psychopathological disorders such as autism (Ward, 1990; unfortunately, it is not mentioned whether this finding is controlled for postnatal effects). Similarly, moderate to severe stressors combined with low levels of social support during pregnancy reduce children's head circumference at birth, pointing to the effects of prenatal stress on brain development (Glynn & Sandman, 2006). Children whose mothers experienced high levels of daily hassles and pregnancy-specific anxiety show lower mental and motor developmental scores at 8 months of age after correcting for postnatal stress (Buitelaar, Huizink, Mulder, Robles de Medina, & Visser, 2003).

Effects of Prenatal Social Stress: Pathology or Adaptation?

Researchers typically interpret the characteristic traits of individuals who were exposed to adverse environmental stimuli (stressors) during pregnancy as deviations from some standard considered optimal, and phenotypic differences in offspring are frequently called pathological. Alternatively, and in accordance with current evolutionary theory, these traits might also represent adaptive maternal effects; that is, the offspring's fitness is enhanced by maternal adjustments to the current environmental conditions.

Adaptation through maternal effects—that is, control and/or modulation of the offspring's phenotype—has become a key

concept in modern evolutionary biology (see, e.g., Groothuis, Müller, von Engelhardt, Carere, & Eising, 2005; Mousseau & Fox, 1998) and numerous studies to reveal the mechanism underlying these phenomena are currently underway. Particular maternal hormonal responses to environmental stimuli represent a potential tool by which development of offspring can be influenced. Indeed, in different bird species, mothers' deposition of androgens into the yolk of their eggs varies with environmental factors or social conditions, and experimental studies have shown effects of enhanced androgen levels on offspring traits such as competitiveness or growth (Groothuis, Müller, von Engelhardt, Carere, & Eising, 2005). Results of two recent studies in wild spotted hyenas and guinea pigs suggest that prenatal androgen exposure can adaptively influence offspring phenotype (in terms of aggression, sexual behavior, and testosterone responsiveness to social challenge) regularly in mammals as well (Dloniak, French, & Holekamp, 2006; Kemme, Kaiser, & Sachser, 2007). If such traits result in enhancement of fitness parameters such as social dominance or reproductive benefits, we can speak of an adaptive phenotype.

Possible Benefits of Altered Phenotypes

The questions arise: What is the benefit of being a masculinized daughter? And what is the benefit for sons who show less pronounced expression of male-typical traits and/or a delay in development?

Consider the case of fluctuations in the density of natural populations of mammals. Under high-density conditions, social instability is a common trait, whereas low population densities are characterized by stable social situations (von Holst, 1998). Hence, different pregnant females may experience very different degrees of social stability in their natural habitats. If a pregnant female living in a high-density population has the possibility of preprogramming her daughters in such a way that they will gain maximum reproductive success in that high-density situation, it would seem reasonable for her to masculinize them in order to make them more robust and/or more competitive. These and other masculine traits facilitate the attainment of dominant social positions, which in turn help to defend important resources such as food and shelter (which are scarce in high-density situations) more efficiently. However, frequently a characteristic feature of masculinized females is impairment of reproductive function later in life (Kaiser & Sachser, 2005). Thus, under high-density conditions, there is likely to be a trade-off between the benefits of a behaviorally and endocrinologically masculinized phenotype and the costs of decreased reproductive success. Although decreased reproductive success might seem inconsistent with the idea of enhanced fitness, under such conditions, masculinized females might fare better than nonmasculinized females; the latter may often fail to reproduce at all because of lower social status that prevents access to resources necessary for reproduction. Under low-density conditions, however, sufficient resources are available and competitive abilities are less important. Under such conditions, it would seem more beneficial to invest time and energy in reproductive effort rather than to build and maintain a male-typical phenotype for defending resources. Thus, under low-density conditions, reproductive success would be higher in nonmasculinized females than in masculinized ones (Kaiser & Sachser, 2005).

The argument is similar for sons. Around the time of sexual maturity, they can find themselves in different situations. Consider a low-density condition with only a few males of the same age and some females present. In such a situation, the best strategy to maximize reproductive success would be to fight for the access to a copulation partner, because usually the winners will mate. Under such conditions, mothers will maximize their own fitness if they program their sons prenatally in a way that maximizes the timely expression of male-typical traits. In contrast, when animals live at high densities in large, age-graded populations, a different situation exists: Under such conditions, in many species, high-ranking (alpha) males almost exclusively sire all the offspring. Remarkably, males usually do not attain an alpha position until well beyond the age of sexual maturity (e.g., mandrills; Setchell, Charpentier, & Wickings, 2005). A male born in a high-density population should avoid agonistic encounters at too early an age, because this will not result in reproductive success. By neither signaling sexual interest in females nor displaying other signs of sexual maturity, a pubescent male is less likely to be attacked by the alpha males. This strategy should change, however, around the time of social maturity in order to attain the alpha position that is required for reproductive success. Thus, under conditions of high density, mothers may provide their sons with a more adaptive reproductive strategy by programming them prenatally in a way that delays development and/or diminishes expression of male-typical traits until social maturity is attained (Kaiser & Sachser, 2005).

Currently, much experimental animal research is being conducted to test such hypotheses on the adaptive value of prenatal maternal programming (Dloniak, French, & Holekamp, 2006; Kemme, Kaiser, & Sachser, 2007).

Human Studies

Similar arguments for the adaptive value of the response to prenatal-stress effects in humans have been put forward. For example, Bateson et al. (2004) hypothesize that a period of starvation during pregnancy tells the developing fetus that food is probably going to be scarce in the future. Babies of such mothers often show small body weight and correspondingly modified metabolism. These traits are not necessarily pathological, inasmuch as they help the baby to cope with environments of low food availability. The proposed mechanism for these persistent effects into adulthood involves alteration in set points for various aspects of basic metabolism (e.g., glucoregulation, adiposity, and blood pressure; Roseboom, de Rooij, & Painter, 2006).

For ethical reasons, in humans it is not feasible to experimentally manipulate hormonal levels during early development or exposure to stress in pregnant mothers. Nevertheless, good evidence that the behavioral phenotype of daughters can be shaped by prenatal androgens does exist. For example, girls with congenital adrenal hyperplasia (an autosomal recessive disorder that causes elevated adrenal androgens) are exposed to elevated androgen concentrations during fetal development, and this results in a masculinized phenotype—revealed, for example, by increased rough-and-tumble play (Hines, 2006). Other evidence shows that androgen levels in women can be affected by environmental situations: Testosterone concentrations increase, for example, in periods of high-intensity exercise (Bergeron et al., 1991). We therefore propose that androgen concentrations in pregnant women may change as a result of environmental factors and that these changed androgen concentrations may influence fetal central-nervous-system differentiation during early development, thereby shaping the behavioral phenotype of the offspring later in life. Whether or not this specific phenotype represents an adaptive adjustment to the environmental conditions under which the mother has lived during pregnancy remains to be determined.

Conclusion

Studies of animals and humans clearly show that severe stressors acting upon a pregnant female can have profoundly negative effects on the later development and health of her offspring. In such cases, prenatal stress results in pathology and no discussion about adaptive function seems appropriate. Recent experimental animal studies of prenatal stress, when considered from an evolutionary perspective, draw attention to an additional hypothesis: that variation in behavioral phenotype brought about by prenatal stressors may represent an adaptation to the prevailing environmental situation. From this point of view, deviations from the behavioral and physiological standard, such as masculinized daughters and infantilized sons, should not be regarded as pathological but may rather be seen as representing adaptations to the offspring's likely environment. It is timely and exciting to test whether some of the individual variation among members of our species might not reflect the action of similar, and perhaps now vestigial, processes. Accordingly the central hypothesis is this: We share the same mechanisms with nonhuman mammals that allow infants to be preadapted to the world their mothers live in during pregnancy. In particular, we assume that the environment in which a pregnant woman lives affects her endocrine state, which in turn influences fetal brain development, thereby adapting the infant's behavior and physiology to cope successfully with the challenges of the environmental niche of the mother. If so, children of mothers who have lived in a stable social situation during pregnancy will cope better with conditions of social stability later in life than will children whose mothers have lived under unstable social conditions. However, children whose mothers have lived under unstable social conditions during pregnancy might cope better with conditions of social instability later in life than might children of mothers who have lived in stable social situations. Future studies are required to test these hypotheses.

Recommended Reading

Bateson, P., Barker, D., Clutton-Brock, T., Deb, D., D'Udine, B., Foley, R.A., et al. (2004). Developmental plasticity and human health. *Nature, 430,* 419–421. Discusses developmental plasticity and human health in more details than the current article.

Champagne, F.A., & Curley, J.P. (2005). How social experiences influence the brain. *Current Opinion in Neurobiology, 15,* 704–709. A clearly written, user-friendly, and relatively comprehensive review for readers who wish to expand their knowledge on influences of social experiences on brain development.

de Kloet, E.R., Sibug, R.M., Helmerhorst, F.M., & Schmidt, M. (2005). (See References). A clearly written, user-friendly, and relatively comprehensive review for readers who wish to expand their knowledge on long-lasting effects of early stress on brain programming.

Dufty, A.M., Jr., Clobert, J., & Møller, A.P. (2002). Hormones, developmental plasticity and adaptation. *Trends in Ecology & Evolution, 17,* 190–196. A clearly written, user-friendly, and relatively comprehensive review for readers who wish to expand their knowledge on developmental plasticity and adaptation.

Kaiser, S., & Sachser, N. (2005). (See References). A comprehensive, highly accessible overview of what is known about mechanisms and function of the effects of prenatal social stress.

References

Bateson, P., Barker, D., Clutton-Brock, T., Deb, D., D'Udine, B., Foley, R.A., et al. (2004). Developmental plasticity and human health. *Nature, 430,* 419–421.

Bergeron, M.E., Maresh, C.M., Kraemer, W.J., Abraham, A., Conroy, B., & Gabaree, C. (1991). Tennis: A physiological profile during match play. *International Journal of Sports Medicine, 12,* 474–479.

Buitelaar, J.K., Huizink, A.C., Mulder, E.J., Robles de Medina, P.G., & Visser, G.H.A. (2003). Prenatal stress and cognitive development and temperament in infants. *Neurobiology of Aging, 24,* S53–S60.

de Kloet, E.R., Sibug, R.M., Helmerhorst, F.M., & Schmidt, M. (2005). Stress, genes and the mechanism of programming the brain for later life. *Neuroscience and Biobehavioral Reviews, 29,* 271–281.

de Weerth, C., Buitelaar, J.K., & Mulder, E.J.H. (Eds.). (2005). Prenatal programming of behaviour, physiology and cognition. *Neuroscience and Biobehavioral Reviews, 29,* 207–384.

Dloniak, S.M., French, J.A., & Holekamp, K.E. (2006). Rank-related maternal effects of androgens on behaviour in wild spotted hyaenas. *Nature, 449,* 1190–1193.

Glynn, L.M., & Sandman, C.A. (2006). The influence of prenatal stress and adverse birth outcome on human cognitive and neurological development. *International Review of Research in Mental Retardation, 32,* 109–129.

Groothuis, T.G.G., Müller, W., von Engelhardt, N., Carere, C., & Eising, C. (2005). Maternal hormones as a tool to adjust offspring phenotype in avian species. *Neuroscience and Biobehavioral Reviews, 29,* 329–352.

Hines, M. (2006). Prenatal testosterone and gender-related behaviour. *European Journal of Endocrinology, 155,* S115–S121.

Huizink, A.C., Mulder, E.J.H., & Buitelaar, J.K. (2004). Prenatal stress and risk for psychopathology: Specific effects or induction of general susceptibility? *Psychological Bulletin, 130,* 115–142.

Kaiser, S., Kruijver, F.P.M., Straub, R.H., Sachser, N., & Swaab, D.F. (2003). Early social stress in male guinea pigs changes social behaviour, and autonomic and neuroendocrine functions. *Journal of Neuroendocrinology, 15,* 761–769.

Kaiser, S., Kruijver, F.P.M., Swaab, D.F., & Sachser, N. (2003). Early social stress in female guinea pigs induces a masculinization of adult behavior and corresponding changes in brain and neuroendocrine function. *Behavioral Brain Research, 144,* 199–210.

Kaiser, S., & Sachser, N. (2005). The effects of prenatal social stress on behaviour: Mechanisms and function. *Neuroscience and Biobehavioral Reviews, 29,* 283–294.

Kemme, K., Kaiser, S., & Sachser, N. (2007). Prenatal maternal programming determines testosterone response during social challenge. *Hormones and Behavior, 51,* 387–394.

Mousseau, T.A., & Fox, C.W. (1998). The adaptive significance of maternal effects. *Trends in Ecology and Evolution, 13,* 403–407.

Roseboom, T., de Rooij, S., & Painter, R. (2006). The Dutch famine and its long-term consequences for adult health. *Early Human Development, 82,* 485–491.

Setchell, J.M., Charpentier, M., & Wickings, E.J. (2005). Sexual selection and reproductive careers in mandrills (*Mandrillus sphinx*). *Behavioral Ecology and Sociobiology, 58,* 474–485.

von Holst, D. (1998). The concept of stress and its relevance for animal behavior. *Advances of the Study of Behavior, 27,* 1–131.

Wadhwa, P.D. (2005). Psychoneuroendocrine processes in human pregnancy influence fetal development and health. *Psychoneuroendocrinology, 30,* 724–743.

Ward, A.J. (1990). A comparison and analysis of the presence of family problems during pregnancy of mothers of "autistic" children and mothers of normal children. *Child Psychiatry and Human Development, 20,* 279–288.

Address correspondence to **Sylvia Kaiser**, Department of Behavioral Biology, University of Muenster, Badestrasse 13, D-48149 Muenster, Germany; e-mail: kaisesy@uni-muenster.de.

From *Current Directions in Psychological Science*, April 2009, pp. 118–121. Copyright © 2009 by the Association for Psychological Science. Reprinted by permission of Wiley-Blackwell.

UNIT 2

Cognition, Language, and Learning

Unit Selections

Key Points to Consider

- Recently, researchers have shown the importance of supporting early interactions and experiences during infancy and preschool to support brain development. How has this information changed or not changed your perceptions and interactions with babies as a result? If you were a parent of an infant or toddler, explain in more detail what you would do to optimize their early development.

- Given that infants experience very limited visual stimuli in the womb, at what point in infancy might they exhibit preferences for human faces? Do you think babies might distinguish and/or prefer female vs. male faces and if so, when and why? What are infants' responses to faces of people of difference racial or ethnic groups?

- It seems that the pressure to raise bright, high-achieving kids continues to increase. Do you think exposing kids to computers and the Internet will make kids smarter? Suppose your child fails at a math task. As a parent, should you emphasize the importance of math ability or effort? Since much of what is on the Internet is text-based, how do you think this might improve children's reading and language skills? Did your parents ever reward you with more allowance or other material rewards for bringing home A's on your report card? How did this make you feel? Did it work? Did money make you want to learn more and perform better?

- When do children first understand other people's feelings and mental states or how to evaluate other people's abilities? Do you think parents and teachers help teach children to promote this awareness and assessment of others? Do you view yourself as having a high emotional IQ? Explain why or why not. Did you have parents or siblings who talked to you about feelings and people and helped you understand others and learn how to behave in productive ways? If not, did you have friends, teachers, or other adults who helped you develop and build your social skills? Do you think you can improve your social skills as an adult or not? Explain your answer and give examples.

We have come a long way from the days when the characterization of cognition of infants and young children included phrases like "tabula rasa" and "booming, buzzing confusion." Infants and young children are no longer viewed by researchers as blank slates, passively waiting to be filled up with knowledge. Today, experts in child development are calling for a reformulation of assumptions about children's cognitive abilities, as well as calling for reforms in the ways we teach children in our schools. Hence, the articles in the first subsection highlight some of the new knowledge of the cognitive abilities of infants and young children, while the second subsection focuses on schooling and learning.

Researchers today continue to discover that babies are developing an impressive array of early social, emotional, and cognitive skills during infancy. In "Infants' Differential Processing of Female and Male Faces," and "The Other-Race Effect Develops during Infancy: Evidence of Perceptual Narrowing," the authors describe new findings showing that infants' and young children's earliest interactions and experiences are critical in helping them develop normal social-emotional milestones and other linguistic, perceptual, and cognitive skills. From this perspective, babies are not as passive as once thought, and parents and teachers can provide environments that nurture and support their babies' developing abilities.

Researchers describe the complex interplay between brain maturational development and external experience in determining the emergence of abilities such as language acquisition, neonate imitation, and factors related to stress reactivity in "New Advances in Understanding Sensitive Periods in Brain Development" and "Contributions of Neuroscience to Our Understanding of Cognitive Development." For example, nurturing touch during infancy has been shown to be a very important factor in promoting growth, reducing stress, and reducing depression and other cognitive deficits later in life.

We learn from research in "Language and Children's Understanding of Mental States" that maternal conversation and language interventions play a key role in helping children develop a theory of mind or the ability to understand other people's points of view and emotional states. Children advance in their understanding of mental states—a critical ingredient for building appropriate social skills and understanding people's good and bad actions—when their parents and teachers engage in rich conversations with them about others who have varying points of view and different emotions as discussed in both "Social Cognitive Development: A New Look" and "Social Awareness + Emotional Skills = Successful Kids." Growing

© Bananastock/PictureQuest

research shows that children need to develop social and emotional intelligence to succeed.

In "Future Thinking in Young Children" researcher Cristina Atance reviews data showing that preschoolers begin to develop concepts about the future that permit them to begin to mentally project to plan and act now in anticipation of future events. The data indicate that this ability to think and prepare for the future begins to develop and increase in efficiency by the ages of 4 and 5 years.

In "It's Fun, but Does it Make You Smarter?" the author discusses the merits and pitfalls of exposing children to computers and the Internet as well as the dangers of over-focusing on intelligence and talent in children.

With increasing pressures for children to do well in school, parents are asking questions such as, "Should I hold my child back from kindergarten for a year?" The author of "When Should a Kid Start Kindergarten?" addresses this question head on.

Student Website
www.mhhe.com/cls

Internet References

Educational Resources Information Center (ERIC)
www.ed.gov/about/pubs/intro/pubdb.html

National Association for the Education of Young Children (NAEYC)
www.naeyc.org

Parent's Action for Children
http://store.parentsactionstore.org/prostores/servlet/StoreFront

Project Zero
http://pzweb.harvard.edu

Vandergrift's Children's Literature Page
www.scils.rutgers.edu/special/kay/sharelit.html

Infants' Differential Processing of Female and Male Faces

Infants show an interesting asymmetry in face processing: They are more fluent in processing female faces than they are at processing male faces. We hypothesize that such processing asymmetry results from greater experience with female faces than with male faces early in development. Asymmetrical face processing may have long-lasting implications for development of face recognition, development of knowledge structures regarding females and males, and social-information processing. We encourage researchers to use both female and male faces in their face-perception research and to conduct separate analyses for female and male faces.

JENNIFER L. RAMSEY-RENNELS AND JUDITH H. LANGLOIS

Categorization is a fundamental information-processing capability that allows reliable recognition and response to novel examples of familiar category members. For example, if Ariana walks into an unfamiliar room containing a telephone, she knows she can use the phone to talk to someone even though she has never before seen this particular telephone. Categorization of objects enables people to allocate cognitive resources efficiently—Ariana will expend more energy in figuring out what to say on the phone than in determining how it works.

Because of the adaptive nature of categorization, it is not surprising that categorization abilities emerge early in infancy (e.g., Quinn, 2002). Such abilities facilitate infants' early and rapid learning about the many different objects in the world. But what about categorization of people? Like categorizing objects, categorizing people has important benefits. For example, categorizing age allows one to interact with infants and children in a developmentally appropriate manner. Categorizing gender allows one to determine if a person would be an appropriate mate. There are, however, problems related to categorization of people—these categories could become linked to positive and negative attributions that might not be accurate characterizations of a particular member of that group. Thus, one byproduct of this otherwise adaptive process of categorization is the formation of stereotypes (e.g., Bargh & Chartrand, 1999).

Our work has focused on infants and the early origins of stereotypes, particularly on how infants recognize, evaluate, and categorize the facial appearance of adults. Our research in this area has led us to conclude that there is a potentially important asymmetry in how infants process male and female faces. Most of our research successes involved infants' responses to female faces (e.g., Rubenstein, Kalakanis, & Langlois, 1999). Yet, our research failures were equally illuminating because they almost always involved infants' responses to male faces (see Ramsey, Langlois, & Marti, 2005, for an overview).

Asymmetries in Infant Processing of Faces

Two different types of studies illustrate the asymmetry we observed. First, as part of our research program to understand the cognitive mechanisms underlying infants' preferences for attractive faces, we examined infants' ability to abstract an averaged (summary) representation, or prototype, of sets of female or male faces. Abstracting a facial prototype from category examples is important because a prototype (a) can facilitate processing of new exemplar faces from that category; and (b) may guide interest toward faces, as infants visually prefer faces most similar to their prototype (Rubenstein et al., 1999). Although we found that infants formed prototypes of female faces (Rubenstein et al., 1999), we could not find evidence that they formed prototypes of male faces. This asymmetry suggests that infants' initial prototype or representation of faces may be more female-like than male-like (Ramsey et al., 2005).

A second type of study, in which infants view male and female faces when they are paired together, shows another asymmetry: Infants look longer at female faces than they do at male faces (Quinn, Yahr, Kuhn, Slater, & Pascalis, 2002). We posit that infants visually prefer female faces to male faces because female faces are more similar than male faces are to the infant's facial prototype. Interestingly, however, when infants view female faces only or male faces only, they spend more time looking at male faces than they do at female faces, particularly when the task is complex (Ramsey et al., 2005). Because female faces are not available to "compete" for infants' attention in studies presenting male faces, longer looking times may reflect infants' lack of expertise and lack of efficiency in processing male faces. Longer looking at male faces in the absence of female faces is particularly evident when the task requires recognition or categorical abstraction, perhaps because infants do not yet have a fully developed male face prototype to facilitate processing (Ramsey et al., 2005).

These asymmetries in our work and that of Quinn et al. (2002) prompted us to explore the infant face-perception literature further for asymmetries in other areas of face processing. We discovered that most studies use only female faces to evaluate infants' reactions to faces. The lack of male-face studies caused us to question whether conclusions about infants' face recognition, interest in faces, understanding of emotion, and development of social expectancies from the existing infant face-perception literature really generalized to all faces, male and female, as is typically assumed.

When we examined the few studies that included male stimulus faces, we found further evidence of differences in infants' processing of female and male faces. First, 3- to 4-month-olds have more difficulty discriminating among male faces and subsequently recognizing them than they do female faces (Quinn et al., 2002). Second, older infants are more skilled at categorizing female faces than they are at categorizing male faces: Whereas 10-month-olds easily recognize that a sex-ambiguous female face does not belong with a group of sex-typical female faces, they have more difficulty excluding a sex-ambiguous male face from a group of sex-typical male faces (data interpretation of Younger & Fearing, 1999, by Ramsey et al., 2005). In addition, there is a lag between when infants recognize that female voices are associated with female faces and when male voices are associated with male faces; infants reliably match female faces and voices at 9 months (Poulin-Dubois, Serbin, Kenyon, & Derbyshire, 1994) but do not reliably match male faces and voices until 18 months. Even at 18 months, infants are more accurate at matching female faces and voices than they are at matching male faces and voices (Poulin-Dubois, Serbin, & Derbyshire, 1998).

Thus, the infant perception literature shows that (a) infants have more difficulty processing male faces than female faces, (b) infants prefer female to male faces, and (c) differential processing of male and female faces is related to the fluency with which infants form categories of male versus female faces. Why?

The Role of Experience with Faces

Early visual experience with faces appears to be very important for specialized processing of upright relative to inverted faces and within-species face recognition (e.g., Nelson, 2001; Pascalis, de Haan, & Nelson, 2002). In most instances, infants have significantly more exposure to adult female faces than they have to adult male faces. For example, the primary caregiver is female for the majority of infants, and infants spend approximately 50% of their personal interactions with her

during the first year. Also, parents of 2-, 5-, 8-, and 11-month-olds report twice as many interactions between their infant and female strangers than between their infant and male strangers during a typical week (Ramsey & Simmons, 2005). There are also qualitative differences in how adults interact with infants (e.g., females play more visual games than males), which may cause females to elicit more attention from infants during social interactions than males do (Ramsey et al., 2005). Therefore, we posit that infants' typical experience with female faces early in development facilitates expert processing (discrimination, recognition, and categorization) of female faces. Greater experience with female faces than with male faces should result in more fluent processing of female faces.

An alternate hypothesis is that experience with faces is not formative; rather, evolution has predisposed infants to attend to female faces because mothers were generally the primary caregivers. Research, however, shows that experience is important for face processing: Babies who have fathers as their primary caregivers show more interest in male faces than in female faces (Quinn et al., 2002). Moreover, 3-month-olds more easily recognize faces from the race with which they are most familiar than they recognize faces from a different race (Sangrigoli & de Schonen, 2004). Thus, it seems unlikely that experience is irrelevant. Rather, predominant experience with faces from a particular sex, race, species, orientation, etc. should result in more fluent processing of the commonly experienced faces.

Once infants become more expert at processing female faces than male faces, the asymmetry may cascade because ease of processing is linked to affective preferences (Winkielman & Cacioppo, 2001). Increased positive affect toward female faces increases the likelihood that infants will look at female faces, further skewing experience and expertise with female faces. Infants' lack of experience with male faces may be compounded by an additional complexity: Male faces are more variable and less perceptually similar than female faces (Ramsey et al., 2005). Measurements of male faces show greater deviation from the mean than measurements of female faces do. This greater deviation means male faces are less prototypical (i.e., less representative of their sex category on average) than female faces are. Thus, infants not only have less experience with male faces than with female faces, but their experience with male faces is less productive because categories with more variable members can be difficult for infants to learn (e.g., Quinn, 2002). Such impediments may cause developmental delays in the attainment of coherent prototype formation for male faces (Ramsey et al., 2005).

Much as how early language input causes specialized processing of the native language, abundant experience with certain faces (e.g., female) during infancy results in expert processing of those faces (Nelson, 2001). Indeed, 9-month-olds perform almost like adults in being better able to recognize human faces than monkey faces, whereas 6-month-olds perform equally well in their recognition of human and monkey faces (Pascalis et al., 2002). The similarities between 9-month-olds and adults in their poorer recognition of monkey faces, as compared to 6-month-olds, is likely due to their greater experience with and specialization in processing human faces over monkey faces.

Unlike infants' experience with the native language relative to other languages and with human faces relative to monkey faces, the disparity between infants' experience with female faces and their experience with male faces is not as large, making this a unique type of problem regarding discrepancies in experience. We suggest, therefore, that differences in early experience with faces can have qualitative, long-lasting impact on how male and female faces are processed, but that these processing disparities may be subtle.

Implications of Early Differential Processing

What might be the enduring implications of differential processing of female and male faces? The fluency or ease with which infants more expertly discriminate, recognize, and categorize female faces relative to male faces has the potential to contribute to later face-recognition abilities, knowledge acquisition of the sex categories, and social-information processing.

Early fluency in processing female faces during infancy should contribute to a later advantage in adults' recognition of female faces. Indeed, adult females are better at recognizing female faces than they are at recognizing male faces, and they perform better than males do at recognizing female faces (e.g., Lewin & Herlitz, 2002). Why should the advantage seen in both female and male infants' recognition of female faces be sustained only in female adults? An important developmental task for young children is to learn about their gender. Because preschoolers typically learn about their own gender before they learn about the other gender (Martin & Halverson, 1981), girls may maintain or enhance their processing of female faces whereas boys may "lose" some of their expertise in processing female faces as male faces begin to compete for their attention. Obviously this proposed developmental pathway requires investigation and there are other mediating variables, but in a legal system that places great reliance on eyewitness testimony, a clear understanding of why females may possess an advantage in recognizing female faces relative to male faces is needed (e.g., Lewin & Herlitz, 2002).

Fluent processing of female faces should allow infants to more easily structure the female face category than the male face category, which should enable infants and young children to more readily learn about females than males because it is less effortful to make associations to the female face category (e.g., Quinn, 2002). Lack of experience with male faces will make it difficult to attain conceptual knowledge about the male face category, suggesting that knowledge structures associated with females should emerge earlier and be more elaborate than those associated with males, at least early in development. Furthermore, the variability of the male face category should make it difficult to associate and organize the conceptual knowledge that is attained. These proposed differences in knowledge structures for females and males would suggest that linking, organizing, and retrieving information should occur with greater ease when processing social information about female targets, relative to male targets.

Future Directions

Infants' differential experience with female and male faces influences their discrimination, recognition, and categorization of faces, although more work is needed to understand the full extent and origins of those differences. We suggest that particular attention be paid to experience with faces and to when interactions with males increase during development. Examining when (or if) the visual preference for female faces over male faces subsides or reverses should provide insight into face-processing changes due to experience and will likely require testing older children and perhaps even adults. Because categorization is inherently linked to knowledge acquisition, it is also important to investigate how the category structure for female and male faces develops, evolves, and reorganizes over time, with attention to both perceptual and conceptual components of the categories.

Unlike other research assessing the role of experience when there is overwhelming exposure to the commonly experienced category (e.g., native language) and minimal experience with alternate categories (e.g., foreign languages), the difference between infants' experience with female and male faces is more subtle. Understanding how subtleties in early exposure subsequently impact later face processing could be informative for researchers interested in sensitive periods in development. One question concerns whether limited early exposure to male faces extends the window for expert processing of male faces to develop or if fluency of processing male faces never develops to the same level that it does for female faces. Testing older children and adults, who should have more experience with male faces, is necessary for addressing this issue, but methods assessing reaction time or psychophysiological responses may be necessary to capture subtle differences in fluency of processing female and male faces.

Regardless of the age group being studied, we urge face-perception researchers to use both female and male faces in their studies, to make a priori hypotheses about potential differences in processing, and to conduct separate analyses for female and male faces in order to carefully examine the nature of any disparities in processing female and male faces (quantitative or qualitative divergence). Because aspects of adult face processing have roots in infancy, we suggest that researchers check the developmental literature for clues when they cannot identify why face-processing discrepancies occur among adult participants.

References

Bargh, J.A., & Chartrand, T.L. (1999). The unbearable automaticity of being. *American Psychologist, 54,* 462–479.

Lewin, C., & Herlitz, A. (2002). Sex differences in face recognition—women's faces make the difference. *Brain & Cognition, 50,* 121–128.

Martin, C.L., & Halverson, C.F., Jr. (1981). A schematic processing model of sex-typing and stereotyping in children. *Child Development, 52,* 1119–1134.

Nelson, C.A. (2001). The development and neural bases of face recognition. *Infant & Child Development, 10,* 3–18.

Pascalis, O., de Haan, M., & Nelson, C.A. (2002). Is face processing species-specific during the first year of life? *Science, 296,* 1321–1323.

Poulin-Dubois, D., Serbin, L.A., & Derbyshire, A. (1998). Toddlers' intermodal and verbal knowledge about gender. *Merrill-Palmer Quarterly, 44,* 338–354.

Poulin-Dubois, D., Serbin, L.A., Kenyon, B., & Derbyshire, A. (1994). Infants' intermodal knowledge about gender. *Developmental Psychology, 30,* 436–442.

Quinn, P.C. (2002). Beyond prototypes: Asymmetries in infant categorization and what they teach us about the mechanisms guiding knowledge acquisition. In R. Kail & H. Reese (Eds.), *Advances in child development and behavior: Vol. 29* (pp. 161–193). San Diego: Academic Press.

Quinn, P.C., Yahr, J., Kuhn, A., Slater, A.M., & Pascalis, O. (2002). Representation of the gender of human faces by infants: A preference for female. *Perception, 31,* 1109–1121.

Ramsey, J.L., Langlois, J.H., & Marti, C.N. (2005). Infant categorization of faces: Ladies first. *Developmental Review, 25,* 212–246.

Ramsey, J.L., & Simmons, R.E. (2005). [Two, 5, 8, and 11 month olds' interactions with familiar and unfamiliar individuals during a typical week]. Unpublished raw data.

Rubenstein, A.J., Kalakanis, L., & Langlois, J.H. (1999). Infant preferences for attractive faces: A cognitive explanation. *Developmental Psychology, 35,* 848–855.

Sangrigoli, S., & de Schonen, S. (2004). Recognition of own-race and other-race faces by three-month-old infants. *Journal of Child Psychology and Psychiatry, 45,* 1219–1227.

Winkielman, P., & Cacioppo, J.T. (2001). Mind at ease puts smile on the face: Psychophysiological evidence that processing facilitation elicits positive affect. *Journal of Personality and Social Psychology, 81,* 989–1000.

Younger, B.A., & Fearing, D.D. (1999). Parsing items into separate categories: Developmental change in infant categorization. *Child Development, 70,* 291–303.

Address correspondence to **JENNIFER L. RAMSEY-RENNELS,** Department of Psychology, University of Nevada, Las Vegas, 4505 Maryland Parkway Box 455030, Las Vegas, NV 89154-5030; e-mail: ramseyj2@unlv.nevada.edu.

Acknowledgments—Preparation of this manuscript was supported by two grants from the National Institute of Child Health and Human Development, one to Jennifer Ramsey-Rennels (HD48467) and one to Judith Langlois (HD21332).

The Other-Race Effect Develops during Infancy

Evidence of Perceptual Narrowing

Experience plays a crucial role in the development of face processing. In the study reported here, we investigated how faces observed within the visual environment affect the development of the face-processing system during the 1st year of life. We assessed 3-, 6-, and 9-month-old Caucasian infants' ability to discriminate faces within their own racial group and within three other-race groups (African, Middle Eastern, and Chinese). The 3-month-old infants demonstrated recognition in all conditions, the 6-month-old infants were able to recognize Caucasian and Chinese faces only, and the 9-month-old infants' recognition was restricted to own-race faces. The pattern of preferences indicates that the other-race effect is emerging by 6 months of age and is present at 9 months of age. The findings suggest that facial input from the infant's visual environment is crucial for shaping the face-processing system early in infancy, resulting in differential recognition accuracy for faces of different races in adulthood.

DAVID J. KELLY ET AL.

Human adults are experts at recognizing faces of conspecifics and appear to perform this task effortlessly. Despite this impressive ability, however, adults are more susceptible to recognition errors when a target face is from an unfamiliar racial group, rather than their own racial group. This phenomenon is known as the *other-race effect* (ORE; see Meissner & Brigham, 2001, for a review). Although the ORE has been widely reported, the exact mechanisms that underlie reduced recognition accuracy for other-race faces, and precisely when this effect emerges during development, remain unclear.

The ORE can be explained in terms of a modifiable face representation. The concept of a multidimensional *face-space* architecture, first proposed by Valentine (1991), has received much empirical support. According to the norm-based coding model, individual face exemplars are represented as vectors within face-space according to their deviation from a prototypical average. The prototype held by each person represents the average of all faces that person has ever encoded and is therefore unique. Although it is unclear which dimensions are most salient and used for recognition, it is likely that dimensions vary between individuals and possibly within each person over time. The prototype (and therefore the entire face-space) continually adapts and is updated as more faces are observed within the environment. Consequently, individuating face-space dimensions of a person living in China are expected to be optimal for recognition of other Chinese persons, but not, for example, for recognition of African individuals.

Other authors have hypothesized that the dimensions of the face prototype present at birth are broad and develop according to the type of facial input received (Nelson, 2001). According to this account, predominant exposure to faces from a single racial category tunes face-space dimensions toward that category. Such tuning might be manifested at a behavioral level in differential responding to own- versus other-race faces, for example, in spontaneous visual preference and a recognition advantage for own-race faces.

Recent findings regarding spontaneous preference have confirmed the impact of differential face input on the tuning of the face prototype during early infancy. It has been demonstrated that selectivity based on ethnic facial differences emerges very early in life, with 3-month-old infants preferring to look at faces from their own group, as opposed to faces from other ethnic groups (Bar-Haim, Ziv, Lamy, & Hodes, 2006; Kelly et al., 2005, 2007). We (Kelly et al., 2005) have shown that this preference is not present at birth, which strongly suggests that own-group preferences result from differential exposure to faces from one's particular ethnic group. In addition, Bar-Haim et al. (2006) tested a population of Ethiopian infants who had been raised in an absorption center while their families awaited housing in Israel. These infants were frequently exposed to both Ethiopian and Israeli adults and subsequently demonstrated no preference for either African or Caucasian faces when presented simultaneously.

Collectively, these results provide strong evidence that faces observed in the visual environment have a highly influential role in eliciting face preferences during infancy. Additional evidence supporting this conclusion comes from a study concerning gender preference (Quinn, Yahr, Kuhn, Slater, & Pascalis, 2002), which showed that 3- to 4-month-old infants raised primarily by a female caregiver demonstrate a visual preference for female over male faces, whereas infants raised primarily by a male caregiver prefer to look at male rather than female faces.

Although the literature on differential face recognition contains discrepancies regarding the onset of the ORE, evidence points toward an early inception. Some of the initial investigations reported onset at 8 (Feinman & Entwhistle, 1976) and 6 (Chance, Turner, & Goldstein, 1982) years of age. More recent studies have found the ORE to be present in 5-year-olds (Pezdek, Blandon-Gitlin, & Moore, 2003) and 3-year-olds (Sangrigoli & de Schonen, 2004a). In addition, Sangrigoli and de Schonen (2004b) showed that 3-month-old Caucasian infants were able to recognize an own-race face, but not an Asian face, as measured by the visual paired-comparison (VPC) task. However, the effect disappeared if infants were habituated to three, as opposed to one, other-race face exemplars. Thus, although the ORE may be present at 3 months of age, it is weak enough to be eliminated after only a few instances of exposure within an experimental session.

Additional lines of evidence indicate that the face representation undergoes change throughout development. At 6 months of age, infants are able to individuate human and monkey faces, and although the ability to individuate human faces is maintained in later development, the ability to individuate monkey faces is absent in 9-month-old infants and in adults (Pascalis, de Haan, & Nelson, 2002). Although the face-processing system appears to adapt toward own-species faces, it still retains flexibility for within-species categories of faces (i.e., other-race faces). Korean adults adopted by French families during childhood (ages 3–9 years) demonstrated a recognition deficit for Korean faces relative to their ability to recognize European faces (Sangrigoli, Pallier, Argenti, Ventureyra, & de Schonen, 2005). Their pattern of performance was comparable to that of the native French people who were tested in the same study.

The purpose of the study reported here was to clarify the developmental origins of the ORE during the first months of life. Using the VPC task, we assessed the ability of 3-, 6-, and 9-month-old Caucasian infants to discriminate within own-race (Caucasian) faces and within three categories of other-race faces (African, Middle Eastern, and Chinese). This task measures relative interest in the members of pairs of stimuli, each consisting of a novel stimulus and a familiar stimulus observed during a prior habituation period. Recognition of the familiar stimulus is inferred from the participant's tendency to fixate on the novel stimulus. Previous studies have found that 3-month-old infants can perform this task even when they are exposed to different views of faces (e.g., full view vs. 3/4 profile) during the habituation period and the recognition test (Pascalis, de Haan, Nelson, & de Schonen, 1998). We also varied face views between familiarization and testing, a procedure that is preferable to using identical pictures in the habituation and testing

phases because it ensures that face recognition—as opposed to picture recognition (i.e., image matching)—is tested. Our selection of which age groups to test was based on previous research demonstrating that the ORE is found in infancy (3-month-olds; Sangrigoli & de Schonen, 2004b) and that the face-processing system appears to undergo a period of tuning between 6 and 9 months of age (Pascalis et al., 2002).

Method
Participants

In total, 192 Caucasian infants were included in the final analysis. There were 64 subjects in each of three age groups: 3-month-olds (age range = 86–102 days; 33 females, 31 males), 6-month-olds (age range = 178–196 days; 31 females, 33 males), and 9-month-olds (age range = 268–289 days; 30 females, 34 males). All participants were healthy, full-term infants. Within each age group, the infants were assigned in equal numbers ($n = 16$) to the four testing conditions (Caucasian, African, Middle Eastern, and Chinese). The infants were recruited from the maternity wing of the Royal Hallamshire Hospital, Sheffield, United Kingdom. In each age group, we tested additional infants who were excluded from the final analysis. Twenty-two 3-month-old infants were excluded because of failure to habituate ($n = 4$), side bias during testing ($> 95\%$ looking time to one side; $n = 15$), or fussiness ($n = 3$); sixteen 6-month-old infants were excluded because of failure to habituate ($n = 7$), side bias during testing ($n = 3$), parental interference ($n = 2$), or fussiness ($n = 4$); and eleven 9-month-old infants were excluded because of a failure to habituate ($n = 3$) or fussiness ($n = 8$).

Stimuli

The stimuli were 24 color images of male and female adult faces (age range = 23–27 years) from four different ethnic groups (African, Asian, Middle Eastern, and Caucasian). All faces had dark hair and dark eyes so that the infants would be unable to demonstrate recognition on the basis of these features. The images were photos of students. The Africans were members of the African and Caribbean Society at the University of Sheffield; the Asians were Han Chinese students from Zhejiang Sci-Tech University, Hangzhou, China; the Middle Easterners were members of the Pakistan Society at the University of Sheffield; and the Caucasians were psychology students at the University of Sheffield.

For each ethnic group, we tested male and female faces in separate conditions. The images for each combination of ethnic group and gender consisted of a habituation face and two test faces, a novel face and the familiar face in a new orientation. The two faces in the test phase were always in the same orientation, and this orientation differed from the orientation of the face seen during habituation. In one orientation condition, infants were habituated to full-view faces and saw test faces in 3/4-profile views; in the other orientation condition, the views were reversed. Equal numbers of infants were assigned to the two orientation conditions.

All photos were taken with a Canon S50 digital camera and subsequently cropped using Adobe Photoshop to remove the neck and background details. All individual pictures were then mounted on a uniform dark-gray background, and the stimuli were resized to the same dimensions to ensure uniformity. Sixteen independent observers rated a pool of 32 faces for attractiveness and distinctiveness, using a scale from 1 to 10, and the final set of 24 faces was selected so as to match gender, attractiveness, and distinctiveness within each face pair.

Procedure

All infants were tested in a quiet room at the department of psychology at the University of Sheffield. They were seated on their mother's lap, approximately 60 cm from a screen onto which the images were projected. Each infant was randomly assigned to one of the four ethnic-group conditions (African, Asian, Middle Eastern, or Caucasian). Within each of these four conditions, infants were tested with either male or female faces; testing was counterbalanced appropriately, with half the infants assigned to the male-faces condition and half the infants assigned to the female-faces condition. Equal numbers of infants were tested in the male and female conditions. Before the session started, all mothers were instructed to fixate centrally above the screen and to remain as quiet as possible during testing.

Habituation Phase

Each infant was first presented with a single face projected onto a screen measuring 45 cm × 30 cm. The face measured 18 cm × 18 cm (14° visual angle). The experimenter observed the infant's eye movements on a control monitor from a black-and-white closed-circuit television camera (specialized for low-light conditions) that was positioned above the screen. Time was recorded and displayed on the control monitor using a Horita (Mission Viejo, CA) II TG-50 time coder; video was recorded at 25 frames per second.

The experimenter recorded the infant's attention to the face by holding down the "z" key on a keyboard whenever the infant fixated on the image. When the infant looked away from the image, the experimenter released the key. If the infant's attention was averted for more than 2 s, the image disappeared from the screen. The experimenter then presented the image again and repeated the procedure. The habituation phase ended when the infant's looking time on a presentation was equal to or less than 50% of the average looking time from the infant's first two presentations. Thus, our measure of looking time was the sum of looking time across all presentations until the habituation criterion was reached.

Test Phase

The test phase consisted of two trials. First, two face images (novel and familiar), each measuring 18 cm × 18 cm (14° visual angle), were presented on the screen. The images were separated by a 9-cm gap and appeared in the bottom left and bottom right corners of the screen. When the infant first looked at the images, the experimenter pressed a key to begin a 5-s countdown. At the end of the 5 s, the images disappeared from the screen. The faces then appeared with their left/right position on the screen reversed.

As soon as the infant looked at the images, another 5-s countdown was initiated. Eye movements were recorded throughout, and the film was digitized for frame-by-frame analysis by two independent observers who used specialized computer software to code looking time to each of the two faces. The observers were blind to both gender and ethnic-group condition and to the screen positions of the faces being viewed by the infants. The average level of interobserver agreement was high (Pearson $r = .93$). Recognition was inferred from a preference for the novel face stimulus across the two 5-s test trials.

Results

Habituation Trials

A preliminary analysis revealed no significant gender differences for stimuli or participants, so data were collapsed across stimulus gender and participant's gender in subsequent analyses. Habituation time (total looking time across trials) was analyzed in a 3 (age: 3, 6, or 9 months) × 4 (face ethnicity: African, Middle Eastern, Chinese, or Caucasian) × 2 (face orientation: full face or 3/4 profile) between-subjects analysis of variance (ANOVA). The ANOVA yielded only a significant effect of age, $F(2, 189) = 73.193$, $p < .0001$, $\eta^2 = .535$. Post hoc Tukey's honestly significant difference (HSD) tests revealed that the habituation times of 6- and 9-month-old infants did not differ significantly, but both 6-month-old ($M = 42.67$ s) and 9-month-old ($M = 38.88$ s) infants habituated significantly more quickly ($p < .0001$) than 3-month-old infants ($M = 70.74$ s). There were no main effects of face ethnicity or face orientation, nor were there any interactions.

Test Trials

Again, a preliminary analysis yielded no significant gender differences for stimuli or participants, so data were collapsed across stimulus gender and participant's gender in subsequent analyses. Percentage of time spent looking at the novel stimulus, combined from both trials of the test phase, was analyzed in a 3 (age: 3, 6, or 9 months) × 4 (face ethnicity: African, Middle Eastern, Chinese, or Caucasian) × 2 (face orientation: full face or 3/4 view) between-subjects ANOVA. The ANOVA yielded a significant effect of age, $F(2, 189) = 5.133$, $p < .007$, $\eta^2 = .058$. Post hoc Tukey's HSD tests revealed that 3-month-olds ($M = 60.15\%$) showed significantly greater preference for the novel face ($p < .003$) than did 9-month-olds ($M = 53.19\%$). There were no main effects of face ethnicity or face orientation.

To investigate novelty preferences within each age group, we conducted one-way between-groups ANOVAs on the percentage of time spent looking at the novel stimuli in the four face-ethnicity conditions. A significant effect of face ethnicity was found for 9-month-old infants, $F(3, 60) = 3.105$, $p < .033$, $\eta^2 = .134$, but not for 3- or 6-month-old infants. These results suggest that novelty preferences differed between face-ethnicity conditions only within the group of 9-month-old infants.

To further investigate novelty preferences within each age group, we conducted a series of two-tailed t tests to determine whether the time spent looking at novel stimuli differed from

TABLE 1 Results of the Novelty-Preference Test, by Age Group and Face Ethnicity

Age and Face Ethnicity	Mean Time Looking at the Novel Face (%)	t(15)	p	p_rep
3 months				
African	60.88 (16.52)	2.635	.019*	.942
Middle Eastern	57.31 (11.37)	2.572	.021*	.937
Chinese	58.72 (14.07)	2.479	.026*	.929
Caucasian	63.71 (13.47)	4.072	.001*	.988
6 months				
African	55.35 (11.40)	1.880	> .05	.840
Middle Eastern	56.70 (12.89)	2.079	> .05	.871
Chinese	56.42 (7.79)	3.295	.005*	.965
Caucasian	58.27 (8.88)	3.725	.002*	.979
9 months				
African	51.33 (10.53)	0.505	> .05	.414
Middle Eastern	53.51 (8.47)	1.658	> .05	.799
Chinese	48.23 (13.31)	0.530	> .05	.642
Caucasian	59.70 (11.16)	3.476	.003*	.971

Note. Standard deviations are given in parentheses. Asterisks highlight conditions in which the infants viewed novel faces significantly more often than predicted by chance.

the chance level of 50% (see Table 1). The results showed that 3-month-old infants demonstrated significant novelty preferences in all four face-ethnicity conditions, 6-month-old infants demonstrated significant novelty preferences in two of the four conditions (Chinese and Caucasian), and 9-month-old infants demonstrated a novelty preference for Caucasian faces only.

Discussion

The aim of the current study was to investigate the onset of the ORE during the first months of life, following up on previous findings that 3-month-olds already show a preference for own-race faces (Bar-Haim et al., 2006; Kelly et al., 2005, 2007). The results reported here do not provide evidence for the ORE (as measured by differential recognition capabilities for own- and other-race faces) in 3-month-old infants, but they do indicate that the ORE emerges at age 6 months and is fully present at age 9 months.

Our results are consistent with the notion of general perceptual narrowing during infancy (e.g., Nelson, 2001). Our findings are also consistent with those of Pascalis et al. (2002), further demonstrating that the face-processing system undergoes a period of refinement within the 1st year of life. Collectively, these findings lend weight to the concept of a tuning period between 6 and 9 months of age. However, differences between the present study and the work by Pascalis et al. should be noted. For example, there is the obvious difference that Pascalis et al. found between-species effects, and our study focused on within-species effects. It should not be assumed that identical mechanisms necessarily underlie the reductions in recognition accuracy observed in the two cases. In addition, once the ability to discriminate between nonhuman primate faces has

diminished, it apparently cannot be recovered easily (Dufour, Coleman, Campbell, Petit, & Pascalis, 2004; Pascalis et al., 2002), whereas the ORE is evidently modifiable through exposure to other-race populations (Sangrigoli et al., 2005) or simple training with other-race faces (Elliott, Wills, & Goldstein, 1973; Goldstein & Chance, 1985; Lavrakas, Buri, & Mayzner, 1976). Furthermore, event-related potential (ERP) studies have shown that in 6-month-olds, the putative infant N170 (a face-selective ERP component elicited in occipital regions) is sensitive to inversion for both human and monkey faces, whereas the N170 recorded in adults is sensitive to inversion only for human faces (de Haan, Pascalis, & Johnson, 2002). An adult-like N170 response is not observed in subjects until they are 12 months of age (Halit, de Haan, & Johnson, 2003). The ERP response for other-race faces has not yet been investigated during infancy, but studies with adults have revealed no differences in the N170 response to own- and other-race faces (Caldara et al., 2003; Caldara, Rossion, Bovet, & Hauert, 2004).

Our findings differ from those reported by Sangrigoli and de Schonen (2004b) in the only other study to have investigated the emergence of the ORE during infancy. In their initial experiment, Sangrigoli and de Schonen found that 3-month-old infants discriminated own-race faces, but not other-race faces, as measured by the VPC task. However, numerous methodological differences between our study and theirs (e.g., color stimuli in our study vs. gray-scale stimuli in theirs) could have contributed to these contrasting results. Furthermore, Sangrigoli and de Schonen were able to eliminate the ORE with only a few trials of exposure to multiple exemplars, which suggests that even if the ORE is already present in 3-month-olds, it is weak and reversible. Between Sangrigoli and de Schonen's work and our own, there are now three VPC experiments (one here, two in Sangrigoli & de Schonen)[1] that have been conducted with 3-month-old infants, yet only one has yielded evidence for the ORE. The weight of the evidence thus suggests that a strong and sustainable ORE may not be present at 3 months of age, but rather develops later.

One might ask whether the ORE arises from differences in the variability of faces from different ethnic groups. However, the available evidence indicates that no category of faces has greater homogeneity than any other (Goldstein, 1979a, 1979b). Moreover, the data suggest that the ORE does not exclusively reflect a deficit for non-Caucasian faces: Individuals from many ethnic groups demonstrate poorer recognition of other-race than own-race faces (Meissner & Brigham, 2001). Evidently, a full account of the ORE will involve factors other than heterogeneity.

We have argued elsewhere (Kelly et al., 2007) that the ORE may develop through the following processes: First, predominant exposure to faces from one's own racial group induces familiarity with and a visual preference for such faces. Second, a preference for faces within one's racial group produces greater visual attention to such faces, even when faces from other racial groups are present in the visual environment. Third, superior recognition abilities develop for faces within one's racial group, but not for faces from groups that are infrequently encountered. Although supporting evidence for the first two processes has been obtained previously (Bar-Haim et al., 2006; Kelly et al., 2005, 2007), the data reported here provide the first direct evidence for the third. According to our account, the ORE can be explained by a modifiable face prototype (Valentine, 1991). If each person's face prototype is an average of all faces that person has encoded during his or her lifetime, then one may assume that it will resemble the race of the faces most commonly encountered. Furthermore, one would expect that individuating dimensions will be optimized for recognition of own-race faces, but not other-race faces.

An alternative to the single-prototype account is that people may possess multiple face-spaces that represent different face categories (e.g., gender, race) separately within a global space. In this contrasting scheme, rather than individuating dimensions being unsuitable for recognition of other-race faces, a face-space for other-race faces (e.g., Chinese faces) either does not exist or is insufficiently formed because of a general lack of exposure to those face categories. In both accounts, recognition capabilities improve through exposure to other-race faces. In the case of the single-prototype account, individuating dimensions acquire properties of newly encountered other-race faces that facilitate recognition. Alternatively, in the multiple-face-spaces account, a relevant space for other-race faces develops through similar exposure.

In summary, this is the first study to investigate the emergence of the ORE during infancy by comparing three different age groups' ability to recognize faces from their own race and a range of other races. The data reported here support the idea that very young infants have a broad face-processing system that is capable of processing faces from different ethnic groups. Between 3 and 9 months of age, this system gradually becomes more sensitive to faces from an infant's own ethnic group as a consequence of greater exposure to such faces than to faces from other racial groups. This shift in sensitivity is reflected in the emergence of a deficit in recognition accuracy for faces from unfamiliar groups.

Future research should address whether the pattern of results we obtained with Caucasian infants is universal, or whether the ORE emerges at different ages in other populations.

Note

1. But note that in a recent study using morphed stimuli, Hayden, Bhatt, Joseph, and Tanaka (2007) demonstrated that 3.5-month-old infants showed greater sensitivity to structural changes in own-race faces than in other-race faces.

References

Bar-Haim, Y., Ziv, T., Lamy, D., & Hodes, R.M. (2006). Nature and nurture in own-race face processing. *Psychological Science, 17,* 159–163.

Caldara, R., Rossion, B., Bovet, P., & Hauert, C.A. (2004). Event-related potentials and time course of the 'other-race' face classification advantage. *Cognitive Neuroscience and Neuropsychology, 15,* 905–910.

Caldara, R., Thut, G., Servoir, P., Michel, C.M., Bovet, P., & Renault, B. (2003). Faces versus non-face object perception and the 'other-race' effect: A spatio-temporal event-related potential study. *Clinical Neurophysiology, 114,* 515–528.

Chance, J.E., Turner, A.L., & Goldstein, A.G. (1982). Development of differential recognition for own- and other-race faces. *Journal of Psychology, 112,* 29–37.

de Haan, M., Pascalis, O., & Johnson, M.H. (2002). Specialization of neural mechanisms underlying face recognition in human infants. *Journal of Cognitive Neuroscience, 14,* 199–209.

Dufour, V., Coleman, M., Campbell, R., Petit, O., & Pascalis, O. (2004). On the species-specificity of face recognition in human adults. *Current Psychology of Cognition, 22,* 315–333.

Elliott, E.S., Wills, E.J., & Goldstein, A.G. (1973). The effects of discrimination training on the recognition of White and Oriental faces. *Bulletin of the Psychonomic Society, 2,* 71–73.

Feinman, S., & Entwhistle, D.R. (1976). Children's ability to recognize other children's faces. *Child Development, 47,* 506–510.

Goldstein, A.G. (1979a). Race-related variation of facial features: Anthropometric data I. *Bulletin of the Psychonomic Society, 13,* 187–190.

Goldstein, A.G. (1979b). Facial feature variation: Anthropometric data II. *Bulletin of the Psychonomic Society, 13,* 191–193.

Goldstein, A.G., & Chance, J.E. (1985). Effects of training on Japanese face recognition: Reduction of the other-race effect. *Bulletin of the Psychonomic Society, 23,* 211–214.

Halit, H., de Haan, M., & Johnson, M.H. (2003). Cortical specialisation for face processing: Face-sensitive event-related potential components in 3- and 12-month-old infants. *NeuroImage, 19,* 1180–1193.

Hayden, A., Bhatt, R.S., Joseph, J.E., & Tanaka, J.W. (2007). The other-race effect in infancy: Evidence using a morphing technique. *Infancy, 12,* 95–104.

Kelly, D.J., Ge, L., Liu, S., Quinn, P.C., Slater, A.M., Lee, K., et al. (2007). Cross-race preferences for same-race faces extend beyond the African versus Caucasian contrast in 3-month-old infants. *Infancy, 11,* 87–95.

Kelly, D.J., Quinn, P.C., Slater, A.M., Lee, K., Gibson, A., Smith, M., et al. (2005). Three-month-olds, but not newborns, prefer own-race faces. *Developmental Science, 8,* F31–F36.

Lavrakas, P.J., Buri, J.R., & Mayzner, M.S. (1976). A perspective on the recognition of other-race faces. *Perception & Psychophysics, 20,* 475–481.

Meissner, C.A., & Brigham, J.C. (2001). Thirty years of investigating the own-race bias in memory for faces: A meta-analytic review. *Psychology, Public Policy, and Law, 7,* 3–35.

Nelson, C.A. (2001). The development and neural bases of face recognition. *Infant and Child Development, 10,* 3–18.

Pascalis, O., de Haan, M., & Nelson, C.A. (2002). Is face processing species-specific during the first year of life? *Science, 296,* 1321–1323.

Pascalis, O., de Haan, M., Nelson, C.A., & de Schonen, S. (1998). Long-term recognition assessed by visual paired comparison in 3- and 6-month-old infants. *Journal of Experimental Psychology: Learning, Memory, and Cognition, 24,* 249–260.

Pezdek, K., Blandon-Gitlin, I., & Moore, C. (2003). Children's face recognition memory: More evidence for the cross-race effect. *Journal of Applied Psychology, 88,* 760–763.

Quinn, P.C., Yahr, J., Kuhn, A., Slater, A.M., & Pascalis, O. (2002). Representation of the gender of human faces by infants: A preference for female. *Perception, 31,* 1109–1121.

Sangrigoli, S., & de Schonen, S. (2004a). Effect of visual experience on face processing: A developmental study of inversion and non-native effects. *Developmental Science, 7,* 74–87.

Sangrigoli, S., & de Schonen, S. (2004b). Recognition of own-race and other-race faces by three-month-old infants. *Journal of Child Psychology and Psychiatry and Allied Disciplines, 45,* 1219–1227.

Sangrigoli, S., Pallier, C., Argenti, A.M., Ventureyra, V.A.G., & de Schonen, S. (2005). Reversibility of the other-race effect in face recognition during childhood. *Psychological Science, 16,* 440–444.

Valentine, T. (1991). A unified account of the effects of distinctiveness, inversion, and race in face recognition. *The Quarterly Journal of Experimental Psychology, 43A,* 161–204.

DAVID J. KELLY: University of Sheffield, Sheffield, United Kingdom; **PAUL C. QUINN:** University of Delaware; **ALAN M. SLATER:** University of Exeter, Exeter, United Kingdom; **KANG LEE:** University of Toronto, Toronto, Ontario, Canada; **LIEZHONG GE:** Zeijiang Sci-Tech University, Hangzhou, People's Republic of China; and **OLIVER PASCALIS:** University of Sheffield, Sheffield, United Kingdom

Address correspondence to David J. Kelly, University of Sheffield, Psychology Department, Western Bank, Sheffield, South Yorkshire S10 2TP, United Kingdom, e-mail: david.kelly@sheffield.ac.uk.

Acknowledgments—This work was supported by National Institutes of Health Grants HD-46526 and HD-42451 and by an Economic and Social Research Council studentship awarded to David J. Kelly.

New Advances in Understanding Sensitive Periods in Brain Development

Michael S. C. Thomas and Mark H. Johnson

The idea that there are "critical" or sensitive periods in neural, cognitive, and behavioral development has a long history. It first became widely known with the phenomenon of *filial imprinting* as famously described by Konrad Lorenz: After a relatively brief exposure to a particular stimulus early in life, many birds and mammals form a strong and exclusive attachment to that stimulus. According to Lorenz, a critical period in development has several features, including the following: Learning or plasticity is confined to a short and sharply defined period of the life cycle, and this learning is subsequently irreversible in the face of later experience. Following the paradigmatic example of filial imprinting in birds, more recent studies on cats, dogs, and monkeys, as well as investigations of bird song and human language development, have confirmed that critical periods are major phenomena in brain and behavioral development (see Michel & Tyler, 2005, for review). However, it rapidly became evident that, even in the prototypical case of imprinting, critical periods were not as sharply timed and irreversible as first thought. For example, the critical period for imprinting in domestic chicks was shown to be extendable in time in the absence of appropriate stimulation, and the learning is reversible under certain circumstances (for review, see Bolhuis, 1991). These and other modifications of Lorenz's original views have led most current researchers to adopt the alternative term *sensitive periods* to describe these widespread developmental phenomena.

A fundamental debate that continues to the present is whether specific mechanisms underlie sensitive periods or whether such periods are a natural consequence of functional brain development. Support for the latter view has come from a recent perspective on developing brain functions. Relating evidence on the neuroanatomical development of the brain to the remarkable changes in motor, perceptual, and cognitive abilities during the first decade or so of a human life presents a formidable challenge. A recent theory, termed *interactive specialization*, holds that postnatal functional brain development, at least within the cerebral cortex, involves a process of increasing specialization, or fine-tuning, of response properties (Johnson, 2001, 2005). According to this view, during postnatal development, the response properties of cortical regions change as they interact and compete with each other to acquire their roles in new computational abilities. That is, some cortical regions begin with poorly defined functions and consequently are partially activated in a wide range of different contexts and tasks. During development, activity-dependent interactions between regions sharpen up their functions, such that a region's activity becomes restricted to a narrower set of stimuli or task demands. For example, a region originally activated by a wide variety of visual objects may come to confine its response to upright human faces. The termination of sensitive periods is then a natural consequence of the mechanisms by which cortical regions become increasingly specialized and finely tuned. Once regions have become specialized for their adult functions, these commitments are difficult to reverse. If this view is correct, sensitive periods in human cognitive development are intrinsic to the process that produces the functional structure of the adult brain.

In order to better understand how sensitive periods relate to the broader picture of vertebrate functional brain development, researchers have addressed a number of specific questions. In any given species are there multiple sensitive periods or just a few (e.g., one per sensory modality)? If there are multiple sensitive periods, do they share common underlying mechanisms? What are the processes that underlie the end of sensitive periods and the corresponding reduction in plasticity?

Varieties of Sensitive Period

Recent work indicates that there are multiple sensitive periods in the sensory systems that have been studied. For example, within the auditory domain in humans, there are different sensitive periods for different facets of speech processing and other sensitive periods, having different timing, related to basic aspects of music perception. Similarly, in nonhuman-primate visual systems there are, at a minimum, different sensitive periods related to amblyopia (a condition found in early childhood in which one eye develops good vision but the other does not), visual acuity, motion perception, and face processing (see Johnson, 2005, for review).

How these different and varied sensitive periods relate to each other is still poorly understood. But high-level skills like human language involve the integration of many lower-level systems, and plasticity in language acquisition is therefore likely to be the combinatorial result of the relative plasticity of underlying auditory, phonological, semantic, syntactic, and motor systems, along with the developmental interactions among these components. The literature currently available suggests that plasticity tends to reduce in low-level sensory systems before it reduces in high-level cognitive systems (Huttenlocher, 2002).

While it is now agreed that there are multiple sensitive periods even within one sensory modality in a given species, there is still considerable debate as to whether these different sensitive periods reflect common underlying mechanisms or whether different mechanisms and principles operate in each case.

Mechanisms Underlying Sensitive Periods

A major feature of sensitive periods is that plasticity appears to be markedly reduced at the end of the period. There are three general classes of explanation for this: (a) termination of plasticity due to maturation, (b) self-termination of learning, and (c) stabilization of constraints on plasticity (without a reduction in the underlying level of plasticity).

According to the first view, endogenous changes in the neurochemistry of the brain region in question could increase the rate of pruning of synapses, resulting in the "fossilization" of existing patterns of functional connectivity. Thus, the termination of sensitive periods would be due to endogenous factors, would have a fixed time course, and could be specific to individual regions of the cortex. Empirical evidence on neurochemical changes associated with plasticity (such as expression of glutamatergic and GABA receptors in the human visual cortex) indicate that the periods of neurochemical change can occur around the age of functional sensitive periods. However, this does not rule out the possibility that these neurochemical changes are a consequence of the differences in functional activity due to termination of plasticity for some other reason, rather than its primary cause (Murphy, Betson, Boley, & Jones, 2005).

The second class of mechanism implies that sensitive periods involve self-terminating learning processes. By this, we mean that the process of learning itself could produce changes that reduce the system's plasticity. These types of mechanisms are most consistent with the view of sensitive periods as a natural consequence of typical functional brain development. An important way to describe and understand self-terminating learning comes from the use of computer-simulated neural networks (Thomas & Johnson, 2006). These models demonstrate mechanistically how processes of learning can lead to neurobiological changes that reduce plasticity, rather than plasticity changing according to a purely maturational timetable. Such computer models have revealed that, even where a reduction in plasticity emerges with increasing experience, a range of different specific mechanisms may be responsible for this reduction (see Thomas & Johnson, 2006). For example, it may be that the neural system's computational resources, which are critical for future learning, have been claimed or used up by existing learning, so that any

new learning must compete to capture these resources. Unless earlier-learned abilities are neglected or lost, new learning may always be limited by this competition. Another mechanism discovered through modeling is called entrenchment. In this case, prior experience places the system into a state that is nonoptimal for learning the new skill. It takes time to reconfigure the system for the new task and learning correspondingly takes longer than it would have done had the system been in an uncommitted state. A third mechanism is assimilation, whereby initial learning reduces the system's ability to detect changes in the environment that might trigger further learning.

Evidence from humans relevant to self-terminating sensitive periods is reported by Lewis and Maurer (2005), who have studied the outcome of cases of human infants born with dense bilateral cataracts in both eyes. Such dense bilateral cataracts restrict these infants to near blindness, but fortunately the condition can be rectified with surgery. Despite variation in the age of treatment from 1 to 9 months, infants were found to have the visual acuity of a newborn immediately following surgery to remove the cataracts. However, after only 1 hour of patterned vision, acuity had improved to the level of a typical 6-week-old; and after a further month of visual experience, the gap to age-matched controls was very considerably reduced. These findings correspond well with experiments showing that rearing animals in the dark appears to delay the end of the normal sensitive period. Thus, in at least some cases, plasticity seems to wait for the appropriate type of sensory stimulation. This is consistent with the idea that changes in plasticity can be driven by the learning processes associated with typical development.

Returning to the paradigmatic example of filial imprinting in birds, O'Reilly and Johnson (1994) constructed a computer model of the neural network known to support imprinting in the relevant region of the chick brain. This computer model successfully simulated a range of phenomena associated with imprinting behavior in the chick. Importantly, in both the model and the chick, the extent to which an imprinted preference for one object can be "reversed" by exposure to a second object depends on a combination of the length of exposure to the first object and the length of exposure to the second object (for review, see Bolhuis, 1991). In other words, in the model, the sensitive period was dependent on the respective levels of learning and was self-terminating. Additionally, like the chick, the network generalised from a training object to one that shared some of its features such as color or shape. By gradually changing the features of the object to which the chick was exposed, the chick's preference could be shifted even after the "sensitive period" had supposedly closed. The simulation work demonstrated the sufficiency of simple learning mechanisms to explain the observed behavioral data (McClelland, 2005).

The third class of explanation for the end of sensitive periods is that it represents the onset of stability in constraining factors rather than a reduction in the underlying plasticity. For example, while an infant is growing, the distance between her eyes increases, thereby creating instability in the information to visual cortical areas. However, once the inter-eye distance is fixed in development, the visual input becomes stable. Thus, brain plasticity may be "hidden" until it is revealed by some perturbation to another constraining factor that disrupts vision.

This mechanism offers an attractive explanation of the surprising degree of plasticity sometimes observed in adults, for instance after even brief visual deprivation. Sathian (2005) reported activity in the visual cortex during tactile perception in sighted human adults after brief visual deprivation—activity similar to that observed in those who have suffered long-term visual deprivation. While this line of research initially appears consistent with life-long plasticity, it is important to note that this tactile-induced visual-cortex activity is much greater if vision is lost early in life or was never present. Thus, although there appears to be residual connectivity between sensory systems that can be uncovered by blocking vision in sighted people, there is also a sensitive period during which these connections can be more drastically altered.

Sensitive Periods in Second Language Acquisition

Given the variety of mechanisms that may underlie sensitive periods, it would be interesting to know how such periods affect the acquisition of higher cognitive abilities in humans. Recent research on learning a second language illustrates one attempt to answer this question. If you want to master a second language, how important is the age at which you start to learn it? If you start to learn a second language as an adult, does your brain process it in a different way from how it processes your first language?

It is often claimed that unless individuals acquire a second language (L2) before mid-childhood (or perhaps before puberty), then they will never reach native-like levels of proficiency in the second language in pronunciation or grammatical knowledge. This claim is supported by deprivation studies showing that the acquisition of a first language (L1) is itself less successful when begun after a certain age. Further, functional brain-imaging studies initially indicated that in L2 acquisition, different areas of the cortex were activated by the L2 than by the L1; only in individuals who had acquired two languages simultaneously were common areas activated (e.g., Kim, Relkin, Lee, & Hirsch, 1997).

However, subsequent research has painted a more complex picture. First, claims for sensitive periods have tended to rely on assessing final level of attainment rather than speed of learning. This is because there is evidence that adults can learn a second language more quickly than children can, even if their final level of attainment is not as high. Indeed adults and children appear to learn a new language in different ways. Children are relatively insensitive to feedback and extract regularities from exposure to large amounts of input, whereas adults adopt explicit strategies and remain responsive to feedback (see, e.g., Hudson Kam & Newport, 2005).

Second, even when the final level of L2 attainment is considered, it has proved hard to find an age after which prospective attainment levels off. That is, there is no strong evidence for a point at which a sensitive period completely closes (see, e.g.,

Birdsong, 2006). Instead, L2 attainment shows a linear decline with age: The later you start, the lower your final level is likely to be (Birdsong, 2006).

Third, recent functional imaging research has indicated that at least three factors are important in determining the relative brain-activation patterns produced by L1 and L2 during comprehension and production. These are the age of acquisition, the level of usage/exposure to each language, and the level of proficiency attained in L2. Overall, three broad themes have emerged (Abutalebi, Cappa, & Perani, 2005; Stowe & Sabourin, 2005): (a) The same network of left-hemisphere brain regions is involved in processing both languages; (b) a weak L2 is associated with more widespread neural activity compared to L1 in production (perhaps because the L2 is more effortful to produce) but less activation in comprehension (perhaps because the L2 is less well understood); and (c) the level of proficiency in L2 is more important than age of acquisition in determining whether L1 and L2 activate common or separate areas. In brief, the better you are at your L2, the more similar the activated regions become to those activated by your L1. This finding fits with the idea that certain brain areas have become optimized for processing language (perhaps during the acquisition of L1) and that, in order to become very good at L2, you have to engage these brain areas. The idea that later plasticity is tempered by the processing structures created by earlier learning fits with the interactive-specialization explanation for the closing of sensitive periods.

Finally, in line with the idea that language requires integration across multiple subskills, increasing evidence indicates that sensitive periods differ across the components of language (Neville, 2006; Wartenburger et al., 2003; Werker & Tees, 2005). Plasticity may show greater or earlier reductions for phonology and morphosyntax than it does for lexical-semantics, in which there may indeed be no age-related change at all. In other words, for the late language learner, new vocabulary is easier to acquire than new sounds or new grammar.

Conclusion

It is important to understand the mechanisms underlying sensitive periods for practical reasons. Age-of-acquisition effects may shape educational policy and the time at which children are exposed to different skills. The reversibility of effects of deprivation on development has important implications for interventions for children with congenital sensory impairments or children exposed to impoverished physical and social environments. And there are clinical implications for understanding the mechanisms that drive recovery from brain damage at different ages.

Exciting vistas for the future include the possibility of using genetic and brain-imaging data to identify the best developmental times for training new skills in individual children, and the possibility that a deeper understanding of the neurocomputational principles that underlie self-terminating plasticity will allow the design of more efficient training procedures (McClelland 2005).

Recommended Readings

Birdsong, D. (2006). (See References). Discusses recent research on sensitive periods and second-language acquisition.

Huttenlocher, P.R. (2002). (See References). An overview of neural plasticity.

Johnson, M.H. (2005). *Developmental cognitive neuroscience* (2nd ed.). Oxford, UK: Blackwell. An introduction to the relationship between brain development and cognitive development.

Knusden, E.I. (2004). Sensitive periods in the development of brain and behavior. *Journal of Cognitive Neuroscience, 16,* 1412–1425. A discussion of mechanisms of plasticity and sensitive periods at the level of neural circuits.

References

Abutalebi, J., Cappa, S.F., & Perani, D. (2005). What can functional neuroimaging tell us about the bilingual brain? In J.F. Kroll & A.M.B. de Groot (Eds.), *Handbook of bilingualism* (pp. 497–515). Oxford, UK: Oxford University Press.

Birdsong, D. (2006). Age and second language acquisition and processing: A selective overview. *Language Learning, 56,* 9–49.

Bolhuis, J.J. (1991). Mechanisms of avian imprinting: A review. *Biological Reviews, 66,* 303–345.

Hudson Kam, C.L., & Newport, E.L. (2005). Regularizing unpredictable variation: The roles of adult and child learners in language formation and change. *Language Learning and Development, 1,* 151–195.

Huttenlocher, P.R. (2002). *Neural plasticity: The effects of the environment on the development of the cerebral cortex.* Cambridge, MA: Harvard University Press.

Huttenlocher, P.R., & Dabholkar, A.S. (1997). Regional differences in synaptogenesis in human cerebral cortex. *Journal of Comparative Neurology, 387,* 167–187.

Johnson, M.H. (2001). Functional brain development in humans. *Nature Reviews Neuroscience, 2,* 475–483.

Johnson, M.H. (2005). Sensitive periods in functional brain development: Problems and prospects. *Developmental Psychobiology, 46,* 287–292.

Kim, K.H.S., Relkin, N.R., Lee, K.M., & Hirsch, J. (1997). Distinct cortical areas associated with native and second languages. *Nature, 388,* 171–174.

Lewis, T.L., & Maurer, D. (2005). Multiple sensitive periods in human visual development: Evidence from visually deprived children. *Developmental Psychobiology, 46,* 163–183.

McClelland, J.L. (2005). How far can you go with Hebbian learning and when does it lead you astray? In Y. Munakata & M.H. Johnson (Eds.), *Attention and Performance XXI: Processes of change in brain and cognitive development* (pp. 33–59). Oxford, UK: Oxford University Press.

Michel, G.F., & Tyler, A.N. (2005). Critical period: A history of the transition from questions of when, to what, to how. *Developmental Psychobiology, 46,* 156–162.

Murphy, K.M., Betson, B.R., Boley, P.M., & Jones, D.G. (2005). Balance between excitatory and inhibitory plasticity mechanisms. *Developmental Psychobiology, 46,* 209–221.

Neville, H.J. (2006). Different profiles of plasticity within human cognition. In Y. Munakata & M.H. Johnson (Eds.), *Attention and Performance XXI: Processes of change in brain and cognitive development* (pp. 287–314). Oxford, UK: Oxford University Press.

O'Reilly, R., & Johnson, M.H. (1994). Object recognition and sensitive periods: A computational analysis of visual imprinting. *Neural Computation, 6,* 357–390.

Sathian, K. (2005). Visual cortical activity during tactile perception in the sighted and the visually deprived. *Developmental Psychobiology, 46,* 279–286.

Stowe, L.A., & Sabourin, L. (2005). Imaging the processing of a second language: Effects of maturation and proficiency on the neural processes involved. *International Review of Applied Linguistics in Language Teaching, 43,* 329–353.

Thomas, M.S.C., & Johnson, M.H. (2006). The computational modelling of sensitive periods. *Developmental Psychobiology, 48,* 337–344.

Wartenburger, I., Heekeren, H.R., Abutalebi, J., Cappa, S.F., Villringer, A., & Perani, D. (2003). Early setting of grammatical processing in the bilingual brain. *Neuron, 37,* 159–170.

Werker, J.F., & Tees, R.C. (2005). Speech perception as a window for understanding plasticity and commitment in language systems of the brain. *Developmental Psychobiology, 46,* 233–251.

Address correspondence to **MICHAEL S. C. THOMAS,** Developmental Neurocognition Laboratory, School of Psychology, Birkbeck College, University of London, Malet Street, Bloomsbury, London WC1E 7HX, United Kingdom; e-mail: m.thomas@bbk.ac.uk.

Acknowledgments—This research was supported by Medical Research Council (MRC) Career Establishment Grant G0300188 to Michael S.C. Thomas, and MRC Grant G9715587 to Mark H. Johnson.

Contributions of Neuroscience to Our Understanding of Cognitive Development

ADELE DIAMOND AND DIMA AMSO

Neuroscience research has made its greatest contributions to the study of cognitive development by illuminating mechanisms (providing a "how") that underlie behavioral observations made earlier by psychologists. It has also made important contributions to our understanding of cognitive development by demonstrating that the brain is far more plastic at all ages than previously thought—and thus that the speed and extent by which experience and behavior can shape the brain is greater than almost anyone imagined. In other words, rather than showing that biology is destiny, neuroscience research has been at the forefront of demonstrating the powerful role of experience throughout life. Besides the surprising evidence of the remarkable extent of experience-induced plasticity, rarely has neuroscience given us previously unknown insights into cognitive development, but neuroscience does offer promise of being able to detect some problems before they are behaviorally observable.

Providing Mechanisms That Can Account for Behavioral Results Reported by Psychologists

Here we describe two examples of behavioral findings by psychologists that were largely ignored or extremely controversial until underlying biological mechanisms capable of accounting for them were provided by neuroscience research. One such example concerns cognitive deficits documented in children treated early and continuously for phenylketonuria (PKU). The second example involves neonatal imitation observed by psychologists and mirror neurons discovered by neuroscientists.

Prefrontal Dopamine System and PKU Cognitive Deficits

Since at least the mid-1980s, psychologists were reporting cognitive deficits in children with PKU that resembled those associated with frontal cortex dysfunction (e.g., Pennington, VanDoornick, McCabe, & McCabe, 1985). Those reports did not impact medical care, however. Doctors were skeptical. No one could imagine a mechanism capable of producing what psychologists claimed to be observing.

PKU is a disorder in the gene that codes for phenylalanine hydroxylase, an enzyme essential for the conversion of phenylalanine (Phe) to tyrosine (Tyr). In those with PKU, that enzyme is absent or inactive. Without treatment, Phe levels skyrocket, resulting in gross brain damage and mental retardation. Phe is an amino acid and a component of all dietary protein. PKU treatment consists primarily of reducing dietary intake of protein to keep Phe levels down, but that has to be balanced against the need for protein. For years, children with PKU were considered adequately treated if their blood Phe levels were below 600 micromoles per liter (μmol/L; normal levels in the general public being 60–120 μmol/L). Such children did not have mental retardation and showed no gross brain damage, although no one disputed that their blood Phe levels were somewhat elevated and their blood Tyr levels were somewhat reduced (Tyr levels were not grossly reduced because even though the hydroxylation of Phe into Tyr was largely inoperative, Tyr is also available in protein). Since Phe and Tyr compete to cross into the brain, a modest increase in the ratio of Phe to Tyr in the bloodstream results in a modest decrease in how much Tyr can reach the brain. Note that this is a global effect—the entire brain receives somewhat too little Tyr. How was it possible to make sense of psychologists' claims that the resulting cognitive deficits were not global but limited to the cognitive functions dependent on prefrontal cortex?

Neuroscience provided a mechanism by which psychologists' findings made sense. Research in neuropharmacology had shown that the dopamine system in prefrontal cortex has unusual properties not shared by the dopamine systems in other brain regions such as the striatum. The dopamine neurons that project to prefrontal cortex have higher rates of firing and dopamine turnover. This makes prefrontal cortex sensitive to modest reductions in Tyr (the precursor of dopamine) that are too small to affect the rest of the brain (Tam, Elsworth, Bradberry, & Roth, 1990). Those unusual properties of the prefrontal dopamine system provide a mechanism by which children treated for PKU could show selective deficits limited to prefrontal cortex. The moderate imbalance in the bloodstream between Phe and Tyr causes a reduction in the amount of Tyr reaching the brain that is large enough to impair the functioning of the prefrontal dopamine system but not large enough to affect the rest of the brain. Diamond and colleagues provided evidence for this mechanism in animal models of PKU and longitudinal study of children (Diamond, 2001). That work, presenting a mechanistic explanation and providing convincing evidence to support it, resulted in a change in the medical guidelines for the treatment of PKU (blood Phe levels should be kept between 120 and 360 µmol/L) that has improved children's lives (e.g., Stemerdink et al., 2000). Also, by shedding light on the role of dopamine in the prefrontal cortex early in development, such work offers insights on the development of cognitive control (executive function) abilities that are relevant to all children.

Mirror Neurons and Neonate Imitation

In 1977, Meltzoff and Moore created a sensation by reporting that human infants just 12 to 21 days old imitated facial expressions they observed adults making. That was followed by a second demonstration of such imitation in infants as young as 42 minutes (Meltzoff & Moore, 1983). For years, those reports met strong resistance. Such imitation was thought to be far too sophisticated an accomplishment for a neonate. After all, infants can feel but not see their own mouth and tongue movements, and they can see but not feel the mouth and tongue movements of others. To equate their own motor movements with the perception of those same movements by others would seem to involve high-level cross-modal matching.

The discovery of mirror neurons by Rizzolatti and his colleagues, Fadiga, Fogassi, and Gallese (for review, see Rizzolatti & Craighero, 2004) provided a mechanism that could conceivably underlie newborns' ability to show such imitation rather automatically. Mirror neurons fire when an individual executes an action or when an individual observes someone else executing that action. The cross-modal association occurs at the neuronal, single-cell level. It has since been demonstrated that 3-day-old rhesus monkeys also imitate the facial movements of adult humans (Ferrari et al., 2006) and that the close link between perception and action is not limited to vision; hearing a sound associated with an action activates mirror neurons associated with that action just as does the sight of that action (Kohler et al., 2002).

Whereas the preceding examples are of neuroscience elucidating possible neurobiological bases for observed psychological phenomena, we move on to describe phenomena—concerning plasticity and environmental influences—that neuroscientists have brought to the attention of developmentalists.

Powerful Effects of Early Experience on Brain, Body, Mind, Behavior, and Gene Expression

Ironically, one of the most important findings to emerge from neurobiology is that biology is not destiny. Neuroscience research has shown that experience plays a far larger role in shaping the mind, brain, and even gene expression than was ever imagined. This insight is particularly important in advancing theory in cognitive development, where debates have raged about the importance of nature versus nurture.

Examples of striking experience-induced plasticity abound—for example, the groundbreaking work of Greenough, Merzenich, Maurer, Neville, Pascual-Leone, Taub, Sur, and Kral. Here we highlight work by Schanberg and Meaney, in part because that work emphasizes a sensory system that has received far less attention by psychologists than have vision and audition: the sense of touch.

Nurturing Touch and its Importance for Growth

Two independent, elegant lines of work have demonstrated the powerful effects of touch. Schanberg and colleagues have shown that the licking behavior of rat mothers is essential for the growth of rat pups. If rat pups are deprived of this touch for even just 1 hour, DNA synthesis is reduced, growth-hormone secretion is inhibited, and bodily organs lose their capacity to respond to exogenously administered growth hormone (Butler, Suskind, & Schanberg, 1978; Kuhn, Butler, & Schanberg, 1978). Schanberg and colleagues have identified molecular mechanisms through which deprivation of the very specific kind of touch rat mothers administer to their pups produces these effects (e.g., Schanberg, Ingledue, Lee, Hannun, & Bartolome, 2003).

Nurturing Touch and its Importance for Reducing Stress Reactivity and for Cognitive Development

Meaney and colleagues have demonstrated that rat moms who more frequently lick and groom their pups produce offspring who, throughout their lives, explore more, are less fearful, show milder reactions to stress, perform better cognitively as adults, and preserve their cognitive skills better into old age (Liu, Diorio, Day, Francis, & Meaney, 2000). It is the mother's behavior that produces these effects rather than a particular genetic profile that produces both a particular mothering style and particular offspring characteristics. Pups of high-licking-and-grooming moms raised by low-licking-and-grooming moms do not show these characteristics, and pups of low-touch moms raised by high-touch moms do show this constellation of attributes (Francis, Diorio, Liu, & Meaney, 1999).

Furthermore, rats tend to raise their offspring the way they themselves were raised, so these effects are transmitted intergenerationally, not through the genome but through behavior. Biological offspring of low-touch moms who are cross-fostered to high-touch moms lick and groom their offspring a lot; in this way the diminished stress response and cognitive enhancement is passed down through the generations (Francis et al., 1999).

Meaney and colleagues have elegantly demonstrated that maternal behavior produces these behavioral consequences through several mechanisms that alter gene expression. Not all genes in an individual are expressed—many are never expressed. Experience can affect which genes are turned on and off, in which cells, and when. For example, methylation (attaching a methyl group to a gene's promoter) stably silences a gene; demethylation reverses that process, typically leading to the gene being expressed. High licking by rat mothers causes demethylation (i.e., activation) of the glucocorticoid receptor gene, hence lowering circulating glucocorticoid (stress hormone) levels as receptors for the stress hormone remove it from circulation.

Nurturing Touch and Human Cognitive and Emotional Development

Unlike newborn rats, human newborns can see, hear, and smell, as well as feel touch. Yet despite the additional sensory information available to them, touch is still crucial. Human infants who receive little touching grow more slowly, release less growth hormone, and are less responsive to growth hormone that is exogenously administered (Frasier & Rallison, 1972). Throughout life, they show larger reactions to stress, are more prone to depression, and are vulnerable to deficits in cognitive functions commonly seen in depression or during stress (Lupien, King, Meaney, McEwen, 2000).

Touch plays a powerful role for human infants in promoting optimal development and in counteracting stressors. Massaging babies lowers their cortisol levels and helps them gain weight (Field et al., 2004). The improved weight gain from neonatal massage has been replicated cross-culturally, and cognitive benefits are evident even a year later. It is not that infants sleep or eat more; rather, stimulating their body through massage increases vagal (parasympathetic nervous system) activity, which prompts release of food-absorption hormones. Such improved vagal tone also indicates better ability to modulate arousal and to attend to subtle environmental cues important for cognitive development. Passive bodily contact also has substantial stress-reducing, calming, and analgesic effects for infants and adults (e.g., Gray, Watt, & Blass, 2000). Thus, besides "simple touch" being able to calm our jitters and lift our spirits, the right kind of touch regularly enough early in life can improve cognitive development, brain development, bodily health throughout life, and gene expression.

Future Directions

Neuroscience may be able to make extremely important contributions to child development by building on repeated demonstrations that differences in neural activity patterns precede and predict differences in cognitive performance. Often, when the brain is not functioning properly, people can compensate so their performance does not suffer until the neural system becomes too dysfunctional or until performance demands become too great. Thus, an underlying problem may exist but not show up behaviorally until, for example, the academic demands of more advanced schooling exceed a child's ability to compensate.

So far, differences in neural activity patterns have been demonstrated to precede and predict differences in cognitive performance only in adults. For example, Bookheimer and colleagues tested older adults (ranging in age from 47 to 82 years) with a genetic predisposition for Alzheimer's disease, selected because they performed fully comparably to controls across diverse cognitive tasks. Nevertheless, functional neuroimaging revealed that the brains of several of the genetically predisposed individuals already showed predicted differences. Two years later, those individuals showed the cognitive impairments predicted by their earlier neural activity patterns (Bookheimer et al., 2000). Similarly, adults in the early stages of other disorders may show no behavioral evidence of a cognitive deficit while neuroimaging shows their brains are compensating or working harder to achieve that behavioral equivalence. As the disease progresses, the compensation is no longer sufficient and the cognitive deficit becomes evident (e.g., Audoin et al., 2006).

What this suggests is that functional neuroimaging in developing children may perhaps be able to detect evidence of learning disorders—such as attentional, sensory-processing, language, or math deficits—before there is behavioral evidence of a problem. Already, research is being undertaken to see if infants' neural responses to auditory stimuli might be predictive of later linguistic problems (e.g., Benasich et al., 2006). The earlier a problem can be detected, the better the hope of correcting it or of putting environmental compensations in place.

Recommended Readings

Diamond, A. (2001). (See References). Summarizes studies with young children and animals showing the role of maturation of prefrontal cortex in the early emergence of executive function abilities and the importance of dopamine for this.

Grossman, A.W., Churchill, J.D., Bates, K.E., Kleim, J.A., & Greenough, W.T. (2002). A brain adaptation view of plasticity: Is synaptic plasticity an overly limited concept? *Progress in Brain Research, 138,* 91–108. Argues that synaptic, even neuronal, plasticity is but a small fraction of the range of brain changes that occur in response to experience, and that there are multiple forms of brain plasticity governed by mechanisms that are at least partially independent, including non-neuronal changes.

Meaney, M.J. (2001). Maternal care, gene expression, and the transmission of individual differences in stress reactivity across generations. *Annual Review of Neuroscience, 24,* 1161–1192. Provides an overview of research demonstrating that naturally occurring variations in maternal care modify the expression of genes affecting offspring's cognitive development as well as their ability to cope with stress throughout life, and that these changes are passed down intergenerationally (epigenetic inheritance).

Meltzoff, A.N., & Decety, J. (2003). What imitation tells us about social cognition: A rapprochement between developmental psychology and cognitive neuroscience. *Philosophical Transactions of the Royal Society of London – B: Biological Sciences, 358,* 491–500. Reviews the psychological evidence concerning imitation in human neonates and the neurophysiological evidence of a common coding at the single cell level (in mirror neurons) between perceived and generated actions.

Neville, H.J., & Bavelier, D. (2002). Human brain plasticity: Evidence from sensory deprivation and altered language experience. *Progress in Brain Research, 138,* 177–188. Summarizes research, using behavioral measures and neuroimaging, on individuals with altered visual, auditory, and/or language experience, showing ways in which brain development can, and cannot, be modified by environmental input, and how that varies by the timing of the altered input and by specific subfunctions within language or vision.

References

Audoin, B., Au Duong, M.V., Malikova, I., Confort-Gouny, S., Ibarrola, D., Cozzone, P.J., et al. (2006). Functional magnetic resonance imaging and cognition at the very early stage of MS. *Journal of the Neurological Sciences, 245,* 87–91.

Benasich, A.A., Choudhury, N., Friedman, J.T., Realpe Bonilla, T., Chojnowska, C., & Gou, Z. (2006). Infants as a prelinguistic model for language learning impairments: Predicting from event-related potentials to behavior. *Neuropsychologia, 44,* 396–441.

Bookheimer, S.Y., Strojwas, M.H., Cohen, M.S., Saunders, A.M., Pericak-Vance, M.A., Mazziota, J.C., et al. (2000). Patterns of brain activation in people at risk for Alzheimer's disease. *New England Journal of Medicine, 343,* 450–456.

Butler, S.R., Suskind, M.R., & Schanberg, S.M. (1978). Maternal behavior as a regulator of polyamine biosynthesis in brain and heart of the developing rat pup. *Science, 199,* 445–447.

Diamond, A. (2001). A model system for studying the role of dopamine in prefrontal cortex during early development in humans. In C. Nelson & M. Luciana (eds.), *Handbook of developmental cognitive neuroscience* (pp. 433–472). Cambridge, MA: MIT Press.

Field, T., Hernandez-Reif, M., Diego, M., Feijo, L., Vera, Y., & Gil, K. (2004). Massage therapy by parents improves early growth and development. *Infant Behavior & Development, 27,* 435–442.

Ferrari, P.F., Visalberghi, E., Paukner, A., Fogassi, L., Ruggiero, A., & Suomi, S. (2006). Neonatal imitation in rhesus macaques. *PLoS Biology, 4,* 1501–1508.

Francis, D., Diorio, J., Liu, D., & Meaney, M.J. (1999). Nongenomic transmission across generations of maternal behavior and stress responses in the rat. *Science, 286,* 1155–1158.

Frasier, S.D., & Rallison, M.L. (1972). Growth retardation and emotional deprivation: Relative resistance to treatment with human growth hormone. *Journal of Pediatrics, 80,* 603–609.

Gray, L., Watt, L., & Blass, E.M. (2000). Skin-to-skin contact is analgesic in healthy newborns. *Pediatrics, 105,* 1–6.

Kohler, E., Keysers, C., Umiltà, M.A., Fogassi, L., Gallese, V., & Rizzolatti, G. (2002). Hearing sounds, understanding actions: Action representation in mirror neurons. *Science, 297,* 846–848.

Kuhn, C.M., Butler, S.R., & Schanberg, S.M. (1978). Selective depression of serum growth hormone during maternal deprivation in rat pups. *Science, 201,* 1034–1036.

Liu, D., Diorio, J., Day, J.C., Francis, D.D., & Meaney, M.J. (2000). Maternal care, hippocampal synaptogenesis and cognitive development in rats. *Nature Neuroscience, 3,* 799–806.

Lupien, S.J., King, S., Meaney, M.J., & McEwen, B.S. (2000). Child's stress hormone levels correlate with mother's socioeconomic status and depressive state. *Biological Psychiatry, 48,* 976–980.

Meltzoff, A.N., & Moore, M.K. (1977). Imitation of facial and manual gestures by human neonates. *Science, 198,* 75–78.

Meltzoff, A.N., & Moore, M.K. (1983). Newborn infants imitate adult facial gestures. *Child Development, 54,* 702–709.

Pennington, B.F., VanDoornick, W.J., McCabe, L.L., & McCabe, E.R.B. (1985). Neuropsychological deficits in early treated phenylketonuric children. *American Journal of Mental Deficiency, 89,* 467–474.

Rizzolatti, G., & Craighero, L. (2004). The mirror-neuron system. *Annual Review of Neuroscience, 27,* 169–192.

Schanberg, S.M., Ingledue, V.F., Lee, J.Y., Hannun, Y.A., & Bartolome, J.V. (2003). PKC mediates maternal touch regulation of growth-related gene expression in infant rats. *Neuropsychopharmacology, 28,* 1026–1030.

Stemerdink, B.A., Kalverboer, A.F., van der Meere, J.J., van der Molen, M.W., Huisman, J., de Jong, L.W., et al. (2000). Behaviour and school achievement in patients with early and continuously treated phenylketonuria. *Journal of Inherited Metabolic Disorders, 23,* 548–562.

Tam, S.Y., Elsworth, J.D., Bradberry, C.W., & Roth, R.H. (1990). Mesocortical dopamine neurons: High basal firing frequency predicts tyrosine dependence of dopamine synthesis. *Journal of Neural Transmission, 81,* 97–110.

Address correspondence to **ADELE DIAMOND,** Canada Research Chair Professor of Developmental Cognitive Neuroscience, Department of Psychiatry, University of British Columbia, 2255 Wesbrook Mall, Vancouver, British Columbia, V6T 2A1, Canada; e-mail: adele.diamond @ubc.ca.

Acknowledgments—AD gratefully acknowledges grant support from the National Institute on Drug Abuse (R01 #DA19685) during the writing of this paper.

It's Fun, but Does It Make You Smarter?

Researchers find a relationship between children's Internet use and academic performance.

Erika Packard

For most children and teenagers, using the Internet has joined watching television and talking on the phone in the repertoire of typical behavior. In fact, 87 percent of 12- to 17-year-olds are now online, according to a 2005 Pew Research Center report. That's a 24 percent increase over the previous four years, leading parents and policy-makers to worry about the effect access to worlds of information—and misinformation—has on children.

Psychologists are only beginning to answer that question, but a study led by Michigan State University psychologist Linda Jackson, PhD, showed that home Internet use improved standardized reading test scores. Other researchers have found that having the Internet at home encourages children to be more self-directed learners.

"We had the same question for television decades ago, but I think the Internet is more important than television because it's interactive," says Jackson. "It's 24/7 and it's ubiquitous in young people's lives."

The positive effects of Internet use appear especially pronounced among poor children, say researchers. Unfortunately, these children are also the least likely to have home computers, which some experts say may put them at a disadvantage.

"The interesting twist here is that the very children who are most likely to benefit from home Internet access are the ones least likely to have it," says Jackson. "It's a classic digital divide issue."

Point, Click and Read

In her research, published in a 2006 *Developmental Psychology* (Vol. 42, No. 3, pages 429–435) special section on Internet use, Jackson studied 140 urban children as part of HomeNetToo, a longitudinal field study designed to assess the effects of Internet use in low-income families. Most of the child participants were African American and around 13 years old; 75 percent lived in single-parent households with an average annual income of $15,000 or less. The children were also underperforming in school, scoring in the 30th percentile on standardized reading tests at the beginning of the study.

Jackson and her colleagues provided each family with a home computer and free Internet access. The researchers automatically and continuously recorded the children's Internet use, and participants completed periodic surveys and participated in home visits.

They found that children who used the Internet more had higher scores on standardized reading tests after six months, and higher grade point averages one year and 16 months after the start of the study than did children who used it less. More time spent reading, given the heavily text-based nature of Web pages, may account for the improvement. Jackson also suggests that there may be yet-undiscovered differences between reading online and reading offline that may make online reading particularly attractive to children and teenagers.

"What's unique about the Internet as compared with traditional ways of developing academic performance skills is that it's more of a fun environment," she says. "It's a play tool. You can learn without any pain. Beneficial academic outcomes may just be a coincidental effect of having a good time."

> **"The interesting twist here is that the very children who are most likely to benefit from home Internet access are the ones least likely to have it. It's a classic digital divide issue."**
>
> Linda Jackson
> Michigan State University

What's more, online reading may enhance skills that traditional book reading doesn't tap, says Donald Leu, PhD, the John and Maria Neag Endowed Chair in Literacy and Technology at the University of Connecticut and director of the New Literacies Research Lab. He's found no substantial association between online reading comprehension performance and performance on state reading assessments, as described in a 2005 report submitted to the North Central Regional Educational Laboratory/Learning Point Associates (available online at www.newliteracies.uconn .edu/ncrel_files/FinalNCRELReport.pdf). That's because online reading takes different skills than traditional book reading, he says. Online reading relies heavily on information-location skills, including how to use search engines, as well as information-synthesis and critical evaluation skills.

"The studies that just look at learning fail to recognize that you have to have these online reading comprehension strategies in place before you can really learn very much with Internet information," says Leu.

Leu is looking for ways to improve adolescents' Internet reading comprehension through a three-year, U.S. Department of Education-funded research project, co-led by reading education expert David Reinking, PhD, Eugene T. Moore Professor of Teacher Education at Clemson University.

About half of the children the team studies don't use search engines, Leu says, preferring to use an ineffective "dot com strategy." For example, if they are searching for information on the Iraq War, they will enter the URL "iraqwar.com." This often leads to ad-filled trap sites that provide incorrect or irrelevant information, says Leu. And, the 50 percent of children who do use search engines use a "click and look strategy" of opening each returned site instead of reading the search engine synopsis. If a site appears as the children imagine it should, they believe it's reliable, he says.

Leu and colleagues asked 50 top-reading seventh-graders from school districts in rural South Carolina and urban Connecticut to assess the reliability of a slickly designed website on the mythical "endangered Pacific Northwest Tree Octopus." Though the site is a known hoax, all but one child claimed it was scientifically valid. And even after the researchers informed the participants that the site was a joke, about half of the children were adamant that it was indeed truthful, says Leu.

Self-Directed Learners

To help children winnow the tree octopus sites from legitimate information, they must develop online reading comprehension skills. These skills are particularly crucial because other researchers have found that children go online to clarify what they're being taught in school.

"Instead of waiting for a tutor or someone to help them, they are very proactive in seeking help for themselves," says Kallen Tsikalas, director of research and learning services for Computers for Youth (CFY), a national educational nonprofit organization.

Home Internet use during the middle-school years appears to empower students and re-engage them in learning at an age when their academic achievement traditionally drops, adds Tsikalas.

Indeed, 70 percent of students in CFY's program consistently say that having a home computer helps them become more curious and feel more confident, and nearly two-thirds of students report working harder in school because they have a home computer, the organization reports.

Though researchers have found encouraging evidence that Internet use can help children stay interested in school and develop reading skills, it's not an easy area to study, say experts.

"A big challenge to researchers here is that we are dealing with a major generational gap—we are still struggling to catch up with evolving technology and how young people are using it," says Elisheva Gross, PhD, of the Children's Digital Media Center at the University of California, Los Angeles.

The publication lag of scholarly research is also at odds with a technology that's changing and expanding by the day.

"Especially when you talk about books published on this topic, they are historical documents at this point," says Gross.

Is America Lagging?

Although the challenges of studying Internet use abound, Leu argues that America needs to catch up with other countries that are harnessing the Internet for educational purposes. In Finland, for example, teachers take five weeks of paid leave to complete professional development training on teaching online reading comprehension and Internet-use skills. In Japan, the government provides 98 percent of its households with broadband access for only $22 a month.

"The government knows that kids read more out of school than they do in school, and they want to make certain that kids are reading online when they are at home," says Leu. "Most developed nations . . . know their kids will have to compete in a global information environment and they are trying to prepare them for that."

By contrast, America's "report card," the National Assessment of Educational Progress, just defined its framework for the 2009–19 assessment and chose not to include a measure of online reading skills.

"This is supposed to be the gold standard of our performance on reading, and until 2019 we are not going to have a handle on how our kids are doing on the most important information resource we have available," says Leu.

Language and Children's Understanding of Mental States

Children progress through various landmarks in their understanding of mind and emotion. They eventually understand that people's actions, utterances, and emotions are determined by their beliefs. Although these insights emerge in all normal children, individual children vary in their rates of progress. Four lines of research indicate that language and conversation play a role in individual development: (a) Children with advanced language skills are better at mental-state understanding than those without advanced language skills, (b) deaf children born into nonsigning families lag in mental-state understanding, and (c) exposure to maternal conversation rich in references to mental states promotes mental-state understanding, as do (d) experimental language-based interventions. Debate centers on the mechanism by which language and conversation help children's understanding of mental states. Three competing interpretations are evaluated here: lexical enrichment (the child gains from acquiring a rich mental-state vocabulary), syntactic enrichment (the child gains from acquiring syntactic tools for embedding one thought in another), and pragmatic enrichment (the child gains from conversations in which varying perspectives on a given topic are articulated). Pragmatic enrichment emerges as the most promising candidate.

PAUL L. HARRIS, MARC DE ROSNAY, AND FRANCISCO PONS

I n the past 20 years, a large body of research has shown that normal children progress through a series of landmarks in their understanding of mental states. At around 4 years of age, children understand that people's actions and utterances are guided by their beliefs, whether those beliefs are true or false. At around 5 to 6 years of age, they come to realize that people's emotions are also influenced by their beliefs (Pons, Harris, & de Rosnay, 2003). This gradual acquisition of what is now routinely known as a *theory of mind* can be illustrated with the classic fairy tale of Little Red Riding Hood. When 3-year-olds are told that the wolf is waiting for Little Red Riding Hood, they typically fail to realize that she mistakenly expects to be greeted by her grandmother as she knocks at the cottage door. By contrast, 4- and 5-year-olds understand Little Red Riding Hood's false belief. Yet many 4-year-olds and some 5-year-olds say that when she knocks, she must be afraid of the wolf—the very wolf that she does not know about! By the age of 6 years, however, most children fully grasp Little Red Riding Hood's naiveté. They understand not only that she fails to realize that a wolf is waiting to eat her, but also that she feels no fear.

Children's acquisition of a theory of mind emerges in orderly steps (Wellman & Liu, 2004; Pons et al., 2003), but individual children vary markedly in their rate of progress. In this article, we review four lines of evidence indicating that language and conversation play a key role in helping children develop an understanding of mental states. We then ask about the causal mechanism involved.

Children's Language Skill and Mental-State Understanding

Among normal children and children with autism, accuracy in the attribution of beliefs and emotions has been correlated with language skill (Happe, 1995; Pons, Lawson, Harris, & de Rosnay, 2003). It could be argued that this correlation shows that a theory of mind facilitates language acquisition. However, longitudinal research has offered little support for such an interpretation. Astington and Jenkins (1999) found that preschoolers' theory-of-mind performance was not a predictor of subsequent gains in language. Rather, the reverse was true: Language ability was a good predictor of improvement in theory-of-mind performance. Children with superior language skills—particularly in the domain of syntax—made greater progress over the next 7 months than other children did in their conceptualization of mental states.

Restricted Access to Language: The Case of Deafness

Does a child's access to language, as well as a child's own language skill, affect his or her theory of mind? When children are born deaf, they are often delayed in their access to language, including sign language. Late signers are particularly common among deaf children born to hearing parents because the parents themselves rarely master sign language. Late signers—like children with autism—are markedly delayed in their understanding of mental states. By contrast, deaf children who learn to sign in a home with native signers are comparable to normal children in their performance on theory-of-mind tasks (Peterson & Siegal, 2000).

Even when efforts are made to bypass problems that late signers might have in grasping the language of such tasks—for example, by substituting a nonverbal (Figueras-Costa & Harris, 2001) or pictorial (Woolfe, Want, & Siegal, 2002) test of mental-state understanding—late signers still have marked difficulties. By implication, late-signing children are genuinely delayed in their conceptualization of mental states; it is not simply that they have difficulty in conveying their understanding when the test is given in sign language.

Maternal Conversation and Mental-State Understanding

Two recent studies show that, even when children have normal access to language, mothers vary in their language style and this style appears to affect children's mental-state understanding. Ruffman, Slade, and Crowe (2002) studied mother-child pairs on three occasions when the children ranged from 3 to 4 years of age. On each occasion, they recorded a conversation between mother and child about a picture book and measured the child's theory-of-mind performance and linguistic ability. Mothers' use or nonuse of mental-state language-terms such as *think, know, want,* and *hope*—at earlier time points predicted children's later theory-of-mind performance. Moreover, the reverse pattern did not hold.

The experimental design used in this study allowed the role of maternal conversation to be clarified in important ways. First, it was specifically mental-state references that predicted children's theory-of-mind performance; other aspects of maternal discourse, such as descriptive comments (e.g., "She's riding a bicycle") or causal comments (e.g., "They have no clothes on because they're in the water"), had no impact on children's theory-of-mind performance over and above the effect of mental-state utterances. Second, children's earlier language abilities also predicted their later theory-of-mind performance independently of their mothers' mental-state discourse.

The study by Ruffman et al. (2002) focused on false-belief tasks mastered somewhere between 3 and 4 years of age. We investigated whether mothers' mental-state discourse is linked to children's performance on a more demanding task typically mastered at around 5 or 6 years of age. Recall the story of Little Red Riding Hood: Only around the age of 5 or 6 years do many children realize that Little Red Riding Hood feels no fear of the wolf when she knocks at the door of grandmother's cottage. In a study of children ranging from 4½ to 6 years (de Rosnay, Pons, Harris, & Morrell, 2004), we found that mothers' use of mentalistic terms when describing their children (i.e., references to their children's psychological attributes as opposed to their behavior or physical attributes) and their children's own verbal ability were positively associated not only with correct false-belief attributions, but also with correct emotion attributions in tasks utilizing stories akin to that of Little Red Riding Hood. Moreover, mothers' mentalistic descriptions predicted children's correct emotion attributions

even when the sample was restricted to children who had mastered the simpler false-belief task. So, even after children have mastered the false-belief task, there is still scope for maternal discourse to help the child make further progress in understanding mental states.

Four important conclusions emerge from these studies. First, mothers who talk about psychological themes promote their children's mental-state understanding. Second, it is unlikely that psychologically precocious children prompt more mental-state language in their mothers; rather, the direction of causation is from mother to child. Third, mere talkativeness on the part of a mother does not promote mental-state understanding—it is the mother's psychological language that is critical. Fourth, mothers' psychological orientation has sustained influence: This influence is evident among 3-year-olds and 6-year-olds alike. The effect of maternal language is not restricted to false-belief understanding. It also applies to the later understanding of belief-based emotions.

Language-Based Interventions

So far, we have summarized correlational findings demonstrating a link between language and mental-state understanding. However, experimental language interventions also produce gains in mental-state understanding. In one study, Lohmann and Tomasello (2003) pretested a large group of 3-year-olds. Those who failed a standard test of false-belief received various types of intervention and were then retested using other false-belief tasks. The most effective intervention for improving children's understanding of false belief combined two factors: (a) the presentation of a series of objects, some of which had a misleading appearance (e.g., an object that looked initially like a flower but turned out to be a pen); and (b) verbal comments on what people would say, think, and know about the perceptible properties and actual identity of these objects. Hale and Tager-Flusberg (2003) also found that language-based interventions were effective in improving children's false-belief understanding. In one intervention, children discussed story protagonists who held false beliefs. In a second intervention, they discussed story protagonists who made false claims. In each case, the children were given corrective verbal feedback if they misstated what the protagonists thought or said. Both interventions proved very effective in promoting 3-year-olds' grasp of false belief.

These intervention studies confirm that conversation about people's thoughts or statements has a powerful effect on children's understanding of belief. One additional finding underscores the critical role of conversation. When Lohmann and Tomasello (2003) presented children with various misleading objects but offered minimal verbal comment—other than a request to look at the objects—the impact on children's mental-state understanding was negligible.

How Does Language Help?

Given the converging evidence just described, the claim that language makes a difference for children's developing theory of mind is convincing. Not only do children's own language abilities predict their rate of progress in understanding the mind, but their access to conversation, especially conversation rich in mentalistic words and concepts, is an equally potent and independent predictor.

Despite this solid evidence for the role of language, there is disagreement over how exactly it helps. Consider the type of comments that a mother might make as she and her preschool child look at a picture book—"I think it's a cat" or "I don't know whether it's a dog" (Ruffman et al., 2002, p. 740). It could be argued that such comments help the child develop an understanding of mental states because the words *think* and *know* draw the child's attention to mental processes. But there are other possible explanations. For example, such comments are also syntactically distinctive: They embed a proposition ("... it's a cat" or "... whether it's a dog") in another clause containing a mental verb ("I think ..." or "I don't know ..."). Mastery of the way propositions can be embedded in other clauses might help children to conceptualize mental states that take particular states of affairs as their target. Mental-state understanding often calls for an appreciation of the way in which a mental state such as a thought, a belief, or a hope is targeted at a particular state of affairs. But also, such comments play a role in the pragmatics of conversation. More specifically, they set out a claim (e.g., "... it's a cat") and they convey the particular perspective of the speaker toward that claim. Accordingly, such comments might underline the way people can vary in the mental stance or perspective they adopt toward a given claim. In short, mentalistic comments contain distinctive words (e.g., *think* and *know*), grammatical constructions (e.g., embedded propositions), and pragmatic features (e.g., the enunciation of individual perspectives). Which factor is critical? It is too early to draw firm conclusions, but the evidence increasingly points to the importance of pragmatic features.

First, two recent studies with children speaking languages other than English suggest that the syntax of embedded propositions is not the reason why language skill correlates with theory-of-mind understanding. In German, *want* sentences such as "Mother wants George to go to bed" must be rendered with a *that* proposition—"Mutter will, dass George ins Bett geht" (literally, "Mother wants that George into the bed goes"). Perner, Sprung, Zauner, and Haider (2003) studied whether early exposure to, and understanding of, the *want–that* structure is associated with good performance on standard theory-of-mind tasks, but they found no evidence supporting such a relationship. Similarly, a study of Cantonese-speaking children failed to uncover any link between mastery of verbs that can serve to embed another proposition and theory-of-mind understanding, once general language competence had been taken into account (Cheung et al., 2004).

Second, our findings (de Rosnay et al., 2004) make both the lexical and the syntactic explanations problematic. Maternal usage of terms like *think* and *know* together with their embedded propositions might plausibly help children to understand false beliefs because when they attribute a false belief to someone, children will need to use the same linguistic constructions. For example, to describe Little Red Riding Hood's mistaken belief, it is appropriate to say: "She thinks that it's her grandmother" or "She doesn't know that it's a wolf." However, the attribution of emotion, including belief-based emotion, does not call for the use of mental-state terms with embedded propositions. It simply calls for appropriate use of particular emotion terms: "Little Red Riding Hood felt happy as she knocked at the cottage." Yet we found that mothers' mental discourse not only helped children understand false beliefs, but also helped them move on to understand belief-based emotions. An emphasis on pragmatics can readily explain this twofold impact: Mothers disposed to talk about varying individual beliefs regarding a given situation will probably also articulate the feelings that flow from those individual beliefs.

Conclusions

People often observe other people's facial expressions and bodily postures for clues to their mental life. Indeed, a great deal of research on the early development of a theory of mind has focused on infants' skill at interpreting these nonverbal clues. However, in contrast to any other species, human beings are also able to talk to each other about their mental lives. They can talk about their feelings, compare their beliefs, and share their plans and intentions.

The research reviewed here shows that such conversations play a key role in helping children to make sense of mental states. We are on the brink of designing longitudinal and intervention studies that will help us determine just how conversation helps children in this endeavor. So far, research on children's mental-state understanding has mainly focused on the milestone of understanding false beliefs. We have shown here, however, that maternal discourse is also linked with how well children attribute belief-based emotions to other people, and specifically that this link holds true even among children who have already mastered false beliefs.

In the future, it will be important to study various other milestones in children's mental-state understanding. For example, only around age 5 or 6 do children understand that the emotions people actually feel may not correspond to the emotions that they express. Also, it is not until middle childhood that children fully understand self-conscious emotions such as guilt—or understand that it is possible to feel conflicting emotions about the same situation. In the future, researchers can focus on these developmental advances to better understand the influence of parents' conversation on children's mental-state understanding. If it is found that the same type of parental conversation style (e.g., coherent psychological discourse) has a pervasive influence across different aspects of mental-state understanding, then it will become less likely that specific lexical or semantic features of discourse are the crucial factor. Instead, as we have noted, it will be more plausible to assume that some parents elucidate a variety of mental states in conversation with their children. That elucidation is not tied to particular lexical terms or syntactic constructions. Instead, it reflects a wide-ranging sensitivity to individual perspectives and nurtures that same sensitivity in children.

Researchers may also consider the implications of mental-state understanding for children's behavior and social relationships. An increasing body of evidence indicates that good performance on theory-of-mind tasks is correlated with the ability to form relationships with peers (Pons, Harris, & Doudin, 2002). A plausible—but as yet untested—interpretation is that children's mental-state understanding helps them both to initiate and to maintain friendships. This hypothesis can be tested by assessing the impact of a discourse-based intervention not just on children's mental-state understanding, but also on their relationships with peers.

Finally, researchers may look forward to an important bridge between developmental and clinical psychology. The mother who is alert to her child's mental states, who accurately puts thoughts and feelings into words, and who nurtures her child's sensitivity to different mental perspectives may have an effect on her child that is not unlike that of a clinician or therapist who fosters a reflective stance in his or her patients.

References

Astington, J.W., & Jenkins, J.M. (1999). A longitudinal study of the relation between language and theory-of-mind development. *Developmental Psychology, 35,* 1311–1320.

Cheung, H., Hsuan-Chih, C., Creed, N., Ng, L., Wang, S.P, & Mo, L. (2004). Relative roles of general and complementation language in theory-of-mind development: Evidence from Cantonese and English. *Child Development, 75,* 1155–1170.

de Rosnay, M., Pons, F., Harris, P.L., & Morrell, J. (2004). A lag between understanding false belief and emotion attribution in young children: Relationships with linguistic ability and mothers' mental state language. *British Journal of Developmental Psychology, 22,* 197–218.

Figueras-Costa, B., & Harris, P.L. (2001). Theory of mind in deaf children: A non-verbal test of false belief understanding. *Journal of Deaf Studies and Deaf Education, 6,* 92–102.

Hale, C.M., & Tager-Flusberg, H. (2003). The influence of language on theory of mind: A training study. *Developmental Science, 6,* 346–359.

Happé, F.G.E. (1995). The role of age and verbal ability in the theory of mind task performance of subjects with autism. *Child Development, 66,* 843–855.

Lohmann, H., & Tomasello, M. (2003). The role of language in the development of false belief understanding: A training study. *Child Development, 74,* 1130–1144.

Perner, J., Sprung, M., Zauner, P., & Haider, H. (2003). Want that is understood well before say that, think that, and false belief: A test of de Villiers's linguistic determinism on German-speaking children. *Child Development, 74,* 179–188.

Peterson, C.C., & Siegal, M. (2000). Insights into theory of mind from deafness and autism. *Mind and Language, 15,* 123–145.

Pons, F., Harris, P.L., & de Rosnay, M. (2003). Emotion comprehension between 3 and 11 years: Developmental periods and hierarchical organization. *European Journal of Developmental Psychology, 2,* 127–152.

Pons, F., Harris, P.L., & Doudin, P.-A. (2002). Teaching emotion understanding. *European Journal of Psychology of Education, 17,* 293–304.

Pons, F., Lawson, J., Harris, P.L., & de Rosnay, M. (2003). Individual differences in children's emotion understanding: Effects of age and language. *Scandinavian Journal of Psychology, 44,* 347–353.

Ruffman, T., Slade, L., & Crowe, E. (2002). The relation between children's and mothers' mental state language and theory-of-mind understanding. *Child Development, 73,* 734–751.

Wellman, H.M., & Liu, D. (2004). Scaling of theory of mind tasks. *Child Development, 75,* 523–541.

Woolfe, T., Want, S.C., & Siegal, M. (2002). Signposts to development: Theory-of-mind in deaf children. *Child Development, 73,* 768–778.

PAUL L. HARRIS, Harvard University, **MARC DE ROSNAY,** Cambridge University, and **FRANCISCO PONS,** University of Aalborg, Denmark.

From *Current Directions in Psychological Science,* February 2005, pp. 69–73. Copyright © 2005 by the Association for Psychological Science. Reprinted by permission of Wiley-Blackwell.

Developmental Narratives of the Experiencing Child

KATHERINE NELSON

Every developmental theory reflects an implicit narrative about the course of development, typically beginning at birth and ending variously at points along the way toward adulthood. Critical to narrative are action and meaningful causal relations, or as Bruner described it, the "landscape of action" and the "landscape of consciousness"— what happens, when, and why (Bruner, 1986). Keeping in mind the underlying narrative of development poses critical theoretical questions and highlights explanations of both general trends and individual variations in continuity and change over time, as the present emerges from the past and intersects with the future.

The narrative account I espouse is that of an experiencing child in a social-cultural world, cared for and guided by elders. This account is largely consistent with other social-cultural theories but differs in viewing the drama from the perspective of the child who, from birth, faces a series of challenging experiences that must be negotiated along the developmental pathway from infant solipsism to the shared meanings, knowledge, and cultural tools of society.[1]

Many other narratives are implicit in developmental theories of other kinds. Some, with roots in Piaget's classic theory, see the child as similar to a working scientist investigating specific domains of the physical and social worlds, gathering data, testing theories, and changing theories as necessary to fit reality (Gopnik, Meltzoff, & Kuhl, 1999; Wellman & Gelman, 1992). In contrast to social-cultural narratives, the child as scientist appears as a lone worker, coming to the correct theory on her or his own. (Of course, real scientists are not alone but are dependent on the aid and work of associates and a vast social network of scientists from the past and present.) In some nativist views, the basic building blocks of these theories are "built in," hard-wired and present at birth. In this case, the drama of change is eschewed in favor of the stability of underlying structure.

The classic social-cultural-historical theory and narrative is more complex and more focused on change (Luria, 1976; Stetsenko, 2004; Vygotsky, 2004). The child, embedded in a cultural and historical context, embarks on a path that has been well trodden in cultural history, participating in the activities of the social world, learning to use the tools of society, specifically, the symbolic tools, including language. Adults actively guide and teach the child, who begins to use these tools to achieve higher levels of thought.

Experience as Developmental Constant

The shift in focus from what is available to the child in the social-cultural world to what the child experiences in specific interactive encounters is the key motif in the narrative of the experiencing child, with important consequences for the emerging theory. First, this perspective emphasizes the complexity and individuality of any experience of an "objective" situation. It provides for the mechanism of change over time, and it provides for the child's active role in his or her own development. Finally, it places meaning—both communal (social-cultural) and personal—at the heart of significant change.

Basically, the process works as follows. The child gains experiential knowledge derived from social and cultural encounters and interactions, retaining from these experiences what is personally meaningful. Meaning is person specific but reflects social and cultural contributions in varying ways as the person appropriates aspects that resonate meaningfully for situated life interests at a specific point in time while remaining ignorant of other potential contributions. Meaning changes as the person grows and develops. The theory of bio-social-cultural development that emerges from this view is "naturalist," in that persons are guided by specific needs and interests in seeking knowledge of their world, and are guided as well by social and cultural companions in their efforts to make sense, in turn motivating efforts to make and keep relationships.

The Composition of Meaningful Experience

The basic proposition here is that children (and adults) experience not the "world" but specific encounters in specific instantiations of the world in interaction with other people and things. Over time, these encounters add up to a subjective accumulation of experience in memory. Memory reflects the subjective meanings of experience, the perspective of a private, but also pre-eminently social, self.

The encounter is central; its transformation into meaningful experience is conditioned by a multitude of developmental systems (see Figure 1). These systems are interactive and interdependent, multileveled and multicausal. They impinge on the child's experience of the encounter, not on some notion of an objective reality of what happens. Each system constrains, limits, and promotes the infant's experience in the world in distinct interacting ways.

In Figure 1, six metasystems are viewed as jointly—and interactively—impinging on children's experience in their encounters in the world. Three of these systems (memory, species-typical inheritance, and personal embodied conditions) are "internal," and three are—at least initially—"external" (ecological, social, and cultural conditions including language). Together they form a hexagonal surround of the child's encounter, constituting conditions for the experience that merges internal and external into a whole. All such systems or collections of systems, including those of the child's own growing and changing body and brain, are themselves undergoing change over time, but all at different rates and time scales (Oyama, Griffiths, & Gray, 2001). The essential point is that experience is affected by change at all levels and from all directions, continuously challenging the ongoing process of self-organization.

Most developmental systems and theories recognize some or all of these influences on development, with some theories focused more on the biological and internal influences and others focused more on the external influences. The different focus here is on two aspects: the complexity involved in the simultaneous interactions of all six constraining systems and the continuing changes in each system occurring at different rates and at different times. In addition, the inclusion of past experience (meaning and memory) as part of the overall experiential condition is in some sense obvious but rarely explicitly acknowledged. More fundamentally, as envisioned here, the systems are not abstractions producing developmental outcomes but are active forces, present moment to moment, shaping the child's experience, which, in turn, conditions future experience and development, as well as shaping ongoing interactions in the present.

In Figure 1, the left and top sides of the hexagon (evolved, embodied, ecological) represent physical and biological systems. The lower left segment (evolved) signifies the biological inheritance of the human species, together with the specific genetic and epigenetic conditions that produce an individual organism. This component determines limits, constraints, and potentialities—for example, the range of sounds and light accessible to humans. These constraints and potentials are lifelong but also undergo change with age and interaction with environments; for example, vision stabilizes and matures during infancy, at puberty rapid growth and hormonal change vary along an individuated time and rate.

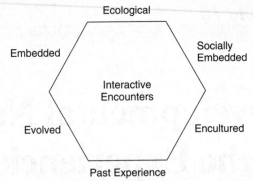

Figure 1   Depiction of the conditions or constraints on the experience of any encounter in the environment.

Note. Based on Figure 1.1 of Nelson (2007). See text for explanation and discussion.

The top left position—embodiment—signifies the body and brain in their changing size, power, and skills at the time of the experience. Both developmental and individual variations are important in this segment, with rapid change during some periods of development, such as infancy and puberty, and slower growth at other times (Stiles, 2008). In turn, the plasticity of the human brain—more immature at birth than in other primates—depends on interactive experience of the organism for its organization. The immaturity of both body and brain systems at birth requires an extended period of dependency on caregivers that has huge consequences for overall psychological development (Hrdy, 1999). Significant differences in embodiment and skills among individuals, including sex differences, can affect many experiences.

The ecological site (top of Figure 1) conditions both the potential for experience and the particulars of what can be experienced in a specific environment. The variety of human cultures and geographical settings is too diverse and changeable over time to be heritable (Plotkin, 1982). Different languages, different cultural practices and technologies, and different geographies require individual learning and specific adaptations. These conditions vary within societies as well, with consequences for what can be experienced (Heath, 1983).

On the right-hand side of Figure 1 are the social and cultural systems that both promote and condition experience. The child is embedded in the social world from birth (and before) and will not survive without caretaking that ensures food, warmth, and the embrace that signals attachment and love (Hrdy, 1999). Throughout early childhood, the child's experience is often confined to the social interactions of family and intimate groups with consequences for communicative developments (Dunn, 1988). The child's perspective on social conditions and interactions changes over time in light of prior social experience. The social presence, in turn, is always changing in respect to the child, making new demands, offering new experiences, imposing new expectations, and broadening in scope from family to institutions.

Cultural systems are omnipresent in the child's environment through institutions, cultural roles, artifacts, and symbolic structures, including language. Culture is present in all the child's experiences of the world, mediated through social figures as well as artifacts. Yet cultural meanings must be learned, both implicitly and explicitly; at birth and for many months and years thereafter, the child encounters cultural symbols but does not experience them as such. Language is pervasive, found throughout these systems, in the evolved and embodied brain, in social interactions, and in memory. Language is dependent on social models for its development, and is itself also a cultural carrier (Heath, 1983; Tomasello, 1999).

The base position in Figure 1 signifies memory remnants of past experience that are specific to the individual person. What is retained from an experience, either as general knowledge or as individual memory, is what has meaning for the individual child. Meaning is thus made through the history of the individual's past experience, and this meaning, in turn, affects what may be experienced in future encounters.

Meaning in Memory

A major advantage of the experiencing-child view of development is the role of memory in preserving experience for future use—for serving action in similar situations, for reflecting on the meaning of an experience, for reconstructing and representing in thought or language. Memory is highly constrained; not all that is encountered in a situation is experienced, and not all that is experienced is retained in memory. How then does memory identify what needs to be preserved? This problem, when formulated in terms of information, is often seen as a critical one in developmental theory (Carey & Gelman, 1991). The typical formula conceptualizes information as existing in infinite degrees in the world we inhabit, posing a potential problem: How do we choose what information to process? In particular, how does the infant choose from the infinite array of potential information in the environment?

When these questions are reformulated in terms of meaning, the problem begins to disappear. The biology of the body/brain system provides initial guidance toward meaningful aspects of the environment defined in terms of the organism's umwelt (Clark, 1997; von Ueskull, 1957). The umwelt defines the environment from the perspective of the organism, given its interactive possibilities. The umwelt of the growing child changes over time, both with experience and with growing competences and consciousness. In infancy, patterns that have meaning for the infant's "lifesphere" within its limited umwelt (e.g., linguistic prosody) attract attention. Later in infancy and throughout life experience-dependent meaning directs what is attended to and subsequently learned. Meaning thus shifts the problem from that of infinite meaningless potential distinctions (information) to what is meaningful for the organism to extract as a pattern from the perceptual array, to recognize, to learn, and to know.

Meaning begins then as a biological given (and in this sense meaning applies to all organisms). It is continually reconstrued as experience enriches what is initially meaningful by what is later seen to be meaningful through interactions and social guidance. Once experience has been meaningfully entered in memory, memory itself begins to guide further meaning explorations. Throughout this process, we can view meaning as a filter on experience and on associated learning processes. Thus, memory absorbs and retains meaning and also makes new meaning.

Language and Shared Meaning

Sharing knowledge appears to be a universal disposition of human infants and young children, through both verbal and nonverbal (e.g., pointing, showing, imitating) means (Hobson, 2003). Sharing behaviors become notable toward the end of the 1st year of the baby's life, emerging spontaneously—they do not need to be taught.[2] These ways of social engagement are followed by the beginnings of the acquisition of first words, the first step in the process of meaningful productive language learning. Sharing knowledge requires externally representing one's own mental contents so that another can understand them. Representing and sharing one's mental contents (ideas, knowledge, feelings) may be a unique characteristic of humans, one that preceded the symbolic systems of natural language (Donald, 1991). Other primates give little or no evidence of attempting to convey knowledge one to another, to teach another, or even to point to draw another's attention to something. Other animals learn, but do not attempt to share their learning (Tomasello, 2008).

A revolution in the child's experience takes place when language becomes available as a symbolic representing and communicating system. External symbolic representations and their effects on the form and function of internal representations radically change the cognitive systems of individual children as they learn their native language, just as they radically changed human intelligence in its evolutionary history (Donald, 1991; Nelson, 1996). Language enables the establishment of shared meaning. Without language, children may share attention with others, share activities, and share goals as they retain individual meanings of their experiences. From infancy to school age, the path is one of broadening opportunities for shared minds and meanings through language. The child makes sense of the world through direct experience guided by attentive caregivers. Mastery of speech makes mutual communication of ideas, thoughts, feelings, and goals. Representing these private concerns in language makes them public and available for sharing with another, or with groups of others. In addition, external representation enables the representer to reflect on his or her own mental constructions.

Thus, language—for the species and for each child—enables a level of shared minds made possible through sharing the same mode of representation in both communication and cognition. Language serves a mediating function that crosses the public–private gap. For both speaker and hearer, language both represents and communicates, both internally and externally. It thus serves as a critical mind-changing system. These dual functions of language have profoundly changed the nature of our mentality as well as the nature of our social and emotional lives, and do so for each child in the course of development. This process can be understood only in terms of a bio-social-cultural experiential approach to developmental change.

Expanding the Scope of Consciousness[3]

Understanding the developmental outcome of the experiential process is clarified by considering the process of expanding consciousness from birth through preschool years. The expansion of consciousness described here refers to changing degrees of conscious awareness from the perspective of the experiencing child. In this sense, it differs from limits on consciousness considered in terms of cognitive operations. Rather, the present concern is with the limits and potentials of what is meaningful to the child in experience or in reflection, and how narrow or broad that perspective may be. The basic idea here is that the very young infant is aware of a few things—the body, significant others, and a small bit of the physical ecology with which she or he comes in visual, auditory, and tactile contact. The horizons of the child's experience expand over time and through an expanding repertoire of behaviors, as the child responds to more of the parents' signals, notices more aspects of the physical world, and explores through action and locomotion parts of the ecology not previously encountered. Thus, the scope of consciousness first expands from limited awareness to interactive social engagement and shared attention, setting the stage for still further expansion in collaborative play, imitation, and early words (Hobson, 2003; Werner & Kaplan, 1963). These shared activities open up private consciousness to shared consciousness, that is, to shared meanings within activities.

During the child's 2nd and 3rd years, parents and others begin to engage the child in conversation eliciting the child's reflection on the meaning of words and sentences. Understanding of repeated stories and personal narratives begins (Nelson, 1989). Through practice at this reflective level of consciousness, the child becomes sufficiently proficient in the representational use of language (generally in the 4th year) to be able to understand a novel narrative presented orally from text. This is a wonderful achievement in its own right. Through this new experiential mode—of personal narratives of the past or future or fictional narratives of other times and places—the child begins to achieve the more advanced level of narrative consciousness, a level that integrates knowledge of people's actions and motivations, and of situations in time and space detached from the present (Nelson, 2003; Nelson & Fivush, 2004).

Narrative, like language itself, is a cultural product. Personal narratives—autobiographical memories—recall personally significant events, but the content and form of autobiographical memory is strongly influenced by its place in cultural life (Fivush & Nelson, 2004). "Narrative consciousness" emerges from social experiences with narratives that incorporate cultural frameworks, among them the structure of time, self, and mind. The emergence of autobiographical memory toward the end of the preschool period reflects a new conscious view of the self as a continuing person with a unique past and future and with experiences distinctly different from those of others, in the present or past, in other times and places.

A more expanded level of consciousness is seen as children enter into participation in adult "communities of minds," where the concepts and complexities of how people see themselves and others, and how they conduct their affairs in the world are talked about and made explicit (Nelson, 2005). Narratives incorporate these matters in terms of specific thoughts, hopes, wants, goals, reasons, whys, hows, and misunderstandings that lie behind the action in everyday life as well as in stories. Whereas children may begin as personal pragmatists, attending to, aware of, and experiencing aspects of the world that have personal meaning, they are not indifferent to the meanings that the adult world conveys or to the fascination of experimenting—in play or "for real"—with how that world works. One of the extraordinary benefits of becoming part of the communities of minds, where sharing minds and meanings is common, is extending consciousness to the nonobservable and hypothetical worlds of science, history, philosophy, and psychology (e.g., reasoning about others' mental states, otherwise known as "theory of mind").

Implicit in this brief overview of expanding consciousness is the notion that, at each level, the child is faced with encounters that incorporate new challenges to old understandings, whether through individual explorations or the presentations of new shared meanings. Such challenges to current understandings of the world require reorganization and exploration of the new meaning landscape and related expansion of consciousness. Recognition of new horizons may be subtle or sudden; development may appear continuous or steplike at different times for different children.

Implications

One of the main considerations in outlining this experiential narrative account is to lay bare the endless variability and complexity of different ways of using potentials and meeting constraints to achieve what is generally considered to be a "normal" or "typical" course of achievements. The narrative view of development places the experiencing child in the center of the action, the necessary perspective for such study. Inevitable variability of experience intrudes at two levels. The first level consists of the singularity of the composition of any given experience for any given child by virtue of its variable constituents. Researchers have been alerted to this aspect of variability in part through the work of systems theorists. The second level of the variability of experience appears over the long term in the composition of solutions to developmental challenges. This is the narrative component, which has also been illuminated by dynamic systems theory. Ultimately, we should be able to show how variability in paths to achievement explains patterns in types and timing of these achievements, as well as predicting their effects on future pathways. The concern here is not specifically about individuals and their possible pathologies but about development itself—how it operates within variable biological systems in interaction with social and cultural experiences.

Notes

1. A more detailed consideration of these ideas may be found in Nelson (2007).

2. In contrast, concealing knowledge, for example, by hiding or lying, must be learned. This is evident from the behavior of 2-year-old children engaged by mothers in a "find the toy" game (Kessler Shaw, unpublished data). When it was the child's turn to hide the toy from the mother, the 2-year-olds invariably showed the mother where the toy was hidden. Three-year-olds in the same situation kept the toy hidden. Similarly, in a hide-and-seek game with 2-year-olds, the child invariably reveals her hiding place (undocumented observations).

3. This section presents a theoretical conception based in Nelson (2007). It is expanded in other forthcoming works. Space restrictions here prevent the discussion of other current and past conceptions of consciousness development (e.g., Zelazo, Gao, & Todd, 2007) or the relation of this to other theories.

References

Bruner, J. S. (1986). *Actual minds, possible worlds.* Cambridge, MA: Harvard University Press.

Carey, S., & Gelman, R. (1991). *The epigenesis of mind: Essays on biology and cognition.* Hillsdale, NJ: Erlbaum.

Clark, A. (1997). *Being there: Putting brain, body, and world together again.* Cambridge, MA: MIT Press.

Donald, M. (1991). *Origins of the modern mind.* Cambridge, MA: Harvard University Press.

Dunn, J. (1988). *The beginnings of social understanding.* Cambridge, MA: Harvard University Press.

Fivush, R., & Nelson, K. (2004). Culture and language in the emergence of autobiographical memory. *Psychological Science, 15,* 573–577.

Gopnik, A., Meltzoff, A., & Kuhl, P. K. (1999). *The scientist in the crib: Minds, brains, and how children learn.* New York: Morrow.

Heath, S. B. (1983). *Ways with words.* Cambridge, UK: Cambridge University Press.

Hobson, P. R. (2003). *The cradle of thought: Exploring the origins of thinking.* New York: Oxford University Press.

Hrdy, S. B. (1999). *Mother nature: A history of mothers, infants, and natural selection.* New York: Pantheon Books.

Luria, A. R. (1976). *Cognitive development: Its cultural and social foundations.* Cambridge, MA: Harvard University Press.

Nelson, K. (Ed.). (1989). *Narratives from the crib.* Cambridge, MA: Harvard University Press.

Nelson, K. (1996). *Language in cognitive development: The emergence of the mediated mind.* New York: Cambridge University Press.

Nelson, K. (2003). Narrative and self, myth and memory. In R. Fivush & C. Haden (Eds.), *Autobiographical memory and the construction of a narrative self: Developmental and cultural perspectives* (pp. 3–28). Mahwah, NJ: Erlbaum.

Nelson, K. (2005). Language pathways to the community of minds. In J. W. Astington & J. Baird (Eds.), *Why language matters to theory of mind* (pp. 26–49). New York: Oxford University Press.

Nelson, K. (2007). *Young minds in social worlds: Experience, meaning, and memory.* Cambridge, MA: Harvard University Press.

Nelson, K., & Fivush, R. (2004). The emergence of autobiographical memory: A social cultural developmental theory. *Psychological Review, 111,* 486–511.

Oyama, S., Griffiths, P. E., & Gray, R. D. (Eds.). (2001). Cycles of contingency: Developmental systems and evolution. Cambridge, MA: MIT Press.

Plotkin, H. C. (Ed.). (1982). *Learning, development, and culture: Essays in evolutionary epistemology.* Chichester, NY: Wiley.

Stetsenko, A. (2004). Scientific legacy: Tool and sign in the development of the child. In R. W. Rieber & D. K. Robinson (Eds.), *The essential Vygotsky* (pp. 501–512). New York: Kluwer Academic/Plenum.

Stiles, J. (2008). *The fundamentals of brain development.* Cambridge, MA: Harvard University Press.

Tomasello, M. (1999). *The cultural origins of human cognitions.* Cambridge, MA: Harvard University Press.

Tomasello, M. (2008). *The origins of human communication.* Cambridge, MA: MIT Press.

von Ueskull, J. (1957). A stroll through the worlds of animals and men. In C. H. Schiller (Ed.), *Instinctive behavior: The development of a modern concept* (pp. 5–80). New York: International Universities Press.

Vygotsky, L. (2004). The function of signs in the development of higher mental processes. In R. W. Rieber & D. K. Robinson (Eds.), *The essential Vygotsky* (pp. 539–550). New York: Kluwer Academic/Plenum.

Wellman, H. M., & Gelman, S. A. (1992). Cognitive development: Foundational theories of core domains. *Annual Review of Psychology, 43,* 337–375.

Werner, H., & Kaplan, B. (1963). *Symbol formation: An organismic-developmental approach to language and the expression of thought.* New York: Wiley.

Zelazo, P. D., Gao, H. H., & Todd, R. (2007). The development of consciousness. In P. D. Zelazo, M. Moscovitch, & E. Thompson (Eds.), *The Cambridge handbook of consciousness* (pp. 405–434). Cambridge, UK: Cambridge University Press.

Social Cognitive Development: A New Look

Kristina R. Olson and Carol S. Dweck

The study of social cognitive development is undergoing a renaissance. A large part of this renaissance stems from research employing methods and theories from the study of cognitive development to ask questions of importance for children's social development. Of course, research on theory of mind (Leslie, 1987; Wellman, 1990; Wimmer & Perner, 1983), imitation (Gergely, Bekkering, & Kiraly, 2002; Meltzoff, 1995; Meltzoff & Borton, 1979), and intentionality and agency (Baldwin, 2000; Gergely, Nadasdy, Csibra, & Biro, 1995; Johnson, Slaughter, & Carey, 1998; Premack & Premack, 1997; Tomasello, Carpenter, Call, Behne, & Moll, 2005; Woodward, 1998) has been thriving for some time, and, in many researchers' minds, social cognitive development is synonymous with these concepts. However, never before have so many researchers in the area of cognitive development brought their tools and perspectives to bear on children's social development. In this article, we focus on emerging work, providing a "thin slice" of research coming from a cognitive development perspective that examines the development of children's social judgments and representations.[1] This work is exciting not only because it brings the ingenious methods of cognitive development to the social domain but also because it illuminates children's social functioning and relationships, topics that cognitive developmentalists have seldom addressed in the past.

As we describe elsewhere (Olson & Dweck, 2008), social cognitive development is the study of socially relevant mental representations and mental processes across development. Key aspects of social cognitive development concern how these representations and processes are shaped by particular antecedents (such as culture or parental practices) and how these representations and processes influence important outcomes for the child (such as children's well-being or relationships). Thus, here, we highlight current work on social judgments and representations because we see it as having important implications for both.

Judgments of Goodness and Badness

A noteworthy body of work is emerging on infants' and young children's social judgments. At the simplest level, this work is concerned with how children decide who is good or bad or helpful or harmful; it examines when these kinds of social judgments first emerge and what information children use to make them.

In some of the most provocative work on social judgments, Kuhlmeier, Wynn, and Bloom (2003) showed infants episodes in which a "climber" (a geometric, self-propelled figure) was attempting, but failing, to go up a hill. In one episode, a "helper" aided the climber, and in another episode, a "hinderer" pushed the climber back down. Through use of looking-time measures, the researchers found that 12-month-old infants (but not 5-month-old infants) looked longer when the climber approached the helper than when it approached the hinderer, indicating, the authors suggest, that the 12-month-olds found the reunion with the helper to be the more satisfying ending. This work was replicated and extended by Hamlin, Wynn, and Bloom (2007), who found that both 6- and 10-month-olds, when encouraged to choose their preferred object, reached for the helper over the hinderer. These results suggest that infants as young as 6 months attend to the good or bad actions of individuals and that perhaps some of the bases of social and moral judgments emerge quite early.

Do children distinguish between different kinds of "good" actors, for example, those who differ in the degree of their generosity? McCrink, Santos, and Bloom (2006) had children receive rewards from two puppets and then select the puppet that was "nicer." In key trials, the puppets differed in the number of rewards they possessed and the number they gave to the participant. The experimenters varied the absolute number and the proportion of rewards given. They discovered that whereas 4-year-olds preferred a puppet who had given a greater absolute number of rewards, 5-year-olds used a combination of absolute number and proportion and adults relied on proportion only. These results suggest that children's understanding of important moral concepts such as sharing changes across development and, as a result, their social evaluations of sharers do as well.

Do children use only people's *actions* to decide whether those people are good or bad? New research with preschoolers and elementary-aged children has asked whether children might also evaluate people on the basis of things that happen to them, even things that may be out of their control, such as lucky or unlucky events that befall them (Olson, Banaji, Dweck, & Spelke, 2006; Olson, Dunham, Dweck, Spelke, & Banaji, 2008). This work has found that children as young as 3 years judge lucky individuals to be nicer than unlucky individuals and that this preference for the lucky holds regardless of whether the events are trivial (e.g., getting splashed by a passing car) or more extreme (such as having one's house destroyed by a tornado). This phenomenon has also been shown in children in Japan (Olson et al., 2008). Finally, the luck preference appears to spread to new members of groups; children prefer an individual who merely shares group membership with lucky people over an individual who shares group membership with unlucky people, despite the fact that the individuals being evaluated were themselves neither lucky nor unlucky (Olson et al., 2006). Understanding the extent of this generalization and the relationship between luck attitudes and prejudice is a task for future research. For example, it could exacerbate prejudice and discrimination if members of disadvantaged groups experience more unlucky events and receive more negative evaluations as a result.

As the Olson et al. (2006) work suggests, often one learns about a person as part of a community of people. Does it matter for social judgments if that community is portrayed in subtly different ways? Master, Markman, and Dweck (2008) asked how young children represent individuals depending on whether they are presented as members of a continuum or members of a category. In a series of studies, they showed 4-year-olds a set of six schematized faces that ranged from broadly smiling to seriously frowning, with the two middle faces crossing the boundary from smiling to frowning. They then either described the first three, one at a time, as "nice" and the last three as "mean" (category condition) or described them in gradations from "really nice" to "really mean" (continuum condition).

They then assessed social expectations and judgments: Who would share, who would hit, with whom did the participant want to play, how much did the participants like each one, and how would participants distribute presents to them? Those in the category condition made a much sharper differentiation between the middle two faces on all measures than did those in the continuum condition, whereas those in the continuum condition showed more differentiation *within* the categories. Future work can explore how the "continuum" representation, which captures many social stimuli, may lead children both to maintain important distinctions among people that category representations may obscure and to avoid the sharp breaks between groups that the category representation encourages.

Evaluations of Similar and Dissimilar Others

Social judgments can also be made on the basis of similarity or dissimilarity to the self. Thus, another topic that is receiving considerable attention is the extent to which children prefer similar to dissimilar others. For example, Markson and Fawcett (2007) discovered that 3-year-old children view those with shared toy preferences, food preferences, or hair color as more desirable playmates than those with different preferences. Thus, early on children can make important social judgments on the basis of common interests and perceptual similarity.

Other researchers have been concerned with the extent to which children prefer others who share their group membership. Historically, these studies have focused on racial, ethnic, and gender groups (e.g., Clark & Clark, 1947; Maccoby & Jacklin, 1974;

for reviews, see Aboud, 1988; Ruble, Martin, & Berenbaum, 2006). New work in these areas, coming from a cognitive development perspective, is employing looking-time, reaching, and choice tasks with young children. These studies ask questions about when children notice group differences and when they use these differences to make decisions, such as whom to play with or what toys or activities are desirable (e.g., Bar-Haim, Ziv, Lamy, & Hodes, 2006; Diesendruck & ha Levi, 2006; Kelly et al., 2007; Shutts, Banaji, & Spelke, 2007).

Another direction this work has moved in is to examine social categories other than race and gender. For example, work by Kinzler, Dupoux, and Spelke (2007) has examined native language and native accent as social category markers. Using an array of different methods appropriate to different ages, they have found that 5- to 6-month-olds preferentially attend to the face of someone speaking their language with a native accent over the face of someone speaking a different language or speaking with a foreign accent and that 10-month-old infants will select toys from a native speaker over a foreign-accented speaker of their language. These preferences appear to continue, as 5-year-old children indicate that they would prefer to be friends with speakers of their native language and those with native accents. An important question for future research is how powerful these biases will be in children's actual relationships and what kinds of information can override them.

Several other researchers have been investigating whether young children will even infer liking from an arbitrary similarity. This work builds on past research demonstrating that older children and adolescents will prefer members of their own groups even when those groups have been arbitrarily assigned by the experimenter (Sherif, Harvey, White, Hood, & Sherif, 1961; Turner, Brown, & Tajfel, 1979). Patterson and Bigler (2006) put 3- to 5-year-old children into arbitrary groups by having them wear one of two colors of T-shirts to preschool every day for 3 weeks. At the end of that time, children made more favorable evaluations of peers wearing the same-color T-shirt than of peers wearing the other-color T-shirt, suggesting that even an arbitrary similarity, such as experimentally assigned T-shirt color, can influence even young children's evaluations of others. Dunham (2007) has found similar results with 5-year-olds, but with an even smaller manipulation. He simply asked children to draw a colored coin out of a bag to assign a T-shirt color and then measured children's attitudes and sharing behavior toward members of both groups.

Across these studies, it is clear that early in life, children can and often do make important social judgments, such as whom to approach, whom to play with, and whom they like, on the basis of similarity, be it a common interest or group membership. As we have noted, it will now be important to see how features of children's environment influence these social judgments and how these judgments play out in social interactions.

Representations of Social Relationships

Exciting new findings are also emerging from the study of infants' and young children's *representations* of people and relationships. Here, too, methods from cognitive development have been used (such as looking-time tasks, resource allocation tasks, and evaluation tasks), and they have illuminated children's expectations of how people will behave and their understanding of the relationships between people.

Attachment theory and research have a long history in social development (e.g., Ainsworth & Bell, 1970; De Wolff & van IJzendoorn, 1997; Main, Kaplan, & Cassidy, 1985; Sroufe, 1985). However, one aspect of Bowlby's (1958) groundbreaking proposal had never been directly investigated in infants: the hypothesis that infants form "internal working models" or mental representations of attachment relationships based on their early experiences with caretakers. These working models are said to consist of children's expectations of how caretakers will behave toward stressed or distressed children (e.g., will they approach them?) and how children under stress will behave toward the caretaker (e.g., will they seek proximity?). Could we detect these internal working models in infants?

Johnson, Dweck, and Chen (2007) employed a looking-time procedure to assess infants' mental representations of attachment relationships. In one study, 14-month-old infants were shown a video interaction between a "child" (represented by a small abstract form) and a "parent" (represented by a larger abstract form). The parent moved away from the child, who was unable to follow, and the child cried repeatedly. Infants watched this episode again and again until they were habituated to (got bored with) the event. Then, on the test trials, the participants either observed the parent return to the distressed child or observed the parent continue to move away from the child. Children previously identified as securely attached to their caregiver looked longer (were more "surprised") when the parent continued moving away from the distressed child than when the parent returned to the child. In contrast, children previously identified as insecurely attached showed little discrimination between the two events. In fact, in follow-up work, they showed the opposite pattern—more surprise when the parent returned (Johnson, 2007)! These results suggest that infants have indeed formed expectations for how caretakers will react to a child in distress.

In a second study, Johnson (2007) showed infants similar videos, except that this time during the habituation trials, the parent returned to a spot near the crying child. During the test trials, as the parent returned, the child either approached or fled from the parent. Consistent with different representations of attachment relationships, securely attached infants expected the distressed child to approach the parent and insecurely attached infants did not. These results importantly demonstrate that infants already have well-formed expectations about human interactions. Although we do not yet know how malleable or how stable these representations are across development, it is reasonable to think that these early representations can have important influences on children's interpersonal interactions. Whereas securely attached infants, when stressed, may be likely to approach others and expect to be helped by them, insecurely attached infants may not recognize or tap into social resources, even when they are available.

Of course, attachment relationships are not the only relationships children understand at an early age. New research by Olson and Spelke (2008) has discovered that children represent reciprocal relationships between unknown individuals. Evolutionary biologists and economists have long argued that it is beneficial to engage in cooperative behaviors including reciprocation (sharing with someone who shared with you) and indirect reciprocation (sharing with someone who shared with someone else). However, in order to engage in these behaviors, individuals must be able to track and represent who has given resources and to whom. As a test of these representations in children, these researchers asked 3.5-year-old children to help a target doll distribute rewards to a series of dolls that had been described as previously sharing with the target, sharing with another doll, or not sharing at all. Although children favored reciprocity over indirect reciprocity, their sharing behavior was consistent with both principles, indicating that they were able to represent these important social relationships. Such behavior suggests that young children have a tendency to reward one another's sharing and that they can track the costs and benefits of sharing with specific individuals.

Other Sources of New Social Cognitive Developmental Research

In addition to work coming from a cognitive development perspective, the recent surge in research on social cognitive development has been influenced by methods from adult cognitive psychology and from adult social cognition. For example, new research is applying neuroimaging and comparative methods from cognitive psychology to address questions about the underlying mechanisms and phylogenetic origins of social cognitive development. Researchers have recently conducted developmental social cognitive neuroscience studies that examined such topics as differences in how children and adults represent self and social knowledge (Pfeifer, Lieberman, & Dapretto, 2007), differences in children's and adult's understanding of a speaker's intention (Wang, Lee, Sigman, & Dapretto, 2006), and differences in the neural circuitry underlying emotion recognition and display in children with and without autism spectrum disorders (Dapretto et al., 2006; Dawson, Webb, Carver, Panagiotides, & McPartland, 2004). We look forward to what this work can contribute to our understanding of the mechanisms underlying social cognitive development and the light it may shed on similarities and differences between children's and adults' social functioning.

Similarly, by investigating basic social cognitive abilities in other primates, researchers can develop better theories about the causes and uses of such abilities and may even change their theories entirely (e.g., Brosnan & de Waal, 2003; Tomasello, Call, & Hare, 2003; Warneken & Tomasello, 2006). For example, some theories have suggested that cognitive dissonance reduction is the result of complex self-related processes; however, recent evidence of cognitive dissonance reduction in capuchins, who are generally considered to lack a sense of self, suggests either that evaluations of capuchin's sense of self are wrong or that a self-based theory of cognitive dissonance is not likely (Egan, Santos, & Bloom, 2007).

Another source, as we have noted, is the field of adult social cognition. Researchers from this tradition have recently begun to ask about the origins of social cognitive phenomena. For example, a key topic in social cognition research over the past decade has been the measurement of implicit or nonconscious attitudes (e.g., Dovidio, Kawakami, Johnson, Johnson, & Howard, 1997;

Fazio & Olson, 2003; Greenwald, McGhee, & Schwartz, 1998). Researchers have now begun to investigate the development of implicit social attitudes (Baron & Banaji, 2006; Rutland, Cameron, Milne, & McGeorge, 2005) in order to understand how attitudes toward specific social groups develop, to understand how explicit and implicit attitudes diverge during development, and to understand the relationship between attitudes and behavior. Such findings may also be of importance for informing future intervention studies that aim to reduce prejudice and stereotyping.

Although modern neuroscience, comparative, and adult social cognitive approaches have not always been concerned with human developmental issues, we see many ways in which they are likely to contribute to the methodological toolbox and theoretical claims of the "new" social cognitive development.

Conclusions

We believe that the recent surge in work on social cognitive development represents an emerging approach that is unique, that is likely to have staying power, and that builds bridges to other fields including social cognition, comparative psychology, and neuroscience. We are optimistic that the work on social cognitive development will not only continue to identify important socially relevant mental representations and cognitive processes but will also (a) examine the influence of specific antecedents, such as culture or parental practices, on the development of these representations and (b) identify the real-world consequences of these processes, with the goal of promoting greater well-being and more positive social interactions. Our hope is that as the research projects we have described become flourishing research programs—and as others adopt a social cognitive approach—we will have increasingly vigorous methods to address the origins of social outcomes that are meaningful for children.

Note

1. Much of the work presented here is current work that has been presented at recent conferences, including the 2007 Society for Research in Child Development meeting, the 2007 Cognitive Development Society meeting, the 2007 and 2008 Society for Personality and Social Psychology meetings, and the 2008 International Conference on Infant Studies meeting.

References

Aboud, F. E. (1988). *Children and prejudice.* New York: Blackwell.

Ainsworth, M. D., & Bell, S. M. (1970). Attachment, exploration, and separation: Illustrated by the behavior of one-year-olds in a strange situation. *Child Development, 41,* 49–67.

Baldwin, D. A. (2000). Interpersonal understanding fuels knowledge acquisition. *Current Directions in Psychological Science, 9,* 40–45.

Bar-Haim, Y., Ziv, T., Lamy, D., & Hodes, R. M. (2006). Nature and nurture in own-race face processing. *Psychological Science, 17,* 159–163.

Baron, A. S., & Banaji, M. R. (2006). The development of implicit attitudes: Evidence of race evaluations from ages 6 and 10 and adulthood. *Psychological Science, 17,* 53–58.

Bowlby, J. (1958). The nature of the child's ties to his mother. *International Journal of Psychoanalysis, 39,* 350–373.

Brosnan, S. F., & de Waal, F. B. (2003). Monkeys reject unequal pay. *Nature, 425,* 297–299.

Clark, K., & Clark, M. (1947). Racial identification and preference in Negro children. In T. M. Newcomb & E. I. Hartley (Eds.), *Readings in social psychology* (pp. 169–178). New York: Holt.

Dapretto, M., Davies, M. S., Pfeifer, J. H., Scott, A. A., Sigman, M., Bookheimer, S. Y., et al. (2006). Understanding emotions in others: Mirror neuron dysfunction in children with autism spectrum disorders. *Nature Neuroscience, 9,* 28–30.

Dawson, G., Webb, S. J., Carver, L., Panagiotides, H., & McPartland, J. (2004). Young children with autism show atypical brain responses to fearful versus neutral facial expressions of emotion. *Developmental Science, 7,* 340–359.

De Wolff, M., & van IJzendoorn, M. H. (1997). Sensitivity and attachment: A meta-analysis on parental antecedents of infant attachment. *Child Development, 68,* 571–591.

Diesendruck, G., & ha Levi, H. (2006). The role of language, appearance, and culture in children's social category-based induction. *Child Development, 77,* 539–553.

Dovidio, J. F., Kawakami, K., Johnson, C., Johnson, B., & Howard, A. (1997). On the nature of prejudice: Automatic and controlled processes. *Journal of Experimental Social Psychology, 33,* 510–540.

Dunham, Y. (2007). *Minimal group biases in childhood.* Talk presented at the meeting of the Cognitive Development Society, Santa Fe, NM.

Egan, L. C., Santos, L. R., & Bloom, P. (2007). The origins of cognitive dissonance: Evidence from children and monkeys. *Psychological Science, 18,* 978–983.

Fazio, R. H., & Olson, M. A. (2003). Implicit measures in social cognition research: Their meaning and uses. *Annual Review of Psychology, 54,* 297–327.

Gergely, G., Bekkering, H., & Kiraly, I. (2002). Rational imitation in preverbal infants. *Nature, 415,* 755.

Gergely, G., Nadasdy, Z., Csibra, G., & Biro, S. (1995). Taking the intentional stance at 12 months of age. *Cognition, 56,* 165–193.

Greenwald, A. G., McGhee, D. E., & Schwartz, J. L. K. (1998). Measuring individual differences in implicit cognition: The implicit association test. *Journal of Personality and Social Psychology, 74,* 1464–1480.

Hamlin, J. K., Wynn, K., & Bloom, P. (2007). Social evaluation in preverbal infants. *Nature, 450,* 557–559.

Johnson, S. C. (2007). *Evidence for infants' working model of attachment.* Presented at the meeting of the Child Development Society, Santa Fe, NM.

Johnson, S. C., Dweck, C. S., & Chen, F. S. (2007). Evidence for infants' internal working models of attachment. *Psychological Science, 18,* 501–502.

Johnson, S. C., Slaughter, V., & Carey, S. (1998). Whose gaze will infants follow? The elicitation of gaze-following in 12-month-olds. *Developmental Science, 1,* 233–238.

Kelly, D. J., Liu, S., Ge, L., Quinn, P. C., Slater, A. M., Lee, K., et al. (2007). Cross-race preferences for same-race faces extend beyond the African versus Caucasian contrast in 3-month-old infants. *Infancy, 11,* 87–95.

Kinzler, K. D., Dupoux, E., & Spelke, E. S. (2007). The native language of social cognition. *Proceedings of the National Academy of Sciences of the United States of America, 104,* 12577–12580.

Kuhlmeier, V., Wynn, K., & Bloom, P. (2003). Attribution of dispositional states by 12-month-olds. *Psychological Science, 14,* 402–408.

Leslie, A. M. (1987). Pretense and representation: The origins of "theory of mind." *Psychological Review, 94,* 412–426.

Maccoby, E. E., & Jacklin, C. N. (1974). *The psychology of sex differences.* Stanford, CA: Stanford University Press.

Main, M., Kaplan, N., & Cassidy, J. (1985). Security in infancy, childhood, and adulthood: A move to the level of representation. *Monographs of the Society for Research in Child Development,* (Serial No. 209), *50,* 66–104.

Markson, L., & Fawcett, C. (2007). *Social influences on children's preferences.* Presented at the meeting of the Cognitive Development Society, Santa Fe, NM.

Master, A., Markman, E. M., & Dweck, C. S. (2008, February). *How thinking in categories or along a continuum affects children's social judgments.* Poster presented at the conference of the Society for Personality and Social Psychology, Albuquerque, NM.

McCrink, K., Santos, L., & Bloom, P. (2006). *Cues to generosity in children and adults.* Presented at the conference of the Society for Research in Child Development, Boston.

Meltzoff, A. (1995). Understanding of the intentions of others: Re-enactment of intended acts by 18-month-old children. *Developmental Psychology, 31,* 838–850.

Meltzoff, A., & Borton, R. W. (1979). Intermodal matching by human neonates. *Nature, 282,* 403–404.

Olson, K. R., Banaji, M. R., Dweck, C. S., & Spelke, E. S. (2006). Children's bias against lucky vs. unlucky people and their social groups. *Psychological Science, 17,* 845–846.

Olson, K. R., Dunham, Y., Dweck, C. S., Spelke, E. S., & Banaji, M. R. (2008). Judgments of the lucky across development and culture. *Journal of Personality and Social Psychology, 94,* 757–776.

Olson, K. R., & Dweck, C. S. (2008). A blueprint for social cognitive development. *Perspectives on Psychological Science, 3,* 193–202.

Olson, K. R., & Spelke, E. S. (2008). Foundations of cooperation in preschool children. *Cognition, 108,* 222–231.

Patterson, M. M., & Bigler, R. S. (2006). Preschool children's attention to environmental messages about groups: Social categorization and the origins of intergroup bias. *Child Development, 77,* 847–860.

Pfeifer, J. H., Lieberman, M. D., & Dapretto, M. (2007). "I know you are but what am I?": Neural bases of self- and social knowledge retrieval in children and adults. *Journal of Cognitive Neuroscience, 19,* 1323–1337.

Premack, D., & Premack, A. J. (1997). Infants attribute value? To the goal-directed actions of self-propelled objects. *Journal of Cognitive Neuroscience, 9,* 848–856.

Ruble, D. N., Martin, C. L., & Berenbaum, S. A. (2006). Gender development. In N. Eisenberg, W. Damon, & R. M. Lerner (Eds.), *Handbook of child psychology: Vol. 3. Social, emotional, and personality development* (6th ed., pp. 858–932). New York: Wiley.

Rutland, A., Cameron, L., Milne, A., & McGeorge, P. (2005). Social norms and self-presentation: Children's implicit and explicit intergroup attitudes. *Child Development, 76,* 451–466.

Sherif, M., Harvey, O. J., White, B. J., Hood, W. R., & Sherif, C. W. (1961). *Intergroup cooperation and competition: The Robbers Cave experiment.* Norman, OK: University Book Exchange.

Shutts, K., Banaji, M. R., & Spelke, E. S. (2007). *Social categories guide young children's preferences for novel objects.* Presented at the meeting of the Cognitive Development Society, Santa Fe, NM.

Sroufe, L. A. (1985). Attachment classification from the perspective of infant-caregiver relationships and infant temperament. *Child Development, 56,* 1–14.

Tomasello, M., Call, J., & Hare, B. (2003). Chimpanzees understand psychological states—The question is which ones and to what extent. *Trends in Cognitive Sciences, 7,* 153–156.

Tomasello, M., Carpenter, M., Call, J., Behne, T., & Moll, H. (2005). Understanding and sharing intentions: The origins of cultural cognition. *Behavioral and Brain Sciences, 28,* 675–735.

Turner, J. C., Brown, R. J., & Tajfel, H. (1979). Social comparison and group interest in ingroup favouritism. *European Journal of Social Psychology, 9,* 187–204.

Wang, A. T., Lee, S. S., Sigman, M., & Dapretto, M. (2006). Developmental changes in the neural basis of interpreting communicative intent. *Social Cognitive and Affective Neuroscience, 1,* 107–121.

Warneken, F., & Tomasello, M. (2006). Altruistic helping in human infants and young chimpanzees. *Science, 311,* 1301–1303.

Wellman, H. (1990). *The child's theory of mind.* Cambridge, MA: MIT Press.

Wimmer, H., & Perner, J. (1983). Beliefs about beliefs: Representation and constraining function of wrong beliefs in young children's understanding of deception. *Cognition, 13,* 103–128.

Woodward, A. L. (1998). Infants selectively encode the goal object of an actor's reach. *Cognition, 69,* 1–34.

Correspondence concerning this article should be addressed to **KRISTINA R. OLSON,** Psychology Department, Box 208205, Yale University, New Haven, CT 06520; e-mail: kristina.olson@yale.edu.

Future Thinking in Young Children

Cristina M. Atance

Humans spend a great deal of time anticipating, planning for, and contemplating the future. Our future thinking is directed toward such ordinary events as what to wear the next day or where to go for lunch, but also toward more significant choices that will potentially impact our long-term happiness and success, such as accepting a job or getting married. The fact that we think (and often ruminate) about these and numerous other aspects of our personal futures is argued to be a reflection of our cognitive capacity for mental time travel (e.g., Atance & Meltzoff, 2005; Suddendorf & Corballis, 2007; Tulving, 2005).

Mental Time Travel

Tulving's (1984) distinction between "semantic" and "episodic" memory has deeply influenced theory and research in human cognition. Semantic memory is described as an early-developing system that allows one to retrieve facts about the world (e.g., knowing that Paris is the capital of France). It is often contrasted with episodic memory, which is described as a later-developing system that mediates one's memory for personally experienced events (e.g., remembering the first time I strolled down the Champs-Elysées). Episodic memory is argued to be unique to humans and critical to mental time travel (Tulving, 2005). Although research and theory have focused almost exclusively on mental time travel into the past, the adaptive significance of the episodic system may be that it allows humans to mentally travel into the future and thus anticipate and plan for needs not currently experienced (e.g., imagining a state of hunger when currently satiated; Suddendorf & Corballis, 2007; Tulving, 2005).

Although other animal species engage in future-oriented behaviors (e.g., food hoarding, nest building, and planning), there is substantial debate about whether these behaviors are carried out with the future in mind. For example, food hoarding may be driven by genetically programmed, species-specific behavioral tendencies (Roberts, 2002), whereas planning (e.g., a chimpanzee preparing a stick for retrieving termites) may be driven largely by the animal's current motivational state rather than by an anticipated future one (e.g., Roberts, 2002; but see Mulcahy & Call, 2006; and Raby, Alexis, Dickinson, & Clayton, 2007). Debates about mental time travel in nonhuman animals have led to the interesting question of when this capacity emerges in human development.

The Development of Mental Time Travel

Busby and Suddendorf (2005) tested preschoolers' ability to mentally project into the future by asking them to verbally report something that they would do "tomorrow." Whereas 4- and 5-year-olds were quite successful in providing reports that their parents judged as plausible (69% and 63% of total reports, respectively), 3-year-olds were not (31%). Meltzoff and I (Atance & Meltzoff, 2005) adopted a different approach requiring verbal and nonverbal responses. Preschoolers were asked to pretend that they would make an outing to various locations (e.g., mountains, desert) and were asked to choose one item from a set of three to bring with them. Only one of these could be used to address a future physiological state. For example, in the mountain scenario, a lunch—which could address the future state of hunger—was the correct choice, whereas a bowl and a comb were incorrect. Scenarios were designed to be ones for which children would have little direct experience, thus reducing the likelihood that children could succeed based on semantic knowledge alone. Across scenarios, 3-year-olds chose the correct item significantly more often than would be expected by chance, with the performance of the older children being nearly perfect. Moreover, to explicitly test whether children recognized that the correct item could be used to address a future state, they were asked to verbally explain their choices. Four- and 5-year-olds were significantly more likely (62% and 71% respectively) than 3-year-olds (35%) to reference a future state of the self (e.g., "I might get hungry").

These two studies suggest that 4- and 5-year-olds are able to mentally travel into the future to consider what they may do the next day and to anticipate a variety of states that could arise across different situations. In contrast, 3-year-olds only show the rudiments of these abilities.

Mental Time Travel and Verbal Ability

Might limitations in verbal ability mask young children's understanding of the future? Comprehension of temporal terms such as *tomorrow* and *yesterday* emerges only gradually during the preschool and early school years. *Tomorrow,* in particular, is understood by most 3-year-olds to refer to the future, but not necessarily the next day (Harner, 1975). Asking a young child to report an event that will occur "tomorrow" may result in the child stating an anticipated event, but not necessarily one that falls within the conceptual boundaries of this term. At the other end of the spectrum is debate about whether a child who *can* talk about the future should be credited with mental time travel into the future (e.g., Suddendorf & Busby, 2005). Children as young as 2 years of age talk about the future, but such talk may reflect preexisting knowledge (or "scripts") of how routine activities such as "bedtime" unfold, rather than a true projection into the future (Atance & O'Neill, 2001). To guard against under- or over-estimating children's future thinking ability, researchers have strived to create tasks that rely as little as possible on verbal ability and that are structured to test when children's *behavior* evidences the anticipation of a state that they are not currently experiencing—the litmus test of mental time travel into the future.

Acting Now *in Anticipation of* Later

Suddendorf and Busby (2005) tested preschoolers' ability to act in the present to avoid a future state of boredom. Children in the experimental group were led to an empty room (Room A) containing only a puzzle board, whereas children in the control group were also led to Room A, but with no puzzle board present. After a brief stay in Room A, children were led to Room B. Several minutes later, they were told that they would return to Room A and were asked to select an item to bring with them—one of these being puzzle pieces. Whereas 4- and 5-year-olds in the experimental group chose puzzle pieces significantly more often than those in the control group, 3-year-olds' choices did not differ across groups, suggesting that only the older children were able to act in the present (i.e., choose puzzle pieces) in anticipation of a future state (i.e., play/avoid boredom).

Using a different behavioral paradigm, Meltzoff and I (Atance & Meltzoff, 2006) manipulated preschoolers' current state to observe how this would impact their choices for the future. Three-, 4-, and 5-year-olds were assigned either to intervention groups, in which they were given pretzels to snack on, or baseline groups, in which they were not. After a delay (which allowed children in the intervention groups to eat the thirst-inducing pretzels), one group of intervention children and one group of baseline children were asked to choose between pretzels and water. Most intervention children, who were presumably thirsty, chose water, whereas most baseline children chose pretzels. More importantly, the remaining two groups of children (one intervention and one baseline) were asked to choose for *tomorrow*. Again, most baseline children chose pretzels, showing that when they were not in a state of thirst they preferred pretzels. In contrast, the intervention children were unable to override their current desire for water to anticipate that pretzels would be desirable the next day (see Figure 1). This was true of all three age groups, despite the fact that most 4- and 5-year-olds correctly responded to comprehension questions about *tomorrow,* which suggests that their difficulty did not lie in an inability to comprehend the temporal reference of the test question.

Rather, the 4- and 5-year-olds' difficulty may involve what social psychologists (e.g., Loewenstein & Schkade, 1999) refer to as "empathy gaps." This term captures the difficulty that people experience when trying to imagine themselves in a

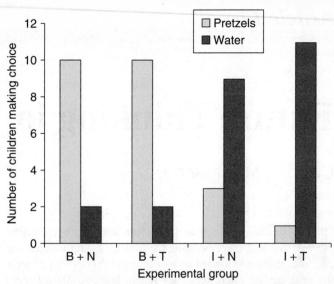

Figure 1 Number of children choosing pretzels or water as a function of whether they had been given pretzels to snack on (intervention groups) or not (baseline groups), and whether they had been asked to choose for *now* or *tomorrow.* B + N = Baseline + Choice for Now; B + T = Baseline + Choice for *Tomorrow;* I + N = Intervention + Choice for *Now;* I + T = Intervention + Choice for *Tomorrow.*

different state than their current one. Most notably, people in a "hot" state (e.g., hunger or thirst) tend to have difficulty imagining that they will eventually "cool off" (i.e., become satiated or quenched). Consequently, predictions, or choices, for the future are biased in the direction of current states. Buying more groceries when hungry than when satiated is a common consequence of empathy gaps. It is likely that the children in our study (Atance & Meltzoff, 2006) were falling prey to this very phenomenon (i.e., they could not imagine a future desire for pretzels while in a state of thirst). Arguably, the children in Suddendorf and Busby's (2005) "two rooms" study did not need to bridge as wide an empathy gap because imagining playing with the puzzle (or avoiding boredom) was not directly conflicting with their current state, nor was their current state one as salient as thirst or hunger. Our (Atance & Meltzoff, 2006) findings do not contradict the claim that mental time travel emerges in the preschool years, but they identify conditions in which the capacity to do so is compromised.

Mental Time Travel and Future-Oriented Behaviors
Planning

Studies examining the development of planning rarely discuss how it is affected by children's growing knowledge about the future (cf. Haith, 1997). Because components of planning, including goal representation and the envisioning of actions necessary to achieve a goal, require thought about the future, planning capacity should shift qualitatively at ages 4 or 5, mirroring episodic-memory development and the emergence of mental time travel. Reinterpretation of data from Hudson, Shapiro, and

Sosa (1995) is consistent with this claim. One group of 3- to 5-year-olds was asked to provide scripts for going to the beach and going grocery shopping (e.g., "Can you tell me what happens when you go to the beach?"), whereas another group was asked to formulate plans (e.g., "Can you tell me a plan for going to the beach?"). Because plans are more future-oriented than scripts, and arguably rely more heavily on the episodic system, a prediction is that they should show more development than scripts during the preschool years.

Results are consistent with this prediction: Children's scripts did not improve significantly with age, whereas their plans did. Moreover, by age 5, children's plans and scripts for the same event were noticeably different. According to Hudson et al., this difference reflected the awareness that planning an event entails more than simply recounting "what happens." Indeed, the older children's plans included more mention of advance preparations than did their scripts, suggesting foresight. Their planning behavior was also more flexible, as evidenced by the capacity to state both how they could remedy an occurrence (e.g., forgetting to bring food to the beach) and prevent its recurrence. This suggests that older children were not merely drawing on their knowledge of how an event typically unfolds (semantic system) but rather were able to imagine different outcomes and how these could be addressed. The foresight and flexibility of the older preschoolers' plans are characteristic of the episodic system and may signal that it, and the mental time travel that it supports, are in place. In contrast, in the absence of a well-developed episodic system, the younger children may have been drawing largely on the semantic system for both script and plan construction.

Delay of Gratification

Future thinking may also be crucial for an important aspect of self-control: delaying gratification. In a delay of gratification paradigm, children are asked to choose between a smaller (e.g., one mini-marshmallow) or a larger (e.g., 10 mini-marshmallows) reward. They are then told that the larger reward can only be obtained after a delay. Although children's ability to delay for the larger, more desirable reward improves with age (e.g., Mischel, Shoda, & Rodriguez, 1989; Moore, Barresi, & Thompson, 1998), there is also individual variability due to self-regulatory strategies (e.g., not looking directly at the reward), for example (Mischel, Shoda, & Rodriguez, 1989). Might an additional source of variability stem from differences in mental time travel capacity? Mischel, Shoda, and Peake (1988) report that 4-year-olds who were good at delaying gratification became adolescents whose parents rated them as being, among other characteristics, better at planning and thinking ahead than the adolescents who were less able to delay gratification. Although these results do not address whether these adolescents also planned more and were future-oriented as preschoolers (an interesting issue for future research), they suggest a mutual interdependence between future thinking and delaying gratification. Indeed, were an organism not able to conceptualize a time other than the present, then delaying would make little sense. These findings also raise the interesting issue of individual differences in mental time travel capacity in both children and adults.

Future Directions

An intriguing issue to consider is the overlap between adopting the perspective of one's future self and the perspective of another person. Research suggests that people experience not only "intrapersonal" empathy gaps but also "interpersonal" ones, such that judgments about the emotional states of others are influenced by one's own (Van Boven & Loewenstein, 2003). Our (Atance & Meltzoff, 2006) state-manipulation paradigm offers a potential means of addressing this issue from a developmental perspective. For instance, do children's current states (e.g., thirst) affect judgments about not only their own future desires but also those of others (both current and future)? A related issue is how thinking about, or planning, one's own future may differ from planning someone else's (e.g., that of one's child or elderly parent). Both processes likely draw on mental time travel but may draw differentially on theory of mind (i.e., mental state attribution).

Because research on the development of future thinking is in its early phases, a primary goal has been to devise methods to assess what young children know about the future. However, in addition to refining existing methodologies, it is important to explore how this knowledge develops. According to Suddendorf and Corballis (2007), mental time travel is not an encapsulated capacity but relies on a host of cognitive processes such as theory of mind, inhibitory control, and working memory. By this view, an organism that lacks some (or all) of these processes will have impaired mental time-travel ability. Exploring whether children's mental time-travel ability is related to individual differences in such skills as theory of mind and inhibitory control will be useful in evaluating this claim.

There is also growing consensus from neurophysiological (e.g., Addis, Wong, & Schacter, 2007) and behavioral (e.g., Busby & Suddendorf, 2005) data that thinking about the future and thinking about the past are intricately entwined; our memories form the basis from which we construct possible futures. Young children (and arguably nonhuman animals) who are limited in their sense of the past will likely also show limitations with respect to the future. Despite this proposed overlap, research findings also suggest neural differentiation between thinking about the past and imagining the future, which may be due to the fact that future events involve some novelty (Addis, Wong, & Schacter, 2007). This view echoes that of Haith (1997), who noted that humans do not just base their future thinking on past events but can also "imagine and create things and events that have never occurred before" (p. 34). Future research efforts will undoubtedly result in significant increases in our knowledge about how the human brain is capable of such a feat, when it becomes attainable in development, and why it may be unattainable for nonhuman animals.

Recommended Readings

Atance, C.M., & Meltzoff, A.N. (2006). (See References). This paper introduces a paradigm to test how children's current states affect their reasoning about the future.

Atance, C.M., & O'Neill, D.K. (2001). (See References). This paper discusses the role of future thinking in different areas of human cognition and behavior.

Haith, M.M., Benson, J.B., Roberts, R.J., Jr., & Pennington, B.F. (Eds.). (1994). *The development of future-oriented processes.* Chicago, IL: University of Chicago Press. A comprehensive volume outlining different aspects of future orientation.

Suddendorf, T., & Corballis, M.C. (2007). (See References). A thorough, highly accessible overview of mental time travel.

Tulving, E. (2005). (See References). A recent, comprehensive review of episodic memory.

References

Addis, D.R., Wong, A.T., & Schacter, D.L. (2007). Remembering the past and imagining the future: Common and distinct neural substrates during event construction and elaboration. *Neuropsychologia, 45,* 1363–1377.

Atance, C.M., & Meltzoff, A.N. (2005). My future self: Young children's ability to anticipate and explain future states. *Cognitive Development, 20,* 341–361.

Atance, C.M., & Meltzoff, A.N. (2006). Preschoolers' current desires warp their choices for the future. *Psychological Science, 17,* 583–587.

Atance, C.M., & O'Neill, D.K. (2001). Episodic future thinking. *Trends in Cognitive Sciences, 5,* 533–539.

Busby, J., & Suddendorf, T. (2005). Recalling yesterday and predicting tomorrow. *Cognitive Development, 20,* 362–372.

Haith, M.M. (1997). The development of future thinking as essential for the emergence of skill in planning. In S.L. Friedman & E. Kofsky Scholnick (Eds.), *The developmental psychology of planning: Why, how, and when do we plan?* (pp. 25–42). Mahwah, NJ: Erlbaum.

Harner, L. (1975). Yesterday and tomorrow: Development of early understanding of the terms. *Developmental Psychology, 11,* 864–865.

Hudson, J.A., Shapiro, L.R., & Sosa, B.B. (1995). Planning in the real world: Preschool children's scripts and plans for familiar events. *Child Development, 66,* 984–998.

Loewenstein, G., & Schkade, D. (1999). Wouldn't it be nice? Predicting future feelings. In D. Kahneman, E. Diener, & N. Schwarz (Eds.), *Well-being: The foundations of hedonic psychology* (pp. 85–105). New York, NY: Russell Sage Foundation.

Mischel, W., Shoda, Y., & Peake, P.K. (1988). The nature of adolescent competencies predicted by preschool delay of gratification. *Journal of Personality and Social Psychology, 54,* 687–696.

Mischel, W., Shoda, Y., & Rodriguez, M.L. (1989). Delay of gratification in children. *Science, 244,* 933–938.

Moore, C., Barresi, J., & Thompson, C. (1998). The cognitive basis of future-oriented prosocial behavior. *Social Development, 7,* 198–218.

Mulcahy, N.J., & Call, J. (2006). Apes save tools for future use. *Science, 312,* 1038–1040.

Raby, C.R., Alexis, D.M., Dickinson, A., & Clayton, N.R. (2007). Planning for the future by western scrub jays. *Nature, 445,* 919–921.

Roberts, W.A. (2002). Are animals stuck in time? *Psychological Bulletin, 128,* 473–489.

Suddendorf, T., & Busby, J. (2005). Making decisions with the future in mind: Developmental and comparative identification of mental time travel. *Learning and Motivation, 36,* 110–125.

Suddendorf, T., & Corballis, M.C. (2007). The evolution of foresight: What is mental time travel and is it unique to humans? *Behavioral and Brain Sciences, 30,* 299–351.

Tulving, E. (1984). Précis of elements of episodic memory. *Behavioral and Brain Sciences, 7,* 223–268.

Tulving, E. (2005). Episodic memory and autonoesis: Uniquely human? In H.S. Terrace & J. Metcalfe (Eds.), *The missing link in cognition: Origins of self-reflective consciousness* (pp. 3–56). New York, NY: Oxford University Press.

Van Boven, L., & Loewenstein, G. (2003). Social projection of transient drive states. *Personality and Social Psychology Bulletin, 29,* 1159–1168.

Address correspondence to **CRISTINA M. ATANCE,** School of Psychology, University of Ottawa, 120 University, Room 407, Ottawa, Ontario, Canada KIN 6N5; e-mail: atance@uottawa.ca.

Acknowledgments—The writing of this article was supported in part by a Discovery Grant from the Natural Sciences and Engineering Research Council of Canada. I thank Daniel Bernstein, Christopher Fennell, Andrew Meltzoff, Julie Scott, and two anonymous reviewers for their comments.

Talking about Science in Museums

CATHERINE A. HADEN

Recent years have seen an increase in questions about what children learn from visiting museums and how this learning occurs. Motivating this trend to a considerable extent is a growing recognition that museums are unique institutions of learning where people of all ages and backgrounds can expand their understanding of culture and science. Museums represent one of a range of important "informal learning environments" where children can broaden their cultural horizons and discover science, technology, engineering, and mathematics (STEM) years before they do so in school (Ash, 2002; Callanan & Jipson, 2001; Callanan & Oakes, 1992; Crowley, Callanan, Jipson, et al., 2001; Palmquist & Crowley, 2007). Moreover, museums—and other such institutions, including zoos, aquariums, and nature centers—are ubiquitous in children's lives. For example, there are more than 1,100 informal science institutions in the United States (http://pbskids.org/dragonflytv/gps/gps_localize.php) that, in addition to serving more than 12 million school children on field trips, offer other wide-ranging educational opportunities, including parent workshops, outreach programs in schools, professional development for teachers, science demonstrations, camps, and after-school programs (Association of Science-Technology Centers, 2008). Given their potential to reach large numbers of children and their families, museums figure prominently in discussions of how to enhance children's cultural understanding and scientific literacy.

Interest in learning in museums has strengthened alongside a growing movement in developmental science for researchers to become more involved with educators to address authentic practical problems. Unique partnerships have been forged, and new systematic museum research on learning is rooted in fresh cross-disciplinary and cross-institutional collaborations between university-based developmentalists within psychology and other divisions, and museum professionals with backgrounds in diverse fields, including science education, the natural sciences, anthropology, and museum education. The questions arising in museum research bridge across varied areas of developmental science from the "cognitive," such as objects-centered learning, to the "social," including motivation and identity development (see, e.g., Leinhardt, Crowley, & Knutson, 2002; Paris, 2002, for reviews). What is more, research in museums has advanced a critical effort in developmental science to move beyond the characterization of various competencies of children at different ages, to elucidate the kinds of experiences and conditions that promote children's learning processes and outcomes. Attempts to capture some of the richness of the social-communicative context in which children learn in museums are transforming definitions of learning beyond single indicators (such as facts retained or recognized) and illuminating multiple influences that bring about learning.

Research in museums presents a considerable opportunity to address serious gaps in our current understanding of how children learn in everyday settings. To illustrate, I offer a focused review of a growing body of research on the fundamental role that parent–child conversational interactions may play in mediating children's knowledge about and approach to science. I begin the review with a description of the empirical and theoretical backdrop for research on talk in museums, and conclude it by pointing to fertile ground for further studies in these informal learning environments.

Empirical and Theoretical Underpinnings

A substantial corpus of work documents clear age-related differences in almost every facet of children's scientific thinking. Older children outperform younger children in terms of the appropriateness of the hypotheses they generate, the experiments they design, and the inferences they draw based on evidence (Dunbar & Klahr, 1989; Klahr, Fay, & Dunbar, 1993; Penner & Klahr, 1996; Schauble, 1996; Zimmerman, 2000). In fact, children under the age of 10 frequently conduct scientific investigations without any explicit hypotheses at all (Penner & Klahr, 1996), and when permitted to do so, tend to end experimentation early, usually after conducting a confounded test to achieve a desired outcome (e.g., Dunbar & Klahr, 1989; Schauble, 1996). With age, children instigate a greater range of experimental tests of hypotheses that include target variables that they do not understand well (Klahr et al., 1993; Schauble, 1996). Children also less frequently jump to a conclusion after a single experiment as they get older (e.g., Gleason & Schauble, 2000). However, throughout the elementary school years, they remain conspicuously poorer than adults in designing studies that control one variable at a time (Schauble, 1996) and in making observations and recording and evaluating data (Garcia-Mila & Andersen, 2007;

Gleason & Schauble, 2000; Klahr et al., 1993; Zimmerman, 2000). Nevertheless, a distillation of evidence from various training studies suggests that children's scientific skills can be improved with appropriate instruction and support, especially during hands-on experiences (e.g., Chen & Klahr, 1999).

This and more of what we have learned about children's scientific thinking at different ages stems from studies carried out in laboratory settings. The importance of this work notwithstanding, it is limited in its focus on individual children working alone to design controlled experiments, make valid inferences, generate new hypotheses, and so forth, and in its emphasis on cognitive processes "within" the children (such as metacognition) that may explain their learning and development (Crowley & Galco, 2001). Indeed, the bulk of the literature on children's scientific thinking has little to say about the experiences in children's everyday lives—including parent–child conversational interactions—that may promote the development of early scientific understanding. Museum research can inform questions about how parent–child conversations can foster children's learning of scientific information on one hand and more general skills for scientific thinking on the other. But it can also bridge to topics that studies of "scientific reasoning" do not typically address, such as whether conversations about science affect children's motivations, aspirations, interest, and productive dispositions toward science (e.g., National Research Council, 2007). It might further provide multiple insights into the implicit messages children may receive about the value of curiosity, inquiry, explanation, reason, and personal meaning-making in parent–child conversational interactions.

Over the past 10 years, in research in museums, developmental psychologists and museum educators have increasingly focused on children's conversations with their caregivers that may promote early science learning (see Leinhardt et al., 2002, for a review). This work has been guided by sociocultural theory (e.g., Berk, 2001; Gauvain, 2000; Rogoff, 1990; Vygotsky, 1978), which emphasizes that to understand learning one must focus in detail on the process of learning. In this view, children construct new understandings in everyday conversations with their parents (and other more knowledgeable members of society), in which they are "scaffolded" (Wood, Bruner, & Ross, 1976) to do and think things that they would not be able to on their own. This scaffolding is evident when parents, for example, help children to focus on what is there to learn, provide important information in response to questions, make useful analogies, tap prior knowledge, offer encouragement, and so forth, in conversations that can to a great extent influence the meaning that children make of their experiences. Put in other terms, when parents engage with their children in richly embellished and elaborated discussions of experiences as they unfold and after they occur, children are able to make sense of their experiences in ways that are likely to make them highly memorable, and what is remembered is learned (Ornstein, Haden, & Hedrick, 2004; see also Leinhardt & Knutson, 2004). Conversational interactions between parents and children in museums (and elsewhere) constitute a mechanism—a process—by which learning occurs (Fivush, Haden, & Reese, 2006; Thompson, 2006).

In addition, sociocultural theory underscores the importance of individual differences such that learning processes and outcomes can be expected to vary with the knowledge and interests children and their parents bring to an experience, and the activities and conversations they engage in during and afterward. Parents' willingness to take on the role of scaffolder, which may be driven by their knowledge but also by beliefs about their role in mediating learning, is further implicated by sociocultural approaches as predictive of learning (see Gaskins, 2008, for further discussion). Individual differences may be reflected in how much parents and children say, what they say, and how they say what they say about their experiences as they unfold and after they have occurred, as well as in what children are able to appropriate about their experiences. For example, the frequency with which parents talk about science with their children should be linked to children's science talk. Moreover, children who hear more and richer talk about science have different opportunities than those who hear less to talk about and think about science in ways that, in turn, should enhance specific literacy-related skills (Tenenbaum & Callanan, 2008; Tenenbaum & Leaper, 2003) and perhaps foster more generally productive attitudes and approaches toward learning.

Parent–Child Conversations about Science in Museums

Museums offer a unique vantage point from which to study parent–child conversations, making it possible for researchers to obtain a precise and dynamic record of how parents and children interact verbally (and nonverbally) during museum experiences. Although we know little about how children develop scientific literacy in everyday settings, new research in museums suggests that—consistent with sociocultural theory—the conversations children have with their parents can both reflect and change what they understand about science (e.g., Ash, 2002; Borun, Chambers, Dristas, & Johnson, 1997; Callanan & Jipson, 2001; Crowley, Callanan, Jipson, et al., 2001; Crowley & Jacobs, 2002; Palmquist & Crowley, 2007; Tenenbaum, Snow, Roach, & Kurland, 2005; Valle & Callanan, 2006). It is clear that particular types of museum exhibits can promote different kinds of conversation, and some can even thwart collaboration and learning altogether (e.g., Crowley & Callanan, 1998; Gelman, Massey, & McManus, 1991; Humphrey & Gutwill, 2005). Even so, experiences in museums can offer significant opportunities for what Leinhardt and Crowley (1998, p. 5) have called "conversational elaboration"—an expression they use to define learning in terms of the richness of the discussions parents engage in with their children during and after museum experiences.

One way that elaborative conversations may be important is that they involve the posing of questions. Children's questions reflect curiosities and interests that can be critical in initiating scientific discovery (Callanan & Jipson, 2001). They can also involve seeking needed help, such as requesting information about one step in an iterative experimental process before proceeding to the next. Parents' questions can facilitate children's understanding as well, by focusing attention on salient aspects of a problem and eliciting information from the child in an effort to diagnose what a child knows and needs to know to make sense of a science exhibit or activity (see Ornstein et al., 2004, for related arguments). Interestingly enough, observations of families in museums have shown that whereas some parents will, in a quiz-like fashion, ask narrowly focused questions that they know the answers to, others asked open-ended *Wh-* questions that elicit collaborative dialog that may extend beyond the facts, to infuse the discussion with personal meaning (Diamond, 1986; Falk & Dierking, 2002). Moreover, although most of the research in museums on parents' questions is descriptive, other work involving observations of parent–child conversations during exhibit-like activities in families' homes (e.g., a camping event; Boland, Haden, & Ornstein, 2003; Haden, Ornstein, Eckerman, & Didow, 2001; Hedrick, San Souci, Haden, & Ornstein, 2009) supports the idea that parents who ask more open-ended *Wh-* question about why things happen, how things work, and what the child thought or felt during science activities should have children who understand more and learn more about science than those whose parents do not ask these sorts of questions. In addition, caregivers' open-ended questions that follow up on children's interest may be essential in motivating sustained engagement in science-related activities in a way that may be remarkably consequential for scientific thinking (e.g., Humphrey & Gutwill, 2005; Schauble, 1996).

Conversational elaboration may also move parents and children beyond simple labeling or listing of objects or activities to explanations of them (Leinhardt & Crowley, 1998). Consistent with this view, Crowley and Callanan (1998; see also Crowley, Callanan, Jipson, et al., 2001) found that children were twice as likely to talk about what they were seeing in a museum exhibit when their parents offered explanations. Moreover, although the children rarely offered explanations themselves, in almost every case when they did, they were responding to a parent explanation. Subsequent museum work has shown that U.S. parents will sometimes offer explanations in response to children's "why?" questions, but more often, parents' explanations are spontaneous (Callanan & Jipson, 2001) and frequently involve specific information to describe, interpret, and apply prior knowledge to an unfolding experience (e.g., Callanan & Jipson, 2001; Callanan, Shrager, & Moore, 1995).

Regarding the content of elaborative talk, Crowley and Callanan (1998; Crowley, Callanan, Jipson, et al., 2001) identified three types of parental explanations in conversations with their 4- to 8-year-old children about a zoetrope— a simple animation device that in this case featured a series of frames of a running horse inside a cylinder that spins. Some explanations involve the use of causal language to link together related events ("The horse looks like it's running backward because you spun this thing the wrong way"). Others refer to unobserverable scientific principles, such as the illusion of motion ("Your mind, your eye, put together each of these little pictures and that's why it looks like it's moving"). Still others make connections between an exhibit and the children's prior knowledge and experiences ("This is how cartoons work"; all examples from Crowley, Callanan,

Jipson, et al., 2001, pp. 719–720). In museums, researchers have found that any of the explanations that parents supply can be quite brief, incomplete, "explanatoids" (p. 409), falling well short of what would be deemed acceptable in a science classroom or text (Crowley & Galco, 2001). Nevertheless, even partial or fragmentary explanations can serve to scaffold children's early understanding of scientific concepts (Callanan & Jipson, 2001; Callanan & Oakes, 1992; Crowley, Callanan, Jipson, et al., 2001; Fender & Crowley, 2008) and may predict later skills (Tenenbaum et al., 2005).

Interestingly enough, in studies that generally include children aged 3–10 years, there are not apparent differences in the number of explanations parents offer for older and younger children (Jipson & Callanan, 2003; Tenenbaum & Leaper, 2003), although parents' question asking and explaining may nonetheless depend on their perceptions of their children's skills and interests (Crowley, Callanan, Tenenbaum, & Allen, 2001; Palmquist & Crowley, 2007). In this regard, parents are more likely to believe that science is less difficult and more interesting for their sons than their daughters (Tenenbaum & Leaper, 2003), and in science tasks in homes (Tenenbaum & Leaper, 2003) and museums (Crowley, Callanan, Jipson, et al., 2001; Crowley, Callanan, Tenenbaum, et al., 2001), parents will explain more often to boys than to girls. Moreover, the frequency of parent–child elaborative conversations about science varies with cultural background and the education level and prior museum experiences of parents (e.g., Tenenbaum, Callanan, Alba-Speyer, & Sandoval, 2002). Specifically, Tenenbaum and Callanan (2008) studied families of Mexican descent living in the United States and found that in both museums and their homes, they engaged in explanatory talk equally with older and younger children. However, the subset of these parents who had completed high school offered more causal and other explanations to their children in the museum than did parents with less schooling. In addition, parents who had prior museum experience made more explanations in this setting than those who had not. Although the reasons underlying the latter two findings are debatable, they may in part result from variations in the parents' understandings of how children learn and their own role in facilitating learning (Gaskins, 2008).

What do children learn from the kinds of explanations that researchers have observed in museum settings? Causal explanations have been linked to increased conceptual understanding, especially in the domain of science (e.g., Chi, de Leeuw, Chiu, & LaVancher, 1994) and to the development and revision of children's intuitive theories of how the world works (Callanan & Jipson, 2001). Scientific principle explanations offer children domain-specific scientific information (Klahr, 2000) that children may, in turn, be able to generalize beyond the immediate learning context (Crowley & Siegler, 1999). Moreover, evidence suggests that parents' use of explanations that connect ongoing activities to children's unique interests and prior knowledge may be especially important in fostering understanding of new experiences (e.g., Tessler & Nelson, 1994). Crowley and Jacobs (2002), for example, found in a museum-like setup that 4- to 12-year-olds who heard their parents explain fossils in ways that included connecting them to previous experiences were more likely to remember the names of the fossils than children who did not receive such explanations. Similarly, Valle and Callanan (2006) found that in a homework-type activity, parents sometimes linked their 4- to 9-year-old children's past experiences to an unfamiliar science topic, and that overall, parents' efforts to point out "analogies" contributed to children's understanding. Thus, there is a good reason to suspect that parents' explanations to children in museums affect learning.

Future Directions

As this brief summary indicates, in recent years there has been an obvious increase in research aimed at describing the nature of parent–child conversations about science in museum settings. Nevertheless, there are limits to the current understanding of how parents may influence children's science learning both in and out of museums. In particular, there is a terrific opportunity in future research to take this work further by examining *what it is* about elaborative conversation (such as *Wh-* questions, explanations) that may serve to mediate learning outcomes, and to look at the processes involved in learning as they extend in time and space. Also, although a few museum researchers have begun to call attention to questions about the impact of visitor diversity on learning in museums (e.g., Gaskins, 2008; Tenenbaum & Callanan, 2008), we must coordinate efforts to obtain detailed descriptions of conversational interactions with information about how these may vary as a function of cultural background, parental education, and museum experience, and why.

One potentially fruitful approach derives from the notion that it is not just how many elaborative questions that parents ask but how children respond to them that predicts learning. For example, Ornstein et al. (2004) have argued that by posing elaborative *Wh-* questions that ask for new information about an ongoing event, a parent may call a child's attention to specific aspects of an event and determine what she or he may or may not understand. But learning may be best enhanced when this questioning results in a "joint" verbal exchange, particularly one in which the parent's *Wh-* question is followed by the child's verbal provision of the (correct) requested information. Investigations of conversations during events have emphasized the importance of joint verbal exchanges between parents and children as being more strongly related to children's later retention of event information than interactions characterized as primarily involving mother-only talk, child-only talk, or no talk (e.g., Haden et al., 2001; Hedrick et al., 2009). Indeed, Tessler and Nelson (1994) found that 3-year-olds who were observed as they visited a museum with their mothers later recalled only the objects that both the mother and the child had talked about during the experience. By looking at, for example, how parents and children discuss STEM-related concepts (e.g., mass, velocity, and building engineering) in joint conversations, and particularly focusing on the patterns of parent *Wh-* questions and child responses, we may be able to gain greater understanding about how elaborative talk facilitates science and other learning.

Another future research direction springs from the idea that the type of learning museums wish to motivate does not stop when visitors leave the museum but rather extends beyond the museum walls, becoming elaborated through multiple conversations after a museum visit, and with other experiences (Crowley & Jacobs, 2002). We need to study such "extended encoding" of experiences (Ornstein & Haden, 2001) in a developmental analysis of children's conversations with their parents about their museum experiences in the days, weeks, and months after the visit. Theoretically, such efforts marry the information-processing framework for the flow of information within the memory system to an emphasis drawn from sociocultural perspectives to examine conversational interactions as a process by which representations are established, maintained, elaborated, and even modified over repeated discussions. Empirically, such designs can address the difficult challenge of obtaining strong evidence that learning is taking place in conversation during exhibit (and other) experiences, by revealing what the child retains. Whereas parent–child conversations in museums can offer a unique vantage point from which to observe how parents guide and support children's learning, it seems critical to explore the impact of the "linguistic milieu"—which includes parent–child conversations about events both in the present and in the past—to adequately characterize both the learning process and learning outcomes of everyday experience.

In conclusion, future research in museums has the potential to address a range of unanswered questions about what aspects of parent–child conversational interactions may be especially important for the development of children's scientific literacy, and more general attitudes and meaning-making skills. As I have argued here, answers will likely require a movement toward detailed analyses of the form and content of parent–child conversational interactions both during and after experiences that illuminate critical mechanisms that link to learning outcomes. When we think we have found these potential mediators, experimental research studies should be launched to permit casual statements, a research strategy we have found in our work to be quite promising (e.g., Boland et al., 2003; Benjamin, Haden, & Wilkerson, in press; see also Fender & Crowley, 2008). In doing so, it should be possible to shed light on the difficult but important developmental question of "What forces propel children's learning in everyday settings?" and to inform parents, educators, and policy makers how we might create more influential learning environments for children in museums and elsewhere.

References

Ash, D. (2002). Negotiation of biological thematic conversations in informal learning settings. In G. Leinhardt, K. Crowley, & K. Knutson (Eds.), *Learning conversations in museums* (pp. 357–400). Mahwah, NJ: Erlbaum.

Association of Science-Technology Centers. (2008). *2007 ASTC sourcebook of statistic & analysis.* Washington, DC: Association of Science-Technology Centers.

Benjamin, N., Haden, C. A., & Wilkerson, E. (in press). Enhancing building, conversation, and learning through caregiver–child interactions in a children's museum. *Developmental Psychology.*

Berk, L. E. (2001). *Awakening children's minds: How parents and teachers can make a difference.* Oxford, UK: Oxford University Press.

Boland, A. M., Haden, C. A., & Ornstein, P. A. (2003). Boosting children's memory by training mothers to use and elaborative conversational style as an event unfolds. *Journal of Cognition and Development, 4,* 39–65.

Borun, M., Chambers, M. B., Dristas, J., & Johnson, J. I. (1997). Enhancing family learning through exhibits. *Curator, 40,* 279–295.

Callanan, M. A., & Jipson, J. (2001). Explanatory conversations and young children's developing scientific literacy. In K. Crowley, C. D. Schunn, & T. Okada (Eds.), *Designing for science: Implications from everyday, classroom, and professional science* (pp. 21–49). Mahwah, NJ: Erlbaum.

Callanan, M. A., & Oakes, L. A. (1992). Preschoolers' questions and parents' explanations: Causal thinking in everyday activity. *Cognitive Development, 7,* 231–233.

Callanan, M. A., Shrager, J., & Moore, J. (1995). Parent–child collaborative explanations: Methods of identification and analysis. *Journal of the Learning Sciences, 4,* 105–129.

Chen, Z., & Klahr, D. (1999). All other things being equal: Children's acquisition of the control of variables strategy. *Child Development, 70,* 1098–1120.

Chi, M. T. H., de Leeuw, N., Chiu, M. H., & LaVancher, C. (1994). Eliciting self-explanations improves understanding. *Cognitive Science, 18,* 439–477.

Crowley, K., & Callanan, M. A. (1998). Identifying and supporting collaborative scientific thinking in parent–child interactions. *Journal of Museum Education, 23,* 12–17.

Crowley, K., Callanan, M., Jipson, J., Galco, J., Topping, K., & Shrager, J. (2001). Shared scientific thinking in everyday parent–child activity. *Science Education, 85,* 712–732.

Crowley, K., Callanan, M. A., Tenenbaum, H. R., & Allen, E. (2001). Parents explain more often to boys than to girls during shared scientific thinking. *Psychological Science, 12,* 258–261.

Crowley, K., & Galco, J. (2001). Family conversations and the emergence of scientific literacy. In K. Crowley, C. Schunn, & T. Okada (Eds.), *Designing for science: Implications from everyday, classroom, and professional science* (pp. 393–413). Mahwah, NJ: Erlbaum.

Crowley, K., & Jacobs, M. (2002). Islands of expertise and the development of family scientific literacy. In G. Leinhardt, K. Crowley, & K. Knutson (Eds.), *Learning conversations in museums* (pp. 333–356). Mahwah, NJ: Erlbaum.

Crowley, K., & Siegler, R. S. (1999). Explanation and generalization in young children's strategy learning. *Child Development, 70,* 304–316.

Diamond, J. (1986). The behavior of families in science museums. *Curator, 29,* 139–154.

Dunbar, K., & Klahr, D. (1989). Developmental differences in scientific discovery strategies. In D. Klahr & K. Kotovsky (Eds.), *Complex information processing: The impact of Herbert A. Simon* (pp. 109–143). Hillsdale, NJ: Erlbaum.

Falk, J., & Dierking, L. (2002). *Learning from museums. Visitor experiences and the making of meaning.* Walnut Creek, CA: AltaMira Press.

Fender, J. G., & Crowley, K. (2008). How parent explanation changes what children learn from everyday scientific thinking. *Journal of Applied Developmental Psychology, 28,* 189–210.

Fivush, R., Haden, C. A., & Reese, E. (2006). Elaborating on elaborations: Role of maternal reminiscing style in cognitive and socioemotional development. *Child Development, 77,* 1568–1588.

Garcia-Mila, M., & Andersen, C. (2007). Developmental change in notetaking during scientific inquiry. *International Journal of Science Education, 29,* 1035–1058.

Gaskins, S. (2008). Designing exhibitions to support families' cultural understandings. *Exhibitionist, 27,* 11–19.

Gauvain, M. (2000). *The social context of cognitive development.* New York: Guilford.

Gelman, R., Massey, C., & McManus, M. (1991). Characterizing supporting environments for cognitive development: Lessons from children in a museum. In L. Resnick, J. Levine, & S. Teasley (Eds.), *Perspectives on socially shared cognition* (pp. 712–732). Washington, DC: APA.

Gleason, M. E., & Schauble, L. (2000). Parents' assistance of their children's scientific reasoning. *Cognition and Instruction, 17,* 343–378.

Haden, C. A., Ornstein, P. A., Eckerman, C. O., & Didow, S. M. (2001). Mother–child conversational interactions as events unfold: Linkages to subsequent remembering. *Child Development, 72,* 1016–1031.

Hedrick, A. M., San Souci, P., Haden, C. A., & Ornstein, P. A. (2009). Mother–child joint conversational exchanges during events: Linkages to children's event memory over time. *Journal of Cognition and Development, 10*(3), 143–161.

Humphrey, T., & Gutwill, J. (2005). *Fostering active prolonged engagement: The art of creating APE exhibits.* San Francisco: Exploratorium Press.

Jipson, J., & Callanan, M. (2003). Mother–child conversation and children's understanding of biological and non-biological changes in size. *Child Development, 74,* 629–644.

Klahr, D. (2000). *Exploring science: The cognition and development of discovery processes.* Cambridge: MIT Press.

Klahr, D., Fay, A., & Dunbar, K. (1993). Heuristics for scientific experimentation: A developmental study. *Cognitive Psychology, 25,* 111–146.

Leinhardt, G., & Crowley, K. (1998). *Conversational elaboration as a process and an outcome of museum learning.* Museum Learning Collaborative Technical Report (MLC-01). Pittsburgh, PA: Learning Research and Development Center, University of Pittsburgh.

Leinhardt, G., Crowley, K., & Knutson, K. (2002). *Learning conversations in museums.* Mahwah, NJ: Erlbaum.

Leinhardt, G., & Knutson, K. (2004). *Listening in on museum conversations.* Walnut Creek, CA: Alta Mira Press.

National Research Council. (2007). *Taking science to school: Learning and teaching science in Grades K-8.* Washington, DC: National Academies Press.

Ornstein, P. A., & Haden, C. A. (2001). The development of memory: Towards an understanding of children's testimony. In M. L. Eisen, G. S. Goodman, & J. A. Quas (Eds.), *Memory and suggestibility in the forensic interview* (pp. 29–61). Mahwah, NJ: Erlbaum.

Ornstein, P. A., Haden, C. A., & Hedrick, A. M. (2004). Learning to remember: Social-communicative exchanges and the development of children's memory skills. *Developmental Review, 24,* 374–395.

Palmquist, S. D., & Crowley, K. (2007). From teachers to testers: Parents' role in child expertise development in informal settings. *Science Education, 91*(5), 712–732.

Paris, S. G. (Ed.). (2002). *Perspectives on object-centered learning in museums.* Mahwah, NJ: Erlbaum.

Penner, D. E., & Klahr, D. (1996). The interaction of domain-specific knowledge and domain-general discovery strategies: A study with sinking objects. *Child Development, 67,* 2709–2727.

Rogoff, B. (1990). *Apprenticeship in thinking: Cognitive development in social context.* Oxford, UK: Oxford University Press.

Schauble, L. (1996). The development of scientific reasoning in knowledge-rich contexts. *Developmental Psychology, 32,* 102–119.

Tenenbaum, H. R., & Callanan, M. A. (2008). Parents' science talk to their children in Mexican-descent families residing in the United States. *International Journal of Behavioral Development, 32,* 1–12.

Tenenbaum, H. R., Callanan, M., Alba-Speyer, C., & Sandoval, L. (2002). The role of educational background, activity, and past experiences in Mexican-descent families' science conversations. *Hispanic Journal of Behavioral Sciences, 24,* 225–248.

Tenenbaum, H. R., & Leaper, C. (2003). Parent–child conversations about science: Socialization of gender inequities. *Developmental Psychology, 39,* 34–47.

Tenenbaum, H. R., Snow, C. E., Roach, K., & Kurland, B. (2005). Talking and reading science: Longitudinal data on sex differences in mother–child conversations in low-income families. *Journal of Applied Developmental Psychology, 26,* 1–19.

Tessler, M., & Nelson, K. (1994). Making memories: The influence of joint encoding on later recall by young children. *Consciousness and Cognition, 3,* 307–326.

Thompson, R. (2006). Conversation and developing understanding: Introduction to the special issue. *Merrill-Palmer Quarterly, 52,* 1–16.

Valle, A., & Callanan, M. A. (2006). Similarity comparisons and relational analogies in parent–child conversations about science topics. *Merrill-Palmer Quarterly, 52,* 96–124.

Vygotsky, L. S. (1978). *Mind in society: The development of higher psychological processes.* Cambridge, MA: Harvard University Press.

Wood, D., Bruner, J. S., & Ross, G. (1976). The role of tutoring in problem-solving. *Journal of Child Psychology and Psychiatry, 17,* 89–100.

Zimmerman, C. (2000). The development of scientific reasoning skills. *Developmental Review, 20,* 99–149.

When Should a Kid Start Kindergarten?

Elizabeth Weil

According to the apple-or-coin test, used in the Middle Ages, children should start school when they are mature enough for the delayed gratification and abstract reasoning involved in choosing money over fruit. In 15th- and 16th-century Germany, parents were told to send their children to school when the children started to act "rational." And in contemporary America, children are deemed eligible to enter kindergarten according to an arbitrary date on the calendar known as the birthday cutoff—that is, when the state, or in some instances the school district, determines they are old enough. The birthday cutoffs span six months, from Indiana, where a child must turn 5 by July 1 of the year he enters kindergarten, to Connecticut, where he must turn 5 by Jan. 1 of his kindergarten year. Children can start school a year late, but in general they cannot start a year early. As a result, when the 22 kindergartners entered Jane Andersen's class at the Glen Arden Elementary School near Asheville, N.C., one warm April morning, each brought with her or him a snack and a unique set of gifts and challenges, which included for some what's referred to in education circles as "the gift of time."

After the morning announcements and the Pledge of Allegiance, Andersen's kindergartners sat down on a blue rug. Two, one boy and one girl, had been redshirted—the term, borrowed from sports, describes students held out for a year by their parents so that they will be older, or larger, or more mature, and thus better prepared to handle the increased pressures of kindergarten today. Six of Andersen's pupils, on the other hand, were quite young, so young that they would not be enrolled in kindergarten at all if North Carolina succeeds in pushing back its birthday cutoff from Oct. 16 to Aug. 31.

Andersen is a willowy 11-year teaching veteran who offered up a lot of education in the first hour of class. First she read Leo Lionni's classic children's book "An Extraordinary Egg," and directed a conversation about it. Next she guided the students through: writing a letter; singing a song; solving an addition problem; two more songs; and a math game involving counting by ones, fives and tens using coins. Finally, Andersen read them another Lionni book. Labor economists who study what's called the accumulation of human capital—how we acquire the knowledge and skills that make us valuable members of society—have found that children learn vastly different amounts from the same classroom experiences and that those with certain advantages at the outset are able to learn more, more quickly, causing the gap between students to increase over time. Gaps in achievement have many causes, but a major one in any kindergarten room is age. Almost all kindergarten classrooms have children with birthdays that span 12 months. But because of redshirting, the oldest student in Andersen's class is not just 12 but 15 months older than the youngest, a difference in age of 25 percent.

After rug time, Andersen's kindergartners walked single-file to P.E. class, where the children sat on the curb alongside the parking circle, taking turns running laps for the Presidential Fitness Test. By far the fastest runner was the girl in class who had been redshirted. She strode confidently, with great form, while many of the smaller kids could barely run straight. One of the younger girls pointed out the best artist in the class, a freckly redhead. I'd already noted his beautiful penmanship. He had been redshirted as well.

States, too, are trying to embrace the advantages of redshirting. Since 1975, nearly half of all states have pushed back their birthday cutoffs and four—California, Michigan, North Carolina and Tennessee—have active legislation in state assemblies to do so right now. (Arkansas passed legislation earlier this spring; New Jersey, which historically has let local districts establish their birthday cutoffs, has legislation pending to make Sept. 1 the cutoff throughout the state.) This is due, in part, to the accountability movement—the high-stakes testing now pervasive in the American educational system. In response to this testing, kindergartens across the country have become more demanding: if kids must be performing on standardized tests in third grade, then they must be prepping for those tests in second and first grades, and even at the end of kindergarten, or so the thinking goes. The testing also means that states, like students, now get report cards, and they want their children to do well, both because they want them to be educated and because they want them to stack up favorably against their peers.

Indeed, increasing the average age of the children in a kindergarten class is a cheap and easy way to get a small bump in test scores, because older children perform better, and states' desires for relative advantage is written into their policy briefs. The California Performance Review, commissioned by Gov. Arnold Schwarzenegger in 2004, suggested moving California's birthday cutoff three months earlier, to Sept. 1 from Dec. 2, noting that "38 states, including Florida and Texas, have kindergarten entry dates prior to California's." Maryland's proposal to move its date mentioned that "the change . . . will align the 'cutoff' date with most of the other states in the country."

All involved in increasing the age of kindergartners—parents, legislatures and some teachers—say they have the best interests of children in mind. "If I had just one goal with this piece of legislation it would be to not humiliate a child," Dale Folwell, the Republican North Carolina state representative who sponsored the birthday-cutoff bill, told me. "Our kids are younger when they're taking the SAT, and they're applying to the same colleges as the kids from Florida and Georgia." Fair enough—governors and state legislators have competitive impulses, too. Still, the question remains: Is it better for children to start kindergarten later? And even if it's better for a given child, is it good for children in general? Time out of school may not be a gift to all kids. For some it may be a burden, a financial stress on their parents and a chance, before they ever reach a classroom, to fall even further behind.

Redshirting is not a new phenomenon—in fact, the percentage of redshirted children has held relatively steady since education scholars started tracking the practice in the 1980s. Studies by the National Center for Education Statistics in the 1990s show that delayed-entry children made up somewhere between 6 and 9 percent of all kindergartners; a new study is due out in six months. As states roll back birthday cutoffs, there are more older kindergartners in general—and more redshirted kindergartners who are even older than the oldest kindergartners in previous years. Recently, redshirting has become a particular concern, because in certain affluent communities the numbers of kindergartners coming to school a year later are three or four times the national average. "Do you know what the number is in my district?" Representative Folwell, from a middle-class part of Winston-Salem, N.C., asked me. "Twenty-six percent." In one kindergarten I visited in Los Altos, Calif.—average home price, $1 million—about one-quarter of the kids had been electively held back as well. Fred Morrison, a developmental psychologist at the University of Michigan who has studied the impact of falling on one side or the other of the birthday cutoff, sees the endless "graying of kindergarten," as it's sometimes called, as coming from a parental obsession not with their children's academic accomplishment but with their social maturity. "You couldn't find a kid who skips a grade these days," Morrison told me. "We used to revere individual accomplishment. Now we revere self-esteem, and the reverence has snowballed in unconscious ways—into parents always wanting their children to feel good, wanting everything to be pleasant." So parents wait an extra year in the hope that when their children enter school their age or maturity will shield them from social and emotional hurt. Elizabeth Levett Fortier, a kindergarten teacher in the George Peabody Elementary School in San Francisco, notices the impact on her incoming students. "I've had children come into my classroom, and they've never even lost at Candy Land."

For years, education scholars have pointed out that most studies have found that the benefits of being relatively older than one's classmates disappear after the first few years of school. In a literature review published in 2002, Deborah Stipek, dean of the Stanford school of education, found studies in which children who are older than their classmates not only do not learn more per grade but also tend to have more behavior problems. However, more recent research by labor economists takes advantage of new, very large data sets and has produced different results. A few labor economists do concur with the education scholarship, but most have found that while absolute age (how many days a child has been alive) is not so important, relative age (how old that child is in comparison to his classmates) shapes performance long after those few months of maturity should have ceased to matter. The relative-age effect has been found in schools around the world and also in sports. In one study published in the June 2005 Journal of Sport Sciences, researchers from Leuven, Belgium, and Liverpool, England, found that a disproportionate number of World Cup soccer players are born in January, February and March, meaning they were old relative to peers on youth soccer teams.

Before the school year started, Andersen, who is 54, taped up on the wall behind her desk a poster of a dog holding a bouquet of 12 balloons. In each balloon Andersen wrote the name of a month; under each month, the birthdays of the children in her class. Like most teachers, she understands that the small fluctuations among birth dates aren't nearly as important as the vast range in children's experiences at preschool and at home. But one day as we sat in her classroom, Andersen told me, "Every year I have two or three young ones in that August-to-October range, and they just struggle a little." She used to encourage parents to send their children to kindergarten as soon as they were eligible, but she is now a strong proponent of older kindergartners, after teaching one child with a birthday just a few days before the cutoff. "She was always a step behind. It wasn't effort and it wasn't ability. She worked hard, her mom worked with her and she still was behind." Andersen followed the girl's progress through second grade (after that, she moved to a different school) and noticed that she didn't catch up. Other teachers at Glen Arden Elementary and elsewhere have noticed a similar phenomenon: not always, but too often, the little ones stay behind.

The parents of the redshirted girl in Andersen's class told a similar story. Five years ago, their older daughter had just made the kindergarten birthday cutoff by a few days, and they enrolled her. "She's now a struggling fourth grader: only by the skin of her teeth has she been able to pass each year," the girl's mother, Stephanie Gandert, told me. "I kick myself every year now that we sent her ahead." By contrast, their current kindergartner is doing just fine. "I always tell parents, 'If you can wait, wait.' If my kindergartner were in first grade right now, she'd be in trouble, too." (The parents of the redshirted boy in Andersen's class declined to be interviewed for this article but may very well have held him back because he's small—even though he's now one of the oldest, he's still one of the shortest.)

Kelly Bedard, a labor economist at the University of California, Santa Barbara, published a paper with Elizabeth Dhuey called "The Persistence of Early Childhood Maturity: International Evidence of Long-Run Age Effects" in *The Quarterly Journal of Economics* in November 2006 that looked at this phenomenon. "Obviously, when you're 5, being a year older is a lot, and so we should expect kids who are the oldest in kindergarten to do better than the kids who are the youngest in kindergarten," Bedard says. But what if relatively older kids keep doing better after the maturity gains of a few months should have ceased to matter? What if kids who are older relative to their classmates still have higher test scores in fourth grade, or eighth grade?

After crunching the math and science test scores for nearly a quarter-million students across 19 countries, Bedard found that relatively younger students perform 4 to 12 percentiles less well in third and fourth grade and 2 to 9 percentiles worse in seventh and eighth; and, as she notes, "by eighth grade it's fairly safe to say we're looking at long-term effects." In British Columbia, she found that the relatively oldest students are about 10 percent more likely to be "university bound" than the relatively youngest ones. In the United States, she found that the relatively oldest students are 7.7 percent more likely to take the SAT or ACT, and are 11.6 percent more likely to enroll in four-year colleges or universities. (No one has yet published a study on age effects and SAT scores.) "One reason you could imagine age effects persist is that almost all of our education systems have ability-groupings built into them," Bedard says. "Many claim they don't, but they do. Everybody gets put into reading groups and math groups from very early ages." Younger children are more likely to be assigned behind grade level, older children more likely to be assigned ahead. Younger children are more likely to receive diagnoses of attention-deficit disorder, too. "When I was in school the reading books all had colors," Bedard told me. "They never said which was the high, the middle and the low, but everybody knew. Kids in the highest reading group one year are much more likely to be in the highest reading group the next. So you can imagine how that could propagate itself."

Bedard found that different education systems produce varying age effects. For instance, Finland, whose students recently came out on top in an Organization for Economic Cooperation and Development study of math, reading and science skills, experiences smaller age effects; Finnish children also start school later, at age 7, and even then the first few years are largely devoted to social development and play. Denmark, too, produces little difference between relatively older and younger kids; the Danish education system prohibits differentiating by ability until students are 16. Those two exceptions notwithstanding, Bedard notes that she found age effects everywhere, from "the Japanese system of automatic promotion, to the accomplishment-oriented French system, to the supposedly more flexible skill-based program models used in Canada and the United States."

The relative value of being older for one's grade is a particularly open secret in those sectors of the American schooling system that treat education like a competitive sport. Many private-school birthday cutoffs are set earlier than public-school dates; and children, particularly boys, who make the cutoff but have summer and sometimes spring birthdays are often placed in junior kindergarten—also called "transitional kindergarten," a sort of holding tank for kids too old for more preschool—or are encouraged to wait a year to apply. Erika O'Brien, a SoHo mother who has two redshirted children at Grace Church, a pre-K-through-8 private school in Manhattan, told me about a conversation she had with a friend whose daughter was placed in junior kindergarten because she had a summer birthday. "I told her that it's really a great thing. Her daughter is going to have a better chance of being at the top of her class, she'll more likely be a leader, she'll have a better chance of succeeding at sports. She's got nothing to worry about for the next nine years. Plus, if you're making a financial investment in school, it's a less risky investment."

Robert Fulghum listed life lessons in his 1986 best seller "All I Really Need to Know I Learned in Kindergarten." Among them were:

Clean up your own mess.

Don't take things that aren't yours.

Wash your hands before you eat.

Take a nap every afternoon.

Flush.

Were he to update the book to reflect the experience of today's children, he'd need to call it "All I Really Need to Know I Learned in Preschool," as kindergarten has changed. The half day devoted to fair play and nice manners officially began its demise in 1983, when the National Commission on Excellence in Education published "A Nation at Risk," warning that the country faced a "rising tide of mediocrity" unless we increased school achievement and expectations. No Child Left Behind, in 2002, exacerbated the trend, pushing phonics and pattern-recognition worksheets even further down the learning chain. As a result, many parents, legislatures and teachers find the current curriculum too challenging for many older 4- and young 5-year-olds, which makes sense, because it's largely the same curriculum taught to first graders less than a generation ago. Andersen's kindergartners are supposed to be able to not just read but also write two sentences by the time they graduate from her classroom. It's no wonder that nationwide, teachers now report that 48 percent of incoming kindergartners have difficulty handling the demands of school.

Friedrich Froebel, the romantic motherless son who started the first kindergarten in Germany in 1840, would be horrified by what's called kindergarten today. He conceived the early learning experience as a homage to Jean-Jacques Rousseau, who believed that "reading is the plague of childhood. . . . Books are good only for learning to babble about what one does not know." Letters and numbers were officially banned from Froebel's kindergartens; the teaching materials consisted of handmade blocks and games that he referred to as "gifts." By the late 1800s, kindergarten had jumped to the United States, with Boston transcendentalists like Elizabeth Peabody popularizing the concept. Fairly quickly, letters and numbers appeared on the wooden blocks, yet Peabody cautioned that a "genuine" kindergarten is "a company of children under 7 years old, who do not learn to read, write and cipher" and a "false" kindergarten is one that accommodates parents who want their children studying academics instead of just playing.

That the social skills and exploration of one's immediate world have been squeezed out of kindergarten is less the result of a pedagogical shift than of the accountability movement and the literal-minded reverse-engineering process it has brought to the schools. Curriculum planners no longer ask, What does a 5-year-old need? Instead they ask, If a student is to pass reading and math tests in third grade, what does that student need to be doing in the prior grades? Whether kindergarten students actually need to be older is a question of readiness, a concept that itself raises the question: Ready for what? The skill set required to succeed in Fulgham's kindergarten—openness, creativity—is well matched to the capabilities of most 5-year-olds but also substantially different from what Andersen's students need. In early 2000, the National Center for Education Statistics assessed 22,000 kindergartners individually and found, in general, that yes, the older children are better prepared to start an academic kindergarten than the younger ones. The older kids are four times as likely to be reading, and two to three times as likely to be able to decipher two-digit numerals. Twice as many older kids have the advanced fine motor skills necessary for writing. The older kids also have important noncognitive advantages, like being more persistent and more socially adept. Nonetheless, child advocacy groups say it's the schools' responsibility to be ready for the children, no matter their age, not the children's to be prepared for the advanced curriculum. In a report on kindergarten, the National Association of Early Childhood Specialists in State Departments of Education wrote, "Most of the questionable entry and placement practices that have emerged in recent years have their genesis in concerns over children's capacities to cope with the increasingly inappropriate curriculum in kindergarten."

Furthermore, as Elizabeth Graue, a former kindergarten teacher who now studies school-readiness and redshirting at the University of Wisconsin, Madison, points out, "Readiness is a relative issue." Studies of early-childhood teachers show they always complain about the youngest students, no matter their absolute age. "In Illinois it will be the March-April-May kids; in California, it will be October-November-December," Graue says. "It's really natural as a teacher to gravitate toward the kids who are easy to teach, especially when there's academic pressure and the younger kids are rolling around the floor and sticking pencils in their ears."

But perhaps those kids with the pencils in their ears—at least the less-affluent ones—don't need "the gift of time" but rather to be brought into the schools. Forty-two years after Lyndon Johnson inaugurated Head Start, access to quality early education still highly correlates with class; and one serious side effect of pushing back the cutoffs is that while well-off kids with delayed enrollment will spend another year in preschool, probably doing what kindergartners did a generation ago, less-well-off children may, as the literacy specialist Katie Eller put it, spend "another year watching TV in the basement with Grandma." What's more, given the socioeconomics of redshirting—and the luxury involved in delaying for a year the free day care that is public school—the oldest child in any given class is more likely to be well off and the youngest child is more likely to be poor. "You almost have a double advantage coming to the well-off kids," says Samuel J. Meisels, president of Erikson Institute, a graduate school in child development in Chicago. "From a public-policy point of view I find this very distressing."

Nobody has exact numbers on what percentage of the children eligible for publicly financed preschool are actually enrolled—the individual programs are legion, and the eligibility requirements are complicated and varied—but the best guess from the National Institute for Early Education Research puts the proportion at only 25 percent. In California, for instance, 76 percent of publicly financed preschool programs have waiting lists, which include over 30,000 children. In Pennsylvania, 35 percent of children eligible for Head Start are not served. A few states do have universal preschool, and among Hillary Clinton's first broad domestic policy proposals as a Democratic presidential candidate was to call for universal pre-kindergarten classes. But at the moment, free high-quality preschool for less-well-to-do children is spotty, and what exists often is aimed at extremely low-income parents, leaving out the children of the merely strapped working or lower-middle class. Nor, as a rule, do publicly financed programs take kids who are old enough to be eligible for kindergarten, meaning redshirting is not a realistic option for many.

One morning, when I was sitting in Elizabeth Levett Fortier's kindergarten classroom in the Peabody School in San Francisco—among a group of students that included some children who had never been to preschool, some who were just learning English and some who were already reading—a father dropped by to discuss whether or not to enroll his fall-birthday daughter or give her one more year at her private preschool. Demographically speaking, any child with a father willing to call on a teacher to discuss if it's best for that child to spend a third year at a $10,000-a-year preschool is going to be fine. Andersen told me, "I've had parents tell me that the preschool did not recommend sending their children on to kindergarten yet, but they had no choice," as they couldn't afford not to. In 49 out of 50 states, the average annual cost of day care for a 4-year-old in an urban area is more than the average annual public college tuition. A RAND Corporation position paper suggests policy makers may need to view "entrance-age policies and child-care polices as a package."

Labor economists, too, make a strong case that resources should be directed at disadvantaged children as early as possible, both for the sake of improving each child's life and because of economic return. Among the leaders in this field is James Heckman, a University of Chicago economist who won the Nobel in economic science in 2000. In many papers and lectures on poor kids, he now includes a simple graph that plots the return on investment in human capital across age. You can think of the accumulation of human capital much like the accumulation of financial capital in an account bearing compound interest: if you add your resources as soon as possible, they'll be worth more down the line. Heckman's graph looks like a skateboard quarter-pipe, sloping precipitously from a high point during the preschool years, when the return on investment in human capital is very high, down the ramp and into the flat line after a person is no longer in school, when the return on investment is minimal. According to Heckman's analysis, if you have limited funds to spend it makes the most economic sense to spend them early. The implication is that if poor children aren't in adequate preschool programs, rolling back the age of kindergarten is a bad idea economically, as it pushes farther down the ramp the point at which we start investing funds and thus how productive those funds will be.

Bedard and other economists cite Heckman's theories of how people acquire skills to help explain the persistence of relative age on school performance. Heckman writes: "Skill begets skill; motivation begets motivation. Early failure begets later failure." Reading experts know that it's easier for a child to learn the meaning of a new word if he knows the meaning of a related word and that a good vocabulary at age 3 predicts a child's reading well in third grade. Skills like persistence snowball, too. One can easily see how the skill-begets-skill, motivation-begets-motivation dynamic plays out in a kindergarten setting: a child who comes in with a good vocabulary listens to a story, learns more words, feels great about himself and has an even better vocabulary at the end of the day. Another child arrives with a poor vocabulary, listens to the story, has a hard time following, picks up fewer words, retreats into insecurity and leaves the classroom even further behind.

How to address the influence of age effects is unclear. After all, being on the older or younger side of one's classmates is mostly the luck of the birthday draw, and no single birthday cutoff can prevent a 12-month gap in age. States could try to prevent parents from gaming the age effects by outlawing redshirting—specifically by closing the yearlong window that now exists in most states between the birthday cutoffs and compulsory schooling. But forcing families to enroll children in kindergarten as soon as they are eligible seems too authoritarian for America's tastes. States could also decide to learn from Finland—start children in school at age 7 and devote the first year to play—but that would require a major reversal, making second grade the old kindergarten, instead of kindergarten the new first grade. States could also emulate Denmark, forbidding ability groupings until late in high school, but unless very serious efforts are made to close the achievement gap before children arrive at kindergarten, that seems unlikely, too.

Of course there's also the reality that individual children will always mature at different rates, and back in Andersen's classroom, on a Thursday when this year's kindergartners stayed home and next year's kindergartners came in for pre-enrollment assessments, the developmental differences between one future student and the next were readily apparent. To gauge kindergarten readiness, Andersen and another kindergarten teacher each sat the children down one by one for a 20-minute test. The teachers asked the children, among other things, to: skip; jump; walk backward; cut out a diamond on a dotted line; copy the word cat; draw a person; listen to a story; and answer simple vocabulary questions like what melts, what explodes and what flies. Some of the kids were dynamos. When asked to explain the person he had drawn, one boy said: "That's Miss Maple. She's my preschool teacher, and she's crying because she's going to miss me so much next year." Another girl said at one point, "Oh, you want me to write the word cat?" Midmorning, however, a little boy who will not turn 5 until this summer arrived. His little feet dangled off the kindergarten chair, as his legs were not long enough to reach the floor. The teacher asked him to draw a person. To pass that portion of the test, his figure needed seven different body parts.

"Is that all he needs?" she asked a few minutes later.

The boy said, "Oh, I forgot the head."

A minute later the boy submitted his drawing again. "Are you sure he doesn't need anything else?" the teacher asked.

The boy stared at his work. "I forgot the legs. Those are important, aren't they?"

The most difficult portion of the test for many of the children was a paper-folding exercise. "Watch how I fold my paper," the teacher told the little boy. She first folded her 8 1/2-by-11-inch paper in half the long way, to create a narrow rectangle, and then she folded the rectangle in thirds, to make something close to a square.

"Can you do it?" she asked the boy.

He took the paper eagerly, but folded it in half the wrong way. Depending on the boy's family's finances, circumstances and mind-set, his parents may decide to hold him out a year so he'll be one of the oldest and, presumably, most confident. Or they may decide to enroll him in school as planned. He may go to college or he may not. He may be a leader or a follower. Those things will ultimately depend more on the education level achieved by his mother, whether he lives in a two-parent household and the other assets and obstacles he brings with him to school each day. Still, the last thing any child needs is to be outmaneuvered by other kids' parents as they cut to the back of the birthday line to manipulate age effects. Eventually, the boy put his head down on the table. His first fold had set a course, and even after trying gamely to fold the paper again in thirds, he couldn't create the right shape.

ELIZABETH WEIL is a contributing writer for the magazine. Her most recent article was about lethal injection.

Should Learning Be Its Own Reward?

DANIEL T. WILLINGHAM

How does the mind work—and especially how does it learn? Teachers' instructional decisions are based on a mix of theories learned in teacher education, trial and error, craft knowledge, and gut instinct. Such gut knowledge often serves us well, but is there anything sturdier to rely on?

Cognitive science is an interdisciplinary field of researchers from psychology, neuroscience, linguistics, philosophy, computer science, and anthropology who seek to understand the mind. In this regular American Educator column, we consider findings from this field that are strong and clear enough to merit classroom application.

Question: In recent months, there's been a big uproar about students being paid to take standardized tests—and being paid even more if they do well. Can cognitive science shed any light on this debate? Is it harmful to students to reward them like this? What about more typical rewards like a piece of candy or five extra minutes of recess?

There has been much debate recently about boosting standardized test scores by paying students. Here are a few examples that I read about in the news. In Coshocton, Ohio, third- and sixth-graders are being paid up to $20 for earning high scores on standardized tests. In New York City, fourth-grade students will receive $5 for each standardized test they take throughout the year, and up to $25 for each perfect score. Seventh-graders will get twice those amounts. In Tucson, Ariz., high school juniors selected from low-income areas will be paid up to $25 each week for attendance. These and similar programs affect just a tiny fraction of students nationwide. But rewarding students with things like small gifts, extra recess time, stickers, certificates, class parties and the like is actually pretty common. Most teachers have the option of distributing rewards in the classroom, and many do. For example, in a recent survey of young adults, 70 percent said that their elementary school teachers had used candy as a reward (Davis, Winsler, and Middleton, 2006).

So whether or not your district offers cash rewards for standardized test scores or attendance, you've probably wondered if rewarding your students for their classwork is a good idea. Some authors promise doom if a teacher rewards students, with the predicted negative effects ranging from unmotivated pupils to a teacher's moral bankruptcy (e.g., Kohn, 1993). Others counter that rewards are harmless or even helpful (e.g., Cameron, Banko, and Pierce, 2001; Chance, 1993). Where does the truth lie? In the middle. There is some merit to the arguments on both sides. Concrete rewards can motivate students to attend class, to behave well, or to produce better work. But if you are not careful in choosing what you reward, they can prompt students to produce shoddy work—and worse, they can cause students to actually like school subjects less. The important guidelines are these: Don't use rewards unless you have to, use rewards for a specific reason, and use them for a limited time. Let's take a look at the research behind these guidelines.

> **Concrete rewards can motivate students to attend class, to behave well, or to produce better work. But if you are not careful in choosing what you reward, they can prompt students to produce shoddy work—and worse, they can cause students to actually like school subjects less.**

Do Rewards Work?

Rewarding students is, from one perspective, an obvious idea. People do things because they find them rewarding, the reasoning goes, so if students don't find school naturally rewarding (that is, interesting and fun), make it rewarding by offering them something they do like, be it cash or candy.

In this simple sense, rewards usually work. If you offer students an appealing reward, the targeted behavior will generally increase (for reviews, see O'Leary and Drabman, 1971; Deci, Koestner, and Ryan, 1999). Teachers typically use rewards like candy, stickers, small prizes, or extra recess time. They use them to encourage student behaviors such as completing assignments, producing good work, and so on. In one example

(Hendy, Williams, and Camise, 2005) first-, second-, and fourth-graders were observed in the school cafeteria to see how often they ate fruits and vegetables. Once this baseline measure was taken, they were rewarded for eating one or the other. Students received a token for each day that they ate the assigned food, and tokens could be redeemed for small prizes at the end of the week. Not surprisingly, students ate more of what they were rewarded for eating.

But things don't always go so smoothly. If you mistakenly offer a reward that students don't care for, you'll see little result. Or, if you reward the wrong behavior, you'll see a result you don't care for. When I was in fourth grade, my class was offered a small prize for each book we read. Many of us quickly developed a love for short books with large print, certainly not the teacher's intent. In the same way, if you reward people to come up with ideas, but don't stipulate that they must be good ideas, people will generate lots of ideas in order to gain lots of rewards, but the ideas may not be especially good (Ward, Kogan, and Pankove, 1972). It's often possible to correct mistakes such as these. Unappealing rewards can be replaced by valued rewards. The target behavior can be changed. My fourth-grade teacher stipulated that books had to be grade-appropriate and of some minimum length.

Because rewards are generally effective, people's objection to them in the classroom is seldom that they won't work. The op-ed newspaper articles I have seen about the student payment plans described above don't claim that you can't get students to go to school by paying them (e.g., Carlton, 2007; Schwartz, 2007). They raise other objections.

The common arguments against rewards fall into three categories. Let me state each one in rather extreme terms to give you the idea, and then I'll consider the merits of each in more detail. The first objection is that using rewards is immoral. You might toss your dog a treat when he shakes hands, but that is no way to treat children. Classrooms should be a caring community in which students help one another, not a circus in which the teacher serves as ringmaster. The second objection is that offering rewards is unrealistic. Rewards can't last forever, so what happens when they stop? Those who make this argument think it's better to help students appreciate the subtle, but real rewards that the world offers for things like hard work and politeness. After all, adults don't expect that someone will toss them a candy bar every time they listen politely, push their chair under a table, or complete a report on time. The third objection is that offering rewards can actually decrease motivation. Cognitive science has found that this is true, but only under certain conditions. For example, if you initially enjoy reading and I reward you for each book you finish, the rewards will make you like reading less. Below, I'll explain how and why that happens. Let's consider each of these arguments in turn.

Are Rewards Immoral?

Don't rewards control students? Aren't rewards dehumanizing? Wouldn't it be better to create a classroom atmosphere in which students wanted to learn, rather than one in which they reluctantly slogged through assignments, doing the minimal work they thought would still earn the promised reward? Cognitive science cannot answer moral questions. They are outside its purview. But cognitive science can provide some factual background that may help teachers as they consider these questions.

It is absolutely the case that trying to control students is destructive to their motivation and their performance. People like autonomy, and using rewards to control people definitely reduces motivation. Even if the task is one students generally like, if they sense that you're trying to coerce them, they will be less likely to do it (e.g., Ryan, Mims, and Koestner, 1983). It is worth pointing out, however, that rewards themselves are not inherently controlling. If students are truly offered a choice—do this and get a reward, don't do it and get no reward—then the student maintains control. Within behavioral science, it is accepted that rewards themselves are coercive if they are excessive (e.g., National Commission for the Protection of Human Subjects of Biomedical and Behavioral Research, 1978). In other words, if I offer you $200 to take a brief survey, it's hard to know that you're freely choosing to take the survey.

Rewards in classrooms are typically not excessive, and so are not, themselves, controlling. Rather, rewards might be an occasion for control if the teacher makes it quite clear that the student is expected to do the required work and collect his or her reward. That is, the teacher uses social coercion. So too, we've all known people we would call "manipulative," and those people seldom manipulate us via rewards. They use social means. In sum, the caution against controlling students is well-founded, but rewards are not inherently controlling.

Are rewards dehumanizing? Again, it seems to me that the answer depends on how the student construes the reward. If a teacher dangles stickers before students like fish before a seal, most observers will likely wince. But if a teacher emphasizes that rewards are a gesture of appreciation for a job well done, that probably would not appear dehumanizing to most observers.[1] Even so, rather than offer rewards, shouldn't teachers create classrooms in which students love learning? It is difficult not to respond to this objection by saying "Well, duh." I can't imagine there are many teachers who would rather give out candy than have a classroom full of students who are naturally interested and eager to learn. The question to ask is not "Why would you use rewards instead of making the material interesting?" Rather, it is "After you've wracked your brain for a way to make the material interesting for students and you still can't do it, then what?" Sanctimonious advice on the evils of rewards won't get chronically failing students to have one more go at learning to read. I think it unwise to discourage teachers from using any techniques in the absolute; rather, teachers need to know what research says about the benefits and drawbacks of the techniques, so that they can draw their own conclusions about whether and when to use them. Considering the merits of the two other objections will get us further into that research.

Sanctimonious advice on the evils of rewards won't get chronically failing students to have one more go at learning to read. I think it unwise to discourage teachers from using any techniques in the absolute; rather, teachers need to know what research says about the benefits and drawbacks of the techniques.

What Happens When Rewards Stop?

This objection is easy to appreciate. If I'm working math problems because you're paying me, what's going to happen once you stop paying me? Your intuition probably tells you that I will stop doing problems, and you're right. In the fruits and vegetables study described earlier, students stopped eating fruits and vegetables soon after the reward program stopped.

Although it might seem obvious that this would happen, psychologists initially thought that there was a way around this problem. Many studies were conducted during the 1960s using token economies. A token economy is a system by which rewards are administered in an effort to change behavior. There are many variants but the basic idea is that every time the student exhibits a targeted behavior (e.g., gets ready to work quickly in the morning), he or she gets a token (e.g., a plastic chip). Students accumulate tokens and later trade them for rewards (e.g., small prizes). Token economies have some positive effects, and have been used not only in classrooms, but in clinical settings (e.g., Dickerson, Tenhula, and Green-Paden, 2005).

When the idea of a token economy was developed, the plan was that the rewards would be phased out. Once the desired behavior was occurring frequently, you would not give the reward every time, but give it randomly, averaging 75 percent of the time, then 50 percent of the time, and so on. Thus, the student would slowly learn to do the behavior without the external reward. That works with animals, but normally not with humans. Once the rewards stop, people go back to behaving as they did before (Kazdin, 1982; O'Leary and Drabman, 1971).[2]

Well, one might counter, it may be true that students won't spontaneously work math problems once we stop rewarding them, but at least they will have worked more than they otherwise would have! Unfortunately, there is another, more insidious consequence of rewards that we need to consider: Under certain circumstances, they can actually decrease motivation.

How Can Rewards Decrease Motivation?

The previous section made it sound like rewards boost desired behavior so long as they are present, and when they are removed behavior falls back to where it started. That's true sometimes, but not always. If the task is one that students like, rewards will, as usual, make it more likely they'll do the task. But after the rewards stop, students will actually perform the previously likable task *less* than they did when rewards were first offered.

A classic study on this phenomenon (Lepper, Greene, and Nisbett, 1973) provides a good illustration. Children (aged 3 to 5 years old) were surreptitiously observed in a classroom with lots of different activities available. The experimenters noted how much time each child spent drawing with markers. The markers were then unavailable to students for two weeks. At the end of the two weeks, students were broken into three groups. Each student in the first group was taken to a separate room and was told that he or she could win an attractive "Good Player" certificate by drawing a picture with the markers. Each was eager to get the certificate and drew a picture. One-by-one, students in a second group were also brought to a separate room, encouraged to draw, and then given a certificate, but the certificate came as a surprise; when they started drawing, they didn't know that they would get the certificate. A third group of students served as a control group. They had been observed in the first session, but didn't draw or get a certificate in this second session. After another delay of about two weeks, the markers again appeared in the classroom, and experimenters observed how much children used them. The students in the first group—those who were promised the certificate for drawing—used the markers about half as much as students in the other two groups. Promising and then giving a reward made children like the markers less. But giving the reward as a surprise (as with the second group of students) had no effect.

This has been replicated scores of times with students of different ages, using different types of rewards, and in realistic classroom situations (see Deci et al., 1999 for a review). What is going on? How can getting a reward reduce your motivation to do something? The answer lies in the students' interpretation of why they chose to use the markers. For students who either didn't get a reward or who didn't expect a reward, it's obvious that they weren't drawing for the sake of the reward; they drew pictures because they liked drawing. But for the children who were promised a reward, the reason is less clear. A student might not remember that he drew because he wanted to draw, but rather he remembered really wanting the certificate. So when the markers were available again but no certificate was promised, the student may well have thought "I drew because I wanted that certificate; why should I draw now for nothing?"

The analogy to the classroom is clear. Teachers seek to create lifelong learners. We don't just want children to read, we want children to learn to love reading. So if, in an effort to get children to read more, we promise to reward them for doing so, we might actually make them like reading less! They will read more in order to get the pizza party or the stickers, but once the teacher is no longer there to give out the rewards, the student will say "Why should I read? I'm not getting anything for it."

The key factor to keep in mind is that rewards only decrease motivation for tasks that students initially like. If the task is dull, motivation might drop back down to its original level once the rewards stop, but it will not drop below its original level. Why does the appeal of the task make a difference? As I mentioned, rewards hurt motivation because of the way students construe the situation: "I drew with markers in order to get a certificate," instead of "I drew with markers because I like to draw with markers." But if the task is dull, students won't make that mistaken interpretation. They never liked the task in the first place. That hypothesis has been confirmed in a number of studies showing that once the reward is no longer being offered, having received a reward in the past harms the motivation for an interesting task, but not for a dull task (e.g., Daniel and Esser, 1980; Loveland and Olley, 1979; Newman and Layton, 1984).

The key factor to keep in mind is that rewards only decrease motivation for tasks that students initially like. If the task is dull, motivation might drop back down to its original level once the rewards stop, but it will not drop below its original level.

This finding might make one wonder whether rewards, in the form of grades, are behind students' lack of interest in schoolwork; by issuing grades, we're making students like school less (Kohn, 1993). It is true that students like school less and less as they get older. But it is wise to remember that motivation is a product of many factors. Researchers often distinguish between extrinsic motivators (e.g., concrete rewards or grades that are external to you) and intrinsic motivators (things that are internal to you such as your interest in a task). The effect described above can be succinctly summarized: Extrinsic rewards can decrease intrinsic motivation. We would thus expect that intrinsic and extrinsic motivation would be negatively correlated. That is, if you work mostly for the sake of getting good grades and other rewards, then you aren't very intrinsically motivated, and if you are highly intrinsically motivated, that must mean you don't care much about rewards. That's true to some extent, but the relationship is far from perfect. College students whose intrinsic and extrinsic motivation have been measured usually show a modest negative correlation, around $-.25$[3] (Lepper, Corpus, and Iyengar, 2005). This seems reasonable since motivation is actually pretty complex—we rarely do things for just one reason.

What Makes Rewards More or Less Effective?

If you decide to use rewards in the classroom, how can you maximize the chances that they will work? Three principles are especially important. Rewards should be desirable, certain, and prompt.

The importance of desirability is obvious. People will work for rewards that appeal to them, and will work less hard or not at all for rewards that are not appealing.[4] That is self-evident, and teachers likely know which rewards would appeal to their students and which would mean little to them.

Less obvious is the importance of the certainty of a reward, by which I mean the probability that a student will get a reward if he or she attempts to do the target behavior. What if you've set a target that seems too difficult to the student, and he won't even try? Or what if the target seems achievable to the student, he makes an attempt and does his best, but still fails? Either reduces the likelihood that the student will try again. Both problems can be avoided if the reward is contingent on the student trying his best, and not on what he achieves. But that has its drawbacks, as well. It means that you must make a judgment call as to whether he tried his best. (And you must make that judgment separately for each student.) It is all too likely that some students will have an inflated view of their efforts, and your differing assessment will lead to mistrust. Ideally, the teacher will select specific behaviors for each student as targets, with the target titrated to each student's current level of ability.

A corollary of rewards being desirable is that they be prompt. A reward that is delayed has less appeal than the same reward delivered immediately. For example, suppose I gave you this choice: "You can have $10 tomorrow, or $10 a week from tomorrow." You'd take the $10 tomorrow, right? Rewards have more "oomph"—that is, more power to motivate—when you are going to get them soon. That's why, when my wife calls me from the grocery store, it's easy for me to say "Don't buy ice cream. I'm trying to lose weight." But when I'm at home it's difficult for me to resist ice cream that's in the freezer. In the first situation, I'm denying myself ice cream sometime in the distant future, but in the second I would be denying myself ice cream right at that moment. The promise of ice cream two minutes from now has higher value for me than the promise of ice cream hours from now.

It is possible to measure how much more desirable a reward is when given sooner rather than later. In one type of experiment, subjects participate in an auction and offer sealed bids for money that will be delivered to them later. Thus, each subject might be asked "What is the maximum you would pay right now for a reward of $10, to be delivered tomorrow?"[5] Subjects are asked to make bids for a variety of rewards to be delivered at delays varying from one to 30 days. Then, researchers use subjects' bids to derive a relationship between the amount of time that the reward is delayed and how much people value the delayed reward. Subjects typically show a steep drop off in how much they value the reward—with a one-day delay, $20 is worth about $18 to most subjects, and with a one-week delay, the value is more like $15 (e.g., Kirby, 1997). In other words, there is a significant cost to the reward value for even a brief delay. Other studies show that the cost

What Is the Difference between Rewards and Praise?

You may have noticed that I have limited my discussion to the effects of concrete rewards—candy, cash, and so on. Isn't praise a reward as well? It can be, but praise as it's usually administered has some important differences. The most important is that praise is usually given unpredictably. The student doesn't think to himself, "If I get 90 percent or better on this spelling test, the teacher will say 'Good job, Dan!'" Rewards are different. There is usually an explicit bargain in the classroom, with the understanding that a particular behavior (e.g., 90 percent or better on a spelling test) merits a reward. As described in the main article, the decrease in motivation for a task only occurs if the reward was expected (and if the students enjoy the task). Since praise is not expected, it does not lead to an immediate decrement to motivation.

Another important difference between praise and concrete rewards is that the former is often taken as a more personal comment on one's abilities. Rewards typically don't impart information to the student. But praise can carry quite a bit of meaning. For starters, it tells the student that she did something noteworthy enough to merit praise. Then too, the student learns what the teacher considers important by listening to what she praises. A student may be told that she's smart, or that she tried hard, or that she's improving. In the short run, sincere praise will provide a boost to motivation (Deci et al., 1999), but in the long run, the content of praise can have quite different effects on the student's self-concept and on future efforts (e.g., Henderlong and Lepper, 2002; Mueller and Dweck, 1998). The key is in what type of praise is given. When faced with a difficult task, a child who has been praised in the past for her *effort* is likely to believe that intelligence increases as knowledge increases and, therefore, will work harder and seek more experiences from which she can learn. In contrast, a student who has been praised for her *ability* will likely believe that intelligence is fixed (e.g., is genetically determined) and will seek to maintain the "intelligent" label by trying to look good, even if that means sticking to easy tasks rather than more challenging tasks from which more can be learned.

A final difference between praise and rewards lies in students' expectations of encountering either in school. At least in the U.S., praise is part of everyday social interaction. If someone displays unusual skill or determination or kindness, or any other attribute that we esteem, it is not unusual to offer praise. In fact, a teacher who never praised her students might strike them as cold, or uncaring. No such expectation exists for rewards, however. It is hard to imagine teaching students without ever praising them. It is easy to imagine teaching students without ever offering them a concrete reward.

For more on praise and its effects, see "Ask the Cognitive Scientist," *American Educator,* Winter 2005–2006, available at www.aft.org/pubs-reports/american_educator/issues/winter05-06/cogsci.htm.

—D.W.

is greater for elementary school students than college students (e.g., Green, Fry and Myerson, 1994). That finding probably matches your intuition: As we get older, we get better at delaying gratification. Distant rewards become more similar to immediate rewards.

In this section I've summarized data showing that rewards should be desirable, certain, and prompt if they are to be effective. These three factors provide some insight into the extrinsic (but non-tangible) rewards that almost all schools offer: grades and graduation. Grades are not as rewarding as we might guess because they are seldom administered right after the required behavior (studying), and the reward of a diploma is, of course, even more distant. Then too, low-achieving students likely perceive these rewards as highly uncertain. That is, hard work does not guarantee that they will receive the reward.

Putting It All Together: Are Rewards Worth It?

When all is said and done, are rewards worth it? I liken using rewards to taking out a loan. You get an immediate benefit, but you know that you will eventually have to pay up, with interest. As with loans, I suggest three guidelines to the use of rewards: 1) try to find an alternative; 2) use them for a specific reason, not as a general strategy; and 3) plan for the ending.

Try to Find an Alternative

It is very difficult to implement rewards without incurring some cost. If the reward system is the same for all class members, it won't work as well as an individualized approach and you will likely reward some students for tasks they already like. If you tailor the rewards to individual students, you vastly increase your workload, and you increase the risk of students perceiving the program as unfair.

The size of the costs to motivation, although real, should not be overstated. As mentioned earlier, there are many contributors to motivation, and putting a smiley sticker on a spelling test will probably not rank high among them. Still, why incur the cost at all, if an alternative is available? The obvious alternative is to make the material intrinsically interesting. Indeed, if you follow that precept, you will never offer an extrinsic reward for an intrinsically interesting task, which is when the trouble with motivation really starts.

It is also worth considering whether student motivation is the real reason you use rewards. Do you put stickers on test papers in the hopes that students will work harder to earn them, or just for a bit of fun, a colorful diversion? Do you throw a class pizza party to motivate students, or to increase the class's sense of community? You might still distribute stickers and throw the party, but not make them explicitly contingent on performance beforehand. Announce to the class that they have done such a good job on the most recent unit that a party seems in order. Thus, the party is still an acknowledgement of good work and still might contribute to a positive class atmosphere, but it is not offered as a reward contingent on performance.

Use Rewards for a Specific Reason

A wise investor understands that taking out a loan, although it incurs a cost, might be strategic in the long run. So too, although a rewards program may incur some cost to motivation, there are times when the cost might be worth it. One example is when students must learn or practice a task that is rather dull, but that, once mastered, leads to opportunities for greater interest and motivation. For example, learning the times tables might be dull, but if students can get over that hump of boredom, they are ready to take on more interesting work. Rewards might also be useful when a student has lost confidence in himself to the point that he is no longer willing to try. If he'll attempt academic work to gain a desirable extrinsic reward and succeeds, his perception of himself and his abilities may change from self-doubt to recognition that he is capable of academic work (Greene and Lepper, 1974). Thereafter, the student may be motivated by his sense of accomplishment and his expectation that he will continue to do well.

Although a rewards program may incur some cost to motivation, there are times that the cost might be worth it. For example, learning the times tables might be dull, but if students can get over that hump of boredom, they are ready to take on more interesting work.

Use Rewards for a Limited Time

No one wants to live with chronic debt, and no one should make rewards a long-term habit. Although the cost of using rewards may not be large, that cost likely increases as rewards are used for a longer time. In addition, there would seem to be an advantage to the program having a natural ending point. For example, students are rewarded for learning their times tables, and once they are learned, the rewards end. The advantage is that any decrease in motivation might stick to the task. In other words, students will think "times tables are boring, and we need to be rewarded to learn them" rather than "math is boring, and we need to be rewarded to learn it." In addition, if students are told at the start of the program when it will end, there may be fewer complaints when the goodies are no longer available.

Notes

1. Such positive framing of rewards does not reverse the negative impact of rewards on motivation, but telling students that rewards signal acknowledgement of good work, rather than the closing of a bargain, seems more in keeping with the spirit of education.

2. Readers who are familiar with interventions to reduce students' aggressive or antisocial behavior may be surprised at this finding. Such interventions do often use rewards and then phase them out. But keep in mind that the rewards are just one part of a complex intervention and that in order to be effective, such interventions must be implemented in full. To learn more about the use of rewards in such an intervention, see "Heading Off Disruption: How Early Intervention Can Reduce Defiant Behavior—and Win Back Teaching Time," *American Educator*, Winter 2003–2004, available at www.aft.org/pubs-reports/american_educator/winter03-04/index.html.

3. A correlation of zero would indicate that they were unrelated, and a correlation of -1.0 would indicate that they were perfectly related.

4. There are exceptions to this generalization, notably in the social realm. People will work hard without reward as part of a social transaction. In such situations a small reward will actually make people less likely to work (e.g., Heyman and Ariely, 2004). For example, if an acquaintance asks you to help her move a sofa, you would assume that she's asking a favor as a friend, and you might well help. But if she offers you $5 to move the sofa you think of the request as a business transaction, and $5 may not seem like enough money. These social concerns could apply to the classroom; some students might work to please the teacher. But such social transactions rest on reciprocity. If your friend with the poorly placed sofa never helps you out, you will get tired of her requests. It would be difficult to set up a classroom relationship that used social reciprocity between teachers and students.

5. The procedure is actually what researchers call a second-bid auction; the highest bidder wins the auction, but pays the price of the second highest bid. This procedure is meant to ensure that people bid exactly what the item is worth to them. The workings of the auction are explained in detail to subjects.

DANIEL T. WILLINGHAM is professor of cognitive psychology at the University of Virginia and author of *Cognition: The Thinking Animal*. His research focuses on the role of consciousness in learning. Readers can pose specific questions to "Ask the Cognitive Scientist," American Educator, 555 New Jersey Ave. N.W., Washington, DC 20001, or to amered@aft.org. Future columns will try to address readers' questions.

Social Awareness + Emotional Skills = Successful Kids

New funding and congressional support are poised to bring the best social and emotional learning research into more classrooms nationwide.

Tori DeAngelis

The sad truth is that most U.S. schools don't foster good mental health or strong connections with friends and nurturing adults. Data show that only 29 percent of sixth-through 12th-grade students report that their schools provide caring, encouraging environments. Another 30 percent of high school students say they engage in high-risk behaviors, such as substance use, sex, violence and even suicide attempts.

For decades, a dedicated group of prevention experts—many of them psychologists—has been trying to improve those statistics through an approach called social and emotional learning, or SEL. They believe that if schools teach youngsters to work well with others, regulate their emotions and constructively solve problems, students will be better equipped to deal with life's challenges, including academic ones.

"It's about creating an environment where a child can learn—because if a child isn't emotionally prepared to learn, he or she is not going to learn," says SEL researcher and program developer Marc Brackett, PhD, head of the Emotional Intelligence Unit at Yale University's Edward Zigler Center in Child Development and Social Policy.

Critics charge that SEL programs are too broad-based and that social and emotional learning shouldn't necessarily fall on teachers' shoulders. Instead, families should oversee their children's social, emotional and character development, they contend. Yet studies show the programs improve mental health and behavior, boost children's social competence, and create more positive school climates. Students who participated in SEL programs gained an average of 11 percentage points more on achievement tests than youngsters who didn't take part in the programs, according to a meta-analysis of 213 studies of SEL programs, in press at Child Development, by prevention experts Joseph A. Durlak, PhD, of Loyola University Chicago; Roger P. Weissberg, PhD, of the University of Illinois at Chicago; and colleagues.

"That's pretty remarkable given how difficult it is to alter achievement test scores," says Mark Greenberg, PhD, director of the Prevention Research Center at Pennsylvania State University and creator of one of the longest-running and most rigorously studied SEL programs, PATHS (Promoting Alternative Thinking Strategies).

Some studies also show major gains long after an SEL program has ended. In the Seattle Social Development Project—a longitudinal study of 808 elementary school children who received a comprehensive SEL intervention in the first through sixth grade starting in 1981—participants reported significantly lower lifetime rates of violence and heavy alcohol use at age 18 than no-intervention controls. In addition, intervention-group students were more likely to complete high school than controls—91 percent compared with 81 percent—and to have lower rates of major depression, post-traumatic stress disorder, anxiety and social phobia at ages 24 and 27. (See the *Archives of Pediatrics and Adolescent Medicine,* Vol. 153, No. 3; Vol. 156, No. 5; and Vol. 159, No. 1).

In a related vein, Greenberg and others are starting to show that the programs affect executive functioning, an ability some researchers think may be even more important than IQ.

"The ability to maintain attention, to shift your set and plan ahead—these are obviously important learning skills that our programs are significantly improving upon," Greenberg says.

Other researchers are starting to examine other untapped areas the programs may be affecting, including health, parenting and even the behavior of children whose parents underwent the original interventions. Researchers are also applying SEL programs abroad, with military families and with special-education populations.

The Tenets of Social and Emotional Learning

Researchers have been studying a version of SEL since the 1970s, but it was first popularized in "Emotional Intelligence," the 1995 best-seller by psychologist Daniel Goleman, PhD. He argued that emotional intelligence can be taught and that schools should teach it systematically.

While SEL programs vary somewhat in design and target different ages, they all work to develop core competencies: self-awareness, social awareness, self-management, relationship skills and responsible decision-making. Instead of focusing on a single negative behavior—such as drug use, sexual risk-taking or aggression, for instance—SEL researchers take a broad-brush approach to tackling these problems. They believe all of these behaviors share common roots: a lack of social and emotional competence, often exacerbated by factors such as family disruption, violent neighborhoods and genetic and biological dispositions. Schools and families can counter these risks, SEL proponents say, by facilitating students' emotional and social skills and providing environments that both nurture and challenge children.

A look at the PATHS program shows how these programs work. Like many SEL programs, it uses easy-to-understand, teacher-led lessons and activities that help students learn to recognize feelings in themselves and others, manage their thoughts and emotions more effectively, and solve interpersonal problems. One activity, for instance, has youngsters construct posters resembling a three-color traffic signal. Each signal light represents a different aspect of constructive problem-solving: Red is "stop and calm down," yellow is "go slow and think," and green is "go ahead, try my plan." Children apply this guide to real-life problems, then evaluate how their solutions worked.

Active strategies like this are embedded in a comprehensive program that teachers share in 131 sequential lessons over a seven-year period, from kindergarten to sixth grade. Children don't just get didactic information but have many chances to practice these skills both in and out of the classroom, Greenberg explains.

"Comprehensive SEL programs create many opportunities for children to practice these skills in the challenging situations they face every day in the classroom and on the playground," he says. "They also build caring, safe school climates that involve everyone in the school."

An interesting synergy results when these programs are offered, Greenberg adds. When children are taught these skills, they learn how to foster their own well-being and become more resilient. That, in turn, builds a more positive classroom climate that better engages children in learning. And as they become more absorbed in learning, children are more likely to do better in school.

"Building emotional awareness, self-control and relationship skills are master skills," Greenberg says. "When we nurture them, children do better in all areas of their daily lives, including school."

The programs, however, are far from perfect, critics and proponents say. While a 2005 review shows that about 59 percent of schools use some kind of SEL programming, the quality varies widely, says Weissberg. In fact, the Collaborative for Academic, Social and Emotional Learning, or CASEL—a nonprofit organization founded by Goleman in 1994 dedicated to advancing the science and evidence base of SEL and promoting the quality of SEL programs—places only 22 of the nation's several hundred SEL programs (including Greenberg's and Hawkins') on its list of exemplary programs for being well-designed and evidence-based,

among other criteria. Researchers also continue to debate whether universal or more targeted curricula are better, since SEL programs tend to have the greatest impact on troubled kids.

Meanwhile, educators are feeling an enormous pressure to have kids do well on standardized testing, even in tight economic times, says Weissberg. "So there are several barriers that make it a challenge to implement SEL programs with high quality and fidelity," he says.

SEL Goes National

That said, more money is pouring into the field, thanks to the positive research findings on social and emotional learning. The NoVo Foundation, a philanthropy headed by Peter and Jennifer Buffett (Peter is investor Warren Buffett's son), has offered $10 million in grants: $3.4 million in research funds and $6.3 million in development funds for CASEL.

Potentially more far-reaching is the Academic, Social, and Emotional Learning Act (H.R. 4223), announced at a CASEL forum in Washington, D.C., in December. The bill, introduced by Rep. Dale Kildee (D-Mich.) and co-sponsored by Rep. Tim Ryan (D-Ohio) and Rep. Judy Biggert (R-Ill.), would authorize the U.S. Department of Education to establish a national SEL training center and provide grants to support evidence-based SEL programs, as well as evaluate their success.

"I don't think I could have imagined that our field would have come this far," says Weissberg, CASEL's president.

In an effort to make the best SEL programming available nationwide, CASEL leaders plan to collaborate with evidence-based SEL providers, work with model school districts, share research to inform federal legislation and state policy, and think realistically about how to implement these programs on a broad scale, says Weissberg. If the legislation passes, it should enhance these efforts, he adds.

The December CASEL forum underscored the field's growing clout and psychologists' central role in it, adds APA Chief Executive Officer Norman Anderson, PhD, who attended the meeting. There, psychologists and other SEL researchers and practitioners rubbed elbows with legislators, philanthropists, national media and even some Hollywood celebrities, including Goldie Hawn, who heads her own SEL-related organization.

"This group of experts is doing an outstanding job of moving the SEL model forward and making a real difference in the lives of our children," says Anderson. He is particularly pleased that research is starting to show a link between developing children's resilience and academic performance, he says.

"These efforts represent another bridge between the worlds of psychology and education," Anderson adds. "It's all very exciting."

Tori DeAngelis is a writer in Syracuse, N.Y.

From *Monitor on Psychology* by Tori DeAngelis, April 2010, pp. 46–47. Copyright © 2010 by American Psychological Association. Reprinted by permission. No further distribution without permission from the American Psychological Association.

UNIT 3

Social and Emotional Development

Unit Selections

Key Points to Consider

- Adopted children from other countries who were institutionalized as infants often show permanent negative effects. Why would institutionalization cause these deficits? Do you know anyone who has chosen to adopt a previously institutionalized baby? Would you consider adopting such a baby from another country and why or why not?

- In years past, mothers-in-law often scolded new mothers for picking up a crying baby due to fears of raising spoiled children. Research shows, however, that infants not only thrive when touched, but it may be critical to the formation of attachment bonds as well as promoting physical and cognitive growth and reducing stress. Explain how you would use this information to parent your baby.

- Who were the most and least popular children growing up? What made them so popular or so shunned? Were you a lonely child? Think of someone who appeared to be lonely. What can be done to assist lonely children? What about your adult friendships today? Do you see any parallels with your childhood friends? Explain. Do you think your childhood friendships helped you to develop improved social skills? Explain. If you have children, how will you help your children develop friends and build their social skills?

- Look at almost any elementary school playground at recess or junior high lunchroom and you will see boys and girls congregating by gender. Think back to when you were in grade school. What were the rules for girls vs. boys and who enforced these gender-typed behaviors? Did your teachers or parents have different rules for boys and girls? Were girls and boys allowed to play with the same toys? Explain. Will you treat your son and daughter differently? What sorts of toys will you select for your child? As a teacher or parent, how might you introduce different kinds of play for children as a result of the research?

- Assume you are the director of a preschool and kindergarten where your teachers create structured play activities to support children's learning. Explain how you would convince parents that your school is superior for children's learning as compared to a more traditional school setting with children sitting in desks listening to the teacher and doing drills or worksheets.

- Several highly visible cases of tragic school violence across the country have been traced to incidences of bullying in school. Recent studies may indicate that the occurrence of bullying is rising. What factors contribute toward making some children bullies and what can be done to defuse these potentially volatile situations? When you were growing up, what did you or your schoolmates do when confronted with a bully? Did you involve a teacher or a parent to help you or others? Why or why not? What if you have a child who becomes a bully, what could you do as a parent to help your child?

One of the truisms about our species is that we are social animals. From birth, each person's life is a constellation of relationships, from family at home to friends in the neighborhood and school. This unit addresses how children's social and emotional development is influenced by important relationships with parents, peers, and teachers.

When John Donne in 1623 wrote, "No man is an island, entire of itself . . . any man's death diminishes me, because I am involved in mankind," he implied that all humans are connected to each other and that these connections make us who we are. Early in this century, sociologist C. H. Cooley highlighted the importance of relationships with the phrase "looking-glass self" to describe how people tend to see themselves as a function of how others perceive them. Personality theorist Alfred Adler, also writing in the early twentieth century, claimed that personal strength derived from the quality of one's connectedness to others: The stronger the relationships, the stronger the person. The notion that a person's self-concept arises from relations with others also has roots in developmental psychology. As Jean Piaget once wrote, "There is no such thing as isolated individuals; there are only relations." The articles in this unit respect these traditions by emphasizing the theme that a child's development occurs within the context of relationships.

Today's society is more complex than ever and children from at-risk families face growing challenges such as acute poverty, homelessness, foster care, illness, alcohol and substance abuse, abandonment, deprivation, death, and violence in families. Amazingly, in spite of these terrible odds, unlike most children, there are a lucky few who somehow manage to transcend these crushing effects and rise up to bounce back and develop normally. The author of "Children's Capacity to Develop Resiliency" describes how certain key factors such as an understanding of one's strengths and accomplishments, humor, and high, positive expectations can protect children and keep them on the path of normal development.

Unfortunately, infants who suffer severe and sustained early human deprivation and institutionalization will sustain enduring and permanent neurological damage that may result in later developmental problems. Researcher Charles Nelson describes some of these lasting negative effects in "A Neurobiological Perspective on Early Human Deprivation." In "Emotions and the Development of Childhood Depression: Bridging the Gap" and "The Role of Neurobiological Deficits in Childhood Antisocial Behavior" researchers discuss childhood depression and identify risk factors such as specific neurobiological deficits that combined with early adverse environments can contribute to depression and antisocial behavior in early childhood.

A significant milestone of early childhood involves a child's ability to socialize, communicate, and play effectively with peers. In the article "When Girls and Boys Play: What Research Tells Us" researchers Riley and Jones review differences found among girls and boys in terms of social interactions, physical play, and language usage and provide

© Getty Images/Blend Images

useful suggestions for teachers and parents. Similarly, researchers are calling on the critical importance of safeguarding and increasing time for children to play as promoting neurological growth, enhancing cooperation and communication, and strengthening children's social, cognitive, and language development as explained in "Playtime in Peril."

As a result of recent tragic school violence and homicides spurred in part by being the victim of bullying, more schools are developing and implementing intervention programs to assist both the bullies and their potential victims. In "A Profile of Bullying at School," leading expert Dan Olweus outlines the typical process involved with bullying and gives supporting data for a prevention program that he has developed over the past 20 years. Given the serious and detrimental effects of bullying on children's development and adjustment, more schools are implementing bullying prevention programs both in the United States and in other countries such as Norway.

Another major influence in the landscape of childhood is friendship. When do childhood friendships begin? Friends become increasingly important during the elementary school years. If forming strong, secure attachments with family members is an important task of early childhood, then one of the major psychological achievements of middle childhood is a move toward the peer group. Researchers for "Children's Social and Moral Reasoning about Exclusion" present new data on how prosocial or aggressive behavior as well as prejudice and stereotypes contribute to children's popularity standing and social and moral reasoning.

Student Website
www.mhhe.com/cls

Internet References

Max Planck Institute for Psychological Research
www.mpg.de/english/institutesProjectsFacilities/instituteChoice/psychologische_forschung
National Child Care Information Center (NCCIC)
www.nccic.org
Serendip
http://serendip.brynmawr.edu/serendip

A Neurobiological Perspective on Early Human Deprivation

The number of children who are abandoned or orphaned around the world is rapidly increasing owing to war, AIDS, and poverty. Many of these children are placed in institutional settings for lack of individual or societal resources or because of long-standing cultural traditions. It has been known for over half a century that rearing children in institutional care characterized by profound sensory, cognitive, linguistic, and psychosocial deprivation can be deleterious to their development. This article examines the neural mechanisms that likely underlie the maldevelopment many institutionalized children experience.

CHARLES A. NELSON

An extraordinary number of children throughout the world begin their lives in psychologically adverse circumstances. In some cases, these children live with their parents in profound poverty; in others, they either do not have parents (such as those orphaned by war or AIDS) or they are abandoned by their parents. Vast numbers of abandoned or orphaned children living in Eastern Europe, China, and Latin America live in institutional settings. This article describes the effects of profound early deprivation (common in many institutional settings) on brain and behavioral development.

The Nature of the Problem

UNICEF estimates that approximately 1.5 million children in Central and Eastern Europe live in public care (orphanages, group homes, psychiatric units). These include children who have been abandoned by their parents, whose parents have died, who live in hospitals because of chronic illness (e.g., AIDS), and who live in penal institutions. The European Commission for Social Cohesion estimates that 10–20 per 1,000 children birth to age 18 in Bulgaria, Russia, and Romania and 5–10 per 1,000 in Poland, Hungary, Moldova, Lithuania, Latvia, and Estonia live in orphanages, group homes, or psychiatric units.[1] In Sweden, Finland, Ireland, Belgium, The Netherlands, Italy, and Spain, 1.5–3.0 per 1,000 children younger than 3 years are institutionalized (Browne, Hamilton-Giachritsis, Johnson, Leth, & Ostergren, 2004).

Collectively, institutionalizing young children is a common practice throughout many parts of the world. The majority of these children will remain in such settings for many years, whereas a relatively small minority will be adopted, most internationally.[2] Indeed, in 2004, nearly 23,000 international adoptions took place in the United States. Not surprisingly given the figures cited above, the vast majority of these children were from Eastern Europe and Asia (Russia and China in particular).

As it does in families, the quality of care varies among institutions; there is also variability in the nature and degree of deprivation. For example, in some model institutions in Russia, the caregiver-to-child ratio is reasonable and the degree of sensory, cognitive, and linguistic deprivation not severe. At the other end of the spectrum, institutional life can be characterized by profound global deprivation. The ratio of children to caregivers can exceed 15:1; caregivers are generally poorly trained and, in many cases, uncommitted to the welfare of children and unresponsive and insensitive to children's needs. Nutrition can be substandard, cognitive stimulation can be inadequate, and exposure to mature language is frequently lacking owing to a paucity of adult caregivers. Basic sensory stimulation can be lacking across multiple modalities, leading to perceptual deficits (e.g., lack of patterned light stimulation because walls and ceilings are painted white and infants are left in their cribs for long periods of time; infants are not held or touched, leading to tactile deprivation). Finally, institutional care is frequently characterized by strict adherence to conformity (e.g., children are dressed alike) and regimen (e.g., children all eat at the same time, use the toilet at the same time). It would not be unreasonable to suggest that life in institutions that globally deprive young children resembles peer-rearing common in some nonhuman primate studies (e.g., Suomi, 1997). Of course, even this is misleading because nonhuman primates typically huddle together when left without caregivers, whereas human children typically do not.

Effects of Early Institutionalization on Development

For most of the 20th century, clinicians and researchers noted the deleterious effects of institutional rearing on the development of young children. Initially, many of these studies were uncontrolled or poorly controlled, but more rigorous, recent investigations have confirmed earlier findings that institutional care is often associated with a variety of deleterious outcomes (for recent review, see Maclean, 2003).

Contemporary research has documented many problems in young children adopted out of institutions in Eastern Europe and Russia. Abnormalities include a variety of serious medical problems (Johnson,

1997; Johnson et al., 1992), physical and brain growth deficiencies (Benoit, Jocelyn, Moddemann, & Embree, 1996; Johnson, 2000), cognitive problems (Morison, Ames, & Chisholm, 1995; Rutter & The English and Romanian Adoptees Study Team, 1998), speech and language delays (Albers, Johnson, Hostetter, Iverson, & Miller, 1997; Dubrovina et al., 1991; Groze & Ileana, 1996), sensory integration difficulties and stereotypies (Cermak & Daunhauer, 1997; Chisholm & Savoie, 1992), and social and behavioral abnormalities (Fisher, Ames, Chisholm, & Savoie, 1997; O'Connor, Bredenkamp, Rutter, & The English and Romanian Adoption Study Team, 1999). The latter include difficulties with inattention and hyperactivity (Rutter, 1999), disturbances of attachment (Chisholm, 1998; Chisholm, Carter, Ames, & Morison, 1995; O'Connor & Rutter, 2000; O'Connor et al., 1999), and a syndrome that mimics autism (Federici, 1998; Rutter et al., 1999). Some of these abnormalities are associated with risk factors that precede placement in the institutions (e.g., prenatal alcohol exposure), but quality of care is often appalling in these institutions, and many problems seem related to the ecology of institutional life (e.g., Ames, 1997).

Several longitudinal studies have examined the effects of institutionalization on children's development. Tizard and her colleagues compared four groups of young children who had been reared in institutions in the United Kingdom for the first 2–4 years of life: (a) a group that was adopted between ages 2 and 4, (b) a group returned to their biological families between ages 2 and 4, (c) a group that remained institutionalized, and (d) a group of never-institutionalized children of the same age (see, e.g., Tizard, 1977; Tizard & Hodges, 1978; Tizard & Reese, 1974, 1975). Across all domains, the adopted children fared better than the institutionalized children. Unfortunately, as is the case with virtually all studies of institutionalized children, they were not randomly assigned to the groups, and selection factors may have influenced the findings (i.e., more developmentally advanced children may have been the first adopted).

Two longitudinal studies have been conducted recently with children adopted from Romanian institutions. Ames, Chisholm, and colleagues (as cited in Maclean, 2003) included three groups of children adopted by Canadian parents: (a) children adopted after having spent at least 8 months in a Romanian institution, (b) children adopted from Romanian institutions at less than 4 months of age, and (c) a Canadian-born (but not adopted) comparison group matched on age and sex to the first group. They found more behavior problems, disturbances of attachment, and lower IQs in the group of children who had spent 8 months or more in Romanian institutions (Maclean, 2003).

O'Connor and Rutter (2000) compared young children adopted from Romania with those adopted within the United Kingdom (see also Rutter, O'Connor, & The English and Romanian Adoptees Study Team, 2004). They found that at both age 4 and again at age 6, the duration of deprivation was linearly related to the number of signs of attachment disorders. Children exhibiting indiscriminate sociability at age 6 had experienced deprivation for twice as long as those exhibiting no attachment disorder signs ($M = 22$ vs. 11 months). Cognitive recovery was inversely related to age of adoption, although social and emotional problems were less clearly related to timing.

Taken together, these findings suggest that although psychosocial deprivation may be associated with impairment across a range of developmental domains, the degree of impairment and trajectories of recovery may vary. These tentative conclusions must be tempered by the lack of randomization and potential selection bias in who is adopted, as well as by lack of data on individual differences in institutional experiences and lack of adequate comparison groups (i.e., native children who have never been institutionalized).

Recently, Zeanah et al. (2003) launched the Bucharest Early Intervention Project (BEIP), in which they examined three cohorts of children: (a) those abandoned at birth, placed in institutions, and who continue to reside in institutions; (b) those abandoned at birth, placed in institutions, and then randomly assigned to foster care; and (c) a sample of children living with their biological parents in the greater Bucharest community. Randomization and the use of an in-country comparison sample circumvent many of the shortcomings of previous studies. Early findings (Nelson, Zeanah, & Fox, 2007) suggest that institutional care has a profoundly negative effect on physical growth, language, cognitive, social–emotional development, and brain development, and that children placed in foster care show improvements in many (although not all) of the domains that are deleteriously affected by institutional life.

The Effects of Early Institutionalization on Brain Development

Given the dramatic behavioral abnormalities observed in institutionalized and formerly institutionalized children, it seems reasonable to consider the neural systems that might be associated with these behavioral abnormalities. Previous research on institutionalized children has not included measures of brain functioning, although some assessments have been conducted with children adopted from institutions. For example, Chugani et al. (2001) used positron emission tomography (PET) in 10 children (average age was 8 years) who had been adopted from a Romanian institution. PET employs a radioactive isotope to examine brain metabolism, for example, the brain's use of glucose, a form of energy. Nearly all children had been placed in the institution before age 18 months and had lived in the institution for an average of 38 months before being adopted. Compared with a control group of healthy adults and a group of 10-year-old children with medically refractory epilepsy (i.e., who were still experiencing seizures), the adoptees showed significantly reduced brain metabolism in select regions of the prefrontal cortex and the temporal lobe and regions associated with higher cognitive functions, memory, and emotion (e.g., the orbital frontal gyrus, the amygdala, and the hippocampus were all affected). Behaviorally, the adopted children suffered from mild neurocognitive impairments, impulsivity, attention, and social deficits—behaviors that are consistent with the patterns of brain findings.

More recently, this same group of researchers examined the connectivity of brain regions that are myelinated (the so-called white matter) in this same sample of previously institutionalized children (Eluvathingal et al., 2006). The authors found that white matter connectivity was diminished in the *uncinate fasciculus* region of the brain in the early deprivation group compared with the controls. Because this structure provides a major pathway of communication between brain areas involved in higher cognitive and emotional function (e.g., amygdala and frontal lobe), the authors concluded that connectivity between brain regions is negatively affected by early institutionalization. It is important to note, however, that these children all tested in the normal range of IQ (although their verbal IQ was lower than their performance IQ), and they suffered only mild impairments in a variety of neuropsychological domains (e.g., sustained attention), as they did in the PET study. How the functional anisotropy (FA; an index of myelination) and behavioral data relate to one another is unclear.

Collectively, results from these two studies point to the neurobiological sequelae of early and prolonged institutionalization. In particular, these children suffered from metabolic deficits in the areas of the brain believed to be involved in higher cognition, emotion, and emotion regulation. Unfortunately, because this sample was small and because this study suffers from the same methodological shortcomings as other post-adoption studies noted earlier, the generalizability of these findings may be limited.

Pollak and colleagues (as cited in Wismer Fries, Ziegler, Kurian, Jacoris, & Pollak, 2005) have also examined the effects of early institutionalization on neurobiological systems, although not the brain per se. This group examined oxytocin and vasopressin, two hormones long associated with affiliative and positive social behavior, in a sample of previously institutionalized children. The previously institutionalized children showed lower overall levels of vasopressin than controls. In addition, they showed lower levels of oxytocin after interacting with their caregiver compared with controls. Collectively, the authors suggest that "a failure to receive species-typical care disrupts the normal development of the [oxytocin and vasopressin] systems in young children". Unfortunately, because these data were collected several years after adoption and because no current data on children's social behavior (such as attachment) were reported, it is difficult to know if the early experiences caused these hormonal changes.

As noted earlier, the BEIP is designed to examine the effects on brain development of early institutionalization that is characterized by profound sensory, cognitive, linguistic, and psychosocial deprivation.[3] Because of the age of the children and limitations in the neuroimaging tools available for use in this project, we were limited to recording the electroencephalogram (EEG) and the event-related potential (ERP). The EEG assesses general cortical activity, whereas the ERP reflects the functioning of populations of neurons acting synchronously during a cognitive task, such as face processing, memory.

In prior work, we (Marshall, Fox, & The BEIP Core Group, 2004) have reported that the institutionalized group had increased levels of low-frequency power and decreased levels of high-frequency power in the EEG compared with the never-institutionalized group. That is, the institutionalized group had less cortical brain activity than the control group (whether subcortical activity is similarly affected is unknown). Similarly, Parker, Nelson, and The BEIP Core Group (2005a, 2005b) performed two cognitive manipulations while recording ERPs. In one manipulation, researchers presented children with images of different facial expressions. In another, they alternated images of the caregiver's face and the face of a stranger. In both cases, the institutionalized population showed reduced amplitude in several ERP components compared with the never-institutionalized group. In all three studies, then, the institutionalized group showed reduced brain activity, a finding that may be consistent with Chugani et al.'s (2001) PET data.

Collectively, it appears that early institutionalization in severe situations has a profoundly negative effect on brain development—although there is still a paucity of data. Specifically, institutionalization appears to lead to a reduction in cortical brain activity (both metabolically and electrophysiologically) and to dysregulation of neuroendocrine systems that mediate social behavior.

Why Is Institutional Rearing Bad for the Brain?

The initial evidence is compelling that early institutionalization (when characterized by profound sensory, cognitive, linguistic, and psychosocial deprivation) has a negative impact on behavioral development. It is also increasingly clear that some of the deficits and developmental delays that result from such institutional rearing have their origins in compromised brain development. The question I seek to address in this final section is why? To address this question requires that I first summarize what drives brain development.

In brief, postnatal brain development is driven by an interaction of genes and experience. Genes provide for the early specification of structures and circuits, whereas experience provides the specialization and fine-tuning needed to lead to mature function. As has been discussed in a variety of forums (e.g., Nelson et al., 2006), brain development reflects a combination of experience-expectant and -dependent mechanisms. The former refers to features of the environment that are (or at least, should be) common to all members of the species, whereas the latter refers to features of the environment that are unique to the individual. Thus, having access to patterned light information or a caregiver is a feature of the environment common to the species, whereas individual differences in environmental challenges (e.g., quality and quantity of stimulation) are unique to the individual.

A short list of experience-expectant features of the environment might include access to a caregiver, adequate nutrition, sensory stimulation (e.g., visual, auditory, tactile), and linguistic input. It likely also includes an environment that is low in the so-called toxic stress, or it provides the building blocks to cope with stress. Of course, if mental and language development is to occur, the environment requires cognitive and linguistic challenges. This list is far from exhaustive, but by inference, it illustrates a key point: many forms of institutional rearing lack most elements of a mental-health-promoting environment. As a result, the young nervous system, which actively awaits and seeks out environmental input, is robbed of such input. This lack of input leads to underspecification of circuits and the miswiring of circuits. Because children living in institutions lack input (stimulation) on a grand scale, we should not be surprised that they experience a range of problems due to "errors" in brain development.

There is also another potential consequence of early institutional rearing. Typical brain development is characterized by an initial overproduction of both neurons and synapses, followed by a retraction to adult numbers (which varies by area; for elaboration, see Nelson et al., 2006). It is believed that the process of overproducing neurons and synapses is guided by a genetic program, whereas the retraction process may depend more heavily on experience. If true, then it may be that living in a deprived environment can lead to errors in apoptosis (programmed cell death). In the BEIP study, we have observed two findings consistent with this hypothesis: smaller head size (even among children placed in foster care) and reduced brain activity. These findings may reflect apoptosis gone awry, specifically, that too many neurons or synapses, or both, were retracted. Because most regions of the brain do not make new neurons postnatally, it is possible that early institutional rearing may have a permanent effect on cell and synapse numbers.

Of course, institutional environments vary in the quality and quantity of deprivation. In my experience in Romanian institutions, I have seen considerable variability in quality of caregiving and the quality of sensory, linguistic, and cognitive stimulation. This leads to an important qualifier in modeling the neurobiology of early institutionalization: Some domains of function are more experience dependent than others, and domains vary in *when* experience is required to facilitate a typical developmental trajectory. Thus, the long-term development of children with histories of early institutionalization will depend on (a) at what age they were institutionalized, (b) how long they were institutionalized, and (c) the exact features of the environment. Moreover, these three dimensions must be set against a backdrop of a child's genetic makeup and his or her prenatal experience (e.g., Was the mother adequately nourished? Was the fetus exposed to alcohol or other teratogens?). Unfortunately, these last two dimensions are rarely known in most studies of post-institutionalized children because genetic information was not obtained and because no reports exist about prenatal development. However, the combination of these three factors— prenatal experience, postnatal experience, and genetic makeup—likely lead to developmental programming effects that may well set the stage for years to come (see Rutter et al., 2004, for elaboration).

Implications

There are many implications of this research. For example, many children living throughout the world (including North America) experience deprivation owing to neglectful parents. Although perhaps not quite as severe as the conditions in many institutions, these children still experience profound neglect. There is an urgent need for societies to respond to the needs of such children, and doing so may be informed by the results of this research.

A second implication of this work applies to the child protection systems in much of this world. We know that the longer a child lives under adversity, the more that child is at risk and the more difficult it will be to redirect that child's development along a typical trajectory. Most child protection systems, however, pay little heed to this clear evidence and fail to move children into permanent homes more quickly or remove them from abusive homes sooner.

Finally, the lessons learned from the BEIP should be noted by the many countries engaged in war or ravaged by disease. Thus, how the world will handle the thousands of children currently being orphaned in Africa, Afghanistan, and Iraq is unclear, although it is frequently the impulse of such countries (motivated by financial, cultural, or practical forces) to place such children in institutional settings rather than to develop a high-quality foster care or adoption system. Wasil Noor, Deputy Minister of Social Welfare in Afghanistan, estimates that of the 1.6 million orphaned Afghani children, more than 10,000 are living in institutional care. Approximately 85% of these children, he estimates, have surviving parents (often both). The government has recently launched a deinstitutionalization program, reunifying children with their families and providing income generating support.[4]

Overall, we have known for more than half a century that children reared in awful institutions are at great risk for atypical development. Most of this work has been descriptive in nature, with little elucidation of the biological mechanisms responsible for maldevelopment. Advances in neuroscience now make it possible to elucidate why, from a neurobiological perspective, children reared in certain institutions are at risk. Having laid the groundwork for a more mechanistic approach to understanding the effects of such early adversity on development, the next step will be to develop interventions targeted at the neural circuits that have been altered by institutional life, with the ultimate goal to use the science of early development to change the policies countries adopt to address their abandoned or neglected children.

Notes

1. Although Romania has made great strides in reducing the number of children living in institutions—from more than 100,000 a decade ago to 30,000 today—the number of children being abandoned has actually held steady at approximately 8,000 per year.

2. Again, using Romania as an example, because there is a moratorium on international adoption and because domestic adoption remains uncommon, abandoned children typically remain in institutions or, more recently, are placed in state-run foster care or are reunited with their biological parents (although the child protection system in Romania generally does an inadequate job of supporting foster care or policing reunification).

3. It is worth noting that in the data reported to date, an intent to treat design was adopted; thus, not all children relegated to the institutionalized group are currently living in institutions—some have been reunited with their biological families and

others have been placed in state-run foster care. Thus, our findings should be considered conservative.

4. A. L. Greenberg (personal communication, May 15, 2007).

References

1. Albers, L. H., Johnson, D. E., Hostetter, M. K., Iverson, S., & Miller, L. C. (1997). Health of children adopted from the former Soviet Union and Eastern Europe: Comparison with preadoptive medical records. *Journal of the American Medical Association, 278,* 922–924.

2. Ames, E. W. (1997). *The development of Romanian orphanage children adopted into Canada.* Final report to human resources development, Canada. Burnaby, Canada: Simon Fraser University.

3. Benoit, T. C., Jocelyn, L. J., Moddemann, D. M., & Embree, J. E. (1996). Romanian adoption: The Manitoba experience. *Archives of Pediatrics & Adolescent Medicine, 150,* 1278–1282.

4. Browne, K., Hamilton-Giachritsis, C., Johnson, R., Leth, L., & Ostergren, M. (2004). *Harm to young children through early institutionalisation/residential care: A survey of 32 European countries.* Paper presented to the EU/WHO Conference on Young Children in European Residential Care; March 19, 2004. Copenhagen, Denmark: World Health Organisation Regional Office for Europe.

5. Cermak, S. A., & Daunhauer, L. A. (1997). Sensory processing in the post-institutionalized child. *American Journal of Occupational Therapy, 51,* 500–507.

6. Chisholm, K. (1998). A three year follow-up of attachment and indiscriminate friendliness in children adopted from Romanian orphanages. *Child Development, 69,* 1092–1106.

7. Chisholm, K., Carter, M. C., Ames, E. W., & Morison, S. J. (1995). Attachment security and indiscriminately friendly behavior in children adopted from Romanian orphanages. *Development and Psychopathology, 7,* 283–294.

8. Chisholm, K., & Savoie, L. (1992, June). *Behavior and attachment problems of Romanian orphanage children adopted to Canada.* Paper presented at the Canada Symposium on Development of Romanian orphanage children adopted (E. W. Ames, Chair). Quebec City, Canada: Canadian Psychological Association.

9. Chugani, H. T., Behen, M. E., Muzik, O., Juhasz, C., Nagy, F., & Chugani, D. C. (2001). Local brain functional activity following early deprivation: A study of postinstitutionalized Romanian orphans. *Neuroimage, 14,* 1290–1301.

10. Dubrovina, I. et al. (1991). *Psychological development of children in orphanages* [Psychologicheskoe razvitie vospitanikov v detskom dome]. Moscow, Russia: Prosveschenie Press.

11. Eluvathingal, T. J., Chugani, H. T., Behen, M. E., Juhász, C., Muzik, O., Maqbool, M., et al. (2006). Abnormal brain connectivity in children after early severe socioemotional deprivation: A diffusion tensor imaging study. *Pediatrics, 117,* 2093–2100.

12. Federici, R. S. (1998). *Help for the hopeless child: A guide for families.* Alexandria, VA: Author.

13. Fisher, L., Ames, E. W., Chisholm, K., & Savoie, L. (1997). Problems reported by parents of Romanian orphans adopted to British Columbia. *International Journal of Behavioral Development, 20,* 67–82.

14. Groze, V., & Ileana, D. (1996). A follow-up study of adopted children from Romania. *Child and Adolescent Social Work Journal, 13,* 541–565.

15. Johnson, D. E. (1997). Medical issues in international adoption: Factors that affect your child's pre-adoption health. *Adoptive Families, 30,* 18–20.

16. Johnson, D. E. (2000). Medical and developmental sequelae of early childhood institutionalization in international adoptees from Romania and the Russian Federation. In C. A. Nelson (Ed.),

The effects of early adversity on neurobehavioral development (pp. 113–162). Mahwah, NJ: Erlbaum.

17. Johnson, D. E., Miller, L. C., Iverson, S., Thomas, W., Franchino, B., & Dole, K. (1992). The health of children adopted from Romania. *Journal of the American Medical Association, 268,* 3446–3451.

18. Maclean, K. (2003). The impact of institutionalization on child development. *Development and Psychopathology, 15,* 853–884.

19. Marshall, P. J., Fox, N. A., & The BEIP Core Group. (2004). A comparison of the electroencephalogram between institutionalized and community children in Romania. *Journal of Cognitive Neuroscience, 16,* 1327–1338.

20. Morison, S. J., Ames, E. W., & Chisholm, K. (1995). The development of children adopted from Romanian orphanages. *Merrill-Palmer Quarterly, 41,* 411–430.

21. Nelson, C. A., de Haan, M., & Thomas, K. M. (2006). *Neuroscience and cognitive development: The role of experience and the developing brain.* New York: Wiley.

22. Nelson, C. A., Zeanah, C., & Fox, N. A. (2007). The effects of early deprivation on brain-behavioral development: The Bucharest Early Intervention Project. In D. Romer & E. Walker (Eds.), *Adolescent psychopathology and the developing brain: Integrating brain and prevention science* (pp. 197–215). New York: Oxford University Press.

23. O'Connor, T. G., Bredenkamp, D., Rutter, M., & The English and Romanian Adoption Study Team. (1999). Attachment disturbances and disorders in children exposed to early severe deprivation. *Infant Mental Health Journal, 20,* 10–29.

24. O'Connor, T. G., & Rutter, M. (2000). Attachment disorder behavior following early severe deprivation: Extension and longitudinal follow-up. The English and Romanian Adoptees Study Team. *Journal of the American Academy of Child and Adolescent Psychiatry, 39,* 703–712.

25. Parker, S. W., Nelson, C. A., & The BEIP Core Group. (2005a). An event-related potential study of the impact of institutional rearing on face recognition. *Development and Psychopathology, 17,* 621–639.

26. Parker, S. W., Nelson, C. A., & The BEIP Core Group. (2005b). The impact of deprivation on the ability to discriminate facial expressions of emotion: An event-related potential study. *Child Development, 76,* 54–72.

27. Rutter, M. L. (1999). Psychosocial adversity and child psychopathology. *British Journal of Psychiatry, 174,* 480–493.

28. Rutter, M., Andersen-Wood, L., Beckett, C., Bredenkamp, D., Castle, J., Groothues, C., et al. (1999). Quasi-autistic patterns following severe early global privation. *Journal of Child Psychology, Psychiatry and Allied Disciplines, 40,* 537–549.

29. Rutter, M., & The English and Romanian Adoptees Study Team. (1998). Developmental catch-up and delay, following adoption after severe global early privation. *Journal of Child Psychology and Psychiatry, 39,* 465–476.

30. Rutter, M., O'Connor, T., & The English and Romanian Adoptees Study Team. (2004). Are there biological programming effects for psychological development? Findings from a study of Romanian adoptees. *Developmental Psychology, 40,* 81–94.

31. Suomi, S. J. (1997). Early determinants of behaviour: Evidence from primate studies. *British Medical Bulletin, 53,* 170–184.

32. Tizard, B. (1977). *Adoption: A second chance.* New York: Free Press.

33. Tizard, B., & Hodges, J. (1978). The effect of early institutional rearing on the development of eight-year-old children. *Journal of Child Psychology, Psychiatry, and Allied Disciplines, 19,* 99–118.

34. Tizard, B., & Rees, J. (1974). A comparison of the effects of adoption, restoration to the natural mother, and continued institutionalization on the cognitive development of four-year-old children. *Child Development, 45,* 92–99.

35. Tizard, B., & Rees, J. (1975). The effect of early institutional rearing on the behavior problems and affectional relationships of four-year-old children. *Journal of Child Psychology, Psychiatry, and Allied Disciplines, 16,* 61–73.

36. Wismer Fries, A. B., Ziegler, T. E., Kurian, J. R., Jacoris, S., & Pollak, S. D. (2005). Early experience in humans is associated with changes in neuropeptides critical for regulating social behavior. *Proceedings of the National Academy of Sciences, 102,* 17237–17240.

37. Zeanah, C. H., Nelson, C. A., Fox, N. A., Smyke, A. T., Marshall, P., Parker, S. W., et al. (2003). Designing research to study the effects of institutionalization on brain and behavioral development: The Bucharest Early Intervention Project. *Development and Psychopathology, 15,* 885–907.

CHARLES A. NELSON, Harvard Medical School, Development Medicine Center Laboratory of Cognitive Neuroscience, Children's Hospital Boston, Harvard Medical School, 1 Autumn Street, Mailbox #713, Office AU621, Boston, MA 02215-5365; e-mail: charles.nelson@childrens.harvard.edu.

Acknowledgments—This article was made possible in part by grants from the NIH (MH078829 to the author; MH068857 to Megan Gunnar).

Don't!
The Secret of Self-Control

Children who are able to pass the marshmallow test enjoy greater success as adults.

JONAH LEHRER

In the late nineteen-sixties, Carolyn Weisz, a four-year-old with long brown hair, was invited into a "game room" at the Bing Nursery School, on the campus of Stanford University. The room was little more than a large closet, containing a desk and a chair. Carolyn was asked to sit down in the chair and pick a treat from a tray of marshmallows, cookies, and pretzel sticks. Carolyn chose the marshmallow. Although she's now forty-four, Carolyn still has a weakness for those air-puffed balls of corn syrup and gelatine. "I know I shouldn't like them," she says. "But they're just so delicious!" A researcher then made Carolyn an offer: she could either eat one marshmallow right away or, if she was willing to wait while he stepped out for a few minutes, she could have two marshmallows when he returned. He said that if she rang a bell on the desk while he was away he would come running back, and she could eat one marshmallow but would forfeit the second. Then he left the room.

Although Carolyn has no direct memory of the experiment, and the scientists would not release any information about the subjects, she strongly suspects that she was able to delay gratification. "I've always been really good at waiting," Carolyn told me. "If you give me a challenge or a task, then I'm going to find a way to do it, even if it means not eating my favorite food." Her mother, Karen Sortino, is still more certain: "Even as a young kid, Carolyn was very patient. I'm sure she would have waited." But her brother Craig, who also took part in the experiment, displayed less fortitude. Craig, a year older than Carolyn, still remembers the torment of trying to wait. "At a certain point, it must have occurred to me that I was all by myself," he recalls. "And so I just started taking all the candy." According to Craig, he was also tested with little plastic toys—he could have a second one if he held out—and he broke into the desk, where he figured there would be additional toys. "I took everything I could," he says. "I cleaned them out. After that, I noticed the teachers encouraged me to not go into the experiment room anymore."

Footage of these experiments, which were conducted over several years, is poignant, as the kids struggle to delay gratification for just a little bit longer. Some cover their eyes with their hands or turn around so that they can't see the tray. Others start kicking the desk, or tug on their pigtails, or stroke the marshmallow as if it were a tiny stuffed animal. One child, a boy with neatly parted hair, looks carefully around the room to make sure that nobody can see him. Then he picks up an Oreo, delicately twists it apart, and licks off the white cream filling before returning the cookie to the tray, a satisfied look on his face.

Most of the children were like Craig. They struggled to resist the treat and held out for an average of less than three minutes. "A few kids ate the marshmallow right away," Walter Mischel, the Stanford professor of psychology in charge of the experiment, remembers. "They didn't even bother ringing the bell. Other kids would stare directly at the marshmallow and then ring the bell thirty seconds later." About thirty percent of the children, however, were like Carolyn. They successfully delayed gratification until the researcher returned, some fifteen minutes later. These kids wrestled with temptation but found a way to resist.

The initial goal of the experiment was to identify the mental processes that allowed some people to delay gratification while others simply surrendered. After publishing a few papers on the Bing studies in the early seventies, Mischel moved on to other areas of personality research. "There are only so many things you can do with kids trying not to eat marshmallows."

But occasionally Mischel would ask his three daughters, all of whom attended the Bing, about their friends from nursery school. "It was really just idle dinnertime conversation," he says. "I'd ask them, 'How's Jane? How's Eric? How are they doing in school?'" Mischel began to notice a link between the children's academic performance as teen-agers and their ability to wait for the second marshmallow. He asked his daughters to assess their friends academically on a scale of zero to five. Comparing these ratings with the original data set, he saw a correlation. "That's when I realized I had to do this seriously," he says. Starting in 1981, Mischel sent out a questionnaire to all the reachable parents, teachers, and academic advisers of the six hundred and fifty-three subjects who had participated in the marshmallow task, who were by then in high school. He asked about every trait he could think of, from their capacity to plan and think ahead to their ability to "cope well with problems" and get along with their peers. He also requested their S.A.T. scores.

Once Mischel began analyzing the results, he noticed that low delayers, the children who rang the bell quickly, seemed more likely to have behavioral problems, both in school and at home. They got lower S.A.T. scores. They struggled in stressful situations, often had trouble paying attention, and found it difficult to maintain friendships. The child who could wait fifteen minutes had an S.A.T. score that was, on average, two hundred and ten points higher than that of the kid who could wait only thirty seconds.

Carolyn Weisz is a textbook example of a high delayer. She attended Stanford as an undergraduate, and got her PhD. in social psychology at Princeton. She's now an associate psychology professor at the University of Puget Sound. Craig, meanwhile, moved to Los Angeles and has spent his career doing "all kinds of things" in the entertainment industry, mostly in production. He's currently helping to write and produce a film. "Sure, I wish I had been a more patient person," Craig says. "Looking back, there are definitely moments when it would have helped me make better career choices and stuff."

Mischel and his colleagues continued to track the subjects into their late thirties—Ozlem Ayduk, an assistant professor of psychology at the University of California at Berkeley, found that low-delaying adults have a significantly higher body-mass index and are more likely to have had problems with drugs—but it was frustrating to have to rely on self-reports. "There's often a gap between what people are willing to tell you and how they behave in the real world," he explains. And so, last year, Mischel, who is now a professor at Columbia, and a team of collaborators began asking the original Bing subjects to travel to Stanford for a few days of experiments in an fMRI machine. Carolyn says she will be participating in the scanning experiments later this summer; Craig completed a survey several years ago, but has yet to be invited to Palo Alto. The scientists are hoping to identify the particular brain regions that allow some people to delay gratification and control their temper. They're also conducting a variety of genetic tests, as they search for the hereditary characteristics that influence the ability to wait for a second marshmallow.

If Mischel and his team succeed, they will have outlined the neural circuitry of self-control. For decades, psychologists have focussed on raw intelligence as the most important variable when it comes to predicting success in life. Mischel argues that intelligence is largely at the mercy of self-control: even the smartest kids still need to do their homework. "What we're really measuring with the marshmallows isn't will power or self-control," Mischel says. "It's much more important than that. This task forces kids to find a way to make the situation work for them. They want the second marshmallow, but how can they get it? We can't control the world, but we can control how we think about it."

Walter Mischel is a slight, elegant man with a shaved head and a face of deep creases. He talks with a Brooklyn bluster and he tends to act out his sentences, so that when he describes the marshmallow task he takes on the body language of an impatient four-year-old. "If you want to know why some kids can wait and others can't, then you've got to think like they think," Mischel says.

Mischel was born in Vienna, in 1930. His father was a modestly successful businessman with a fondness for café society and Esperanto, while his mother spent many of her days lying on the couch with an ice pack on her forehead, trying to soothe her frail nerves. The family considered itself fully assimilated, but after the Nazi annexation of Austria, in 1938, Mischel remembers being taunted in school by the Hitler Youth and watching as his father, hobbled by childhood polio, was forced to limp through the streets in his pajamas. A few weeks after the takeover, while the family was burning evidence of their Jewish ancestry in the fireplace, Walter found a long-forgotten certificate of U.S. citizenship issued to his maternal grandfather decades earlier, thus saving his family.

The family settled in Brooklyn, where Mischel's parents opened up a five-and-dime. Mischel attended New York University, studying poetry under Delmore Schwartz and Allen Tate, and taking studio-art classes with Philip Guston. He also became fascinated by psychoanalysis and new measures of personality, such as the Rorschach test. "At the time, it seemed like a mental X-ray machine," he says. "You could solve a person by showing them a picture." Although he was pressured to join his uncle's umbrella business, he ended up pursuing a PhD. in clinical psychology at Ohio State.

But Mischel noticed that academic theories had limited application, and he was struck by the futility of most personality science. He still flinches at the naïveté of graduate students who based their diagnoses on a battery of meaningless tests. In 1955, Mischel was offered an opportunity to study the "spirit possession" ceremonies of the Orisha faith in Trinidad, and he leapt at the chance. Although his research was supposed to involve the use of Rorschach tests to explore the connections between the unconscious and the behavior of people when possessed, Mischel soon grew interested in a different project. He lived in a part of the island that was evenly split between people of East Indian and of African descent; he noticed that each group defined the other in broad stereotypes. "The East Indians would describe the Africans as impulsive hedonists, who were always living for the moment and never thought about the future," he says. "The Africans, meanwhile, would say that the East Indians didn't know how to live and would stuff money in their mattress and never enjoy themselves."

Mischel took young children from both ethnic groups and offered them a simple choice: they could have a miniature chocolate bar right away or, if they waited a few days, they could get a much bigger chocolate bar. Mischel's results failed to justify the stereotypes—other variables, such as whether or not the children lived with their father, turned out to be much more important—but they did get him interested in the question of delayed gratification. Why did some children wait and not others? What made waiting possible? Unlike the broad traits supposedly assessed by personality tests, self-control struck Mischel as potentially measurable.

In 1958, Mischel became an assistant professor in the Department of Social Relations at Harvard. One of his first tasks was to develop a survey course on "personality assessment," but Mischel quickly concluded that, while prevailing theories held personality traits to be broadly consistent, the available data didn't back up this assumption. Personality, at least as it was then conceived, couldn't be reliably assessed at all. A few years later, he was hired as a consultant on a personality assessment initiated by the Peace Corps. Early Peace Corps volunteers had sparked several embarrassing international incidents—one mailed a postcard on which she expressed disgust at the sanitary habits of her host country—so the Kennedy Administration wanted a screening process to eliminate people unsuited for foreign assignments. Volunteers were tested for standard personality traits, and Mischel compared the results with ratings of how well the volunteers performed in the field. He found no correlation; the time-consuming tests predicted nothing. At this point, Mischel realized that the problem wasn't the tests—it was their premise. Psychologists had spent decades searching for traits that exist independently of circumstance, but what if personality can't be separated from context? "It went against the way we'd been thinking about personality since the four humors and the ancient Greeks," he says.

While Mischel was beginning to dismantle the methods of his field, the Harvard psychology department was in tumult. In 1960, the personality psychologist Timothy Leary helped start the Harvard Psilocybin Project, which consisted mostly of self-experimentation. Mischel remembers graduate students' desks giving way to mattresses, and large packages from Ciba chemicals, in Switzerland, arriving in the mail. Mischel had nothing against hippies, but he wanted modern psychology to be rigorous and empirical. And so, in 1962, Walter Mischel moved to Palo Alto and went to work at Stanford.

There is something deeply contradictory about Walter Mischel—a psychologist who spent decades critiquing the validity of personality tests—inventing the marshmallow task, a simple test with impressive predictive power. Mischel, however, insists there is no contradiction. "I've always believed there are consistencies in a person that can be looked at," he says. "We just have to look in the right way." One of Mischel's classic studies documented the aggressive behavior of children in a variety of situations at a summer camp in New Hampshire. Most psychologists assumed that aggression was a stable trait, but Mischel found that children's responses depended on the details of the interaction. The same child might consistently lash out when teased by a peer, but readily submit to adult punishment. Another might react badly to a warning from a counsellor, but play well with his bunkmates. Aggression was best assessed in terms of what Mischel called "if-then patterns." If a certain child was teased by a peer, then he would be aggressive.

One of Mischel's favorite metaphors for this model of personality, known as interactionism, concerns a car making a screeching noise. How does a mechanic solve the problem? He begins by trying to identify the specific conditions that trigger the noise. Is there a screech when the car is accelerating, or when it's shifting gears, or turning at slow speeds? Unless the mechanic can give the screech a context, he'll never find the broken part. Mischel wanted psychologists to think like mechanics, and look at people's responses under particular conditions. The challenge was devising a test that accurately simulated something relevant to the behavior being predicted. The search for a meaningful test of personality led Mischel to revisit, in 1968, the protocol he'd used on young children in Trinidad nearly a decade earlier. The experiment seemed especially relevant now that he had three young daughters of his own. "Young kids are pure id," Mischel says. "They start off unable to wait for anything—whatever they want they need. But then, as I watched my own kids, I marvelled at how they gradually learned how to delay and how that made so many other things possible."

A few years earlier, in 1966, the Stanford psychology department had established the Bing Nursery School. The classrooms were designed as working laboratories, with large one-way mirrors that allowed researchers to observe the children. In February, Jennifer Winters, the assistant director of the school, showed me around the building. While the Bing is still an active center of research—the children quickly learn to ignore the students scribbling in notebooks—Winters isn't sure that Mischel's marshmallow task could be replicated today. "We recently tried to do a version of it, and the kids were very excited about having food in the game room," she says. "There are so many allergies and peculiar diets today that we don't do many things with food."

Mischel perfected his protocol by testing his daughters at the kitchen table. "When you're investigating will power in a four-year-old, little things make a big difference," he says. "How big should the marshmallows be? What kind of cookies work best?" After several months of patient tinkering, Mischel came up with an experimental design that closely simulated the difficulty of delayed gratification. In the spring of 1968, he conducted the first trials of his experiment at the Bing. "I knew we'd designed it well when a few kids wanted to quit as soon as we explained the conditions to them," he says. "They knew this was going to be very difficult."

At the time, psychologists assumed that children's ability to wait depended on how badly they wanted the marshmallow. But it soon became obvious that every child craved the extra treat. What, then, determined self-control? Mischel's conclusion, based on hundreds of hours of observation, was that the crucial skill was the "strategic allocation of attention." Instead of getting obsessed with the marshmallow—the "hot stimulus"—the patient children distracted themselves by covering their eyes, pretending to play hide-and-seek underneath the desk, or singing songs from "Sesame Street." Their desire wasn't defeated—it was merely forgotten. "If you're thinking about the marshmallow and how delicious it is, then you're going to eat it," Mischel says. "The key is to avoid thinking about it in the first place."

In adults, this skill is often referred to as metacognition, or thinking about thinking, and it's what allows people to outsmart their shortcomings. (When Odysseus had himself tied to the ship's mast, he was using some of the skills of metacognition: knowing he wouldn't be able to resist the Sirens' song, he made it impossible to give in.) Mischel's large data set from various studies allowed him to see that children with a more accurate understanding of the workings of self-control were better able to delay gratification. "What's interesting about four-year-olds is that they're just figuring out the rules of thinking," Mischel says. "The kids who couldn't delay would often have the rules backwards. They would think that the best way to resist the marshmallow is to stare right at it, to keep a close eye on the goal. But that's a terrible idea. If you do that, you're going to ring the bell before I leave the room."

According to Mischel, this view of will power also helps explain why the marshmallow task is such a powerfully predictive test. "If you can deal with hot emotions, then you can study for the S.A.T. instead of watching television," Mischel says. "And you can save more money for retirement. It's not just about marshmallows."

Subsequent work by Mischel and his colleagues found that these differences were observable in subjects as young as nineteen months. Looking at how toddlers responded when briefly separated from their mothers, they found that some immediately burst into tears, or clung to the door, but others were able to overcome their anxiety by distracting themselves, often by playing with toys. When the scientists set the same children the marshmallow task at the age of five, they found that the kids who had cried also struggled to resist the tempting treat.

The early appearance of the ability to delay suggests that it has a genetic origin, an example of personality at its most predetermined. Mischel resists such an easy conclusion. "In general, trying to separate nature and nurture makes about as much sense as trying to separate personality and situation," he says. "The two influences are completely interrelated." For instance, when Mischel gave delay-of-gratification tasks to children from low-income families in the Bronx, he noticed that their ability to delay was below average, at least compared with that of children in Palo Alto. "When you grow up poor, you might not practice delay as much," he says. "And if you don't practice then you'll never figure out how to distract yourself. You won't develop the best delay strategies, and those strategies won't become second nature." In other words, people learn how to use their mind just as they learn how to use a computer: through trial and error.

But Mischel has found a shortcut. When he and his colleagues taught children a simple set of mental tricks—such as pretending that the candy is only a picture, surrounded by an imaginary frame—he dramatically improved their self-control. The kids who hadn't been able to wait sixty seconds could now wait fifteen minutes. "All I've done is given them some tips from their mental user manual," Mischel says. "Once you realize that will power is just a matter of learning how to control your attention and thoughts, you can really begin to increase it."

Marc Berman, a lanky graduate student with an easy grin, speaks about his research with the infectious enthusiasm of a freshman taking his first philosophy class. Berman works in the lab of John Jonides, a psychologist and neuroscientist at the University of Michigan, who is in charge of the brain-scanning experiments on the original Bing subjects. He knows that testing forty-year-olds for self-control isn't a straightforward proposition. "We can't give these people marshmallows," Berman says. "They know they're part of a long-term study that looks at delay of gratification, so if you give them an obvious delay task they'll do their best to resist. You'll get a bunch of people who refuse to touch their marshmallow."

This meant that Jonides and his team had to find a way to measure will power indirectly. Operating on the premise that the ability to delay eating the marshmallow had depended on a child's ability to banish thoughts of it, they decided on a series of tasks that measure the ability of subjects to control the contents of working memory—the relatively limited amount of information we're able to consciously consider at any given moment. According to Jonides, this is how self-control "cashes out" in the real world: as an ability to direct the spotlight of attention so that our decisions aren't determined by the wrong thoughts.

Last summer, the scientists chose fifty-five subjects, equally split between high delayers and low delayers, and sent each one a laptop computer loaded with working-memory experiments. Two of the experiments were of particular interest. The first is a straightforward exercise known as the "suppression task." Subjects are given four random words, two printed in blue and two in red. After reading the words, they're told to forget the blue words and remember the red words. Then the scientists provide a stream of "probe words" and ask the subjects whether the probes are the words they were asked to remember. Though the task doesn't seem to involve delayed gratification, it tests the same basic mechanism. Interestingly, the scientists found that high delayers were significantly better at the suppression task: they were less likely to think that a word they'd been asked to forget was something they should remember.

In the second, known as the Go/No Go task, subjects are flashed a set of faces with various expressions. At first, they are told to press the space bar whenever they see a smile. This takes little effort, since smiling faces automatically trigger what's known as "approach behavior." After a few minutes, however, subjects are told to press the space bar when they see frowning faces. They are now being forced to act against an impulse. Results show that high delayers are more successful at not pressing the button in response to a smiling face.

When I first started talking to the scientists about these tasks last summer, they were clearly worried that they wouldn't find any behavioral differences between high and low delayers. It wasn't until early January that they had enough data to begin their analysis (not surprisingly, it took much longer to get the laptops back from the low delayers), but it soon became obvious that there were provocative differences between the two groups. A graph of the data shows that as the delay time of the four-year-olds decreases, the number of mistakes made by the adults sharply rises.

The big remaining question for the scientists is whether these behavioral differences are detectable in an fMRI machine. Although the scanning has just begun—Jonides and his team are still working out the kinks—the scientists sound confident. "These tasks have been studied so many times that we pretty much know where to look and what we're going to find," Jonides says. He rattles off a short list of relevant brain regions, which his lab has already identified as being responsible for working-memory exercises. For the most part, the regions are in the frontal cortex—the overhang of brain behind the eyes—and include the dorsolateral prefrontal cortex, the anterior prefrontal cortex, the anterior cingulate, and the right and left inferior frontal gyri. While these cortical folds have long been associated with self-control, they're also essential for working memory and directed attention. According to the scientists, that's not an accident. "These are powerful instincts telling us to reach for the marshmallow or press the space bar," Jonides says. "The only way to defeat them is to avoid them, and that means paying attention to something else. We call that will power, but it's got nothing to do with the will."

The behavioral and genetic aspects of the project are overseen by Yuichi Shoda, a professor of psychology at the University of Washington, who was one of Mischel's graduate students. He's been following these "marshmallow subjects" for more than thirty years: he knows everything about them from their academic records and their social graces to their ability to deal with frustration and stress. The prognosis for the genetic research remains uncertain. Although many studies have searched for the underpinnings of personality since the completion of the Human Genome Project, in 2003, many of the relevant genes remain in question. "We're incredibly complicated creatures," Shoda says. "Even the simplest aspects of personality are driven by dozens and dozens of different genes." The scientists have decided to focus on genes in the dopamine pathways, since those neurotransmitters are believed to regulate both motivation and attention. However, even if minor coding differences influence delay ability—and that's a likely possibility—Shoda doesn't expect to discover these differences: the sample size is simply too small.

In recent years, researchers have begun making house visits to many of the original subjects, including Carolyn Weisz, as they try to better understand the familial contexts that shape self-control. "They turned my kitchen into a lab," Carolyn told me. "They set up a little tent where they tested my oldest daughter on the delay task with some cookies. I remember thinking, I really hope she can wait."

While Mischel closely follows the steady accumulation of data from the laptops and the brain scans, he's most excited by what comes next. "I'm not interested in looking at the brain just so we can use a fancy machine," he says. "The real question is what can we do with this fMRI data that we couldn't do before?" Mischel is applying for an N.I.H. grant to investigate various mental illnesses, like obsessive-compulsive disorder and attention-deficit disorder, in terms of the ability to control and direct attention.

Mischel and his team hope to identify crucial neural circuits that cut across a wide variety of ailments. If there is such a circuit, then the same cognitive tricks that increase delay time in a four-year-old might help adults deal with their symptoms. Mischel is particularly excited by the example of the substantial subset of people who failed the marshmallow task as four-year-olds but ended up becoming high-delaying adults. "This is the group I'm most interested in," he says. "They have substantially improved their lives."

Mischel is also preparing a large-scale study involving hundreds of schoolchildren in Philadelphia, Seattle, and New York City to see if self-control skills can be taught. Although he previously showed that children did much better on the marshmallow task after being taught a few simple "mental transformations," such as pretending the marshmallow was a cloud, it remains unclear if these new skills persist over the long term. In other words, do the tricks work only during the experiment or do the children learn to apply them at home, when deciding between homework and television?

Angela Lee Duckworth, an assistant professor of psychology at the University of Pennsylvania, is leading the program. She first grew interested in the subject after working as a high-school math teacher. "For the most part, it was an incredibly frustrating experience," she says. "I gradually became convinced that trying to teach a teen-ager algebra when they don't have self-control is a pretty futile exercise." And so, at the age of thirty-two, Duckworth decided to become a psychologist. One of her main research projects looked at the relationship between self-control and grade-point average. She found that the ability to delay gratification—eighth graders were given a choice between a dollar right away or two dollars the following week—was a far better predictor of academic performance than I.Q. She said that her study shows that "intelligence is really important, but it's still not as important as self-control."

Last year, Duckworth and Mischel were approached by David Levin, the co-founder of KIPP, an organization of sixty-six public charter schools across the country. KIPP schools are known for their long workday—students are in class from 7:25 A.M. to 5 P.M.—and for dramatic improvement of inner-city students' test scores. (More than eighty percent of eighth graders at the KIPP academy in the South Bronx scored at or above grade level in reading and math, which was nearly twice the New York City average.) "The core feature of the KIPP approach is that character matters for success," Levin says. "Educators like to talk about character skills when kids are in kindergarten—we send young kids home with a report card about 'working well with others' or 'not talking out of turn.' But then, just when these skills start to matter, we stop trying to improve them. We just throw up our hands and complain."

Self-control is one of the fundamental "character strengths" emphasized by KIPP—the KIPP academy in Philadelphia, for instance, gives its students a shirt emblazoned with the slogan "Don't Eat the Marshmallow." Levin, however, remained unsure about how well the program was working—"We know how to teach math skills, but it's harder to measure character strengths," he says—so he contacted Duckworth and Mischel, promising them unfettered access to KIPP students. Levin also helped bring together additional schools willing to take part in the experiment, including Riverdale Country School, a private school in the Bronx; the Evergreen School for gifted children, in Shoreline, Washington; and the Mastery Charter Schools, in Philadelphia.

For the past few months, the researchers have been conducting pilot studies in the classroom as they try to figure out the most effective way to introduce complex psychological concepts to young children. Because the study will focus on students between the ages of four and eight, the classroom lessons will rely heavily on peer modelling, such as showing kindergartners a video of a child successfully distracting herself during the marshmallow task. The scientists have some encouraging preliminary results—after just a few sessions, students show significant improvements in the ability to deal with hot emotional states—but they are cautious about predicting the outcome of the long-term study. "When you do these large-scale educational studies, there are ninety-nine uninteresting reasons the study could fail," Duckworth says. "Maybe a teacher doesn't show the video, or maybe there's a field trip on the day of the testing. This is what keeps me up at night."

Mischel's main worry is that, even if his lesson plan proves to be effective, it might still be overwhelmed by variables the scientists can't control, such as the home environment. He knows that it's not enough just to teach kids mental tricks—the real challenge is turning those tricks into habits, and that requires years of diligent practice. "This is where your parents are important," Mischel says. "Have they established rituals that force you to delay on a daily basis? Do they encourage you to wait? And do they make waiting worthwhile?" According to Mischel, even the most mundane routines of childhood—such as not snacking before dinner, or saving up your allowance, or holding out until Christmas morning—are really sly exercises in cognitive training: we're teaching ourselves how to think so that we can outsmart our desires. But Mischel isn't satisfied with such an informal approach. "We should give marshmallows to every kindergartner," he says. "We should say, 'You see this marshmallow? You don't have to eat it. You can wait. Here's how.'"

Children's Capacity to Develop Resiliency

How to Nurture It

DEIRDRE BRESLIN

Today's world, full of change, uncertainty, and the unexpected challenges everyone's ability to cope. What coping skills must we nurture, enrich, and enhance to help children navigate successfully in a complex society? Resiliency must be primary. Not only is it essential for the children we teach, but it is a vital skill for ourselves as we strive to enable every child to become all that he or she is capable of.

By definition *resiliency* means the capability to rebound or recoil or to spring back, the power of recovery. How can a teacher help young children develop this capacity, the ability to bounce back from set-backs every child experiences in one form or another as a fact of everyday life?

Resiliency is a set of protective mechanisms that modify a person's response to risk situations.

Resiliency is not a fixed attribute. Rather it is a set of protective mechanisms that modify a person's response to risk situations. These mechanisms operate at turning points during the individual's life (Rutter 1984; Garmezy 1991). Resiliency is a valuable coping skill for all young children.

The Defeating Label "At Risk"

"Labeling matters, and the younger the person getting the label is, the more it matters" (Rosenthal & Jacobson 1968, 3). Some educators seek to help a child having difficulty by focusing on the child's inappropriate behavior patterns. The learning approaches and solutions emphasized perpetuate a problem perspective, and children are frequently labeled "at risk." In eradicating behaviors, massive doses of correction are administered to the child. As a result, we minimize or ignore strengths and competencies a child possesses that could promote adaptation and wellness.

Researcher Emmy Werner and her colleague Ruth Smith (1985) document that one in three children considered to be at

risk develops into a competent, capable, caring young person by age 18. In their follow-up work (Werner & Smith 1992), they conclude that of the remaining two out of three high-risk adolescents, two-thirds are successful adults by age 32.

The growing body of research about resiliency provides concise information on the ways individuals develop successfully despite adversity and on the lack of predictive power in risk factors (Rutter 1979; Lanni 1989; McLaughlin, Irbey, & Langman 1994; Meier 1995). These facts have profound implications for deciding what approaches to emphasize when helping today's young children develop positive coping skills.

Children's Adaptive Approaches

For two years I systematically interviewed families and young children age five to eight who were identified by the school administration as functioning well in their urban school settings. Each interviewee had three and sometimes more major, ongoing life stressors in their lives: for example, homelessness, foster care, single parent family, alcohol and substance abuse, family problems, abandonment, and death in the family. Despite negative life events and stress, the children and their families seemed to be adapting and surviving. They displayed resilient behavior through their active participation in classroom activities, consistent high attendance, well-developed listening skills, and cooperative child-to-child and teacher-to-child interactions.

No group of families or individual children interviewed showed identical sets of coping behaviors. Although resiliency is an individualized skill, the resiliency of the individuals interviewed revealed some common factors that are important to examine. Four factors of resiliency that I identified are outlined here, with examples of classroom activities to help develop and enrich each aspect.

1. Heightened Sensory Awareness

The kindergarten boy who first alerted me to this quality of resiliency lived in a very poor area in which the streets contained a great deal of garbage and drug users' paraphernalia. As

Helping Children Realize Potential through Their Multiple Intelligences

Intelligences	Recognition and Reinforcement Suggestions
linguistic	Tell stories. Let children dictate their stories to the teacher or an adult volunteer. Transcribers read back each story and give the child his or her own print copy to illustrate. Create poetry orally and in writing. Imagine a character and play-act the role. Play word games and solve puzzles.
spatial	Ask children to describe the physical characteristics they see in a bird, squirrel, cat, dog. Draw visual likenesses of any objects.
logical-mathematical	Use numbers to create calendars. Make itemized, numbered lists, counting anything and everything. Estimate how many of something (pennies, seeds, pebbles, acorns) are in a jar, box, bowl.
musical	Listen to various types of music. Sing songs and clap to the music. Hum, whistle, or use bodily response to the music. Write about what's fun in dancing or playing basketball and other sports. Make up skits or pantomimes in response to literature or music.
bodily-kinesthetic	Dance in all kinds of movement styles. Play pin-the-tail-on-the-donkey. Throw and catch a ball. Try all kinds of sports. Smell flowers and look closely to concentrate on their colors. Name flowers and notice the many differences (reds, pinks, etc.). Take walks to focus on enhancing and heightening sensory awareness.
interpersonal	Act out situations that children encounter in classroom activities.
intrapersonal	Portray emotions such as sadness, regret, and so forth that everyone experiences.
naturalist	Make books identifying animals, birds, plants, and so on. Write stories and poetry about nature.

I walked to his school, I was startled by what I saw and could only focus on the unpleasantness of the journey. On meeting the child, I was so consumed with repugnance from the walk that my first question was, "What is it like coming to school each day?" He looked at me and smiled.

"It's wonderful," he said. "You know, the streets have been 'glassticized,' and all the little pieces of glass that are in the paving material shine and sparkle—it's like finely chopped diamonds. Every day my grandmother walks with me to school, and we look at the street and count the colors. On sunny days there is silver and gold, but on dark days there are purple and dark colors. We count the colors and name them."

With this boy's positive experience in mind, teachers can transform every trip home from school into an opportunity to heighten and enrich sensory awareness no matter where the child lives. The family member or other adult who accompanies the child to and from school can become an integral partner in the experience.

The walk provides a tool for observation as the teacher follows up on it the next day. How many squares did you see on the way home? How many circles? Where were they? Describe the circle. Which vocabulary words can you use in telling about your trip home? What new words can you teach us about your walk? What else do you do/see/feel on the way home from school?

The school setting provides many opportunities to encourage high, positive expectations.

2. High, Positive Expectations

One of the eight-year-old girls interviewed said that she was going to be a female basketball star. "I know I will be a star, because the gym teacher told me how good I am at basketball."

The importance of teacher expectations and feedback has been the focus of much research, starting with the classic study completed by Rosenthal and Jacobson (1968). This study showed that student performance was affected by teachers' expectations of the child. The effect on student performance was called the Pygmalion effect, referring to the growth in motivation that can occur when a teacher believes in and encourages a student. The name Pygmalion comes from the mythological story of a king who creates a female statue and then with the help of the gods brings it to life. The gym teacher's positive expectations and feedback heightened this girl's motivation and helped her to succeed.

Howard Gardner (1983) describes our multiple intelligences and outlines relevant behaviors that accompany each intelligence. Bodily kinesthetic intelligence is one of these, and the eight-year-old's performance at basketball indicates strength in that area. The gym teacher was reinforcing one of the intelligences this child displayed.

Children's self-concepts result partly from the expectations others have for them. Their self-concepts in turn affect the expectations they have for themselves. The school setting provides many opportunities to encourage high, positive expectations.

Gardner (1983) explores intelligence in terms of different "frames of mind." In the chart above, each of the eight intelligences (including Naturalist, which Gardner proposed later [1998]) is accompanied by suggestions that can be modified and enhanced to match the developmental and unique needs of young children.

3. A Clear and Developing Understanding of One's Strengths Relating to Accomplishment

The most powerful example of this concept came from an eight-year-old who said, "Well, you know I'm not so good at ball games, but I'm an awesome reader." This child understood the concept of knowing one's strengths and ably used his personal interactions with both adults and peers to cast success in the light of what he could accomplish. Developing such a clear understanding supports and reinforces children's high, positive expectations.

4. A Heightened, Developing Sense of Humor

All of the children I interviewed seemed to have a well-developed sense of the playful. Humor is not an innate gift, but it can and should be cultivated. It is a frame that can help keep things in perspective. The more children learn about humor, the more they become sensitized to it, and the more humor enters into everyday life (Kozol 2000). Philosopher Reinhold Neibuhr emphasized the importance of humor and the need for using it when trying to make sense out of some of the incongruities of life (Kleinman 2000). Children need this skill more than ever before.

In a second grade classroom I visited, each week the teacher featured an activity that highlighted humor. I joined the children on a humor walk. The teacher asked students to walk silently and listen for any sounds, notice sidewalk cracks, and watch for signs to present to the class in a humorous manner. After the walk the students shared what they saw and heard that was funny for them. One child imitated a bird in a marvelous way. In a few minutes, the entire class was trying to reproduce the sound, laughing and smiling happily.

The walk not only highlighted humor but also developed listening skills, interpersonal communication skills, and having the fun of a shared experience. The children told about another of their humor curriculum stories. For several weeks, children could act out something that happened to them or their family that they found funny. The class voted on the funniest story, and the humor prize of the week went to the winner. This activity enhanced coping skills, built vocabulary, honed presentation skills, and let the children act as critics and judges.

The more children learn about humor, the more they become sensitized to it, and the more humor enters into everyday life.

I believe that as part of a humor curriculum, each teacher and his students should develop together the group's criteria

Building Children's Resiliency

One effort that focuses on resiliency in children age two to six is an initiative of the Devereux Early Childhood Foundation in Villanova, Pennsylvania. The Devereux Early Childhood Initiative is a strength-based implemented in Head Start and other early childhood programs. The program consists of an integrated approach that not only provides a tool for assessing children's protective factors and screening challenging behaviors but also suggests strategies for fostering resiliency.

The Devereux Early Childhood Assessment (DECA), a nationally normed assessment of within-the-child protective factors in children age two to five, is the program's assessment tool. Supportive materials provide home and classroom approaches for supporting and enhancing resilient behaviors. An infant/toddler version of the DECA is under development.

More information is available online: www.devereuxearlychilhood.org.

for success. This is a meaningful way to introduce the importance of standards. In 2005, standards are critical in every facet of life.

Summary

This look at resiliency development through heightened sensory awareness; high, positive expectations; a clear understanding of one's strengths relating to accomplishment; and a developing sense of humor hopefully can encourage you to foster enriching coping behaviors in children. These four facets of resiliency seem critically important for young children.

But don't be trapped into thinking that there are precisely four resilience factors or seven or three. It is not possible to succinctly categorize human resiliency. Educators today need to help children search for the unique strengths that equip them, no matter the circumstances, to fulfill their individual potential.

However, we must avoid the urge to simplify as we strive to facilitate the resilience of children. Today's teacher must understand that development is part of a very complex unstable phenomenon. Garmezy and Rutter (1983), focusing on the study of competency, give insight into the fact that resiliency may not be fully attainable by all. However, Nobel laureate Albert Camus tells us the worth of trying: "In the midst of winter, I finally learned there was in me an invincible summer."

Educators today need to help children search for the unique strengths that equip them, no matter the circumstances, to fulfill their individual potential.

References

Gardner, H. 1983. *Frames of mind: The theory of multiple intelligences.* New York: Basic.

Gardner, H. 1998. Are there additional intelligences? In *Education, information, and transformation,* ed. J. Kane. Englewood, NJ: Prentice Hall.

Garmezy, N. 1991. Relevance and vulnerability to adverse developmental outcomes with poverty. *Behavioral Scientist* 34 (4): 416–30.

Garmezy, N., & M. Rutter. 1983. *Stress, coping and development in children.* New York: McGraw-Hill.

Kleinman, M.L. 2000. *A world of hope, a world of fear: Henry A. Wallace, Reinhold Neibuhr, and American liberalism.* Columbus: Ohio State University.

Kozol, J. 2000. *Ordinary resurrections.* New York: Crown.

Lanni, F. 1989. *The search for structure: A report on American youth today.* New York: Free Press.

McLaughlin, M., M. Irbey, & J. Langman. 1994. *Urban sanctuaries: Neighborhood organizations in the lives and futures of inner-city youth.* San Francisco: Jossey Bass.

Meier, D. 1995. *The power of their ideas: Lessons for America from a small school in Harlem.* Boston: Beacon.

Rosenthal, R., & L. Jacobson. 1968. *Pygmalion in the classroom.* New York: Rinehart & Winston.

Rutter, M. 1979. *Fifteen thousand hours.* Cambridge: Harvard University Press.

Rutter, M. 1984. Resilient children. *Psychology Today* (March): 57–65.

Werner, E.E., & R.S. Smith. 1985. V*ulnerable but invincible: A study of resilient children.* New York: McGraw-Hill.

Werner, E.E., & R.S. Smith. 1992.*Overcoming the odds.* New York: Cornell University Press.

DEIRDRE BRESLIN, PhD, is an urban educator and director of academic programs for Project ReConnect at St. John's University in New York City. Her primary area of research interest is resilient behavior, with a focus on inner-city children.

From *Young Children,* January 2005, pp. 47–48, 50–52. Copyright © 2005 by National Association for the Education of Young Children. Reprinted by permission.

Emotions and the Development of Childhood Depression: Bridging the Gap

Pamela M. Cole, Joan Luby, and Margaret W. Sullivan

The mental health problems of young children are often unrecognized until they become severe and difficult to treat (e.g., Tolan & Dodge, 2005; U.S. Public Health Service, 2000a, 2000b). There is mounting evidence that early childhood behavioral and emotional difficulties are not always transient phases of normal development but can represent risk for or the presence of psychopathology (Briggs-Gowan, Carter, Bosson-Heenan, Guyer, & Horwitz, 2006; Egger & Angold, 2006; Keenan & Wakschlag, 2000). Yet, there is a significant gap in scientific knowledge that needs to be bridged to help us distinguish among these different developmental pathways. To bridge the gap, we need evidence that *integrates* knowledge of the wide range of individual differences in the functioning of typical children with clinical knowledge of the unique features of disordered functioning. Although this is a challenge during periods when children are going through rapid developmental changes, early identification is important for prevention because certain forms of behavioral and neural plasticity may permit intervention before symptoms crystallize into serious disorders (Cicchetti & Cohen, 2006).

We still have much to learn about when, why, and how early childhood problems constitute dysfunctional behavior that warrants formal diagnosis, signal risk for disorder, or reflect transient periods of difficulty that will resolve themselves without professional intervention. Recently, a published prevalence study indicated that approximately 6% to 7% of Danish toddlers qualified for a psychiatric diagnosis of emotional, behavioral, or attentional disorder on the basis of two recognized classification systems (Skovgaard, Houman, Christiansen, & Andreasen, 2007; see Egger & Angold, 2006, for discussion of the systems). Diagnosing such young children stimulates intense debate. What evidence demonstrates that we can distinguish disorder in processes such as executive attention and self-regulation when they are just emerging and rapidly developing (McClellan & Speltz, 2003)? In order to address this gap in knowledge, we need greater integration of developmental theory, knowledge, and methods with the study of individual differences that include significant risk or impairment. In this way, we avoid "pathologizing" individual differences among

typically developing children and yet address the critical need for evidence-based early identification and intervention (Egger & Angold, 2006).

In this article, we illustrate an approach to the study of emotional development that can address the call for research that aids the accurate classification of problems and prediction of pathways to health, risk, and affective disorder (Costello et al., 2002). A comprehensive, comparative analysis of the emotional profiles of typically developing children and children with or at risk for clinical depression will help distinguish normal transitory problems (such as increased irritability as a developmental phase), indicators of risk or emerging psychopathology (such as predisposition to react negatively or difficulty regulating emotion), and symptom constellations that constitute clinical disorder (such as depression). We briefly summarize (a) what is known about early emotional development, (b) trends in research on childhood depression, and (c) new research directions that integrate the study of typical emotional development with clinical evidence of risk for and presence of affective disorders in young children.

Childhood Depression and Emotional Development

A leading developmental perspective views emotions as adaptive psychological processes that function to support goals for survival and well-being (Barrett & Campos, 1987), and yet, emotions are a salient feature of psychopathological functioning (Berenbaum, Raghavan, Le, Vernon, & Gomez, 2003; Cicchetti, Ganiban, & Barnett, 1991; Cole, Michel, & Teti, 1994; Gross & Muñoz, 1995; Keenan, 2000). Considerable evidence links heightened negative emotion, whether viewed as responses to challenging situations or as a stable temperamental characteristic, to the presence of or risk for psychological problems in children (Cole, Zahn-Waxler, Fox, Usher, & Welsh, 1996; Eisenberg et al., 1993; Luby et al., 2006; Zeman, Shipman, & Suveg, 2002). Yet, because heightened negative emotion is associated with several disorders, it does not identify specific pathways. We share the view that all emotions, including negative ones, are adaptive, and we advocate for research that identifies how normally functional processes become dysfunctional. Specifically, we believe that examining a full range of emotions, specific features of emotional processes (not just valence), and the nature and efficacy of strategies children use to regulate emotional reactions and moods will advance our knowledge of the development of psychopathology in early childhood (Cole & Hall, 2008; Luby & Belden, 2006).

Children who are diagnosed with depression exhibit prolonged sad or irritable mood or anhedonia (loss of pleasure and interest) along with concurrent symptoms involving four or more of the following: significant changes in eating and/or sleeping, changes in motor activity (restlessness or lethargy), difficulty concentrating, feelings of worthlessness or guilt, and recurrent thoughts of death. Although researchers once assumed that children under the age of 6 were too psychologically immature to experience clinical depression (Rie, 1966), evidence now indicates that depression often has a chronic and relapsing course of symptoms, underscoring the need to understand early precursors and first onset (Costello et al., 2002). Indeed, young children can suffer a constellation of symptoms that qualifies for a depressive disorder diagnosis (Luby et al., 2002); it is considerably similar to depression in older individuals and is relatively stable, specific, and distinguishable from disruptive disorders (Costello et al., 2002; Keenan & Wakschlag, 2004; Luby, Mrakotsky, Heffelfinger, Brown, & Spitznagel, 2004; Luby et al., 2003; Stalets & Luby, 2006). It is not clear how common depression is in early childhood, but one study estimated it at 2% (Egger & Angold, 2006).

Our view is that childhood depression results from dysfunctional patterns of normally adaptive emotional processes. Biological and environmental influences, and in most cases both, determine whether a pattern of emotional functioning deviates from the norm and further develops into symptoms that result in significant impairment in functioning. For instance, sadness, even intense or enduring, is not inherently maladaptive. Defined as (a) the appreciation that a goal for well-being is lost and (b) behavioral readiness to relinquish effort to attain it (e.g., Barrett & Campos, 1987), sadness supports realistic behavior in the face of unachievable goals. What distinguishes normal sadness from dysphoric mood is not the presence of sadness but such difficulty resolving it that it becomes pervasive and compromises other domains of functioning. It is therefore important to understand the regulation of emotion, or the ability to alter emotional responses (Cicchetti, Ackerman, & Izard, 1995; Cole, Martin, & Dennis, 2004; Thompson, 1994).

A Brief Synopsis of Early Emotional Development

Emotional development is rapid in the first 5 years of life. From the 1st weeks, nascent emotional capacities are evident (e.g., Gormally et al., 2001). A core set of emotions—anger, sadness, enjoyment, fear, interest, and surprise—and rudimentary strategies for regulating emotions, such as self-soothing, are discernible in infant behavior and expression before the end of the 1st year (Izard, 1991; Lewis & Michalson, 1983; Rothbart, Ziaie, & O'Boyle, 1992; Sroufe, 1996). In the 2nd year, the rudiments of guilt, shame, embarrassment, and pride emerge (Barrett, Zahn-Waxler, & Cole, 1993; Kochanska, 1997; Lewis & Sullivan, 2005; Lewis, Sullivan, Weiss, & Stanger, 1989). Around age 2, toddlers begin to understand prototypical expressions of happiness, sadness, and anger, and then other emotions; how they relate to situational contexts; and how they influence behavior (Lewis & Michalson, 1983). Between ages 2 and 5, children develop skill at regulating emotions (Kopp, 1989), such that by first grade, most children regulate emotion well enough to learn, form and maintain friendships, and obey classroom rules (Calkins & Hill, 2007; Denham, 1998; Shonkoff & Phillips, 2000).

This positive portrait is tempered by the fact that these same capacities contribute to the psychological vulnerability of young children. Emotional receptivity and responsiveness make young children vulnerable to environmental stress and conflict. Yet, young children lack the cognitive and social resources that help older persons cope with stress and conflict, including reflexive self-awareness, analytic reasoning, a social network, and personal autonomy. Thus, young children are emotionally sensitive but lack the skill, experience, and self-sufficiency to deal with strong emotions. Early exposure to adverse circumstances can have long-term deleterious effects on children's physiological and behavioral functioning, including debilitating effects on the neural, cardiovascular, and endocrine processes that support emotional functioning (Gunnar & Quevedo, 2007; Pollak, 2005; Porges, 2001), which is why it is critical for children to have external sources of emotion regulation, such as competent, sensitive caregivers.

During this period of rapid emotional development and vulnerability, it should be possible to specify qualities that distinguish the emotional functioning of typically developing children from those with disorder or risk for disorder. For example, typical children's tantrums appear to be composed of two related but distinct components—anger and distress—that are organized into initial quick peaks in anger intensity that decline as whining and comfort seeking appear (Potegal & Davidson, 2003; Potegal, Kosorok, & Davidson, 2003). The tantrums of depressed preschool-aged children, however, are more violent, self-injurious, destructive, and verbally aggressive, and they have a longer recovery time (Belden, Thompson, & Luby, 2008). Collectively, these findings suggest that the emotional dynamics of depressed and nondepressed children's tantrums differ, which may serve as one indicator of a need for early intervention.

Trends in Research on Emotional Functioning in Children with or at Risk for Depression

Research on emotional functioning in children with or at risk for depression has identified important emotional correlates of depressive symptoms but has not yet fully embraced a developmental perspective that would permit studying the thresholds that distinguish normal and atypical emotional functioning.

Approaches that examine a continuum of symptom profiles across ages, whether cross-sectional or longitudinal, are rare (but see Graber, Brooks-Gunn, & Warren, 2006).

Research on depressed children tends to draw from studies of adult depression rather than research on emotional development. Generally, it reveals that depressive symptoms in children and youth are associated with attending to and remembering both positive and negative emotional content differently (Bishop, Dalgleish, & Yule, 2004; Gotlib, Traill, Montoya, Joormann, & Chang, 2005; Joormann, Talbot, & Gotlib, 2007), reduced performance when other information is also presented that is emotional in nature (Jazbec, McClure, Hardin, Pine, & Ernst, 2005; LaDouceur et al., 2005), and less accurate, more inefficient processing of emotional information (LaDouceur et al., 2006; Pérez-Edgar, Fox, Cohn, & Kovacs, 2006; Pine et al., 2004; Reijntjes, Stegge, Terwogt, & Hurkens, 2007; but see Bishop et al., 2004, and Pine et al., 2004, for exceptions). However, much remains unknown about the consistency and specificity of such differences, as the same effects are often found for anxious children (Dalgleish et al., 2003; Hardin, Schroth, Pine, & Ernst, 2007).

Our view, that difficulty appropriately releasing from and resolving negative emotions is at the core of depression, has some empirical support (Forbes, Fox, Cohn, Galles, & Kovacs, 2006; Park, Goodyer, & Teasdale, 2004; Wilkinson & Goodyer, 2006). Childhood depressive symptoms are linked with less frequent use of and less confidence in effective strategies (such as problem solving and positive reappraisal; Garber, Braafladt, & Weiss, 1995; Garnefski, Rieffe, Jellesma, Terwogt, & Kraiij, 2007; Reijntjes et al., 2007). As with adults, neuroimaging evidence suggests that depression involves greater mental processing and/or less ability to draw on positive emotions or approach motivation when negative emotions are evoked (Forbes et al., 2006; Thibodeau, Jorgensen, & Kim, 2006).

Studies on infants or children who are offspring of depressed parents are particularly important as these groups have heightened risk for depression and, at young ages, it is possible to prospectively examine potential precursors because the children do not yet show symptoms (Goodman & Gotlib, 1999). Observational studies of young children at risk for depression indicate that they differ in emotional responsivity from healthy children, but the studies suggest nuances that are often not captured in neurophysiological and cognitive studies of responses to emotional information. For example, 4-month-olds of depressed mothers smile and vocalize less than infants of nondepressed women do during spontaneous interactions with their mothers (Field et al., 2007b; Moore, Cohn, & Campbell, 2001), a pattern that forecasts symptoms at 18 months (Moore et al., 2001). However, compared to infants who are not at risk, 5-month-old offspring of depressed mothers laugh *more* and fuss *less* when (a) maternal behavior is confined to imitating the infant (behavior that agitates infants of nondepressed mothers) or (b) the interaction is with an animated doll (Field et al., 2007a). Similarly, the emotional reactions of school-aged children with major depressive disorder differ in complex ways from those of children with other disorders. Casey (1996) reported that although depressed children expressed less emotion in peer interaction than children

with attention deficit hyperactivity disorder (ADHD), they did not differ from children with oppositional defiant disorder (ODD). They were *slower* to express emotion than both ADHD and ODD children, although they eventually behaved similarly. Their emotion perception inaccuracies were not random (like those of ADHD children) but biased toward attributing negative emotions to other children.

In sum, evidence indicates unique emotional differences in children with or at risk for depression but does not fully distinguish childhood depression from other problems and does not address how emotional patterns uniquely associated with depression evolve from normal, adaptive emotional processes. An integration of developmental approaches with clinically pertinent aspects of emotional functioning may contribute to filling this gap. It may aid delineation of normal variations and normative boundaries, and the unique emotional characteristics that typify risk for and presence of childhood depression risk. To illustrate, we first take a brief look at the emotional problems of a troubled preschool-aged child.

The Emotional Profile of a Troubled Preschooler

Mr. and Mrs. B sought outpatient services for their 4-year-old son's impulsivity and excessive crying. They reported that A.B. was easily provoked, and that when provoked, he was impulsively aggressive. To illustrate the seriousness of the problem, they described an incident in which A.B. became very frustrated because his 2-year-old brother would not relinquish a toy immediately. In his frustration, A.B. poked his brother's eye with a stick.

In addition, A.B.'s parents stated that he was always unhappy, including frequent periods of excessive crying. They found him inconsolable, particularly during these periods, such that he required constant attention and support that disrupted family life. At these times, they tried unsuccessfully to soothe him or redirect his attention to pleasant activities. The excessive crying often followed his misbehavior, and their descriptions of his behavior suggested he felt intense guilt and shame. This pattern of unhappiness, frustration, misbehavior, and excessive crying was so well established and disruptive that his parents established a "cry room" in the home where A.B. often cried unabated for long periods.

A.B.'s emotional difficulties, which impair his interpersonal functioning, are atypical and, if left unchecked, will arguably compromise his ability to master later developmental tasks (Cicchetti et al., 1991; Cole & Hall, 2008). Typically developing 4-year-olds have their share of impulsive, angry, aggressive behavior with siblings (Dunn, 2002; Miller, Volling, & McElvain, 2000) and get angry when their goals are thwarted, but they modulate anger, frustration, and disappointment well enough that their behavior is easily redirected and not disruptive or destructive (Cole, 1986; Cole, Zahn-Waxler, & Smith, 1994; Skuban, Shaw, Gardner, Supplee, & Nichols, 2006). In fact, among typically developing 3- and 4-year-olds, low-intensity anger is followed by *appropriate* effort and problem solving (Dennis et al., 2008). A.B., in contrast, is not just angry; he is persistently, excessively sad and irritable, and his emotional difficulties may be compounded by anxiety, guilt, and/or shame, particularly in response to his own misbehavior. Furthermore, his capacity for interest and pleasure in typically enjoyable activities appears substantially diminished, including being unresponsive to parental soothing. The available data fail to address such atypical emotional functioning.

Future Directions

Our experience suggests research directions that we believe can shed more light on the clinically significant features of emotional dysfunction that is associated with early childhood depression and, in so doing, cast additional light on the nature of typical emotional development, including mechanisms underlying the development of trajectories toward and away from childhood depression.

Negative Emotions: Anger, Anxiety, Guilt, and Shame

A.B.'s aggression follows intense anger, a characteristic that may distinguish the aggression of young children with disruptive disorders from that of typically developing preschoolers (Wakschlag et al., 2007). What seems different for A.B. is his intense distress after acting angrily. We know little about individual differences in children's normal recovery from anger or the emotions that follow anger (Cole & Hall, 2008). A.B.'s intense and sustained postanger distress raises the question of whether he feels inordinate anxiety, shame, or guilt about his actions, reactions that are common in depressed adults (Gratz & Roemer, 2004). Typical youngsters become sad or clingy after intense anger (Potegal & Davidson, 2003), but A.B.'s responses are different. Emotions such as sadness and anxiety that follow anger are one area worthy of study for understanding clinical risk and dysfunction, as Izard (1972) and Tomkins (1963) first noted. For instance, infants who become sad when their goals are blocked have large cortisol responses, whereas those who express the most anger show little cortisol responses, a difference that suggests sadness in this context may reflect more stress (Lewis, Ramsay, & Sullivan, 2006; Lewis, Sullivan, Ramsay, & Alessandri, 1992). Relatively little is known about the experience and regulation of anger in children with major depression. Poorly regulated anger or persistent frustration can devolve into prolonged hopelessness and sadness or increased aggressiveness (Goodwin, 2006).

During the 2nd year, Children reveal sensitivity to standards, which supports the development of guilt, shame, and embarrassment (e.g., Barrett et al., 1993; Kagan, 1981; Lewis et al., 1989). Researchers have not explored the relation of these emotions to early presence of and risk for depression. Typically developing preschoolers show shame after they have been angry (Bennett, Sullivan, & Lewis, 2005); this may become dysfunctional, however, if it maintains a negative focus on the self and interferes with appropriate, instrumental problem-solving and reparative behavior. Depressed preschoolers display high levels of guilt and shame and lower levels of reparative behavior than preschoolers with other clinical disorders and without disorder (Luby, Belden, Sullivan, Hayden, & McCadney, 2008). In A.B.'s case, his intense personal distress after being aggressive does not aid reparation or even appear to constitute empathic concern. Self-focused distress interferes with prosocial behavior, whereas empathic concern motivates it, probably alleviating shame or guilt (Eisenberg et al., 1988, 1990). Thus, a promising future direction for research is to understand individual differences in young children's emotions about their misbehavior, distinguishing among callousness, personal distress, and empathic concern, and how these relate to other emotions. For example, proneness to fear may inhibit empathic concern in early childhood (Young, Fox, & Zahn-Waxler, 1999).

Positive Emotions: Joy, Interest, and Pride

Another atypical feature of A.B.'s emotions is diminished positive emotion. Most upset 4-year-olds are responsive to efforts to redirect them toward pleasurable activities. A.B. does not enjoy, and is not readily diverted to, activities that most 4-year-olds greet with eagerness and delight. Young children who have or are at risk for depression may have difficulty generating positive emotions, such as enjoyment, enthusiasm, pride, and interest (Forbes & Dahl, 2005). Preschoolers who qualify for diagnosis of depression with anhedonia show the most severe depression (Luby et al., 2004), and the trait of low positive emotionality in 3-year-olds is associated with family history of depression (Durbin, Klein, Hayden, Buckley, & Moerk, 2005).

Temporal and Intensive Dynamics of Emotional Responding

Apart from studying the emotions involved, we also need to study atypical temporal and intensive features of emotional responses (Thompson, 1994). The speed, intensity, and duration of different emotions likely distinguish A.B.'s emotional responses from those of typically developing children. Yet, surprisingly few studies do service to Thompson's (1994) call for studying emotion dynamics (but see Luby & Belden, 2006). In part, this neglect may be due to the emphasis on aggregated negative emotions, such that threshold to a palpable emotional response, intensity (peak and average), and duration are highly correlated with total amount. A more detailed, time-sensitive study of *specific* emotions, and among children with risk or problems, will yield information on the clinical utility of studying temporal and intensive emotion dynamics.

Context Appropriateness

Negative emotions, even intense ones, are appropriate in certain circumstances (Saarni, 1999). A.B.'s lack of pleasure in contexts that please most children can be thought of as context-inappropriate emotion. Adults with major depressive disorder report higher levels of sadness than controls while watching films that generally evoke happy emotions (Rottenberg, Gross, & Gotlib, 2005). We know little about the context appropriateness of young children's emotional responses, although toddlers who react fearfully to situations that other children find enjoyable have more symptoms of anxiety (Buss, Kiel, Williams, & Leuty, 2005; Fox, Henderson, Marshall, Nichols, & Ghera, 2005). Diminished positive emotion in response to normally pleasant events then seems a particularly important aspect of context-inappropriate emotion in the study of depression (Forbes & Dahl, 2005).

Emotion Regulation Strategies

Finally, A.B. shows little effective, age-appropriate self-regulation of emotion, such as self-distraction or support seeking. It would be useful to know whether depressed children lack strategies or whether their strategic attempts are ineffective because of the intensity of emotional reactions. As we noted earlier, school-aged children with depression do not think of effective regulatory strategies and also report lacking confidence in those strategies. Multimethod, time-sensitive studies of strategies, their appropriateness, and their effectiveness are important for understanding typical and atypical emotional development.

In sum, A.B.'s emotional profile involves multiple emotions, with problematic temporal and intensive qualities, and clinically pertinent features such as resistance to change and few effective regulatory strategies (Cole & Hall, 2008; Luby & Belden, 2006). To fully develop a scientific basis for understanding emotional differences among typically developing children and those who are developing depression, research should (a) distinguish the emotional profiles of depressed and high-risk children; (b) specify the range of their emotional differences, including expressive and physiological qualities; (c) trace emotional profiles over time, from early risk to later outcomes; (d) examine the conditions that lead one child's symptoms to be transient and another's to develop into serious emotional dysfunction; and (e) integrate multiple levels of analysis, addressing the complex interplay among environmental, neurobehavioral, and cognitive factors. Integrating developmental and clinical science has enormous potential to address the complex and varied pathways to children's mental health and resilience, symptom development, and psychopathology. In doing so, the forward movement of our fields across the gap will be assured.

References

Barrett, K. C., & Campos, J. J. (1987). Perspectives on emotional development II: A functionalist perspective on emotions. In J. D. Osofsky (Ed.), *Handbook of infant development* (pp. 555–578). Oxford, England: Wiley.

Barrett, K. C., Zahn-Waxler, C., & Cole, P. M. (1993). Avoiders vs. amenders: Implications for the investigation of guilt and shame during toddlerhood? *Cognition and Emotion, 7,* 481–505.

Belden, A. C., Thompson, N. R., & Luby, J. L. (2008). Temper tantrums in healthy versus DSM-IV depressed and disruptive preschoolers: Defining tantrum behaviors associated with clinical problems. *Journal of Pediatrics, 152,* 117–122.

Bennett, D. B., Sullivan, M. W., & Lewis, M. (2005). Young children's emotional-behavioral adjustment as a function of maltreatment, shame, and anger. *Child Maltreatment, 10,* 311–324.

Berenbaum, H., Raghavan, C., Le, H., Vernon, L. L., & Gomez, J. J. (2003). A taxonomy of emotional disturbances. *Clinical Psychology: Science and Practice, 10,* 206–226.

Bishop, S. J., Dalgleish, T., & Yule, W. (2004). Memory for emotional stories in high and low depressed children. *Memory, 12,* 214–230.

Briggs-Gowan, M. J., Carter, A. S., Bosson-Heenan, J., Guyer, A. E., & Horwitz, S. M. (2006). Are infant-toddler socio-emotional and behavioral problems transient? *Journal of the American Academy of Child & Adolescent Psychiatry, 45,* 849–858.

Buss, K. A., Kiel, E. J., Williams, N. A., & Leuty, M. (2005, April). *Using context to identify toddlers with dysregulated fear responses.* Paper presented at the Society for Research in Child Development Conference, Atlanta, GA.

Calkins, S. D., & Hill, A. M. (2007). Caregiver influences on emerging emotion regulation: Biological and environmental transactions in early development. In J. J. Gross (Ed.), *Handbook of emotion regulation* (pp. 229–248). New York: Guilford.

Casey, R. J. (1996). Emotional competence in children with externalizing and internalizing disorders. In M. Lewis & M. W. Sullivan (Eds.), *Emotional development in atypical children* (pp. 161–183). Mahwah, NJ: Erlbaum.

Cicchetti, D., Ackerman, B., & Izard, C. E. (1995). Emotions and emotion regulation in developmental psychopathology. *Development and Psychopathology, 7,* 1–10.

Cicchetti, D., & Cohen, D. (2006). *Developmental psychopathology: Vol. 1. Theory and method.* New York: Wiley.

Cicchetti, D., Ganiban, J., & Barnett, D. (1991). Contributions from the study of high-risk populations to understanding the development of emotion regulation. In J. Garber & K. A. Dodge (Eds.), *The development of emotion regulation and dysregulation* (pp. 15–48). New York: Cambridge University Press.

Cole, P. M. (1986). Children's spontaneous control of facial expression. *Child Development, 57,* 1309–1321.

Cole, P. M., & Hall, S. E. (2008). Emotion dysregulation as a risk factor for psychopathology. In T. P. Beauchaine & S. P. Hinshaw (Eds.), *Child and adolescent psychopathology* (pp. 265–298). New York: Wiley.

Cole, P. M., Martin, S. E., & Dennis, T. D. (2004). Emotion regulation as a scientific construct: Methodological challenges and directions for child development research. *Child Development, 75,* 317–333.

Cole, P. M., Michel, M., & Teti, L. O. (1994). The development of emotion regulation and dysregulation: A clinical perspective. *Monographs of the Society for Research in Child Development, 59*(2–3, Serial No. 240).

Cole, P. M., Zahn-Waxler, C., Fox, N. A., Usher, B. A., & Welsh, J. D. (1996). Individual differences in emotion regulation and behavior problems in preschool children. *Journal of Abnormal Psychology, 105,* 518–529.

Cole, P. M., Zahn-Waxler, C., & Smith, K. D. (1994). Expressive control during a disappointment: Variations related to preschoolers' behavior problems. *Developmental Psychology, 30,* 835–846.

Costello, E. J., Pine, D. S., Hammen, C., March, J. S., Plotsky, P. M., Weissman, M. M., et al. (2002). Development and natural history of mood disorders. *Biological Psychiatry, 52,* 529–542.

Dalgleish, T., Taghavi, R., Neshat-Doost, H., Moradi, A., Canterbury, R., & Yule, W. (2003). Patterns of processing bias for emotional information across clinical disorders: A comparison of attention, memory, and prospective cognition in children and adolescents with depression, generalized anxiety, and posttraumatic stress disorder. *Journal of Clinical Child and Adolescent Psychology, 32,* 10–21.

Denham, S. E. (1998). *Emotional development in young children.* New York: Guilford.

Dennis, T. A., Wiggins, C. N., Cole, P. M., Myftaraj, L., Cushing, A., Cohen, L. C., et al. (2008). *Functional relations between preschool age children's emotions and actions in challenging situations.* Manuscript submitted for publication.

Dunn, J. (2002). Sibling relationships. In P. K. Smith & C. H. Hart (Eds.), *Blackwell handbook of childhood social development* (pp. 223–237). Malden, MA: Blackwell.

Durbin, C. E., Klein, D. N., Hayden, E. P., Buckley, M. E., & Moerk, K. C. (2005). Temperamental emotionality in preschoolers and parental mood disorders. *Journal of Abnormal Psychology, 114,* 28–37.

Egger, H. L., & Angold, A. (2006). Common emotional and behavioral disorders in preschool children: Presentation, nosology, and epidemiology. *Journal of Child Psychology and Psychiatry, 47,* 313–337.

Eisenberg, N., Cumberland, A., Spinrad, T. L., Fabes, R. A., Shepard, S. A., Reiser, M., et al. (1993). The relations of regulation and emotionality to children's externalizing and internalizing problem behavior. *Child Development, 72,* 1112–1134.

Eisenberg, N., Fabes, R. A., Bustamante, D., Mathy, R., Miller, P. A., & Lindholm, E. (1988). Differentiation of vicariously induced emotional reactions in children. *Developmental Psychology, 24,* 237–246.

Eisenberg, N., Fabes, R. A., Miller, P. A., Shell, R., Shea R., May-Plumlee, T., et al. (1990). Preschoolers' vicarious responding and their situational and dispositional prosocial behavior. *Merrill-Palmer Quarterly, 36,* 507–529.

Field, T., Hernandez-Rief, M., Diego, M., Feijo, L., Vera, Y., Gil, K., et al. (2007a). Responses to animate and inanimate faces by infants of depressed mothers. *Early Childhood Development and Care, 177,* 533–539.

Field, T., Hernandez-Rief, M., Diego, M., Feijo, L., Vera, Y., Gil, K., et al. (2007b). Still-face and separation effects on depressed mother-infant interactions. *Infant Mental Health Journal, 28,* 314–323.

Forbes, E. E., & Dahl, R. E. (2005) Neural systems of positive affect: Relevance to understanding child and adolescent depression? *Development and Psychopathology, 17,* 827–850.

Forbes, E. E., Fox, N. A., Cohn, J. F., Galles, S. F., & Kovacs, M. (2006). Children's affect regulation during a disappointment: Psychophysiological responses and relation to parental history of depression. *Biological Psychiatry, 71,* 264–277.

Fox, N. A., Henderson, H. A., Marshall, P. J., Nichols, K. E., & Ghera, M. M. (2005). Behavioral inhibition: Linking biology and behavior within a developmental Framework. *Annual Review of Psychology, 56,* 235–262.

Garber, J., Braafladt, N., & Weiss, B. (1995). Affect regulation in depressed and nondepressed children and young adolescents. *Development and Psychopathology, 7,* 93–115.

Garnefski, N., Rieffe, C., Jellesma, F., Terwogt, M. M., & Kraiij, V. (2007). Cognitive emotion regulation strategies and emotional problems in 9-11-year-old children: The development of an instrument. *European Child and Adolescent Psychiatry, 16,* 1–9.

Goodman, S. H., & Gotlib, I. H. (1999). Risk for psychopathology in children of depressed mothers: A developmental model for understanding mechanisms of transmission. *Psychological Review, 106,* 458–490.

Goodwin, R. D. (2006). Association between coping with anger and feelings of depression among youth. *American Journal of Public Health, 96,* 664–669.

Gormally, S., Barr, R. G., Wertheim, L., Alkawaf, R., Calinoiu, N., & Young, S. N. (2001). Contact and nutrient caregiving effects on newborn pain responses. *Developmental Medicine and Child Neurology, 43,* 28–38.

Gotlib, I. H., Traill, S. K., Montoya, R. L., Joormann, J., & Chang, K. (2005). Attention and memory biases in offspring of parents with bipolar disorder: Implications from a pilot study. *Journal of Child Psychology and Psychiatry, 46,* 84–93.

Graber, J. A., Brooks-Gunn, J., & Warren, M. P. (2006). Pubertal effects on adjustment in girls: Moving from demonstrating effects to identifying pathways. *Journal of Youth and Adolescence, 35,* 413–423.

Gratz, K. L., & Roemer, L. (2004). Multidimensional assessment of emotion regulation and dysregulation: Development, factor structure, and initial validation of the difficulties in emotion regulation scale. *Journal of Psychopathology and Behavioral Assessment, 26,* 41–54.

Gross, J. J., & Muñoz, R. F. (1995). Emotion regulation and mental health. *Clinical Psychology: Science and Practice, 2,* 151–164.

Gunnar, M. R., & Quevedo, K. (2007). The neurobiology of stress and development. *Annual Review of Psychology, 58,* 145–173.

Hardin, M. G., Schroth, E., Pine, D. S., & Ernst, M. (2007). Incentive-related modulation of cognitive control in healthy, anxious, and depressed adolescents: Development and psychopathology related differences. *Journal of Child Psychology and Psychiatry, 48,* 446–454.

Izard, C. E. (1972). *Patterns of emotion in anxiety and depression.* New York: Academic Press.

Izard, C. E. (1991). *The psychology of emotions.* New York; Plenum.

Jazbec, S., McClure, E., Hardin, M., Pine, D. S., & Ernst, M. (2005). Cognitive control under contingencies in anxious and depressed adolescents: An antisaccade task. *Biological Psychiatry, 58,* 632–639.

Joormann, J., Talbot, L., & Gotlib, I. H. (2007). Mood regulation in depression: Differential effects of distraction and recall of happy and sad memories. *Journal of Abnormal Psychology, 116,* 484–490.

Kagan, J. (1981). *The second year: The emergence of self-awareness.* Cambridge, MA: Harvard University Press.

Keenan, K. (2000). Emotion dysregulation as a risk factor for child psychopathology. *Clinical Psychology: Science and Practice, 7,* 418–434.

Keenan, K., & Wakschlag, L. S. (2000). More than the terrible twos: The nature and severity of behavior problems in clinic-referred preschoolers. *Journal of Abnormal Child Psychology, 28,* 33–46.

Keenan, K., & Wakschlag, L. S. (2004). Are oppositional defiant and conduct disorder symptoms normative behaviors in preschoolers? A comparison of referred and non-referred children. *American Journal of Psychiatry, 161,* 356–358.

Kochanska, G. (1997). Multiple pathways to conscience for children with different temperaments: From toddlerhood to age 5. *Developmental Psychology, 33,* 228–240.

Kopp, C. B. (1989). The regulation of distress and negative emotions: A developmental view. *Developmental Psychology, 25,* 343–354.

LaDouceur, C. D., Dahl, R. E., Williamson, D. E., Birmaher, B., Axelson, D. A., Ryan, N. D., et al. (2006). Processing emotional facial expressions influences performance on a Go/No Go task in pediatric anxiety and depression. *Journal of Child Psychology and Psychiatry, 47,* 1107–1115.

LaDouceur, C. D., Dahl, R. E., Williamson, D. E., Birmaher, B., Ryan, N. D., & Casey, B. J. (2005). Altered emotional processing in pediatric anxiety, depression, and comorbid anxiety-depression. *Journal of Abnormal Child Psychology, 33,* 165–177.

Lewis, M., & Michalson, L. A. (1983). *Children's emotions and moods: Developmental theory and measurement.* New York: Plenum.

Lewis, M., Ramsay, D., & Sullivan, M. W. (2006). The relation of ANS and HPS activation to infant anger and sadness response to goal blockage. *Developmental Psychobiology, 48,* 397–405.

Lewis, M., & Sullivan, M. W. (2005). The development of self-conscious and evaluative emotions in early childhood. In A. Elliott and C. Dweck (Eds.), *Handbook of motivation* (pp. 185–201). New York: Guilford.

Lewis, M., Sullivan, M. W., Weiss, M., & Stanger, C. (1989). Self-cognition and the development of self-conscious emotions. *Child Development, 60,* 146–156.

Luby J. L., & Belden, A. (2006). Mood disorders: Phenomenology and a developmental emotion reactivity model. In J. L. Luby (Ed.), *Handbook of preschool mental health: Development, disorders and treatment* (pp. 200–230). New York: Guilford.

Luby, J. L., Belden, A., Sullivan, J., Hayden, R., & McCadney, A. (2008). *Guilt in preschool depression: Evidence for unique patterns in emotional development in early childhood psychopathology.* Manuscript submitted for publication.

Luby, J. L., Heffelfinger, A., Mrakotsky, C., Brown, K., Hessler, M., Wallis, J., et al. (2003). The clinical picture of depression in preschool children. *Journal of the American Academy of Child and Adolescent Psychiatry, 42,* 340–348.

Luby, J. L., Heffelfinger, A., Mrakotsky, C., Hessler, M. J., Brown, K. M., & Hildebrand, T. (2002). Preschool major depressive disorder: Preliminary validation for developmentally modified DSM-IV criteria. *Journal of the American Academy of Child Adolescent Psychiatry, 41,* 928–937.

Luby J. L., Mrakotsky, C. M., Heffelfinger, A., Brown, K., & Spitznagel, E. (2004). Characteristics of depressed preschoolers with and without anhedonia: Evidence for a melancholic depressive sub-type in young children. *American Journal of Psychiatry, 161,* 1998–2004.

Luby, J. L., Sullivan, J., Belden, A., Stalets, M., Blankenship, S., & Spitznagel, E. (2006). An observational analysis of behavior in depressed preschoolers: Further validation of early-onset depression. *Journal of the American Academy of Child and Adolescent Psychiatry, 45,* 203–212.

McClellan, J., & Speltz, M. (2003). Psychiatric diagnosis in preschool children. *Journal of the American Academy of Child and Adolescent Psychiatry, 42,* 127–128.

Miller, A. L., Volling, B. L., & McElvain, N. L. (2000). Sibling jealousy in triadic context with mothers and fathers. *Social Development, 9,* 433–457.

Moore, G. A., Cohn, J. F., & Campbell, S. B. (2001). Infant affective responses to mother's still face at 6 months differentially predict externalizing and internalizing behaviors at 18 months. *Developmental Psychology, 37,* 706–714.

Park, R. J., Goodyer, I. M., & Teasdale, J. D. (2004). Effects of induced rumination and distraction on mood and overgeneral autobiographical memory in adolescent major depressive

disorder and controls. *Journal of Child Psychology and Psychiatry, 45,* 996–1006.

Pérez-Edgar, K., Fox, N. A., Cohn, J. F., & Kovacs, M. (2006). Behavioral and electrophysiological markers of selective attention in children of parents with a history of depression. *Biological Psychiatry, 60,* 1131–1138.

Pine, D. S., Lissek, S., Klein, R. G., Mannuzza, S., Mouton, J. L., III, Guardino, M., et al. (2004). Face-memory and emotion: Associations with major depression in children and adolescents. *Journal of Child Psychology and Psychiatry, 45,* 1199–1208.

Pollak, S. D. (2005). Early adversity and mechanisms of plasticity: Integrating affective neuroscience with developmental approaches to psychopathology. *Development and Psychopathology, 17,* 735–752.

Porges, S. W. (2001). The polyvagal theory: Phylogenetic substrates of a social nervous system. *International Journal of Psychophysiology, 42,* 123–126.

Potegal, M., & Davidson, R. J. (2003). Temper tantrums in young children: 2. Behavioral composition. *Journal of Developmental & Behavioral Pediatrics, 24,* 140–147.

Potegal, M., Kosorok, M., & Davidson, R. J. (2003). Tantrum duration and temporal organization. *Journal of Developmental & Behavioral Pediatrics, 24,* 148–154.

Reijntjes, A., Stegge, H. Terwogt, M. M., & Hurkens, E. (2007). Children's depressive symptoms and their regulation of negative affect in response to vignette depicted emotion-eliciting events. *International Journal of Behavioral Development, 31,* 49–58.

Rie, H. E. (1966). Depression in Childhood: A survey of some pertinent contributions. *Journal of the American Academy of Child and Adolescent Psychiatry, 5,* 653–685.

Rothbart, M. K., Ziaie, H., & O'Boyle, C. G. (1992). Self-regulation and emotion in infancy. In N. Eisenberg & R. A. Fabes (Eds.), *Emotion and its regulation in early development* (pp. 7–23). San Francisco: Jossey-Bass.

Rottenberg, J., Gross, J. J., & Gotlib, I. H. (2005). Emotion context insensitivity in major depressive disorder. *Journal of Abnormal Psychology, 114,* 627–639.

Saarni, C. (1999). *The development of emotional competence.* New York: Guilford.

Shonkoff, J. P., & Phillips, D. A. (2000). *From neurons to neighborhoods: The science of early child development.* Washington, DC: National Academy Press.

Skovgaard, A. M., Houman, T., Christiansen, E., & Andreasen, A. H. (2007). The reliability of the ICD-10 and the DC 0-3 in an epidemiological sample of children 1½ years of age. *Infant Mental Health Journal, 26,* 470–480.

Skuban, E. M., Shaw, D. S., Gardner, F., Supplee, L. H., & Nichols, S. R. (2006). The correlates of dyadic synchrony in high-risk, low-income toddler boys. *Infant Behavior & Development, 29,* 423–434.

Sroufe, L. A. (1996). *Emotional development: The organization of emotional life in the early years.* New York: Cambridge University Press.

Stalets, M. M., & Luby, J. L. (2006). Preschool depression. *Psychiatric Clinics of North America, 15,* 899–917.

Thibodeau, R., Jorgensen, R. S., & Kim, S. (2006). Depression, anxiety, and resting frontal EEG asymmetry: A meta-analytic review. *Journal of Abnormal Psychology, 115,* 715–729.

Thompson, R. A. (1994). Emotion regulation: In theme in search of definition. *Monographs of the Society for Research in Child Development, 59*(2–3, Serial No. 240).

Tolan, P. H., & Dodge, K. A. (2005). Children's mental health as a primary care and concern: A system for comprehensive support and services. *American Psychologist, 60,* 601–614.

Tomkins, S. S. (1963). *Affect, imager, and consciousness: Vol. 2. The negative affects.* New York: Springer.

U.S. Public Health Service. (2000a). *Infant mental health initiative agenda.* Washington, DC: Administration for Children, Youth, and Families. Retrieved November 15, 2007, from www.acf.hhs.gov/programs/opre/ehs/mental_health/mental_hth_overview.html

U.S. Public Health Service. (2000b). *Report of the Surgeon General's conference on children's mental health: A national agenda.* Washington, DC: Government Printing Office. Retrieved November 15, 2007, from www.surgeongeneral.gov/topics/cmh/childreport.htm

Wakschlag, L. S., Briggs-Gown, M. J., Carter, A. S., Hill, C., Danis, B., Keenan, K., et al. (2007). A developmental framework for distinguishing disruptive behavior from normative behavior in preschool children. *Journal of Child Psychology and Psychiatry, 48,* 976–987.

Wilkinson, P. O., & Goodyer, I. H. (2006). Attention difficulties and mood-related ruminative response style in adolescents with unipolar depression. *Journal of Child and Adolescent Psychiatry, 47,* 1284–1291.

Young, S. K, Fox, N. A., & Zahn-Waxler, C. (1999). The relations between temperament and empathy in 2-year-olds. *Developmental Psychology, 35,* 1189–1197.

Zeman, J., Shipman, K., & Suveg, C. (2002). Anger and sadness regulation: Predictions to internalizing and externalizing symptoms in children. *Journal of Clinical Child & Adolescent Psychology, 31,* 393–398.

This article began as a stimulating discussion among the authors at the National Institute of Mental Health Workshop, *Developmental and Translational Models of Emotion Regulation and Dysregulation: Links to Childhood Affective Disorders,* held April 3–4, 2006, in Bethesda, MD. The order of authorship is alphabetic. Support for this work includes National Institutes of Health awards to each of the authors: P. M.C. (MH61388), J.L. (MH64796), and M.W.S. (MH61778).

Correspondence concerning this article should be addressed to **Pamela M. Cole,** Department of Psychology, 309 Moore Building, The Pennsylvania State University, University Park, PA 16802; e-mail: pcole@la.psu.edu.

Children's Social and Moral Reasoning about Exclusion

Developmental research on social and moral reasoning about exclusion has utilized a social-domain theory, in contrast to a global stage theory, to investigate children's evaluations of gender- and race-based peer exclusion. The social-domain model postulates that moral, social-conventional, and personal reasoning coexist in children's evaluations of inclusion and exclusion, and that the priority given to these forms of judgments varies by the age of the child, the context, and the target of exclusion. Findings from developmental intergroup research studies disconfirm a general-stage-model approach to morality in the child, and provide empirical data on the developmental origins and emergence of intergroup attitudes regarding prejudice, bias, and exclusion.

MELANIE KILLEN

How early do individuals become capable of moral reasoning? What is the evidence for morality in the child? Over the past two decades, research on children's moral judgment has changed dramatically, providing new theories and methods for analysis. In brief, the change has been away from a global stage model toward domain-specific models of development. According to Kohlberg's foundational stage model of moral development (Kohlberg, 1984), which followed Piaget's research on moral judgment (Piaget, 1932), children justify acts as right or wrong first on the basis of consequences to the self (preconventional), then in terms of group norms (conventional), and finally in terms of a justice perspective in which individual principles of how to treat one another are understood (postconventional). This approach involved assessing an individual's general scheme (organizing principle) for evaluating social problems and dilemmas across a range of contexts.

By the mid-1980s, however, studies of contextual variation in judgments provided extensive evidence contesting broad stages (Smetana, 2006; Turiel, 1998). For example, young children's evaluations of transgressions and social events reflect considerations of the self, the group, and justice; these considerations do not emerge hierarchically (respectively) but simultaneously in development, each with its own separate developmental trajectory (e.g., self-knowledge, group knowledge, and moral knowledge). Thus, multiple forms of reasoning are applied to the evaluations of social dilemmas and interactions. Social judgments do not reflect one broad template or stage, such as Kohlberg's preconventional stage to characterize childhood morality. Instead, children use different forms of reasoning, moral, conventional, and psychological, simultaneously when evaluating transgressions and social events.

One area of recent empirical inquiry pertains to social and moral evaluations of decisions to exclude others, particularly on the basis of group membership (such as gender, race, or ethnicity), referred to as *intergroup exclusion*. What makes this form of exclusion a particularly compelling topic for investigation from a moral viewpoint is that it reflects, on the one hand, prejudice, discrimination, stereotyping, and bias about groups, and, on the other hand, judgments about fairness, equality, and rights (Killen, Lee-Kim, McGlothlin, & Stangor, 2002). Conceptually, these judgments are diametrically opposed; prejudice violates moral principles of fairness, discrimination violates equality, and stereotyping restricts individual rights. Do both forms of reasoning exist within the child? What do children do when confronted with an exclusion decision that involves moral considerations of fairness and equal treatment, on the one hand, and stereotypic and social-conventional expectations, on the other?

A social-domain model proposes that morality includes fairness, justice, rights, and others' welfare (e.g., when a victim is involved; "It wouldn't be fair to exclude him from the game"); social-conventional concerns involve conventions, etiquette, and customs that promote effective group functioning (e.g., when disorder in the group occurs; "If you let someone new in the group they won't know how it works or what it's about and it will be disruptive"); and psychological issues pertain to autonomy, individual prerogatives, and identity (e.g., acts that are not regulated but affect only the self; "It's her decision who she wants to be friends with"). Social-domain-theory approaches to moral reasoning, along with social-psychological theories about intergroup attitudes, provide a new approach to understanding social exclusion.

Social exclusion is a pervasive aspect of social life, ranging from everyday events (e.g., exclusion from birthday parties, sports teams, social organizations) to large-scale social tragedies (e.g., exclusion based on religion and ethnicity resulting in genocide). These forms of interindividual and intergroup exclusion create conflict, tension, and, in extreme cases, chronic suffering. In the child's world, exclusion has been studied most often in the context of interindividual, rather than intergroup, conflict. Research on peer rejection and victimization, for example, has focused on individual differences and the social deficits that contribute to being a bully (lack of social competence) or a victim (wariness, shyness, fearfulness; Rubin, Bukowski, & Parker, 1998). The findings indicate that the long-term consequences for children and adults who experience pervasive exclusion are negative, resulting in depression, anxiety, and loneliness.

Developmental Approaches

Recently, developmental researchers have investigated children's evaluations of intergroup exclusion (e.g., "You're an X and we don't want Xs in our group"). Decisions to exclude others involve a range of reasons, from group norms and stereotypic expectations to moral assessments about the fairness of exclusion. Much of what is known about group norms has been documented by social psychologists, who have conducted extensive studies on intergroup relationships. The findings indicate that social categorization frequently leads to intergroup bias and that explicit and implicit attitudes about others based on group membership contribute to prejudicial and discriminatory attitudes and behavior (Dovidio, Glick, & Rudman, 2005). Few researchers, however, have examined the developmental trajectory of exclusion from a moral-reasoning perspective.

Social-domain theory has provided a taxonomy for examining the forms of reasoning—moral, social-conventional, and psychological—that are brought to bear on intergroup exclusion decisions. One way that a social-domain model differs from the traditional stage model of moral reasoning, as formulated by Kohlberg in the late 1960s, is that the former provides a theory and a methodology for examining how individuals use different forms of reasons when evaluating everyday phenomena.

Social Reasoning about Exclusion

One of the goals of social-domain research is to identify the conditions under which children give priority to different forms of reasons when evaluating social decisions, events, and interactions. What are the major empirical findings on intergroup exclusion decisions by children? Most centrally, children do not use one scheme ("stage") to evaluate all morally relevant intergroup problems and scenarios; moreover, although some types of decisions are age related, others are not. In a study with children in the 1st, 4th, and 7th grades, the vast majority of students (95%) judged it wrong to exclude a peer from a group solely because of gender or race (e.g., a ballet club excludes a boy because he's a boy; a baseball club excludes a girl because she's a girl), and based their judgment on moral reasons, such as that such exclusion would be unfair and discriminatory (Killen & Stangor, 2001); there were no age-related differences, contrary to what a stage-model approach would predict.

Introducing complexity, however, revealed variation in judgments and justifications. As shown in Figure 1, in an equal-qualifications condition ("What if there was only room for one more to join the club, and a girl and a boy both were equally qualified, who should the group pick?"), most children used moral reasons ("You should pick the person who doesn't usually get a chance

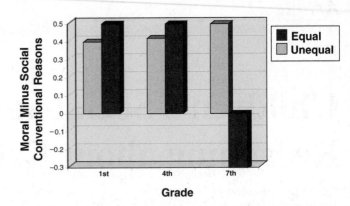

Figure 1 Proportion of moral minus social-conventional reasons given by 1st, 4th, and 7th graders for peer-exclusion judgments based on gender or race. In one condition (equal), participants stated which of two children should be excluded from an after-school club with only one available opening when a stereotypical and nonstereotypical applicant both were equally qualified. In the other (unequal) condition, participants stated which child should be excluded if the child who fit the stereotype for that activity was also more qualified. After-school clubs were baseball/ballet and basketball/math, reflecting gender- and race-associated stereotypes, respectively. Reprinted from Killen & Stangor (2001).

to be in the club because they're both equally good at it"); but in an unequal-qualification condition ("What if X was more qualified, who should the group pick?"), age-related increases in the use of social-conventional reasons ("The group won't work well if you pick the person who is not very good at it") were found. Young adolescents weighed individual merits and considered the functioning of the club or team. Qualifications (e.g., good at ballet or baseball) were considered to be more salient considerations than preserving the "equal opportunity" dimensions (e.g., picking a girl for baseball who has not had a chance to play).

In fact, how children interpret their group's ingroup and outgroup norms (conventions) appears to be related to prejudice and bias (moral transgressions; Abrams, Rutland, Cameron, & Ferrell, in press). Abrams et al. (in press) showed that children's view of whether exclusion is legitimate or wrong was contingent on whether they viewed an individual as supporting or rejecting an ingroup-identity norm. In other related developmental intergroup research, children's lay theories (conventional knowledge) about what it means to work in a group, and whether effort or intrinsic ability is what counts, have been shown to be significantly related to whether they view the denial of allocation of resources as fair or unfair (moral decision making); focusing on intrinsic ability in contrast to effort results in condoning prejudicial treatment (Levy, Chiu, & Hong, 2006). Moreover, adolescents' perceptions of the social status of membership in peer cliques (conventional knowledge) determine whether they view exclusion (e.g., excluding a "goth" from the cheerleading squad) as fair or legitimate (Horn, 2003). These findings demonstrate the nuanced ways in which children make judgments about groups and how group knowledge and group norms bear directly on moral judgments about exclusion and inclusion.

Research on intergroup contact in childhood provides information regarding how social experience influences the mani-

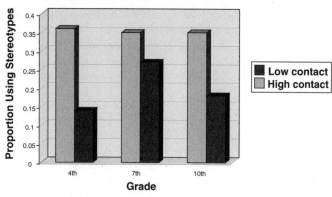

Figure 2 Proportion of European American students who explicitly used stereotypes to explain what it is about interracial interactions that makes their peers uncomfortable, as a function of positive intergroup contact. Positive intergroup contact included cross-race friendship in classrooms, schools, and neighborhoods (based on data reported in Killen et al., 2006).

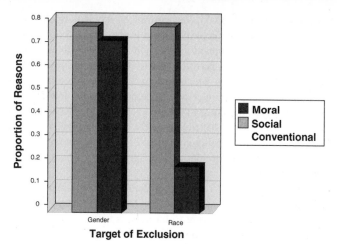

Figure 3 Proportion of moral and social-conventional reasons for gender and racial targets of exclusion in peer-group contexts. Peer-group contexts referred to after-school music clubs that excluded a target child from joining the club due to his or her gender or race. Reasons were moral (unfairness) or social-conventional (group functioning; based on data from Killen, Lee-Kim, McGlothlin, & Stangor, 2002).

festation of children's stereotypes and conventional reasoning to justify exclusion. Intergroup-contact theory states that under certain conditions, contact with members of outgroups decreases prejudice (Pettigrew & Tropp, 2005). In a developmental study with participants enrolled in 13 public schools ($N = 685$) of varying ethnic diversity (see Figure 2), European American students enrolled in heterogeneous schools were more likely to use explicit stereotypes to explain why interracial interactions make their peers uncomfortable, and were less likely to use moral reasons to evaluate peer exclusion, than were European Americans enrolled in homogeneous schools (Killen, Richardson, Kelly, Crystal, & Ruck, 2006). Children's positive experiences with students who are different from themselves, under certain conditions, facilitate moral reasoning about intergroup exclusion and suppress stereotypic expectations as a reason for an exclusion decision.

These findings support a domain-model view of social and moral judgment and challenge stage theory, which proposes that children are limited in their ability to make moral judgments by a general-processing scheme for assimilating information (their "stage"). From a stage view, one would expect children to use conventional or stereotypic (group-expectations) reasons, and expect older children to use moral reasons. Instead, researchers now find that children's reasoning varies by the context and a balance of priorities.

Context has many variables, and determining it involves investigating the role of the target of exclusion as well as participant variables (age, gender, race/ethnicity) on exclusion decisions. Regarding the target of exclusion, a series of findings reveals that gender exclusion is viewed as more legitimate than exclusion based on ethnicity, with more social-conventional reasons and stereotypic expectations used to support the former than the latter (Killen et al., 2002). As shown in Figure 3, children used fewer moral reasons to evaluate exclusion in a peer-group music context with a gender target ("What if the boys' music club will not let a girl join?") than with a race target ("What if the white students in a music club will not let a black student join?"). A significant proportion of students used social-conventional reasons, such as: "A girl/black student likes different music, so she/he won't fit in with the group." Not surprisingly, though, European American females, and minority participants (both males and females),

were more likely to reject these forms of exclusion and to use moral reasons than were European American males. This inclusive orientation may be due to the perspective, empathy, and reciprocity that result from experiencing prior exclusion. Thus, these findings support social-domain-theory propositions that the target of exclusion is influential on evaluations of exclusion, and that specific types of peer experiences may contribute to judgments that exclusion is wrong.

Children reject atypical peers based on stigmatized group identity (Nesdale & Brown, 2004). This finding further indicates that peer experience with exclusion is an important variable for investigation. Nesdale and Brown propose that children who experience extensive exclusion may be at risk for demonstrating prejudicial behavior toward others, and for perpetuating a cycle of negative intergroup attitudes. At the same time, however, adolescents are cognizant of the wrongfulness of discrimination regarding stigmatized peers (Verkuyten & Thijs, 2002).

Although stereotypes and conventions are powerful forces that legitimize exclusion, there is also extensive evidence of how adolescents explain the wrongfulness of discrimination in terms of social justice. Social-reasoning categories provide evidence for the types of norms that children use to justify or reject exclusion decisions and for the conditions that promote children's change from a priority on morality to group functioning, which may, at times, occur at the expense of fairness.

New Directions

Adults frequently use traditions and customs to justify exclusion. Tiger Woods' initial response to playing at the Augusta (Georgia) National Golf Club (host of the legendary Masters Tournament), which excludes women, was "That's just the way it is" (Brown, 2002)—categorized as social-conventional reasoning. More recently, Woods has stated, "Is it unfair? Yes. Do I want to see a female member? Yes" ("Woods Thinks Masters Debate Deserves a Private Meeting," 2005)—categorized as moral reasoning. Yet, he refuses to give up his participation in the event: "They're asking me to give up an opportunity to win the Masters three straight years" (Smith, 2003)—personal priority over the wrongfulness of exclusion. These quotes, which do not reflect coded responses from an in-depth systematic interview, nonetheless reveal how an individual can give different priorities to exclusion decisions and how these priorities change depending on the context (Killen, Sinno, & Margie, in press). Social-conventional or personal reasons do not necessarily reflect a developmentally "primitive" response (as put forth by stage theory).

Are children moral? Yes, children demonstrate spontaneous and elaborated reasons for why it is wrong to exclude others based on group membership, referring to fairness, equality, and rights. Do children have stereotypes about others? Yes; how these stereotypes enter into moral decision making requires an in-depth analysis of how children weigh competing considerations, such as group functioning, traditions, customs, and cultural norms, when evaluating exclusion. What changes as children age is how these considerations are weighed, the contexts that become salient for children and adolescents, and the ability to determine when morality should take priority in a given situation.

What is not well known is how children's intergroup biases (those that are not explicit) influence their judgments about exclusion; what it is about intergroup contact that contributes to children's variation in reliance on stereotypes to evaluate exclusion; and how early intergroup attitudes influence children's awareness of justice, fairness, and equality. Given that stereotypes are very hard to change in adulthood, interventions need to be conducted in childhood. Understanding when children resort to stereotypic expectations is crucial information for creating effective interventions. Developmental findings on social reasoning about exclusion provide a new approach for addressing these complex issues in childhood and adulthood and for creating programs to reduce prejudice.

References

Abrams, D., Rutland, A., Cameron, L., & Ferrell, A. (in press). Older but wilier: Ingroup accountability and the development of subjective group dynamics. *Developmental Psychology.*

Brown, J. (2002, August 16). Should Woods carry the black man's burden? *The Christian Science Monitor* [electronic version]. Retrieved January 5, 2007, from www.csmonitor.com/2002/0816/p01s01-ussc.html

Dovidio, J.F., Glick, P., & Rudman, L. (Eds.). (2005). *Reflecting on the nature of prejudice: Fifty years after Allport.* Malden, MA: Blackwell.

Horn, S. (2003). Adolescents' reasoning about exclusion from social groups. *Developmental Psychology, 39,* 11–84.

Killen, M., Lee-Kim, J., McGlothlin, H., & Stangor, C. (2002). How children and adolescents evaluate gender and racial exclusion. *Monographs for the Society for Research in Child Development* (Serial No. 271, Vol. 67, No. 4). Oxford, England: Blackwell.

Killen, M., Richardson, C., Kelly, M.C., Crystal, D., & Ruck, M. (2006, May). *European-American students' evaluations of interracial social exchanges in relation to the ethnic diversity of school environments.* Paper presented at the annual convention of the Association for Psychological Science, New York City.

Killen, M., Sinno, S., & Margie, N. (in press). Children's experiences and judgments about group exclusion and inclusion. In R. Kail (Ed.), *Advances in child psychology.* New York: Elsevier.

Killen, M., & Stangor, C. (2001). Children's social reasoning about inclusion and exclusion in gender and race peer group contexts. *Child Development, 72,* 174–186.

Kohlberg, L. (1984). *Essays on moral development: Vol. 2. The psychology of moral development—The nature and validity of moral stages.* San Francisco: Harper & Row.

Levy, S.R., Chiu, C.Y., & Hong, Y.Y. (2006). Lay theories and intergroup relations. *Group Processes and Intergroup Relations, 9,* 5–24.

Nesdale, D., & Brown, K. (2004). Children's attitudes towards an atypical member of an ethnic in-group. *International Journal of Behavioral Development, 28,* 328–335.

Pettigrew, T.F., & Tropp, L.R. (2005). Allport's intergroup contact hypothesis: Its history and influence. In J.F. Dovidio, P. Glick, & L. Rudman (Eds.), *Reflecting on the nature of prejudice: Fifty years after Allport* (pp. 262–277). Malden, MA: Blackwell.

Piaget, J. (1932). *The moral judgment of the child.* New York: Free Press.

Rubin, K.H., Bukowski, W., & Parker, J. (1998). Peer interactions, relationships and groups. In W. Damon (Ed.), *Handbook of child psychology: Vol. 3. Social, emotional, and personality development* (5th ed., pp. 619–700). New York: Wiley.

Smetana, J.G. (2006). Social domain theory: Consistencies and variations in children's moral and social judgments. In M. Killen & J.G. Smetana (Eds.), *Handbook of moral development* (pp. 119–154). Mahwah, NJ: Erlbaum.

Smith, T. (2003, February 20). A Master's challenge. *Online NewsHour.* Retrieved July 16, 2006, from www.pbs.org/newshour/bb/sports/jan-june03/golf_2-20.html

Turiel, E. (1998). The development of morality. In W. Damon (Ed.), *Handbook of child psychology: Vol. 3. Social, emotional, and personality development* (5th ed., pp. 863–932). New York: Wiley.

Verkuyten, M., & Thijs, J. (2002). Racist victimization among children in the Netherlands: The effect of ethnic group and school. *Ethnic and Racial Studies, 25,* 310–331.

Woods thinks Masters debate deserves a private meeting. (2005, February 14). *USA Today* [electronic version]. Retrieved January 10, 2007, from www.usatoday.com/sports/golf/2002-10-16-woods-masters_x.htm

Address correspondence to **MELANIE KILLEN,** 3304 Benjamin Building, Department of Human Development, University of Maryland, College Park, MD 20742-1131; e-mail: mkillen@umd.edu.

Acknowledgments—The author would like to thank Judith G. Smetana, Stefanie Sinno, and Cameron Richardson for helpful comments on earlier drafts of this manuscript, and the graduate students in the Social and Moral Development Laboratory for collaborative and insightful contributions to the research reported in this paper. The research described in this manuscript was supported, in part, by grants from the National Institute of Child Health and Human Development (IR01HD04121-01) and the National Science Foundation (#BCS0346717).

From *Current Directions in Psychological Science,* February 2007, pp. 32–36. Copyright © 2007 by the Association for Psychological Science. Reprinted by permission of Wiley-Blackwell.

A Profile of Bullying at School

Bullying and victimization are on the increase, extensive research shows. The attitudes and routines of relevant adults can exacerbate or curb students' aggression toward classmates.

DAN OLWEUS

Bullying among schoolchildren is a very old and well-known phenomenon. Although many educators are acquainted with the problem, researchers only began to study bullying systematically in the 1970s (Olweus, 1973, 1978) and focused primarily on schools in Scandinavia. In the 1980s and early 1990s, however, studies of bullying among schoolchildren began to attract wider attention in a number of other countries, including the United States.

What Is Bullying?

Systematic research on bullying requires rigorous criteria for classifying students as bullies or as victims (Olweus, 1996; Solberg & Olweus, in press). How do we know when a student is being bullied? One definition is that

> a student is being bullied or victimized when he or she is exposed, repeatedly and over time, to negative actions on the part of one or more other students. (Olweus, 1993)

The person who intentionally inflicts, or attempts to inflict, injury or discomfort on someone else is engaging in *negative actions,* a term similar to the definition of *aggressive behavior* in the social sciences. People carry out negative actions through physical contact, with words, or in more indirect ways, such as making mean faces or gestures, spreading rumors, or intentionally excluding someone from a group.

Bullying also entails an *imbalance in strength* (or an *asymmetrical power relationship*), meaning that students exposed to negative actions have difficulty defending themselves. Much bullying is *proactive aggression,* that is, aggressive behavior that usually occurs without apparent provocation or threat on the part of the victim.

Some Basic Facts

In the 1980s, questionnaire surveys of more than 150,000 Scandinavian students found that approximately 15 percent of students ages 8–16 were involved in bully/victim problems with some regularity—either as bullies, victims, or both bully and victim (bully-victims) (Olweus, 1993). Approximately 9 percent of all students were victims, and 6–7 percent bullied other students regularly. In contrast to what is commonly believed, only a small proportion of the victims also engaged in bullying other students (17 percent of the victims or 1.6 percent of the total number of students).

In 2001, when my colleagues and I conducted a new large-scale survey of approximately 11,000 students from 54 elementary and junior high schools using the same questions that we used in 1983 (Olweus, 2002), we noted two disturbing trends. The percentage of victimized students had increased by approximately 50 percent from 1983, and the percentage of students who were involved (as bullies, victims, or bully-victims) in frequent and serious bullying problems—occurring at least once a week—had increased by approximately 65 percent. We saw these increases as an indication of negative societal developments (Solberg & Olweus, in press).

The surveys showed that bullying is a serious problem affecting many students in Scandinavian schools. Data from other countries, including the United States (Nansel et al., 2001; Olweus & Limber, 1999; Perry, Kusel, & Perry, 1988)—and in large measure collected with my Bully/Victim Questionnaire (1983, 1996)—indicate that bullying problems exist outside Scandinavia with similar, or even higher, prevalence (Olweus & Limber, 1999; Smith et al., 1999). The prevalence figures from different countries or cultures, however, may not be directly comparable. Even though the questionnaire gives a detailed definition of bullying, the prevalence rates obtained may be affected by language differences, the students' familiarity with the concept of bullying, and the degree of public attention paid to the phenomenon.

Boys bully other students more often than girls do, and a relatively large percentage of girls—about 50 percent—report that they are bullied mainly by boys. A somewhat higher percentage of boys are victims of bullying, especially in the junior high school grades. But bullying certainly occurs among girls as well. Physical bullying is less common among girls, who typically use more subtle and indirect means of harassment,

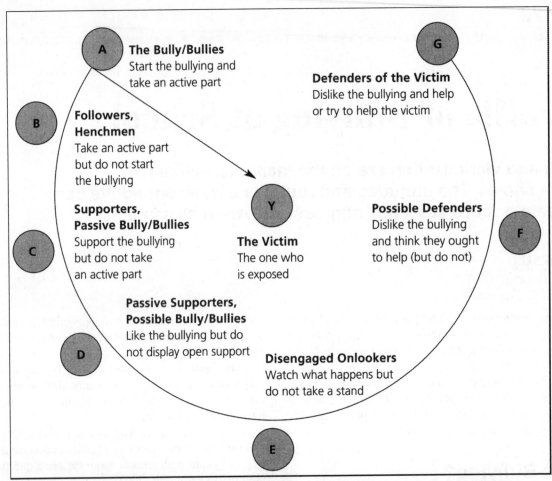

Figure 1 The Bullying Circle. Students' Modes of Reaction/Roles in an Acute Bullying Situation

such as intentionally excluding someone from the group, spreading rumors, and manipulating friendship relations. Such forms of bullying can certainly be as harmful and distressing as more direct and open forms of harassment. Our research data (Olweus, 1993), however, clearly contradict the view that girls are the most frequent and worst bullies, a view suggested by such recent books as *Queen Bees and Wannabes* (Wiseman, 2002) and *Odd Girl Out* (Simmons, 2002).

Common Myths about Bullying

Several common assumptions about the causes of bullying receive little or no support when confronted with empirical data. These misconceptions include the hypotheses that bullying is a consequence of large class or school size, competition for grades and failure in school, or poor self-esteem and insecurity. Many also believe erroneously that students who are overweight, wear glasses, have a different ethnic origin, or speak with an unusual dialect are particularly likely to become victims of bullying.

All of these hypotheses have thus far failed to receive clear support from empirical data. Accordingly, we must look for other factors to find the key origins of bullying problems. The accumulated research evidence indicates that personality characteristics or typical reaction patterns, in combination with physical strength or weakness in the case of boys, are important in the development of bullying problems in individual students. At the same time, environmental factors, such as the attitudes, behavior, and routines of relevant adults—in particular, teachers and principals—play a crucial role in determining the extent to which bullying problems will manifest themselves in a larger unit, such as a classroom or school. Thus, we must pursue analyses of the main causes of bully/victim problems on at least two different levels: individual and environmental.

Victims and the Bullying Circle

Much research has focused on the characteristics and family backgrounds of victims and bullies. We have identified two kinds of victims, the more common being the *passive* or *submissive victim,* who represents some 80–85 percent of all victims. Less research information is available about *provocative victims,* also called *bully-victims* or *aggressive victims,* whose behavior may elicit negative reactions from a large part of the class. The dynamics of a classroom with a provocative victim are different from those of a classroom with a submissive victim (Olweus, 1978, 1993).

Bullies and victims naturally occupy key positions in the configuration of bully/victim problems in a classroom, but other students also play important roles and display different attitudes and reactions toward an acute bullying situation. Figure 1 outlines the "Bullying Circle" and represents the various ways in which most students in a classroom with bully/victim problems are involved in or affected by them (Olweus, 2001a, 2001b).

The Olweus Bullying Prevention Program

The Olweus Bullying Prevention Program,[1] developed and evaluated over a period of almost 20 years (Olweus, 1993, 1999), builds on four key principles derived chiefly from research on the development and identification of problem behaviors, especially aggressive behavior. These principles involve creating a school—and ideally, also a home—environment characterized by

- Warmth, positive interest, and involvement from adults;
- Firm limits on unacceptable behavior;
- Consistent application of nonpunitive, nonphysical sanctions for unacceptable behavior or violations of rules; and
- Adults who act as authorities and positive role models.

We have translated these principles into a number of specific measures to be used at the school, classroom, and individual levels (Olweus, 1993, 2001b). Figure 2 lists the set of core components that our statistical analyses and experience with the program have shown are particularly important in any implementation of the program.

Our research data clearly contradict the view that girls are the most frequent and worst bullies.

The program's implementation relies mainly on the existing social environment. Teachers, administrators, students, and parents all play major roles in carrying out the program and in restructuring the social environment. One possible reason for this intervention program's effectiveness is that it changes the opportunity and reward structures for bullying behavior, which results in fewer opportunities and rewards for bullying (Olweus, 1992).

Research-Based Evaluations

The first evaluation of the effects of the Olweus Bullying Prevention Program involved data from approximately 2,500 students in 42 elementary and junior high schools in Bergen, Norway, and followed students for two and one-half years, from 1983 to 1985 (Olweus, 1991, in press; Olweus & Alsaker, 1991). The findings were significant:

- Marked reductions—by 50 percent or more—in bully/victim problems for the period studied, measuring after 8 and 20 months of intervention.
- Clear reductions in general anti-social behavior, such as vandalism, fighting, pilfering, drunkenness, and truancy.
- Marked improvement in the social climate of the classes and an increase in student satisfaction with school life.

The differences between baseline and intervention groups were highly significant. The research concluded that the registered changes in bully/victim problems and related behavior patterns were likely to be a consequence of the intervention program and not of some other factor. Partial replications of the program in the United States, the United Kingdom, and Germany have resulted in similar, although somewhat weaker, results (Olweus & Limber, 1999; Smith & Sharp, 1994).

In 1997–1998, our study of 3,200 students from 30 Norwegian schools again registered clear improvements with regard to bully/victim problems in the schools with intervention programs. The effects were weaker than in the first project, with averages varying between 21 and 38 percent. Unlike the first study, however, the intervention program had been in place for only six months when we made the second measurement. In addition, we conducted the study during a particularly turbulent year in which Norway introduced a new national curriculum that made heavy demands of educators' time and resources.

Nonetheless, the intervention schools fared considerably better than the comparison schools. Surveys of the comparison schools, which had set up anti-bullying efforts according to their own plans, showed very small or no changes with regard to "being bullied" and a 35 percent increase for "bullying other students" (Olweus, in press). Because we have not yet analyzed the questionnaire information, we cannot fully explain this result, but it is consistent with findings from a number of studies showing that inexpert interventions intended to counteract delinquent and antisocial behavior often have unexpectedly negative effects (Dishion, McCord, & Poulin, 1999; Gottfredson, 1987; Lipsey, 1992).

Most students in a classroom with bully/victim problems are involved in or affected by the problems.

In the most recent (1999–2000) evaluation of the Olweus Bullying Prevention Program among approximately 2,300 students from 10 schools—some of which had large percentages of students with immigrant backgrounds—we found an average reduction by around 40 percent with regard to "being bullied" and by about 50 percent for "bullying other students" (Olweus, in press).

The Need for Evidence-Based Intervention Programs

Coping with bully/victim problems has become an official school priority in many countries, and many have suggested ways to handle and prevent such problems. But because most proposals have either failed to document positive results or have never been subjected to systematic research evaluation, it is difficult to know which programs or measures actually work and which do not. What counts is how well the program works for students, not how much the adults using the program like it.

Recently, when a U.S. committee of experts used three essential criteria (Elliott, 1999) to systematically evaluate more than 500 programs ostensibly designed to prevent violence or other problem behaviors, only 11 of the programs (four of which are school-based) satisfied the specified criteria.[2] The U.S. Department of Justice's Office of Juvenile Justice and Delinquency Prevention and other sources are now providing financial support for the implementation of these evidence-based "Blueprint" programs in a number of sites.

In Norway, an officially appointed committee recently conducted a similar evaluation of 56 programs being used in Norway's schools to counteract and prevent problem behavior (Norwegian Ministry of Education, Research, and Church Affairs, 2000) and recommended without reservation only one program for further use. The Olweus Bullying Prevention Program is one of the 11 Blueprint programs and the program selected by the Norwegian committee.

Norway's New National Initiative against Bullying

In late 2000, Norway's Department of Education and Research and Department of Children and Family Affairs decided to offer the Olweus Bullying Prevention Program on a large scale to Norwegian elementary and junior high schools over a period of several years. In building the organization for this national initiative, we have used a four-level train-the-trainer strategy of dissemination. At Norway's University of Bergen, the Olweus Group Against Bullying at the Research Center for Health Promotion trains and supervises specially selected *instructor candidates,* each of whom trains and supervises key persons from a number of schools. The key persons are then responsible for leading staff discussion groups at each participating school. These meetings typically focus on key components and themes of the program (Olweus, 1993, 2001b).

The training of the instructor candidates consists of 10–11 whole-day assemblies over 16 months. In between the whole-day meetings, the instructor candidates receive ongoing consultation from the Olweus Group by telephone or through e-mail.

In implementing this train-the-trainer model in the United States with financial support from the U.S. Department of

---

The Olweus Bullying Prevention Program

General Prerequisite

- Awareness and involvement of adults

Measures at the School Level

- Administration of the Olweus Bully/Victim Questionnaire (filled out anonymously by students)
- Formation of a Bullying Prevention Coordinating Committee
- Training of staff and time for discussion groups
- Effective supervision during recess and lunch periods

Measures at the Classroom Level

- Classroom and school rules about bullying
- Regular classroom meetings
- Meetings with students' parents

Measures at the Individual Level

- Individual meetings with students who bully
- Individual meetings with victims of bullying
- Meetings with parents of students involved
- Development of individual intervention plans

Figure 2

Justice and the U.S. Department of Health and Human Services, we have made some modifications to accommodate cultural differences and practical constraints. In particular, we have reduced the number of whole-day assemblies to four or five and have granted greater autonomy to individual schools' Bullying Prevention Coordinating Committees than is typical in Norway.

So far, 75 instructor candidates have participated in training, and more than 225 schools participate in the program. Recently, Norway's government substantially increased our funding to enable us to offer the program to more schools starting in 2003.

We see Norway's national initiative as a breakthrough for the systematic, long-term, and research-based work against bully/victim problems in schools. We hope to see similar developments in other countries.

Notes

1. More information about the Olweus Bullying Prevention Program is available at www.colorado.edu/cspv/blueprints/model/ BPPmaterials.html or by contacting nobully @clemson.edu or olweus@psych.uib.no.

2. The four school-based programs are Life Skills Training, Promoting Alternative Thinking Strategies (PATHS), the Incredible Years, and the Olweus Bullying Prevention Program. For more information about the Blueprints for Violence Prevention's model programs, visit www.colorado.edu/cspv/ blueprints/model/overview.html.

References

Dishion, T. J., McCord, J., & Poulin, F. (1999). When interventions harm: Peer groups and problem behavior. *American Psychologist, 54,* 755–764.

Elliott, D. S. (1999). Editor's introduction. In D. Olweus & S. Limber, *Blueprints for violence prevention: Bullying Prevention Program.* Boulder, CO: Institute of Behavioral Science.

Gottfredson, G. D. (1987). Peer group interventions to reduce the risk of delinquent behavior: A selective review and a new evaluation. *Criminology, 25,* 671–714.

Lipsey, M. W. (1992). Juvenile delinquency treatment: A meta-analytic inquiry into the variability of effects. In T. D. Cook, H. Cooper, D. S. Corday, H. Hartman, L. V. Hedges, R. J. Light, T. A. Louis, & F. Mosteller (Eds.), *Meta-analysis for explanation: A casebook* (pp. 83–125). New York: Russell Sage.

Nansel, T. R., Overpeck, M., Pilla, R. S., Ruan, W. J., Simons-Morton, B., & Scheidt, P. (2001). Bullying behaviors among U.S. youth: Prevalence and association with psychosocial adjustment. *Journal of the American Medical Association, 285,* 2094–2100.

Norwegian Ministry of Education, Research, and Church Affairs. (2000). *Rapport 2000: Vurdering av program og tiltak for å redusere problematferd og utvikle sosial kompetanse.* (Report 2000: Evaluation of programs and measures to reduce problem behavior and develop social competence.) Oslo, Norway: Author.

Olweus, D. (1973). *Hackkycklingar och översittare. Forskning om skolmobbing.* (Victims and bullies: Research on school bullying.) Stockholm: Almqvist & Wicksell.

Olweus, D. (1978). *Aggression in the schools: Bullies and whipping boys.* Washington, DC: Hemisphere Press (Wiley).

Olweus, D. (1983). *The Olweus Bully/Victim Questionnaire.* Mimeo. Bergen, Norway: Research Center for Health Promotion, University of Bergen.

Olweus, D. (1991). Bully/victim problems among schoolchildren: Basic facts and effects of a school-based intervention program. In D. Pepler & K. Rubin (Eds.), *The development and treatment of childhood aggression* (pp. 411–448). Hillsdale, NJ: Erlbaum.

Olweus, D. (1992). Bullying among schoolchildren: Intervention and prevention. In R. D. Peters, R. J. McMahon, & V. L. Quincy (Eds.), *Aggression and violence throughout the life span.* Newbury Park, CA: Sage.

Olweus, D. (1993). *Bullying at school: What we know and what we can do.* Cambridge, MA: Blackwell. (Available from AIDC, P.O. Box 20, Williston, VT 05495; (800) 216-2522).

Olweus, D. (1996). *The Revised Olweus Bully/Victim Questionnaire.* Mimeo. Bergen, Norway: Research Center for Health Promotion, University of Bergen.

Olweus, D. (1999). Norway. In P. K. Smith, Y. Morita, J. Junger-Tas, D. Olweus, R. Catalano, & P. Slee (Eds.), *The nature of school bullying: A cross-national perspective* (pp. 28–48). London: Routledge.

Olweus, D. (2001a). Peer harassment: A critical analysis and some important issues. In J. Juvonen & S. Graham (Eds.), *Peer harassment in school* (pp. 3–20). New York: Guilford Publications.

Olweus, D. (2001b). *Olweus' core program against bullying and anti-social behavior: A teacher handbook.* Bergen, Norway: Research Center for Health Promotion, University of Bergen.

Olweus, D. (2002). *Mobbing i skolen: Nye data om omfang og forandring over tid.* (Bullying at school: New data on prevalence and change over time.) Manuscript. Research Center for Health Promotion, University of Bergen, Bergen, Norway.

Olweus, D. (in press). Bullying at school: Prevalence estimation, a useful evaluation design, and a new national initiative in Norway. *Association for Child Psychology and Psychiatry Occasional Papers.*

Olweus, D., & Alsaker, F. D. (1991). Assessing change in a cohort longitudinal study with hierarchical data. In D. Magnusson, L. R. Bergman, G. Rudinger, & B. Törestad (Eds.), *Problems and methods in longitudinal research* (pp. 107–132). New York: Cambridge University Press.

Olweus, D., & Limber, S. (1999). *Blueprints for violence prevention: Bullying Prevention Program.* Boulder, CO: Institute of Behavioral Science.

Perry, D. G., Kusel, S. J., & Perry, L. C. (1988). Victims of peer aggression. *Developmental Psychology, 24,* 807–814.

Simmons, R. (2002). *Odd girl out.* New York: Harcourt.

Smith, P. K., Morita, Y., Junger-Tas, J., Olweus, D., Catalano, R., & Slee, P. (Eds.). (1999). *The nature of school bullying: A cross-national perspective.* London: Routledge.

Smith, P. K., & Sharp, S. (Eds.). (1994). *School bullying: Insights and perspectives.* London: Routledge.

Solberg, M., & Olweus, D. (in press). Prevalence estimation of school bullying with the Olweus Bully/Victim Questionnaire. *Aggressive Behavior.*

Wiseman, R. (2002). *Queen bees and wannabes.* New York: Crown.

DAN OLWEUS is Research Professor of Psychology and Director of the Olweus Group Against Bullying at the Research Center for Health Promotion at the University of Bergen, Christies Gate 13, N-5015 Bergen, Norway; e-mail: olweus@psych.uib.no.

From *Educational Leadership,* March 2003, pp. 12–17. Copyright © 2003 by Dan Olweus. Reprinted by permission of the author.

When Girls and Boys Play: What Research Tells Us

JEANETTA G. RILEY AND ROSE B. JONES

Research on play suggests that children of all ages benefit from engaging in play activities (Bergen, 2004). With the recent emphasis on standards and testing, however, many teachers have felt the increased pressure to spend time on structured learning events, leaving few moments of relaxation in a child's day (Chenfeld, 2006). Many elementary schools have even reduced or eliminated recess times in an effort to give children more time to work on academics (Clements, 2000). That is unfortunate, as findings from studies of play indicate that play helps children to develop social, language, and physical skills.

While beneficial for both, play often differs for girls and boys (see Gallas, 1998; Gurian & Stevens, 2005). This article reviews research related to the differences found between the genders as they play and the benefits that elementary children can gain from play. In addition, the authors include suggestions for educators regarding children's play at school.

Social Development
Girls and Boys Sharing Social Interactions during Play

Researchers have found differences in the way the genders socialize during play. In an early study examining gender and play, Lever (1978) found several differences in how 5th-grade girls and boys play. For example, boys played more competitive, rule-oriented, group games than did girls; girls interacted in smaller groups, had conversations, and walked and talked with friends more often than did boys. Lever concluded that the nature of boys' team games and their experiences with rule-dictated play: 1) allowed for the development of cooperation skills between peers with differing ideas, 2) afforded them opportunities to work independently to accomplish a common task, and 3) provided motivation to abide by established rules.

Other recent studies have found results similar to those of Lever (1978). A study of elementary students at recess conducted by Butcher (1999) indicated that boys more often participated in competitive games, and girls chose activities that allowed them to have conversations. Likewise, Lewis and Phillipsen (1998) found that elementary-age boys at recess played physically active group games with rules more often than did girls. However, in contrast to Lever's (1978) findings on groupings during recess, Lewis and Phillipsen (1998) noted that while girls tended to play in small groups, boys tended to play in groups of various sizes, from dyads to more than five children.

Also consistent with Lever's (1978) findings, a study of 4th-graders by Goodwin (2001) indicated that boys tended to form social structures, wherein the boys who were more skilled at the activity took the lead and directed the players. Boys with less skill were allowed to play but were not allowed a leadership role. In contrast, girls' leadership roles during games of jump rope did not depend on their ability to carry out the physical tasks of the game. Instead of one girl taking the lead, several girls directed the games; however, Goodwin (2001) found that the girls were more likely to exclude others from their play than were the boys.

Even very young children tend to be socially influenced by playing with same-sex peers. For example, Martin and Fabes' (2001) investigation of preschool and kindergarten children at play indicated that playing with same-gender peers affects play behaviors. Their research findings added to the evidence (e.g., Boyatzis, Mallis, & Leon, 1999; Thorne, 1993) that children often choose to play with same-sex peers. Additionally, Martin and Fabes found gender-typical behaviors for children who more often played with same-sex peers. For instance, the girls who most often played with other girls were generally less active during play and chose to play in areas close to adults. Boys who played with other boys more often engaged in play that was more aggressive and farther from adult supervision. This stereotypical play was found less often in children who tended to play with the opposite sex.

Not all students have positive social experiences during play activities. Some students may have difficulty developing the appropriate skills necessary for positive peer interactions. Children with inadequate social skills may tend to behave inappropriately during times of free play, such as recess (Blatchford, 1998). Rather than limit free play due to inappropriate behavior, however, these times can provide opportunities for conflict resolution interventions. In one study by Butcher (1999), the researchers trained college students to use conflict resolution strategies when interacting with 1st- through 6th-graders during recess times. The volunteers provided positive feedback, modeled appropriate social skills, and implemented strategies to increase cooperation among the children. As a result, when the numbers were analyzed, combining all grade levels, the means for the number of incidents of inappropriate targeted behaviors (i.e., violent behavior, verbal abuse, and inappropriate equipment use) declined during interventions. However, it is important to note that when the results were analyzed according to gender, significant differences were found in the reduction of targeted behaviors for boys only. No significant differences were found for girls' behavior. The researchers suggested that this lack of difference for the girls was due to the limited number of negative behaviors the girls initially exhibited (Butcher, 1999).

Overall Play and the Social Development of Children

By the time children reach school age, play typically becomes a social activity (Jarrett & Maxwell, 2000). As children play with others, they begin to learn what behaviors are expected and acceptable in their society. Playing with peers permits children to adjust to the expected norms (Fromberg, 1998).

Opportunities for free play with limited adult intervention provide time for children to explore which behaviors are accepted among their peers (Wortham, 2002). As younger children associate in play situations, they begin to realize that play ends if they do not negotiate behaviors and cooperate; therefore, play helps children learn to regulate their behaviors in order to continue playing together (Heidemann & Hewitt, 1992; Poole, Miller, & Church, 2004).

For older children, recess can be a time for learning about and adjusting to peer expectations. Pellegrini and Blatchford's (2002) findings suggest that recess play provides children with time to enter into social relationships early in the school year, which, in turn, helps them in social situations throughout the year. Pellegrini, Blatchford, Kato, and Baines (2004) also found that recess allowed opportunities for children to increase positive social experiences. For the 7- and 8-year-old participants in their study, basic games played at the beginning of the school year permitted the children time to get acquainted with peers, leading to more advanced play once the children became more familiar with each other. Additionally, Jarrett et al. (1998) speculated that children who move from one school to another find recess times helpful in adjusting and making new friends.

Language Development
Girls and Boys Expressing Language during Play

Research indicates that the types of games in which girls often engage may support language development differently than the types of games boys typically play. Blatchford, Baines, and

Pellegrini (2003) studied playground activities of children in England during the year the children turned 8 years old. The researchers found that girls held significantly more conversations and played significantly more verbal games than did boys. Goodwin (2002) also found that 4th- through 6th-grade girls spent most of their playtime talking with one another. Their games tended to require close proximity to one another, thus allowing for extended conversations. Conversely, some studies found that the games boys tended to choose often involved language usage that was more instruction-oriented, with boys verbally directing the play actions of one another (Boyle, Marshall, & Robeson, 2003; Goodwin, 2001).

Overall Play and Language Skill Development of Children

Play is a natural environment for children's language development (Perlmutter & Burrell, 1995). Children use language during their solitary play as well as in social play encounters (Piaget, 1962). Both expressive and receptive language skills are needed to plan, explain, and execute play activities. Language skills give children the ability to cooperate in creating and prolonging their play episodes (Van Hoorn, Monighan-Nourot, Scales, & Alward, 2003).

Developing language skills facilitates peer relationships. Piaget (1962) theorized that the talk of preschool-age children is egocentric (i.e., talk that is not for the sake of communicating with others). Very young children verbalize without a need for others to enter into the conversation; however, as older children begin to interact more often with adults and peers, the need to communicate arises. Egocentric speech gradually subsides and social speech takes over as children practice using language (Ginsburg & Opper, 1979).

Language in the context of play provides children with the ability to develop strategies for cooperation, engage in varied and complex play themes, and share perspectives about their world.

Language is a major factor in social play scenarios, such as sociodramatic play in which children create pretend play episodes and take on the roles of others. Language in the context of play provides children with the ability to develop strategies for cooperation, engage in varied and complex play themes, and share perspectives about their world (Van Hoorn et al., 2003). Children's language guides their play and provides the communication needed for the continuation of the play (Guddemi, 2000; Heidemann & Hewitt, 1992).

Language usage during play allows children to develop and test their verbal skills. Children experiment with language by telling jokes and riddles, reciting chants and poems, and making up words. As children use language during play, they create meaning for themselves concerning the nature of language and communication (Frost, 1992). Additionally, playing with language develops children's phonological awareness by allowing for experimentation with the sounds of words. Children learn that sounds can be manipulated as they rhyme words and create nonsense words (Johnson, Christie, & Wardle, 2005).

A more complicated form of play, games with rules, also requires children to expand their language skills. Once the egocentrism of earlier childhood diminishes, children can become more proficient at working together to negotiate the rules of games (Van Hoorn et al., 2003). Games with rules provide practice in cooperation, as well as opportunities to build language skills, as children create new games or discuss rules of known games.

Physical Development
Girls and Boys Engaging in Physical Activity during Play

Research indicates gender differences in physical activity during play. Studies have noted that boys, from infancy through adolescence, tend to participate in more physically active play than do girls (Campbell & Eaton, 1999; Frost, 1992; Lindsey & Colwell, 2003). For example, Lindsey and Colwell (2003) observed young children and found that boys playing with one other child engage in more physical play than girls playing with one other child. Additionally, a study by Sarkin, McKenzie, and Sallis (1997) compared gender differences in play levels of 5th-graders during physical education classes and recess. They found no significant differences between the boys' and the girls' activity levels during physical education classes. However, during recess times, boys more often played games requiring higher levels of physical activity than did girls. Girls played less strenuous games or held conversations as they walked around the playground. These results suggested that during times of unstructured activity, such as recess, boys tend to choose more active play than girls do.

Likewise, other researchers also concluded that the physical play of girls and boys often differs. Boys and girls tend to divide into gendered groups during outdoor play, and they often choose different types of activities (Thorne, 1993). Studies suggest that boys engage in play that involves more physical activity (Boyle, Marshall, & Robeson, 2003), more competition (Lever, 1978), and more space (Martin & Fabes, 2001) than do girls. Pellegrini and Smith (1993) suggested that boys tend to prefer playing outdoors, due to the need for open space to participate in their active games. One type of active play in which boys tend to engage in more frequently than girls is rough and tumble play (Martin & Fabes, 2001; Pellegrini, 1989; Thorne, 1993). Rough and tumble play involves such activities as grabbing and wrestling and may be a socially acceptable way for boys to physically demonstrate their feelings of friendship (Reed, 2000).

Overall Active Play and Physical Development in Children

The human body needs movement to stay healthy and well. Findings by the Centers for Disease Control and Prevention (2005) indicate that the incidence of childhood obesity is increasing. In today's world, many children spend most of their time in sedentary activities that do not enhance physical fitness. Active play encourages movement, thereby helping children's fitness. According to Huettig, Sanborn, DiMarco, Popejoy, and Rich (2004), young children need at least "thirty to sixty minutes of physical activity a day" (p. 54). Physical advantages that children gain from active play are increased motor control and flexibility (Brewer, 2001). Furthermore, with the added body control that develops as they play, children often become more competent in their skills and gain the self-confidence to play games with peers (Wortham, 2002).

Physical movement is necessary for the growth and development of the mind as well as the body. The brain needs movement in order to function properly.

Physical movement is necessary for the growth and development of the mind as well as the body. The brain needs movement in order to function properly (Gurian, 2001). Although indoor play encourages creativity and socialization, it provides only a limited amount of space for the type of physical movement children need each day. Time in outdoor play encourages physical activity, which, in turn, increases children's physical fitness. Consequently, outdoor recess periods provide the time and space for children to engage in the physically vigorous active play that is limited indoors (Sutterby & Frost, 2002).

Further Research Needs

Understanding more about how play benefits the social, language, and physical development of children can help teachers as they create learning environments; however, more research is needed to gain a clearer picture of how play enhances children's learning. For example, studies examining the influence of recess on classroom behaviors, such as concentration and amount of work produced, have yielded conflicting results (Jarrett et al., 1998; Pellegrini & Davis, 1993). Therefore, more work is necessary to determine how unstructured play correlates with behavior as well as academic achievement. Additionally, more research needs to be conducted about social interventions during play. Children who have been targeted as requiring assistance in developing positive social behaviors may have more difficulty during times of unstructured activity (Blatchford, 1998). Research to determine how to best assist these children, particularly during recess periods, is needed.

Finally, some researchers have included such variables as race and gender within the framework of their study of play; however, less often has the researcher's main purpose been to examine the educational implications based on the different ways girls and boys play. This aspect of play needs further examination if educators are to gain a better understanding of how to best structure learning environments for both genders.

Implications for Educators

Knowing the research about how children play and what they learn as they play can help educators and parents make sound decisions about how to provide appropriate play opportunities. To create learning environments in which children can thrive, adults must observe children's needs and try to accommodate those needs. The following are some suggestions for educators and parents.

- **Importance of Observations of Play Experiences:** Teachers can use playtimes to observe and assess children's social, emotional, physical, and cognitive development. Observing children's play can provide teachers with information about how to create appropriate learning environments. In some settings, recess may be a prime time to do this.
- **Girls' Play:** Girls have been found to engage in more sedentary, language-oriented activities during recess play than boys. Although this type of activity is important, girls also need to be encouraged to be physically active. While many boys may participate in physical movement through rough and tumble play, educators may need to help girls create activities in which they become more active. Providing areas and equipment for active play is the first step; additionally, ensuring that girls have the opportunity to engage in this type of physical play is necessary.
- **Boys' Play:** Rough and tumble play may provide an outlet for boys' physical, social, emotional, and verbal expression. Schools where all physical contact during play has been banned may need to consider how to reduce aggressive behaviors while allowing for this type of physical contact between boys. Recess monitors may need to be trained to recognize differences between acts of aggression and rough and tumble play. Additionally, the exploration of language that girls enjoy during play may need to be encouraged for boys by creating play environments that support language development. For example, teachers can lead boys in discussing their play activities.
- **Accommodations for Differences:** Children have various interests and styles of play; therefore, schools can provide a variety of play materials and equipment to accommodate the differences. Additionally, an assortment of resources can encourage children to expand and extend their play. Children with special needs should be considered in this process.
- **Parental Awareness:** Parents may be concerned that their young children are "only playing" at school. During Open House, at PTA meetings, and through newsletters, educators can make parents aware of growth and development that takes place as children play, both in classrooms and at recess. It is necessary to make adults aware that natural outdoor play environments are important for girls and boys and that these areas do not always require equipment. Rustic, wooded settings can provide children with many opportunities for creative movement, imaginative growth, and cognitive learning as they participate in such activities as nature walks with adult supervision.
- **Cooperative Activities:** Although research indicates that girls tend to enjoy cooperative activities while boys pursue competitive games, children need to learn about both cooperation and competition. Teachers can incorporate each type of activity into classroom lessons.

Conclusion

While some adults dismiss play as mere fun, much growth and development occurs during playtimes. As children play, they gain knowledge of the world and an understanding of their place in it. Although play may differ generally for girls and boys, it offers both genders opportunities to test and refine their developing social, language, and physical skills, which leads not only to academic achievement but also to a lifetime of success. Thus, play does benefit children.

References

Bergen, D. (2004). *ACEI speaks: Play's role in brain development* [Brochure]. Olney, MD: Association for Childhood Education International.

Blatchford, P. (1998). The state of play in schools. *Child Psychology and Psychiatry Review,* 3(2), 58–67.

Blatchford, P., Baines, E., & Pellegrini, A. (2003). The social context of school playground games: Sex and ethnic differences, and changes over time after entry to junior high school. *British Journal of Developmental Psychology,* 21(4), 481–505.

Boyatzis, C. J., Mallis, M., & Leon, I. (1999). Effects of game type on children's gender-based peer preferences: A naturalistic observational study. *Sex Roles: A Journal of Research,* 40(1–2), 93–105.

Boyle, D. E., Marshall, N. L., & Robeson, W. W. (2003). Gender at play: Fourth-grade girls and boys on the playground. *American Behavioral Scientist,* 46(10), 1326–1345.

Brewer, J. A. (2001). *Introduction to early childhood education: Preschool through primary grades* (4th ed.). Boston: Allyn and Bacon.

Butcher, D. A. (1999). Enhancing social skills through school social work interventions during recess: Gender differences. *Social Work in Education,* 21(4), 249–262.

Campbell, D. W., & Eaton, W. O. (1999). Sex differences in the activity level of infants. *Infant and Child Development,* 8(1), 1–17.

Centers for Disease Control and Prevention. (2005). *Preventing chronic diseases through good nutrition and physical activity.* Retrieved July 18, 2006, from www.cdc.gov/nccdphp/publications/factsheets/Prevention/obesity.htm

Chenfeld, M. B. (2006). Handcuff me, too! *Phi Delta Kappan,* 87(10), 745–747.

Clements, R. L. (Ed.). (2000). *Elementary school recess: Selected readings, games, and activities for teachers and parents.* Boston: American Press.

Fromberg, D. P. (1998). Play issues in early childhood education. In C. Seefeldt & A. Galper (Eds.), *Continuing issues in early childhood education* (2nd ed.) (pp. 190–212). Upper Saddle River, NJ: Merrill Prentice-Hall.

Frost, J. L. (1992). *Play and playscapes.* Albany, NY: Delmar.

Gallas, K. (1998). *Sometimes I can be anything: Power, gender, and identity in a primary classroom.* New York: Teachers College Press.

Ginsburg, H., & Opper, S. (1979). *Piaget's theory of intellectual development* (2nd ed.). Englewood Cliffs, NJ: Prentice-Hall.

Goodwin, M. H. (2001). Organizing participation in cross-sex jump rope: Situating gender differences within longitudinal studies of activities. *Research on Language & Social Interaction, 34(1),* 75–106.

Goodwin, M. H. (2002). Exclusion in girls' peer groups: Ethnographic analysis of language practices on the playground. *Human Development, 45(6),* 392–415.

Guddemi, M. P. (2000). Recess: A time to learn, a time to grow. In R. L. Clements (Ed.), *Elementary school recess: Selected readings, games, and activities for teachers and parents* (pp. 2–8). Boston: American Press.

Gurian, M. (2001). *Boys and girls learn differently! A guide for teachers and parents.* San Francisco: Jossey-Bass.

Gurian, M., & Stevens, K. (2005). *The minds of boys: Saving our sons from falling behind in school and life.* San Francisco: Jossey-Bass.

Heidemann, S., & Hewitt, D. (1992). *Pathways to play: Developing play skills in young children.* St. Paul, MN: Redleaf Press.

Huettig, C. I., Sanborn, C. R, DiMarco, N., Popejoy, A., & Rich, S. (2004). The O generation: Our youngest children are at risk for obesity. *Young Children, 59(2),* 50–55.

Jarrett, O. S., & Maxwell, D. M. (2000). What research says about the need for recess. In R. L. Clements (Ed.), *Elementary school recess: Selected readings, games, and activities for teachers and parents* (pp. 12–20). Boston: American Press.

Jarrett, O. S., Maxwell, D. M., Dickerson, C., Hoge, P., Davies, G., & Yetley, A. (1998). Impact of recess on classroom behavior: Group effects and individual differences. *The Journal of Educational Research, 92(2),* 121–126.

Johnson, J. E., Christie, J. R, & Wardle, F. (2005). *Play, development, and early education.* Boston: Pearson Education.

Lever, J. (1978). Sex differences in the complexity of children's play and games. *American Sociological Review, 43(4),* 471–483.

Lewis, T. E., & Phillipsen, L. C. (1998). Interactions on an elementary school playground: Variations by age, gender, race, group size, and playground area. *Child Study Journal, 2S(4),* 309–320.

Lindsey, E. W., & Colwell, M. J. (2003). Preschoolers' emotional competence links to pretend and physical play. *Child Study Journal, 33(1),* 39–52.

Martin, C. L., & Fabes, R. A. (2001). The stability and consequences of young children's same-sex peer interactions. *Developmental Psychology, 37(3),* 431–446.

Pellegrini, A. D. (1989). Elementary school children's rough-and-tumble play. *Early Childhood Research Quarterly,* 4(2), 245–260.

Pellegrini, A. D., & Blatchford, P. (2002). The developmental and educational significance of recess in schools. *Early Report,* 29(1). Retrieved March 16, 2004, from www.education.umn .edu/ceed/publications/earlyreport/spring02.htm.

Pellegrini, A. D., Blatchford, P., Kato, K., & Baines, E. (2004). A short-term longitudinal study of children's playground games in primary school: Implications for adjustment to school and social adjustment in the USA and the UK. *Social/ Development,* 13(1), 107–123.

Pellegrini, A. D., & Davis, P. (1993). Relations between children's playground and classroom behaviour. *British Journal of Educational Psychology, 63(1),* 88–95.

Pellegrini, A. D., & Smith, P. K. (1993). School recess: Implications for education and development. *Review of Educational Research, 63(1),* 51–67.

Perlmutter, J. C, & Burrell, L. (1995). Learning through 'play' as well as 'work' in the primary grades. *Young Children,* 50(5), 14–21.

Piaget, J. (1962). *Play, dreams, and imitation in childhood* (G. Gattegno & F. M. Hodgson, Trans.). New York: W.W. Norton & Company.

Poole, C., Miller, S., & Church, E. B. (2004). Working through that "It's Mine" feeling. *Early Childhood Today, 18(5),* 28–32.

Reed, T. (2000). Rough and tumble play during recess: Pathways to successful social development. In R. L. Clements (Ed.), *Elementary school recess: Selected readings, games, and activities for teachers and parents* (pp. 45–48). Boston: American Press.

Sarkin, J. S., McKenzie, T. L., & Sallis, J. F. (1997). Gender differences in physical activity during fifth-grade physical education and recess periods. *Journal of Teaching in Physical Education, 17(1),* 99–106.

Sutterby, J. S., & Frost, J. L. (2002). Making playgrounds fit for children and children fit on playgrounds. *Young Children, 57(3),* 36–41.

Thorne, B. (1993). *Gender play: Girls and boys in school.* New Brunswick, NJ: Rutgers University Press.

Van Hoorn, J., Monighan-Nourot, P., Scales, B., & Alward, K. R. (2003). *Play at the center of the curriculum* (3rd ed.). Upper Saddle River, NJ: Merrill Prentice-Hall.

Wortham, S. C. (2002). *Early childhood curriculum: Developmental bases for learning and teaching* (3rd ed.). Upper Saddle River, NJ: Merrill Prentice-Hall.

JEANETTA G. RILEY is Assistant Professor, Department of Early Childhood and Elementary Education, Murray State University. **ROSE B. JONES** is Assistant Professor of Early Childhood Education/ Literacy, The University of Southern Mississippi.

From *Childhood Education,* Fall 2007, pp. 38–43. Copyright © 2007 by the Association for Childhood Education International. Reprinted by permission of Jeanetta G. Riley and Rose B. Jones and the Association for Childhood Education International, 17904 Georgia Avenue, Suite 215, Olney, MD 20832.

Playtime in Peril

LEA WINERMAN

What did your kindergarten look like? For most adults, kindergarten brings back images of Play-doh, building blocks and maybe a teacher reading aloud.

But kindergarten circa 2009 is different, finds a report published by a nonprofit group of psychologists and educators called the Alliance for Childhood. Kindergartners in New York and Los Angeles spend nearly three hours per day on reading and math instruction and test prep, and less than half an hour each day on "choice time," or play, finds the report *Crisis in the Kindergarten: Why Children Need Play in School.*

Those same kids probably don't get much time to play dress-up or make-believe outside of school either. In fact, children today have eight fewer hours of free, unstructured playtime a week than they had 20 years ago, according to Tufts University psychologist David Elkind, PhD—time lost to organized sports, video games and educational computer programs, among other activities.

Now, Elkind and others are trying to resuscitate playtime's reputation among parents and policymakers who often view play as a waste of valuable learning time.

"Play is really important for young children, for social and cognitive development," says psychologist Kathy Hirsh-Pasek, PhD, a child development researcher at Temple University. "And yet we're taking it away."

Whither Playtime?

Disappearing playtime at home and in schools stems from a common root, says Hirsh-Pasek: fear. "As a society and as parents, we believe we're at risk of falling behind," she says.

Marketers of infant and early childhood educational products stress that research on brain development shows a "critical period" before age 3 when neurons grow and develop connections, and they urge parents to make sure they harness this special learning time.

That concern has manifested itself in an ever-widening market for "edutainment" toys, and such products as vocabulary-enriching computers for tots have become the toy market's hottest segment. LeapFrog, one company that specializes in such toys, saw its sales nearly quadruple between 2000 and 2006, prompting industry giants like Mattel to follow them into the edutainment market.

A national fear of falling behind manifests itself in schools as well, Hirsh-Pasek says, via more standardized testing and a push for content to be taught at ever-earlier grade levels—expecting children to learn to read in kindergarten, for example, rather than waiting until first grade.

"We want to make sure that our kids are ready for a globalized society. So what do we do about it? We keep shoving more factoids at them," says Hirsh-Pasek.

The trouble, Hirsh-Pasek and Elkind argue, is that parents and educators are ignoring decades of evidence that young children learn best through active, exploratory play (sometimes guided by an adult) rather than through direct, lecture-style classroom instruction, flash cards and push-button computer learning toys that can push them to memorize facts that they're not cognitively ready to understand.

"The real problem is not that we don't know what's good pedagogy for children," Elkind says. "It's that we don't use what we know."

Tiny Scientists

Educators and researchers alike have long known or suspected that children learn from exploratory play. Italian educator Maria Montessori founded her schools in 1907, where children's own interests and abilities guide the pace of their learning. And beginning in the 1920s, Jean Piaget studied children's exploratory learning through close observations of his own and other children.

In the decades since, psychologists have expanded upon and refined their knowledge of how children learn through play. They've found that children learn spatial skills and counting through activities like playing with blocks, and they can pick up a rich vocabulary simply by hearing books read aloud.

Imaginary play and make-believe have myriad benefits as well, giving children practice working with others, and substituting one object, like a toy hammer, for another, like a phone—a knowledge of symbols that lays the foundation for reading and math.

This learning process is not haphazard, says Laura Schulz, PhD, a psychologist at the Early Childhood Cognition Lab at the Massachusetts Institute of Technology. She's found that preschoolers are, in some ways, rational little scientists in their approach. Children need to learn the properties of objects around them—an oven is hot, ice is cold, etc. Sensibly, they do this by recognizing that objects in similar categories have similar properties: if one ice cube is cold, the next one likely will be too.

In a series of studies, Schulz has investigated how violating these rules by surprising children with an object that has properties that don't fit into its predetermined category cause children to play with—and thus learn about—the object more.

For example, in one study, published last year in *Developmental Psychology* (Vol. 44, No. 5), Schulz showed 3- and 4-year-olds how a magnetic object she called a "blicket" would stick to a table. When she then asked the children to play with a bunch of "blickets" that were not magnetized, the children were surprised to see that the "blickets" failed to stick, and played with the objects longer.

However, when Schulz told the children that the nonmagnetic objects were called "dax," the children weren't surprised that these "new" objects failed to stick and they quickly lost interest in them—even though "dax" looked the same as "blickets."

Meanwhile, correlational research by Hirsh-Pasek and others backs up the claim that children learn best, in their early years, through play. In one study, she found no differences in academic achievement by first grade between children who had gone to "academic" preschools versus those who'd gone to more play-oriented preschools. She did, however, find that the children from academic preschools were more anxious.

Hirsh-Pasek emphasizes, however, that children in play-oriented schools must still learn content.

"I think many [researchers] would say that we cannot have a rich education that consists of solely free play. The evidence here is clear. Preschoolers who are exposed to social problem solving, math and reading are better prepared for the transition to school and do better in early elementary school . . . The issue here is not whether we should have content for children, but how it should be presented."

She adds: "What's happened is that this has become a warring faction between direct instruction, which has a narrow focus on reading and math, and playful learning. But these two foci are not incompatible. Playful learning leads to literacy and math skills."

Champions of Frivolity

Hirsh-Pasek, Elkind and other researchers who agree with them believe they are swimming against the tide when it comes to convincing parents and policymakers to give children the space to explore and play.

In 1981, Elkind published the now-classic book *The Hurried Child,* warning against trying to push children into academics and adulthood too soon. In the 28 years since that book was first published, he says the hurrying has only accelerated. His most recent book, *The Power of Play* (Da Capo Press, 2007), focuses specifically on how children are losing free, unstructured playtime, and the importance of play for children's development.

Hirsh-Pasek, too, has written books, including a guide for parents called *Einstein Never Used Flash Cards* (Rodale Books, 2003), that encourage them to put down the cards and instead play blocks with their children, read to them and encourage make-believe play.

But Elkind worries that efforts like his and Hirsh-Pasek's are "a drop in the bucket" against educational toymakers' marketing millions. Hirsh-Pasek, meanwhile, believes her most difficult opponent is fear—parents' and societies' fear of children falling behind.

"None of us want a kid left behind," she says. "But we have to ask, what are the skills we want our kids to have?"

Parents might think that the most critical skills—reading, writing and math—require early and intense instruction. But according to Hirsh-Pasek, just as important are creativity, critical thinking and the ability to learn from failure—all skills best learned through play.

From *Monitor on Psychology* by Lea Winerman, September 2009, pp. 50–52. Copyright © 2009 by American Psychological Association. Reprinted by permission. No further distribution without permission from the American Psychological Association.

The Role of Neurobiological Deficits in Childhood Antisocial Behavior

STEPHANIE H. M. VAN GOOZEN, GRAEME FAIRCHILD, AND GORDON T. HAROLD

Antisocial behavior is a significant social and clinical concern. Every year, more than 1.6 million people are killed as a result of violence, and many more suffer from physical or mental health problems stemming from violence (World Health Organization, 2002). Antisocial behavior committed by youths is an issue of particular concern. A recent survey showed that citizens of European nations see themselves as having "significant" difficulties with antisocial behavior, and that the problem is above all associated with people under 25 years of age ("Bad behaviour," 2006).

The term *antisocial behavior* refers to the fact that people who are on the receiving end of the behavior are disadvantaged by it, and that social norms and values are violated. Not only aggression but also activities such as theft, vandalism, lying, truancy, running away from home, and oppositional behaviors are involved.

Most normally developing children will occasionally exhibit negative and disobedient behavior toward adults and engage in lying, fighting, and bullying other children. When antisocial behavior forms a pattern that goes beyond the "normal" realm and starts to have adverse effects on the child's functioning, psychiatrists tend to make a diagnosis of conduct disorder (CD) or oppositional defiant disorder (ODD; American Psychiatric Association, 1994). These disorders are relatively common in children, with estimated prevalences ranging from 5 to 10%. The extent to which these disorders can be treated via therapy is limited, and, as a result, these children are at risk for a host of negative outcomes in adolescence and adulthood, including dropping out of school, criminality unemployment, dependence on welfare, and substance abuse (Hill & Maughan, 2001).

There is a growing consensus that both child-specific (i.e., genetic, temperamental) and social (e.g., early adversity) factors contribute to the development and maintenance of antisocial behavior, although most research has focused on identifying specific contextual factors that impinge on the developing child. For example, negative life events, family stress, and parental relationship problems have been associated with antisocial-behavior problems in children. However, there is increasing evidence that factors organic to individual children exacerbate the risk of antisocial behavior to those who live with social adversity. Here, we review evidence relating to the role of neurobiological factors in accounting for the link between early adversity and childhood antisocial behavior and propose that consideration of biological factors underlying this stress-distress link significantly advances understanding of the mechanisms explaining individual differences in the etiology of antisocial behavior.

Research suggests that neurobiological deficits related to the functioning of the stress systems in children with CD are linked to antisocial behavior. We argue that familial factors (e.g., genetic influences, early adversity) are linked to negative outcomes through the mediating and transactional interplay with neurobiological deficits (see Figure 1) and propose that stress hyporeactivity is an index of persistent and serious antisocial behavior.

Stress-Response Systems

There are clear indications that stress plays an important role in explaining individual differences in antisocial behavior. The systems involved in the regulation of stress are the neuroendocrine hypothalamic-pituitary-adrenal (HPA) axis and the paychophysiological autonomic nervous system (ANS). Cortisol is studied in relation to HPA-axis activation, and heart rate (HR) and skin-conductance (SC) responses are used as markers of ANS (re)activity.

The starting point of our approach is that antisocial individuals are less sensitive to stress. This can be deduced from the fact that antisocial individuals engage in risky or dangerous behavior more often than other people do and seem less deterred by its possible negative consequences. There are two explanations for the proposed relationship between lower stress sensitivity and antisocial behavior. One theory claims that antisocial individuals are fearless (Raine, 1996). A lack of fear leads to antisocial behavior because individuals are less sensitive to the negative consequences of their own or other people's behavior in general and to the receipt of punishment in particular. The implications for treatment are clear: Antisocial individuals will have problems learning the association between behavior and punishment, such

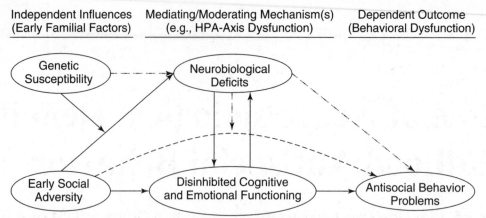

| Independent Influences (Early Familial Factors) | Mediating/Moderating Mechanism(s) (e.g., HPA-Axis Dysfunction) | Dependent Outcome (Behavioral Dysfunction) |

Figure 1 Theoretical model relating early social adversity to later antisocial behavior problems. It is hypothesized that this relationship is explained by the underlying mediating and moderating role of neurobiological factors. The dashed rolled lines emanating from genetic susceptibility to neurobiological deficits and from neurobiological deficits to antisocial behavior problems represent an indirect (or mediating) pathway between these factors. The bold line emanating from genetic susceptibility to the pathway linking early social adversity to neurobiological deficits, and the dashed-dotted line from neurobiological deficits to the pathway linking early social adversity to antisocial behavior problems, represent proposed moderating influences from each source variable (i.e., genetic susceptibility and neurobiological deficits). A moderating influence is the equivalent of statistical interaction between two theoretical constructs. Bold and dashed-dotted lines in all other instances represent direct and indirect pathways linking primary theoretical constructs. For a full exposition of this model, see van Goosen, Fairchild, Snoek, and Harold (2007).

that pointing out the negative consequences of behavior, or punishing unacceptable behavior, is likely to have little or no effect.

The second explanation focuses on stress thresholds and sensation-seeking behavior (Zuckerman, 1979), and argues that antisocial individuals have elevated thresholds for stress. They are more easily bored and less easily put off by situations that normal people find stressful or dangerous.

What evidence is there that dysfunctional stress systems play a role in antisocial behavior? Several studies (e.g., Virkkumen, 1985) have found that antisocial adults have low resting levels of cortisol, SC, and HR. There is also evidence of inverse relationships between these physiological variables and the severity of the behavioral problems shown. Studies investigating the relation between biological stress parameters and antisocial behavior have also been performed in children (e.g., van Goozen et al., 1998), and the predicted (inverse) relations have been found.

Stress variables can also predict antisocial behavior over time. Raine, Venables, and Mednick (1997) measured HR in more than 1,700 three-year-old children. Aggressive behavior was assessed at age 11. Raine et al. found that low resting HR at age 3 predicted aggressive behavior at age 11. In a study of criminals' sons (who are at risk of becoming delinquent), Brenman et al. (1997) found that boys who did not become delinquent had higher HR and SC than did boys who became delinquent. The authors concluded that the boys in the former group were biologically protected by their heightened autonomic responsivity.

Studies of youths who engage in antisocial behavior show that they, like antisocial adults, have less reactive stress systems than do youths who do not engage in antisocial behavior. The question is whether the same applies to children with serious antisocial behavior who have been diagnosed with CD or ODD.

Stress Studies in CD Children

Most studies collect stress data under resting conditions rather than during stress exposure. Antisocial individuals might be different from normal individuals in two respects: A low resting stress level could result in failing to avoid, or even approaching, stressful situations; and low stress reactivity implies that one is more fearless and cares less about possible negative consequences.

Our studies use a paradigm in which psychosocial stress is evoked by exposing children to frustration, provocation, and competition (e.g., van Goozen et al., 1998). The participant competes against a fictitious videotaped "opponent" who behaves in an antagonistic manner. The participant and opponent perform computerized tasks on which they can earn points. The participant is told that the person who earns the most points will receive an attractive prize. Some tasks are impossible to complete, which induces frustration. HR and SC are measured continuously, and cortisol is collected repeatedly in saliva.

CD children show lower HR, SC, and cortisol reactivity to stress than do normal children. Although CD children appear to be less affected at a biological level, they react more angrily and aggressively to provocation than do non-CD children and report feeling quite upset. It is known that CD children are impulsive, have hostile appraisal patterns, and engage in conflictual situations. It is striking that this pattern of appraisal and behavior is not accompanied by contextually appropriate somatic changes.

Genetic factors likely play a role in the functioning of the HPA axis and ANS. There is also evidence that stressful events—by which we mean serious stressors like neglect and traumatization—play an important role in "programming" the stress systems, particularly the HPA axis. This evidence comes mainly from nonhuman animal studies, but the neurobiological consequences of the types of severe stress that can be manipulated in animal studies also occur in humans.

Early Experience and Family Adversity

Physical and biological problems during important phases in development (e.g., birth complications, stress or illness during pregnancy), together with early adversity (e.g., malnutrition, neglect, abuse), contribute importantly to the development of personality and psychopathology. There is increasing evidence that interactions between biological and environmental factors affect the developing brain (Huizink, Mulder, & Buitelaar, 2004).

Nonhuman animal studies show that stressors in early life can have permanent effects on the functioning of the HPA axis, resulting in altered basal and stress-reactivity levels. For example, Liu et al. (1997) varied the amount of licking and grooming behavior in mothers of newborn rats. In adulthood, offspring who had been exposed to normal maternal care were more capable of handling stress than were rats that had received less care. The former also expressed more stress-hormone receptors in the hippocampus, an area important for stress regulation, than did rats that had received less care. Thus, maternal behavior had a direct and lasting effect on the development of the stress systems of the offspring.

Such conclusions are based on data from nonhuman animals, and for obvious reasons it is difficult to conduct similar studies on humans. However, evidence from a handful of studies involving institutionalized children suggests that the processes at work are similar (Carlson & Earls, 1997; Gunnar, Morison, Chisolm, & Schuder, 2001).

Antisocial children are more likely to come from adverse rearing environments involving atypical caregiver–child interactions (Rutter & Silberg, 2002). It is known that CD children are more likely to experience compromised pre- or perinatal development due to maternal smoking, poor nutrition, or exposure to alcohol and/or drugs. It is possible that these factors have affected such children's stress-response systems and resulted in children with a difficult temperament.

Stress Hyporeactivity as a Mediating Factor

We have suggested that physiological hyporeactivity may reflect an inability to generate visceral signals to guide behavior and, in particular, to regulate anger and reactive aggression (van Goozen, Fairchild, Snoek, & Harold, 2007). Evidence from nonhuman animals indicates that abolishing the hormonal response to stress may impair processing of social signals and lead to abnormal patterns of aggression (Haller, Halász, Mikics, & Kruk, 2004). These studies also showed that abnormal aggressive behavior can be prevented by mimicking the hormonal response normally seen during aggressive encounters. These findings have clear parallels with abnormal aggression in humans, in the sense that the behavior is not only excessive but also often risky, badly judged, and callous.

We have proposed an integrative theoretical model linking genetic factors, early adversity, cognitive and neurobiological regulatory mechanisms, and childhood antisocial behavior (van Goozen et al., 2007; see Figure 1). Interactions between genetic predispositions and the environment in which they are expressed appear to be crucial in the etiology of antisocial-behavior problems. A genetic predisposition toward antisocial behavior may be expressed in adverse rearing environments in which the child receives harsh or inconsistent discipline or is exposed to high levels of interparental conflict or marital breakdown (Moffitt, 2005). It is likely that the origin of antisocial behavior in young children lies in this combination of a difficult temperament and a harsh environment in which there is ineffective socialization: A difficult child elicits harsh, inconsistent, and negative socialization behaviors, as a result of which a difficult temperament develops into antisocial behavior (Lykken, 1995). Conversely, the effects of a genetic predisposition may be minimized if the child is raised in an environment in which the parents express warmth or adopt a consistent, authoritative parenting style.

Some children are born with a more easygoing temperament than others. In cases of "hard-to-manage" children, a child's genotype can evoke negative behavior from the environment because genetic influences lead the individual to create, seek out, or otherwise end up in environments that match the genotype (Rutter & Silberg, 2002). These active, evocative gene–environment processes are extremely important in understanding the development and continuity of antisocial behavior (Moffitt, 2005). Social factors occurring independently of the child's genetic makeup or temperament can serve as contributory factors (Harold, Aitken, & Shelton, 2008).

We noted above that early brain development is vulnerable to the effects of environmental stress (Huizink et al., 2004), and that CD children are likely to have been exposed to early stress. A down-regulation of the stress-response system in the face of chronic stress in early life would be an adaptive mechanism, avoiding chronic arousal and excessive energy expenditure that could ultimately result in serious pathophysiological consequences. Given what we know about the background of CD children, it is plausible that these processes have occurred.

We propose that physiological hyporeactivity is a mediating and/or moderating factor for persistent and severe antisocial behavior and that the effects of variations in genetic makeup and early adversity on childhood antisocial behavior occur via this deficit. The primary pathway by which familial factors are linked to antisocial outcome is the reciprocal interplay with neurobiological deficits and resulting disinhibited cognitive (e.g., impulsivity, hostile bias) and emotional (e.g., increased anger) processing, with the latter serving as the psychological gateway through which neurobiological deficits find their expression in antisocial behavior.

Conclusion

Antisocial behavior in children can be persistent and difficult to treat. Although behavioral interventions have been shown to be effective in milder forms of problem behavior, they have limited effectiveness in more seriously disturbed children (Hill & Maughan, 2001).

At present, we do not know what causes the pattern of neurobiological impairments observed in antisocial children, although it is clear that genetic factors are involved (Caspi et al., 2002). An important line of research suggests that psychosocial adversity affects brain development. Knowing that many CD children have problematic backgrounds, it seems possible that exposure to severe stress has had an effect on the development of their stress systems. Longitudinal research in high-risk children is needed to shed more light on this issue.

Future interventions and treatments should benefit from a neurobiological approach: Neurobiological assessment of high-risk children could indicate whether their deficits are such that interventions involving "empathy induction" or "learning from punishment," for example, are unlikely to work. In such cases, pharmacological interventions could be considered as a treatment option. An important line of future research is to establish whether CD children with attenuated stress (re)activity would be more effectively treated by using pharmacological therapies that reinstate normal HPA-axis functioning.

Current interventions for childhood antisocial behavior have limited success because we lack knowledge of the cognitive–emotional problems of these children and their neurobiological bases. We also fail to assess the environmental risk factors that affect individual neurodevelopment. Furthermore, available treatment options do not target the individual's specific neurobiological vulnerabilities. It seems prudent to identify subgroups of children in whom different causal processes initiate and maintain behavioral problems. This should result in a better match between patient and treatment.

A final point is that the understandable tendency to focus on persistence of antisocial behavior runs the risk of overlooking the fact that a substantial proportion of antisocial children do not grow up to be antisocial adults (with prevalence rates for antisocial children who persist into adulthood ranging from 35 to 75%). Neurobiological factors could also account for this: Promising data from a handful of studies show that neurobiological factors differ between children who persist in and desist from antisocial behavior (Brennan et al., 1997; van de Wiel, van Goozen, Matthys, Snoek, & van Engeland, 2004). Expanding on this research base is essential if we are to reach a more adequate understanding of the causes, course, and consequences of childhood antisocial behavior and, most importantly, devise effective ways of reducing the negative consequences for society.

Recommended Reading

Hill, J., & Maughan, B. (2001). *Conduct disorders in childhood and adolescence.* Cambridge, UK: Cambridge University Press. A clearly written and comprehensive review for readers who wish to expand their knowledge on conduct disorders in youngsters.

Moffitt, T.E. (2005). The new look of behavioral genetics in developmental psychopathology: Gene–environment interplay in antisocial behaviors. *Psychological Bulletin, 131,* 533–554. Explains and discusses the gene–environment interplay in antisocial behavior in more detail.

van Goozen, S.H.M., Fairchild, G., Snoek, H., & Harold, G.T. (2007). The evidence for a neurobiological model of childhood antisocial behavior. *Psychological Bulletin, 133,* 149–182. Discusses the neurobiological basis of antisocial behavior in greater detail than the current paper.

References

American Psychiatric Association. (1994). *Diagnostic and statistical manual of mental disorders* (4th ed.). Washington, DC: Author.

Bad behaviour 'worst in Europe'. (2006). BBC News. Downloaded April 30, 2008, from http://news.bbc.co.uk/l/hi/uk/4751315.stm

Brennan, P.A., Raine, A., Schulsinger, F., Kirkegaard-Sorensen, L., Knop, J., Hutchings, B., et al. (1997). Psychophysiological protective factors for male subjects at high risk for criminal behavior. *American Journal of Psychiatry, 154,* 853–855.

Carlson, M., & Earls, F. (1997). Psychological and neuroendocrinological sequelae of early social deprivation in institutionalized children in Romania. *Annals of the New York Academy of Sciences, 807,* 419–428.

Caspi, A., McClay J., Moffitt, T.E., Mill, J., Martin, J., Craig, I.W., et al. (2002). Role of the genotype in the cycle of violence in maltreated children. *Science, 297,* 851–854.

Gunnar, M.R., Morison, S.J., Chisholm, K., & Schuder, M. (2001). Salivary cortisol levels in children adopted from Romanian orphanages. *Development and Psychopathology, 13,* 611–628.

Harold, G.T, Aitken, J.J., & Shelton, K.H. (2008). Inter-parental conflict and children's academic attainment: A longitudinal analysis. *Journal of Child Psychology and Psychiatry, 48,* 1223–1232.

Haller, J., Halász, J., Mikics, E., & Kruk, M.R. (2004). Chronic glucocorticoid deficiency-induced abnormal aggression, autonomic hypoarousal, and social deficit in rats. *Journal of Neuroendocrinology, 16,* 550–557.

Hill, J., & Maughan, B. (2001). *Conduct disorders in childhood and adolescence.* Cambridge, UK: Cambridge University Press.

Huizink, A.C., Mulder, E.J.H., & Buitelaar, J.K. (2004). Prenatal stress and risk for psychopathology: Specific effects or induction of general susceptibility. *Psychological Bulletin, 130,* 115–142.

Liu, D., Diorio, J., Tannenbaum, B., Caldji, C., Francis, D., Freedman, A., et al. (1997). Maternal care, hippocampal glucocorticoid receptors, and hypothalamic-pituitary-adrenal responses to stress. *Science, 277,* 1659–1662.

Lykken, D.T (1995). *The antisocial personalities.* Hillsdale, NJ: Erlbaum.

Moffitt, T.E. (2005). The new look of behavioral genetics in developmental psychopathology: Gene–environment interplay in antisocial behaviors. *Psychological Bulletin, 131,* 533–554.

Raine, A. (1996). Autonomic nervous system activity and violence. In D.M. Stoff & R.B. Cairns (Eds.), *Aggression and violence: Genetic, neurobiological and biological perspectives* (pp. 145–168). Mahwah, NJ: Erlbaum.

Raine, A., Venables, P.H., & Mednick, S.A. (1997). Low resting heart rate at age 3 years predisposes to aggression at age 11 years: Evidence from the Mauritius Child Health Project. *Journal of the American Academy of Child and Adolescent Psychiatry, 36,* 1457–1464.

Rutter, M., & Silberg, J. (2002). Gene–environment interplay in relation to emotional and behavioral disturbance. *Annual Review of Psychology, 53,* 463–490.

van de Wiel, N.M.H., van Goozen, S.H.M., Matthys, W., Snoek, H., & van Engeland, H. (2004). Cortisol and treatment effect in children with disruptive behavior disorders: A preliminary study. *Journal of the American Academy of Child and Adolescent Psychiatry, 43,* 1011–1018.

van Goozen, S.H.M., Fairchild, G., Snoek, H., & Harold, G.T. (2007). The evidence for a neurobiological model of childhood antisocial behaviour. *Psychological Bulletin, 133,* 149–182.

van Goozen, S.H.M., Matthys, W., Cohen-Kettenis P.T, Gispen-de Wied, C., Wiegant, V.M., & van Engeland, H. (1998). Salivary cortisol and cardiovascular activity during stress in oppositional-defiant disorder boys and normal controls. *Biological Psychiatry, 43,* 531–539.

Virkkunen, M. (1985). Urinary free cortisol secretion in habitually violent offenders. *Acta Psychiatrica Scandinavica, 72,* 40–44.

World Health Organization (2002). *World report on violence and health.* E.G. Krug, L.L. Dahlman, J.A. Mercy, A.B. Zwi, & R. Lozano (Eds.). Geneva, Switzerland: Author.

Zuckerman, M. (1979). *Sensation seeking: Beyond the optimum level of arousal.* Hillsdale, NJ: Erlbaum.

Address correspondence to **STEPHANIE H.M. VAN GOOZEN,** School of Psychology Cardiff University, Tower Building, Park Place, Cardiff CF1O 3AT, United Kingdom; e-mail: vangoozens@cardiff.ac.uk.

UNIT 4

Parenting and Family Issues

Unit Selections

Key Points to Consider

- Were your father and mother strict disciplinarians? Explain what methods your parents used to discipline or control your behavior when you were growing up as children. Did other parents you knew from different backgrounds (ethnic or social class) discipline their children in similar or different ways? Explain. What sort of parental discipline (or lack thereof) seemed to result in the most maladjusted children in your neighborhood? What sort of parents produced well behaved, happy children who turned into successful adults? What sort of disciplinary methods do you plan to use with your own children? Explain why and provide supporting evidence for your answer.

- If you have brothers or sisters, have you ever felt your parents favored your siblings over yourself? Does this favoritism continue today as adults? How does this favoritism affect your feelings and relationships with your parents or your siblings today? Explain how you are similar to and different from your siblings. What things did your parents or family do that helped to create or intensify these differences or similarities?

- A significant number of children in the United States will experience the divorce of their parents. Have you or do you know of children who have experienced their parents' divorce? Explain how divorce impacts children at different ages and by gender. Describe factors that can ameliorate the negative effects of divorce. If your parents divorced, at what age were you, how did it make you feel, and explain how you coped with the divorce. Did your parents' divorce influence your feelings about marriage and divorce? If you felt you needed to get a divorce and you have children, explain what could you do to reduce the negative impact to your children.

- Effective parenting is not a function of one's sexual orientation, and children raised by gay or lesbian parents develop normally and are equally well adjusted as children raised by heterosexual parents. How might you help children raised by gay parents cope with the unfair discrimination they often receive from other adults and children? What steps could you take to help educate others of these results?

Student Website
www.mhhe.com/cls

Internet References

The National Association for Child Development (NACD)
  www.nacd.org

National Council on Family Relations
  www.ncfr.com

Parenting and Families
  www.cyfc.umn.edu

Parentsplace.com: Single Parenting
  www.parentsplace.com/family/archive/0,10693,239458,00.html

National Stepfamily Resource Center
  www.stepfam.org

Few people today realize that the potential freedom to choose parenthood—deciding whether to become a parent, deciding when to have children, or deciding how many children to have—is a development due to the advent of reliable methods of contraception and other recent sociocultural changes. Moreover, unlike any other significant job to which we may aspire, few, if any, of us will receive any formal training or information about the lifelong responsibility of parenting. For most of us, our behavior is generally based on our own conscious and subconscious recollections of how we were parented as well as on our observations of the parenting practices of others around us. In fact, our society often behaves as if the mere act of producing a baby automatically confers upon the parents an innate parenting ability, furthermore, that a family's parenting practices should remain private and not be subjected to scrutiny or criticism by outsiders.

Given this climate, it is not surprising that misconceptions about many parenting practices persist. Only within the last 40 years or so have researchers turned their lenses on the scientific study of the family. Social, historical, cultural, and economic forces also have dramatically changed the face of the American family today. In fact, the vast majority of parents never take courses or learn of the research on parenting. This unit helps present some of the research on the many complex factors related to successful parenting.

One of the most fundamental achievements of infancy is for the baby to develop a strong attachment to a parent or primary adult caregiver. Recent data by researchers Johnson, Dweck, and Chen in "Evidence of Infants' Internal Working Models of Attachment" show that infants are capable of developing abstract mental attachment representations in forging an attachment bond.

Each year, children die as a result of being left in an overheated vehicle. Should this be called neglect and should these parents be punished? If punishment is meted out, what form would be appropriate? Gene Weingarten writes about this horrific occurrence in "Fatal Distraction: Forgetting a Child in the Backseat of a Car Is a Horrifying Mistake. Is It a Crime?" and asks readers to consider whether it could happen to them.

Between 43 percent and 50 percent of first marriages will end in divorce in the United States. Researcher Jennifer Lansford summarizes the wealth of data on the effects of divorce on children's development in "Parental Divorce and Children's Adjustment" and makes recommendations that might improve children's adjustment to divorce in the areas of child custody and child support policies and enforcement.

Parental favoritism for some of their children over others is discussed by researchers in "Within-Family Differences in Parent–Child Relations across the Life Course." They review

© Getty Images/Stockbyte

research studies showing that parental favoritism can begin very early in children's development and often continues and grows stronger when children become adults. The authors discuss factors that influence favoritism including gender, birth order, temperament, and health status as well as the positive and negative effects of parental favoritism. Similarly, researchers in "Siblings Play Formative, Influential Role as 'Agents of Socialization'", explain how siblings learn from one another and how this contributes to both differences and similarities among siblings.

Research on lesbian and gay parents demonstrates that children's adjustment and development are not negatively affected by having same-sex parents. In fact, the studies show that children from same-sex parents are equally likely to thrive as children from heterosexual parents. What matters more is the quality of the parenting relationships as described in Patterson's article, "Children of Lesbian and Gay Parents." This important data is being used to assist judges when awarding custody and helping to develop sound family policies.

Very few parents in America or anywhere else on the planet ever take courses in parenting or child development. So how do parents learn to parent? Do we learn to parent from the way our parents treated us as children? Do parents control or discipline their children differently depending on different cultural norms? What forms of discipline or parental control and guidance are least effective or most effective? Researchers answer some of these questions in "The Role of Parental Control in Children's Development in Western and East Asian Countries" and in "The Messy Room Dilemma: When to Ignore Behavior, When to Change It."

Children of Lesbian and Gay Parents

Does parental sexual orientation affect child development, and if so, how? Studies using convenience samples, studies using samples drawn from known populations, and studies based on samples that are representative of larger populations all converge on similar conclusions. More than two decades of research has failed to reveal important differences in the adjustment or development of children or adolescents reared by same-sex couples compared to those reared by other-sex couples. Results of the research suggest that qualities of family relationships are more tightly linked with child outcomes than is parental sexual orientation.

CHARLOTTE J. PATTERSON

Does parental sexual orientation affect child development, and if so, how? This question has often been raised in the context of legal and policy proceedings relevant to children, such as those involving adoption, child custody, or visitation. Divergent views have been offered by professionals from the fields of psychology, sociology, medicine, and law (Patterson, Fulcher, & Wainright, 2002). While this question has most often been raised in legal and policy contexts, it is also relevant to theoretical issues. For example, does healthy human development require that a child grow up with parents of each gender? And if not, what would that mean for our theoretical understanding of parent–child relations? (Patterson & Hastings, in press). In this article, I describe some research designed to address these questions.

Early Research

Research on children with lesbian and gay parents began with studies focused on cases in which children had been born in the context of a heterosexual marriage. After parental separation and divorce, many children in these families lived with divorced lesbian mothers. A number of researchers compared development among children of divorced lesbian mothers with that among children of divorced heterosexual mothers and found few significant differences (Patterson, 1997; Stacey & Biblarz, 2001).

These studies were valuable in addressing concerns of judges who were required to decide divorce and child custody cases, but they left many questions unanswered. In particular, because the children who participated in this research had been born into homes with married mothers and fathers, it was not obvious how to understand the reasons for their healthy development. The possibility that children's early exposure to apparently heterosexual male and female role models had contributed to healthy development could not be ruled out.

When lesbian or gay parents rear infants and children from birth, do their offspring grow up in typical ways and show healthy development? To address this question, it was important to study children who had never lived with heterosexual parents. In the 1990s, a number of investigators began research of this kind.

An early example was the Bay Area Families Study, in which I studied a group of 4- to 9-year-old children who had been born to or adopted early in life by lesbian mothers (Patterson, 1996, 1997). Data were collected during home visits. Results from in-home interviews and also from questionnaires showed that children had regular contact with a wide range of adults of both genders, both within and outside of their families. The children's self-concepts and preferences for same-gender playmates and activities were much like those of other children their ages. Moreover, standardized measures of social competence and of behavior problems, such as those from the Child Behavior Checklist (CBCL), showed that they scored within the range of normal variation for a representative sample of same-aged American children. It was clear from this study and others like it that it was quite possible for lesbian mothers to rear healthy children.

Studies Based on Samples Drawn from Known Populations

Interpretation of the results from the Bay Area Families Study was, however, affected by its sampling procedures. The study had been based on a convenience sample that had been assembled by word of mouth. It was therefore impossible to rule out the possibility that families who participated in the research were especially well adjusted. Would a more representative sample yield different results?

To find out, Ray Chan, Barbara Raboy, and I conducted research in collaboration with the Sperm Bank of California

(Chan, Raboy, & Patterson, 1998; Fulcher, Sutfin, Chan, Scheib, & Patterson, 2005). Over the more than 15 years of its existence, the Sperm Bank of California's clientele had included many lesbian as well as heterosexual women. For research purposes, this clientele was a finite population from which our sample could be drawn. The Sperm Bank of California also allowed a sample in which, both for lesbian and for heterosexual groups, one parent was biologically related to the child and one was not.

We invited all clients who had conceived children using the resources of the Sperm Bank of California and who had children 5 years old or older to participate in our research. The resulting sample was composed of 80 families, 55 headed by lesbian and 25 headed by heterosexual parents. Materials were mailed to participating families, with instructions to complete them privately and return them in self-addressed stamped envelopes we provided.

Results replicated and expanded upon those from earlier research. Children of lesbian and heterosexual parents showed similar, relatively high levels of social competence, as well as similar, relatively low levels of behavior problems on the parent form of the CBCL. We also asked the children's teachers to provide evaluations of children's adjustment on the Teacher Report Form of the CBCL, and their reports agreed with those of parents. Parental sexual orientation was not related to children's adaptation. Quite apart from parental sexual orientation, however, and consistent with findings from years of research on children of heterosexual parents, when parent–child relationships were marked by warmth and affection, children were more likely to be developing well. Thus, in this sample drawn from a known population, measures of children's adjustment were unrelated to parental sexual orientation (Chan et al., 1998; Fulcher et al., 2005).

Even as they provided information about children born to lesbian mothers, however, these new results also raised additional questions. Women who conceive children at sperm banks are generally both well educated and financially comfortable. It was possible that these relatively privileged women were able to protect children from many forms of discrimination. What if a more diverse group of families were to be studied? In addition, the children in this sample averaged 7 years of age, and some concerns focus on older children and adolescents. What if an older group of youngsters were to be studied? Would problems masked by youth and privilege in earlier studies emerge in an older, more diverse sample?

Studies Based on Representative Samples

An opportunity to address these questions was presented by the availability of data from the National Longitudinal Study of Adolescent Health (Add Health). The Add Health study involved a large, ethnically diverse, and essentially representative sample of American adolescents and their parents. Data for our research were drawn from surveys and interviews completed by more than 12,000 adolescents and their parents at home and from surveys completed by adolescents at school.

Parents were not queried directly about their sexual orientation but were asked if they were involved in a "marriage, or marriage-like relationship." If parents acknowledged such a relationship, they were also asked the gender of their partner. Thus, we identified a group of 44 12- to 18-year-olds who lived with parents involved in marriage or marriage-like relationships with same-sex partners. We compared them with a matched group of adolescents living with other-sex couples. Data from the archives of the Add Health study allowed us to address many questions about adolescent development.

Consistent with earlier findings, results of this work revealed few differences in adjustment between adolescents living with same-sex parents and those living with opposite-sex parents (Wainright, Russell, & Patterson, 2004; Wainright & Patterson, 2006). There were no significant differences between teenagers living with same-sex parents and those living with other-sex parents on self-reported assessments of psychological well-being, such as self-esteem and anxiety; measures of school outcomes, such as grade point averages and trouble in school; or measures of family relationships, such as parental warmth and care from adults and peers. Adolescents in the two groups were equally likely to say that they had been involved in a romantic relationship in the last 18 months, and they were equally likely to report having engaged in sexual intercourse. The only statistically reliable difference between the two groups—that those with same-sex parents felt a greater sense of connection to people at school—favored the youngsters living with same-sex couples. There were no significant differences in self-reported substance use, delinquency, or peer victimization between those reared by same- or other-sex couples (Wainright & Patterson, 2006).

Although the gender of parents' partners was not an important predictor of adolescent well-being, other aspects of family relationships were significantly associated with teenagers' adjustment. Consistent with other findings about adolescent development, the qualities of family relationships rather than the gender of parents' partners were consistently related to adolescent outcomes. Parents who reported having close relationships with their offspring had adolescents who reported more favorable adjustment. Not only is it possible for children and adolescents who are parented by same-sex couples to develop in healthy directions, but—even when studied in an extremely diverse, representative sample of American adolescents—they generally do.

These findings have been supported by results from many other studies, both in the United States and abroad. Susan Golombok and her colleagues have reported similar results with a near-representative sample of children in the United Kingdom (Golombok et al., 2003). Others, both in Europe and in the United States, have described similar findings (e.g., Brewaeys, Ponjaert, Van Hall, & Golombok, 1997).

The fact that children of lesbian mothers generally develop in healthy ways should not be taken to suggest that they encounter no challenges. Many investigators have remarked upon the fact that children of lesbian and gay parents may encounter anti-gay sentiments in their daily lives. For example, in a study of 10-year-old children born to lesbian mothers, Gartrell, Deck, Rodas, Peyser, and Banks (2005) reported that a substantial minority had encountered anti-gay sentiments among their peers. Those who had had such encounters were likely to report having felt angry, upset, or sad about these experiences. Children of lesbian and gay parents may be exposed to prejudice against their parents in some settings, and this may be painful for them, but evidence for the idea that such encounters affect children's overall adjustment is lacking.

Conclusions

Does parental sexual orientation have an important impact on child or adolescent development? Results of recent research provide no evidence that it does. In fact, the findings suggest that parental sexual orientation is less important than the qualities of family relationships. More important to youth than the gender of their parent's partner is the quality of daily interaction and the strength of relationships with the parents they have.

One possible approach to findings like the ones described above might be to shrug them off by reiterating the familiar adage that "one cannot prove the null hypothesis." To respond in this way, however, is to miss the central point of these studies. Whether or not any measurable impact of parental sexual orientation on children's development is ever demonstrated, the main conclusions from research to date remain clear: Whatever correlations between child outcomes and parental sexual orientation may exist, they are less important than those between child outcomes and the qualities of family relationships.

Although research to date has made important contributions, many issues relevant to children of lesbian and gay parents remain in need of study. Relatively few studies have examined the development of children adopted by lesbian or gay parents or of children born to gay fathers; further research in both areas would be welcome (Patterson, 2004). Some notable longitudinal studies have been reported, and they have found children of same-sex couples to be in good mental health. Greater understanding of family relationships and transitions over time would, however, be helpful, and longitudinal studies would be valuable. Future research could also benefit from the use of a variety of methodologies.

Meanwhile, the clarity of findings in this area has been acknowledged by a number of major professional organizations. For instance, the governing body of the American Psychological Association (APA) voted unanimously in favor of a statement that said, "Research has shown that the adjustment, development, and psychological well-being of children is unrelated to parental sexual orientation and that children of lesbian and gay parents are as likely as those of heterosexual parents to flourish" (APA, 2004). The American Bar Association, the American Medical Association, the American Academy of Pediatrics, the American Psychiatric Association, and other mainstream professional groups have issued similar statements.

The findings from research on children of lesbian and gay parents have been used to inform legal and public policy debates across the country (Patterson et al., 2002). The research literature on this subject has been cited in amicus briefs filed by the APA in cases dealing with adoption, child custody, and also in cases related to the legality of marriages between same-sex partners. Psychologists serving as expert witnesses have presented findings on these issues in many different courts (Patterson et al., 2002). Through these and other avenues, results of research on lesbian and gay parents and their children are finding their way into public discourse.

The findings are also beginning to address theoretical questions about critical issues in parenting. The importance of gender in parenting is one such issue. When children fare well in two-parent lesbian-mother or gay-father families, this suggests that the gender of one's parents cannot be a critical factor in child development. Results of research on children of lesbian and gay parents cast doubt upon the traditional assumption that gender is important in parenting. Our data suggest that it is the quality of parenting rather than the gender of parents that is significant for youngsters' development.

Research on children of lesbian and gay parents is thus located at the intersection of a number of classic and contemporary concerns. Studies of lesbian- and gay-parented families allow researchers to address theoretical questions that had previously remained difficult or impossible to answer. They also address oft-debated legal questions of fact about development of children with lesbian and gay parents. Thus, research on children of lesbian and gay parents contributes to public debate and legal decision making, as well as to theoretical understanding of human development.

References

American Psychological Association (2004). Resolution on sexual orientation, parents, and children. Retrieved September 25, 2006, from www.apa.org/pi/lgbc/policy/parentschildren.pdf

Brewaeys, A., Ponjaert, I., Van Hall, E.V., & Golombok, S. (1997). Donor insemination: Child development and family functioning in lesbian mother families. *Human Reproduction, 12,* 1349–1359.

Chan, R.W., Raboy, B., & Patterson, C.J. (1998). Psychosocial adjustment among children conceived via donor insemination by lesbian and heterosexual mothers. *Child Development, 69,* 443–457.

Fulcher, M., Sutfin, E.L., Chan, R.W., Scheib, J.E., & Patterson, C.J. (2005). Lesbian mothers and their children: Findings from the Contemporary Families Study. In A. Omoto & H. Kurtzman (Eds.), *Recent research on sexual orientation, mental health, and substance abuse* (pp. 281–299). Washington, DC: American Psychological Association.

Gartrell, N., Deck., A., Rodas, C., Peyser, H., & Banks, A. (2005). The National Lesbian Family Study: 4. Interviews with the 10-year-old children. *American Journal of Orthopsychiatry, 75,* 518–524.

Golombok, S., Perry, B., Burston, A., Murray, C., Mooney-Somers, J., Stevens, M., & Golding, J. (2003). Children with lesbian parents: A community study. *Developmental Psychology, 39,* 20–33.

Patterson, C.J. (1996). Lesbian mothers and their children: Findings from the Bay Area Families Study. In J. Laird & R.J. Green (Eds.), *Lesbians and gays in couples and families: A handbook for therapists* (pp. 420–437). San Francisco: Jossey-Bass.

Patterson, C.J. (1997). Children of lesbian and gay parents. In T. Ollendick & R. Prinz (Eds.), *Advances in clinical child psychology* (Vol. 19, pp. 235–282). New York: Plenum Press.

Patterson, C.J. (2004). Gay fathers. In M.E. Lamb (Ed.), *The role of the father in child development* (4th ed., pp. 397–416). New York: Wiley.

Patterson, C.J., Fulcher, M., & Wainright, J. (2002). Children of lesbian and gay parents: Research, law, and policy. In B.L. Bottoms, M.B. Kovera, & B.D. McAuliff (Eds.), *Children, social science and the law* (pp. 176–199). New York: Cambridge University Press.

Patterson, C.J., & Hastings, P. (in press). Socialization in context of family diversity. In J. Grusec & P. Hastings (Eds.), *Handbook of socialization.* New York: Guilford Press.

Stacey, J., & Biblarz, T.J. (2001). (How) Does sexual orientation of parents matter? *American Sociological Review, 65,* 159–183.

Wainright, J.L., & Patterson, C.J. (2006). Delinquency, victimization, and substance use among adolescents with female same-sex parents. *Journal of Family Psychology, 20,* 526–530.

Wainright, J.L., Russell, S.T., & Patterson, C.J. (2004). Psychosocial adjustment and school outcomes of adolescents with same-sex parents. *Child Development, 75,* 1886–1898.

Address correspondence to **Charlotte J. Patterson,** Department of Psychology, P.O. Box 400400, University of Virginia, Charlottesville, VA 22904; e-mail: cjp@virginia.edu.

From *Current Directions in Psychological Science,* October 2006, pp. 241–244. Copyright © 2006 by the Association for Psychological Science. Reprinted by permission of Wiley-Blackwell.

Evidence of Infants' Internal Working Models of Attachment

Susan C. Johnson, Carol S. Dweck, and Frances S. Chen

Nearly half a century ago, psychiatrist John Bowlby proposed that the instinctual behavioral system that underpins an infant's attachment to his or her mother is accompanied by "internal working models" of the social world—models based on the infant's own experience with his or her caregiver (Bowlby, 1958, 1969/1982). These mental models were thought to mediate, in part, the ability of an infant to use the caregiver as a buffer against the stresses of life, as well as the later development of important self-regulatory and social skills.

Hundreds of studies now testify to the impact of caregivers' behavior on infants' behavior and development: Infants who most easily seek and accept support from their parents are considered secure in their attachments and are more likely to have received sensitive and responsive caregiving than insecure infants; over time, they display a variety of socioemotional advantages over insecure infants (Cassidy & Shaver, 1999). Research has also shown that, at least in older children and adults, individual differences in the security of attachment are indeed related to the individual's representations of social relations (Bretherton & Munholland, 1999). Yet no study has ever directly assessed internal working models of attachment in infancy. In the present study, we sought to do so.

Method

Using a visual habituation technique, we tested expectations of caregivers' responsiveness in 10 securely and 11 insecurely attached 12- to 16-month-old infants (mean age = 403 days; 13 females). Attachment security was measured in the lab using the Strange Situation (Ainsworth, Blehar, Waters, & Wall, 1978).

Following Bowlby (1958, 1969/1982) and Ainsworth (Ainsworth et al., 1978), we predicted that different experiences with their own primary caregivers would lead infants to construct different internal working models, including different expectations of caregivers' responsiveness. Thus, we expected that secure infants, compared with insecure infants, would look longer at a display of an unresponsive caregiver (relatively unexpected) relative to a display of a responsive caregiver (relatively expected).

Given recent demonstrations of the abstractness and generality of infants' reasoning about agents (Gergely, Nádasdy,

Csibra, & Bíró, 1995; Johnson, 2003; Kuhlmeier, Wynn, & Bloom, 2003), we chose to test infants' expectations with displays of animated geometric characters, rather than actual people. Infants were habituated to a video of two animated ellipses enacting a separation event. The large "mother" and small "child" appeared together at the bottom of a steep incline, and then the mother traveled halfway up the incline to a small plateau. As the mother came to rest there, the child below began to cry, an event depicted by a slight pulsation and bouncing and an actual human infant cry. The animation then paused, allowing the participant to look at the scene as long as he or she desired. Once the participant looked away, the sequence was repeated until his or her visual attention to the event declined to half of its initial amount, as measured by the duration of the participant's looks. When an infant reached this criterion of habituation, each of two test outcomes was shown twice. Each test outcome opened with the mother still positioned halfway up the incline, as the child continued to cry. In the *responsive* outcome, the mother returned to the child. In the *unresponsive* outcome, the mother continued up the slope, away from the child. The order in which the outcomes were presented was counterbalanced. Interest in each outcome was measured by looking time.

The Strange Situation sessions of all 21 infants were blind-coded by the third author after training at the Institute of Child Development's Attachment Workshop. A second blind coder, the first author, scored 10 randomly selected sessions. The coders' agreement was 90%, and kappa was .83.

The visual looking times of all infants were coded on-line by an observer blind to attachment status and test event. A second blind observer, also on-line, coded the looking times of 13 of the infants, achieving 93% agreement and a kappa of .82.

Results

Mean looking times for the last three trials of habituation and each outcome were calculated for each infant (see Figure 1). Securely attached infants looked for 5.9 s (SD = 4.1) at the last three habituation events, 10.2 s (SD = 8.9) at the unresponsive-caregiver outcome, and 7.3 s (SD = 7.0) at the responsive-caregiver outcome. The comparable times in insecurely attached infants were 5.4 s (SD = 2.9), 6.6 s (SD = 3.5), and 8.0 s

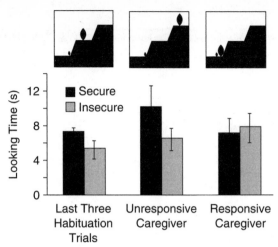

Figure 1 Mean looking times (in seconds) to habituation and test events among secure and insecure infants. Standard error bars are shown. Each illustration depicts the final scene in the video corresponding to the graph below. The large oval represents the "mother," and the small oval represents the "child."

($SD = 5.4$). Preliminary analyses showed no effect of gender or order of presentation on looking times in the outcome trials.

A mixed analysis of variance with attachment status (secure, insecure) and outcome (responsive, unresponsive) as variables revealed no differences between secure and insecure infants in the overall amount of time that they looked at the test displays, $F(1, 19) = 0.31$, n.s., and no differences between the overall looking times (secure and insecure infants combined) to responsive versus unresponsive outcomes, $F(1, 19) = 0.48$, n.s. However, as predicted, infants' relative interest in the two outcomes did vary by group. Secure infants looked relatively longer at the unresponsive outcome than the responsive outcome compared with the insecure infants, $F(1, 19) = 4.76$, $p = .042$.[1] These results constitute direct positive evidence that infants' own personal attachment experiences are reflected in abstract mental representations of social interactions.

The current method opens a new window onto the nature of internal working models of attachment. In addition, these representations can now be traced as they emerge, well before existing behavioral measures of attachment can be employed. The literature on attachment has shown the profound impact of early experience. The method used in the present study provides a means of looking into the mind upon which that experience has left its imprint.

Note

1. Results of additional analyses converged. One-tailed, pair-wise comparisons revealed a significant effect of outcome within the secure group, $t(9) = 1.99$, $p < .04$, but not the insecure group. Also, 7 of the 10 secure infants looked longer at the unresponsive than at the responsive outcome, whereas 7 of the 11 insecure infants showed the opposite result, $p < .07$, Mann-Whitney test. The looking behaviors of the two subtypes of insecure infants (6 avoidant, 5 resistant) did not differ.

References

Ainsworth, M.D.S., Blehar, M.C., Waters, E., & Wall, S. (1978). *Patterns of attachment: A psychological study of the strange situation.* Hillsdale, NJ: Erlbaum.

Bowlby, J. (1958). The nature of the child's ties to his mother. *International Journal of Psychoanalysis, 39,* 350.

Bowlby, J. (1982). *Attachment and loss: Vol. 1. Attachment.* New York: Basic Books. (Original work published 1969)

Bretherton, I., & Munholland, K.A. (1999). Internal working models revisited. In J. Cassidy & P.R. Shaver (Eds.), *Handbook of attachment: Theory, research, and clinical applications* (pp. 89–111). New York: Guilford Press.

Cassidy, J., & Shaver, P.R. (Eds.). (1999). *Handbook of attachment: Theory, research, and clinical applications.* New York: Guilford Press.

Gergely, G., Nádasdy, Z., Csibra, G., & Bíró, S. (1995). Taking the intentional stance at 12 months of age. *Cognition, 56,* 165–193.

Johnson, S.C. (2003). Detecting agents. *Philosophical Transactions of the Royal Society B, 358,* 549–559.

Kuhlmeier, V.A., Wynn, K., & Bloom, P. (2003). Attribution of dispositional states by 12-month-olds. *Psychological Science, 14,* 402–408.

SUSAN C. JOHNSON, CAROL S. DWECK, and FRANCES S. CHEN Stanford University.

Address correspondence to Susan C. Johnson, Department of Psychology, Jordan Hall, Bldg. 420, Stanford University, Stanford, CA 94305; e-mail: scj@psych.stanford.edu.

Acknowledgments—We thank C. Lai, P. Romera, C. Titchenal, and L. Weitzel for assistance.

Parental Divorce and Children's Adjustment

JENNIFER E. LANSFORD

In the United States, between 43% and 50% of first marriages end in divorce (U.S. Census Bureau, 2004), and 50% of American children will experience their parents' divorce (National Center for Health Statistics, 2008). Given the large number of families affected by divorce each year, parents, clinicians, and policymakers alike are concerned with understanding how experiencing parental divorce affects children's adjustment. Indeed, many parents considering divorce ask whether they should stay together for the sake of their children.

Key questions in the research literature have focused on whether divorce per se affects children's adjustment and, if so, why and how. The literature has at times portrayed two extreme positions on whether divorce affects children's adjustment (Cherlin, 1999). The first extreme position holds that the long-term effects of divorce on children are quite debilitating and that children carry a lasting negative burden years after the divorce in terms of mental health and interpersonal relationships (e.g., Glenn, 2001; Popenoe, 1993, 2003; Wallerstein, Lewis, & Blakeslee, 2000). This work has drawn criticism for methodological (e.g., reliance on small samples of clinical populations) and ideological reasons. For example, Coontz (1992) points out that many condemnations of divorce and non-traditional families stem from misguided perceptions of family life in previous decades and that myths about family life in the past reflected reality for only a small subset of middle-class European Americans. At the opposite extreme is the position that divorce has no measurable long-term effects on children (e.g., Harris, 1998). This extreme has been criticized because it appears to conflict with hundreds of empirical studies to the contrary.

Between these two extremes, most researchers have come to the conclusion that divorce has some negative effects on children's adjustment but that these effects may be small in magnitude and not universal. For example, in a meta-analysis of 92 studies conducted in the 1950s through 1980s, Amato and Keith (1991b) reported that 70% of studies found lower well-being for children whose parents had divorced than for children whose parents had not divorced; the median effect size was .14 of a standard deviation. Conduct problems and father–child relationship outcomes showed the largest effect sizes, and psychological adjustment and self-concept outcomes showed the smallest effect sizes (Amato & Keith, 1991b). Amato (2001) updated the meta-analysis using 67 studies published in the 1990s. Although 88% of the effects suggested lower well-being for children whose parents divorced than for children whose parents did not divorce, only 42% of the effects were significant (Amato, 2001). There has been considerable debate in the literature regarding the extent to which these effects are attributable to divorce per se or to correlated factors such as exposure to interparental conflict.

The main purpose of this review is to provide an overview of the nuances represented in the patterns of findings regarding links between parental divorce and children's short-term and long-term adjustment. First, I consider how divorce is related to several different aspects of children's adjustment. Second, I examine the timing of divorce, demographic characteristics, children's adjustment prior to the divorce, and stigmatization as moderators of the links between divorce and children's adjustment. Third, I examine income, interparental conflict, parenting, and parents' well-being as mediators of relations between divorce and children's adjustment. Fourth, I describe the caveats and limitations of the research literature. Finally, I consider the notable policies related to grounds for divorce, child support, and child custody in light of how they might affect children's adjustment to their parents' divorce.

Indicators of Children's Adjustment

Although findings regarding whether and how parental divorce is related to children's adjustment are not always clear in the literature, there is agreement among most researchers that children experiencing parental divorce are at risk for a variety of negative developmental outcomes (see Cherlin, 1999, for a review). However, the magnitude of these effects appears to depend on the indicators of adjustment under consideration, and some studies find no differences on particular outcomes between children whose parents divorce and those whose parents stay together (Ruschena, Prior, Sanson, & Smart, 2005). Externalizing behaviors, internalizing problems, academic achievement, and quality of social relationships are frequently included indicators of adjustment in the divorce literature. Studies that have examined these indicators of adjustment at discrete time points provide some evidence that children whose parents have divorced have more externalizing and internalizing problems, lower academic achievement, and more problematic social relationships than do children whose parents have not divorced (e.g., Cherlin et al., 1991; Emery, Waldron, Kitzmann, & Aaron, 1999).

Meta-analyses have revealed that divorce has larger effects on relationships with nonresidential fathers and externalizing behaviors than it does on internalizing problems or academic achievement (Amato, 2001; Amato & Keith, 1991b). In the earlier meta-analysis (Amato & Keith, 1991b), divorce was found to have larger effects on academic achievement than on internalizing problems, but in the later meta-analysis (Amato, 2001), divorce was found to have larger effects on internalizing problems than on academic achievement. In these meta-analyses, effect sizes depended on the methodological sophistication of the studies under consideration. More methodologically sophisticated studies (e.g., those with multiple-item scales and control variables) showed smaller effect sizes than did less methodologically sophisticated studies. Methodologically unsophisticated studies may overestimate the effects of divorce on children. For example, if socioeconomic status is not controlled, children who have experienced divorce and are living with a single mother may show worse adjustment than do children who are living with two parents in part because of the confounding effect of having fewer economic resources in single-mother families.

A problem with relying on indicators of adjustment measured at a single point in time is that these indicators are likely to look worse if they are assessed in close temporal proximity to the time of the divorce, but they show improvement over time because the short-term effects of divorce tend to look worse than the long-term effects. The examination of developmental trajectories of adjustment has several advantages over the examination of adjustment at discrete points in time. The examination of trajectories makes it possible to track change over time from before the divorce occurs

to some period following the divorce. The inclusion of predivorce adjustment in these models is important because of evidence that children whose parents eventually divorce show poorer adjustment prior to the divorce than do children whose parents do not divorce (e.g., Cherlin, Chase-Lansdale, & McRae, 1998; Doherty & Needle, 1991). Links between parental divorce and children's adjustment are often attenuated or eliminated by controlling for predivorce adjustment. For example, Sun and Li (2001) used longitudinal data from a nationally representative sample and found that differences in academic achievement between children whose parents divorced and children whose parents stayed together could be accounted for almost entirely by children's academic achievement and family functioning prior to the divorce.

Although one can control for prior adjustment in analyses predicting subsequent adjustment at a discrete point in time, such analyses do not allow for an examination of how these effects continue to develop over time. Children often have more short-term adjustment difficulties immediately after their parents' divorce, but these difficulties may lessen in severity or disappear following an initial adjustment period (Chase-Lansdale & Hetherington, 1990). Studying trajectories of adjustment that extend from before the parents' divorce to a period well after the divorce will provide a more complete picture of children's long-term adjustment.

To overcome the limitations of cross-sectional approaches, Cherlin et al. (1998) followed a large sample of children born in 1958 in Great Britain prospectively from childhood to the age of 33. Prior to their parents' divorce, individuals whose parents eventually divorced had more internalizing and externalizing problems than did individuals whose parents did not divorce. However, divorce itself also contributed to higher levels of long-term internalizing and externalizing problems into adulthood. It is important to note that their findings suggested that some of the effects of divorce during childhood may not manifest themselves shortly after the divorce and that they may not become apparent until adolescence or adulthood. The gap between groups of individuals whose parents had and had not divorced widened over the course of several years from childhood to adulthood. Cherlin et al. (1998) suggested that parental divorce may curtail educational achievement or disrupt social relationships in ways that are not apparent until children try to enter the labor market, marry, or have children of their own.

In a sample of American children followed from before kindergarten through Grade 10, Malone et al. (2004) used latent change score models to examine trajectories of teacher-rated externalizing behavior over time. Parental divorce was unrelated to girls' externalizing behavior trajectories, regardless of the timing of divorce. Parental divorce was related to boys' externalizing trajectories differently depending on the timing of the divorce. In particular, parental divorce during elementary school was related to an increase in boys' externalizing behaviors that began in the year of the divorce and persisted for years afterward. Parental divorce during middle school was related to an increase in boys' externalizing behaviors in the year of the divorce that declined below baseline levels in the year following the divorce and persisted into subsequent years.

Several studies also address whether parental divorce during childhood relates to long-term effects on adults' own romantic relationships and their relationships with their parents later in life. Intergenerational studies suggest that parental divorce doubles the risk that one's own marriage will end in divorce, in part because individuals whose parents have divorced are less likely to view marriage as a lifelong commitment (Amato & DeBoer, 2001); the risk is exacerbated if both spouses experienced their parents' divorce (Hetherington & Elmore, 2004). There is also evidence that intergenerational transmission of divorce is mediated by interpersonal skill deficits (e.g., communication patterns not conducive to supporting a long-term intimate relationship) that make it more difficult for individuals whose parents have divorced to sustain their own intimate relationships (Amato, 1996). In addition to being at greater risk for difficulties in romantic relationships, adults whose parents divorced have lower quality relationships with their parents (particularly fathers) during adulthood, on average (Lye, 1996). However, these associations depend on the parents' marital quality prior to the divorce, the gender of the parent, and the gender of the adult child (Booth & Amato, 1994; Orbuch, Thornton, & Cancio, 2000).

To summarize, research suggests that children whose parents have divorced have higher levels of externalizing behaviors and internalizing problems, lower academic achievement, and more problems in social relationships than do children whose parents have not divorced. But, the magnitude of these effects is attenuated after controlling for children's adjustment prior to the divorce and other potential confounds. Furthermore, even though children whose parents divorce have worse adjustment on average than do children whose parents stay together, most children whose parents divorce do not have long-term negative outcomes. For example, in their longitudinal study of a representative sample of 17,414 individuals in Great Britain who were followed from ages 7 to 23, Chase-Lansdale, Cherlin, and Kiernan (1995) reported that the likelihood of scoring in the clinical range on the Malaise Inventory, which measures a wide range of adult emotional disorders,

was 11% for young adults who had experienced their parents' divorce and 8% for young adults who had not experienced their parents' divorce. Nevertheless, analyses using data from this sample after they were followed to age 33 led Cherlin et al. (1998) to conclude that the adjustment gap between individuals who had and had not experienced parental divorce widened over time and that although part of the effect of parental divorce could be attributed to factors prior to the divorce, experiencing parental divorce during childhood was related to worse mental health when the offspring were in their 20s and 30s.

Hetherington and Kelly (2002) concluded that 25% of individuals whose parents divorce have serious long-term social, emotional, or psychological problems in adulthood in comparison with 10% of individuals whose parents have stayed together; still, this means that 75% of individuals whose parents divorce do not have serious long-term impairment during adulthood. Even studies that do find long-term effects of divorce generally report that the effect sizes are small. For example, Allison and Furstenberg (1989) used longitudinal data from a nationally representative sample and concluded that although divorce was related to behavior problems, psychological distress, and low academic achievement, the effect sizes for divorce were smaller than those found for gender differences (but larger than those found for several other demographic variables). Amato (2003) concluded that about 10% of children whose parents divorce grow up to have poorer psychological well-being than would have been predicted if their parents had stayed together, 18% of children whose parents divorce have more marital discord as adults than do children whose parents stayed together, and 35% of children whose parents divorce have worse relationships with their fathers than do children whose parents stayed together. Laumann-Billings and Emery (2000) caution that researchers and clinicians may reach different conclusions regarding the long-term effects of divorce because researchers often study psychological or behavioral problems, whereas clinicians often are faced with clients' subjective impressions of their psychological distress (which may not be manifest in psychological or behavioral disorders). Taken together, these findings indicate that the majority of children whose parents divorce do not have long-term adjustment problems, but the risk of externalizing behaviors, internalizing problems, poorer academic achievement, and problematic social relationships is greater for children whose parents divorce than for those whose parents stay together. Different children may manifest adjustment problems in different ways. Future research should adopt a more person-centered approach to investigate whether, for example, those children whose grades are dropping are the same children whose internalizing or externalizing problems are increasing following their parents' divorce.

Moderators of Links between Divorce and Children's Adjustment

Despite the research suggesting that divorce is related to children's adjustment, there is considerable evidence that these effects do not operate in the same way for all children. Links between divorce and children's adjustment are moderated by several factors, including children's age at the time of their parents' divorce, children's age at the time of the study, the length of time since the divorce, children's demographic characteristics (gender, race/ethnicity), children's adjustment prior to the divorce, and stigmatization of divorce (by location or historical period).

Children's Age at Divorce, Age at the Time of the Study, and Length of Time since Divorce

Studies have shown mixed results with respect to how the timing of divorce affects children's adjustment (see Hetherington, Bridges, & Insabella, 1998). Hetherington (1989) suggests that, in comparison with older children, young children may be less capable of realistically assessing the causes and consequences of divorce, may feel more anxious about abandonment, may be more likely to blame themselves, and may be less able to take advantage of resources outside the family to cope with the divorce. All of these factors may contribute to findings that young children experience more problems after their parents divorce than do children who are older when the divorce occurs (Allison & Furstenberg, 1989). Note that this conclusion applies specifically to divorce; other findings suggest that adjusting to parents' remarriage may be harder for adolescents than for younger children (Hetherington, Stanley-Hagan, & Anderson, 1989). It may be that divorce has effects on particular outcomes that are salient during the developmental period during which the divorce occurs. For example, academic achievement, identity development, and emerging romantic relationships may be affected by divorce that occurs during adolescence because these domains of functioning are developmentally salient then.

A methodological problem is that in many studies, children's reported age reflects their age at the time of the study rather than their age at the time of their parents' divorce. Amato (2001) noted this lack of availability of children's age at the time of the divorce as a limitation in his meta-analysis. The most common approach is to study children in a particular developmental stage (e.g., early childhood, middle childhood, adolescence) and compare the adjustment of children whose parents have divorced with the adjustment of children whose parents have not divorced. A drawback of this strategy is that the length of time between the parents' divorce and the time of the assessment will vary considerably across the sample. Lansford et al. (2006) addressed this limitation by using the time of parental divorce as an anchor point and modeling trajectories of adjustment over a period from 1 year prior to the divorce to 3 years after the divorce. This approach makes it possible to compare children at comparable points of time in relation to their parents' divorce. Lansford et al. (2006) also analyzed a matched group of children whose parents did not divorce. Results suggested that parental divorce occurring from kindergarten to Grade 5 exerted more adverse effects on internalizing and externalizing problems than did parental divorce occurring from Grades 6 to 10, whereas parental divorce occurring from Grades 6 to 10 exerted more adverse effects on grades.

Children's Demographic Characteristics

Researchers have attempted to understand how children's demographic characteristics (primarily gender and race) may moderate the link between parental divorce and children's adjustment. Early research findings suggested that parental divorce was related to more adjustment difficulties for boys than girls but that parents' remarriage was related to more adjustment difficulties for girls than for boys (see Hetherington, Cox, & Cox, 1985). However, recent findings have been more mixed; there is no consistent pattern regarding whether divorce has more adverse effects on girls or boys. Some studies report that boys have more adjustment problems following parental divorce than do girls (Morrison & Cherlin, 1995; Shaw, Emery, & Tuer, 1993). Other studies report that girls have more adjustment problems following parental divorce than do boys (Allison & Furstenberg, 1989). Still other studies report no gender differences (e.g., Amato & Cheadle, 2005; Sun & Li, 2002). There is also evidence that the particular outcomes affected by parental divorce may differ by gender. For example, early childbearing has been found to be associated with parental divorce for girls, and more unemployment has been found to be associated with parental divorce for boys (McLanahan, 1999). In their meta-analysis, Amato and Keith (1991b) found no gender differences except that boys whose parents divorced had a harder time adjusting socially than did girls.

It has been proposed that parental divorce may have a less negative effect on African American children than on European American children (Jeynes, 2002). Specifically, researchers have suggested that because African American children tend to experience less of a decrease in household income following parents' divorce and there is a greater norm for single parenthood in the African American community (Cherlin, 1998; Laosa, 1988), these factors may mitigate the effects of divorce on African American youth. Research assessing these effects has produced mixed results, but a meta-analysis of 37 studies investigating links between parental divorce and adults' well-being found that effect sizes were smaller for African Americans than for European Americans (Amato & Keith, 1991a), which is consistent with the hypothesis that divorce would have a less negative effect on African American children than for European American children.

Children's Adjustment Prior to the Divorce

Some evidence suggests that children whose parents eventually divorce already have more adjustment problems many years before the divorce (Cherlin et al., 1998). Genetic or other environmental factors may be contributing to these adjustment problems, and the children's adjustment may have appeared to be just as problematic even if the parents had not divorced. Chase-Lansdale et al. (1995) found a steeper increase in adjustment problems after parental divorce for children who were well-adjusted prior to the divorce than for children with predivorce adjustment problems (or for children whose parents did not divorce). However, the long-term adjustment of children with predivorce adjustment problems was worse than it was for children who were better adjusted prior to the divorce (Chase-Lansdale et al., 1995). Controlling for children's adjustment prior to their parents' divorce greatly reduces differences between children whose parents divorce and those whose parents stay together (Cherlin et al., 1991).

Children with positive attributes such as attractiveness, easy temperament, and social competence are also more resilient following their parents' divorce (Hetherington et al., 1989). In part, this may be because children with such attributes are more likely to have strong support networks outside the family (e.g., from teachers or peers) and to evoke positive responses from others. In an epidemiological sample of 648 children who were initially assessed when they were 1–10 years old and assessed again 8 years later, Kasen, Cohen, Brook, and Hartmark (1996) found significant interactions between temperament assessed in the first 10 years of life and family structure in the prediction of subsequent adjustment. In particular, the risk of oppositional defiant disorder was exacerbated for children who had early affective problems and were living with a single mother or in a stepfamily; the authors speculated that the stress of adjusting to new living arrangements may have overwhelmed the coping capacities of these already vulnerable children.

On the other hand, Kasen et al. (1996) also found that the risk of overanxiety disorder was reduced for children (especially boys) who were socially immature early in life and were living with a single mother; the authors speculated that needing to play more "adult" roles in a single-parent family may have enhanced the social skills of previously immature children. Thus, children's adjustment can moderate the effects of divorce on subsequent adjustment.

Stigmatization

At a societal level, stigmatization has been considered as a potential moderator of the link between parents' divorce and children's adjustment. Divorce would be expected to have more detrimental effects for children in societal contexts in which family forms other than two-parent biological families are stigmatized than it would in societies that are more accepting of diverse family forms. There is some empirical support for this perspective. For example, Amato and Keith's (1991b) meta-analysis revealed smaller effect sizes for some outcomes in more recent studies than in studies from earlier decades, suggesting that the effects of divorce became less pronounced over time from the 1950s to the 1980s. Amato and Keith also reported that studies conducted outside the United States on average found more problems with conduct, psychological adjustment, and both mother–child and father–child relationships than did studies conducted in the United States. One explanation for these findings is that divorce is less stigmatized in the United States than in many other countries (Amato & Keith, 1991b). On the other hand, Amato (2001) found that although the adjustment of children whose parents had and had not divorced became increasingly similar over time from the 1950s to the 1980s, the gap between these two groups began to increase again in the 1990s (Reifman, Villa, Amans, Rethinam, & Telesca, 2001, reached a similar conclusion). It is not clear that stigmatization increased again over this same time period.

Mediators of Links between Divorce and Children's Adjustment

Most researchers no longer simply compare the adjustment of children whose parents have and have not divorced. Instead, researchers have adopted more complex models of how divorce may be related to children's adjustment and now investigate moderators as described previously or analyze their data to understand the mechanisms through which divorce might affect children's adjustment. Several scholars have argued that processes occurring in all types of families are more important than family structure in relation to the well-being of children and adolescents (e.g., Dunn, Deater-Deckard, Pickering, & O'Connor, 1998; Lansford, Ceballo, Abbey, & Stewart, 2001). Taking family process and other mediating variables into account attenuates the association between the experience of parental divorce and children's adjustment (e.g., Amato & Keith, 1991b; Mechanic & Hansell, 1989). It is also important to keep in mind that divorce can be conceptualized more as a process than as a discrete event, with the family processes leading up to and following the divorce being an integral part of the divorce itself.

Income

In a review of five theoretical perspectives on why marital transitions may be related to children's adjustment, Hetherington et al. (1998) found some support for an economic disadvantage perspective suggesting that a drop in household income often accompanies divorce and mediates the link between parents' divorce and children's adjustment. Twenty-eight percent of single mothers and 11% of single fathers live in poverty in comparison with 8% of two-parent families (Grall, 2007). Following their parents' divorce, children most often live with single mothers who do not have the same financial resources they did prior to the divorce, especially if they are not receiving regular child-support payments from nonresidential fathers. This sometimes necessitates a change for the worse in housing, neighborhoods, and schools. These economic hardships and their sequelae can lead to behavioral and emotional problems in children. For example, Guidubaldi, Cleminshaw, Perry, and McLoughlin (1983) surveyed children whose parents had and had not divorced and found differences between them on 27 out of 34 outcomes before controlling for income, but only found 13 differences between them after controlling for income, suggesting that income plays an important role but does not account for all of the effect of divorce on children's adjustment. Furthermore, children's adjustment often worsens rather than improves following remarriage and its accompanying increase in economic resources (Hetherington et al., 1989). Taken together, these findings suggest that income is important, but there is more contributing to children's adjustment problems following divorce than a decrease in household income.

Interparental Conflict

Interparental conflict has received substantial empirical attention. There is consistent evidence that high levels of interparental conflict have negative and long-lasting implications for children's adjustment (Davies & Cummings, 1994; Grych & Fincham, 1990). Amato (1993) and Hetherington et al. (1998) found more support for a parental conflict perspective on why divorce is related to children's adjustment than for any other theoretical perspective that has been proposed to account for this link. Averaging across measures in their review, children in high-conflict, intact families scored .32 standard deviation below children in low-conflict, intact families and .12 standard deviation below children in divorced families on measures of adjustment, suggesting that exposure to high levels of conflict was more detrimental to children than was parental divorce (Hetherington et al., 1998). To illustrate, using data from the National Survey of Families and Households, Vandewater and Lansford (1998) found that when interparental conflict and family structure (married and never divorced vs. divorced and not remarried) were considered simultaneously after controlling for family demographic covariates and children's prior adjustment, high interparental conflict was related to more externalizing behaviors, internalizing problems, and trouble with peers, but family structure was not significantly related to child outcomes. The finding that children whose parents divorce look worse before the divorce than do comparable children whose parents do not divorce is also consistent with this perspective; worse adjustment prior to the divorce could be accounted for, in part, by exposure to interparental conflict.

If divorce leads to a reduction in children's exposure to interparental conflict, one might expect that their adjustment would improve. Indeed, this issue is at the heart of parents' question of whether they should stay in a conflicted marriage for the sake of the children. In an important longitudinal investigation of this issue, Amato, Loomis, and Booth (1995) found that children's problems decrease when parents in a high-conflict marriage divorce (which encompassed 30%–49% of divorces), whereas children's problems increase when parents in a low-conflict marriage divorce. Booth and Amato (2001) examined correlates of divorce for low-conflict couples and found that factors such as less integration in the community, having fewer friends, not owning a home, and having more positive attitudes toward divorce were related to an increased likelihood of divorce; the authors suggest that because these factors may be less salient to children than conflict between their parents, the divorce may come as more of an unwelcome and unexpected shock, accounting for the more negative effects of divorce on children from low-conflict families than those seen in children from high-conflict families.

Researchers have moved beyond monolithic characterizations of conflict into descriptions of particular types of conflict and specific aspects of interparental conflict that may be especially detrimental to children. Overt conflict may be physical or verbal and includes behaviors and emotions such as belligerence, contempt, derision, screaming, insulting, slapping, threatening, and hitting; exposure to overt conflict has been linked to children's externalizing problems (Buehler et al., 1998). Covert conflict may include passive-aggressive techniques such as trying to get the child to side with one parent, using the child to get information about the other parent, having the child carry messages to the other parent, and denigrating the other parent in the presence of the child; covert conflict has been linked more to internalizing problems than to externalizing problems (Buehler et al., 1998). Amato and Afifi (2006) found that the feeling of being caught between parents even into young adulthood was associated with high-conflict marriages but not with divorce and that it was related to more internalizing problems and worse parent–child relationships. Thus, children whose parents divorce may have better long-term adjustment than do children whose parents remain in high-conflict marriages if divorce enables children to escape from exposure to conflict and feelings of being caught between their parents.

Parenting

Another mechanism that has been proposed many times in the literature as an explanation for the links between parental divorce and children's adjustment is the disruption in parenting practices that may occur following divorce. Divorce can make it more difficult for parents to monitor and supervise children effectively (Buchanan, Maccoby, & Dornbusch, 1996; McLanahan & Sandefur, 1994), to discipline consistently (Hetherington, Cox, & Cox, 1979), and to provide warmth and affection (Forehand, Thomas, Wierson, & Brody, 1990; Hetherington & Stanley-Hagan, 1999). After divorce, parent–child conflict often increases, and family cohesion decreases (Short, 2002).

As with studies of children's adjustment showing that children whose parents eventually divorce have significantly more predivorce adjustment problems than do children whose parents do not divorce, parents who eventually divorce have been found to have more problematic parenting practices as long as 8–12 years before the divorce than do parents who do not divorce (Amato & Booth, 1996; Shaw et al., 1993). Parenting problems contribute to children's adjustment problems in all types of family structures. Several studies provide evidence that controlling for the quality of parenting attenuates the link between parental divorce and children's adjustment (Amato, 1986; Amato & Gilbreth, 1999; Simons, Whitbeck, Beaman, & Conger, 1994; Tschann, Johnson, & Wallerstein, 1989; Videon, 2002). For example, in a study of mothers and their sons in Grades 1–3, Martinez and Forgatch (2002) found that mothers' encouragement of academic skills mediated the relation between marital

transitions and boys' academic achievement and that a more general indicator of effective parenting mediated the link between marital transitions and externalizing and internalizing problems.

Some studies have investigated whether contact with the noncustodial parent and the quality of this relationship also mediate the link between parental divorce and children's adjustment. In a meta-analysis of 63 studies, Amato and Gilbreth (1999) found that improved child adjustment (academic achievement and fewer externalizing and internalizing problems) was unrelated to frequency of contact with nonresident fathers but was associated with nonresident fathers' payment of child support, authoritative parenting, and feelings of father–child closeness.

Parents' Well-Being

Yet another possible mediator of the link between parental divorce and children's adjustment is parents' well-being. Marital conflict and divorce increase parents' depression, anxiety, and stress, which decrease parents' ability to parent well and may in turn negatively affect children's adjustment. Mothers' history of delinquent behavior has also been found to account for much of the link between parental divorce and children's externalizing behaviors (Emery et al., 1999). These relations are complicated. Through assortative mating, parents with problems such as depression, substance use, or antisocial behavior are at risk of selecting spouses with similar problems (Maes et al., 1998). These parental risk factors increase marital conflict and divorce (Merikangas, 1984). Children may share some of these parental characteristics genetically or through shared environmental experiences.

Caveats

Because children cannot be randomly assigned to family structure groups, studies of links between parents' divorce and children's adjustment are necessarily correlational. Despite researchers' attempts to control for potential confounds, it is possible that uncontrolled variables account for associations between divorce and adjustment. Two large bodies of research that present important caveats for understanding links between parental divorce and children's adjustment are studies of children's adjustment in stepfamilies and studies of genetic effects.

Remarriage and Stepfamilies

Much of the literature comparing the adjustment of children whose parents have or have not divorced is complicated by the fact that children are often exposed not only to one marital transition (i.e., their biological parents' divorce) but to multiple marital transitions (e.g., the initial divorce plus subsequent remarriages and divorces). If these multiple transitions are not taken into account, children's adjustment to divorce may be confounded with children's adjustment to remarriage and possibly multiple divorces. The present review focuses on parental divorce rather than stepfamilies, but several excellent reviews provide nuanced information about children's adjustment following their parents' remarriage (e.g., Dunn, 2002; Hetherington & Clingempeel, 1992; Hetherington et al., 1999).

Genetic Effects

Recent research has attempted to estimate the relative contributions of genes and environments in accounting for the likelihood that parents will divorce and the adjustment of their children following the divorce (Neiderhiser, Reiss, & Hetherington, 2007). Lykken (2002) presents evidence that a monozygotic twin has a 250% increase in risk of divorcing if his or her cotwin has divorced. Furthermore, divorce is more concordant between monozygotic than dizygotic twins (McGue & Lykken, 1992). These findings support the role of genetics as a risk factor for divorce, but Jocklin, McGue, and Lykken (1996) further specified the personality mechanisms through which this effect occurs. That is, they found between 30% and 42% of the heritability of divorce to be associated with the heritability of the personality characteristics of positive emotionality, negative emotionality, and less constraint, which were, in turn, associated with divorce (Jocklin et al., 1996).

Research also has begun to examine genotype–environment interactions to understand under what environmental conditions genes may express themselves. An important question is whether the genetic contributions to divorce also account for the poorer adjustment of children whose parents have divorced or whether experiencing parental divorce contributes above and beyond the genetic risks. In a longitudinal study of 398 biological and adoptive families, O'Connor, Caspi, DeFries, and Plomin (2000) found that children who experienced their biological parents' divorce by the age of 12 had higher levels of behavior problems and substance use and lower levels of achievement and social adjustment than did children whose biological parents did not divorce. Children who experienced their adoptive parents' divorce by the age of 12 also had higher levels of behavior problems and substance use than did children who did not experience their adoptive parents' divorce, but these two groups of adopted children did not differ on achievement or social adjustment. These findings suggest the importance of gene–environment interactions in contributing to achievement and social adjustment and suggest the importance of the environment in accounting for links between parental

divorce and children's behavior problems and substance use (O'Connor et al., 2000).

Using a high-risk sample in Australia, D'Onofrio et al. (2005) compared the offspring of adult twins on externalizing, internalizing, and substance-use problems and concluded that environmental (rather than genetic) effects of divorce accounted for the higher rates of problems among the group that experienced their parents' divorce. In a further elaboration of the process involved in genetic versus environmental effects, D'Onofrio et al. (2006) found that the experience of divorce was related to earlier age of first intercourse and more emotional and educational problems, whereas earlier use of drugs and likelihood of cohabitation were predicted by genetic and other selection factors. Using a children of twins design with a population-based American sample, D'Onofrio et al. (2007) found that genetic and other selection factors, rather than divorce per se, accounted for differences in internalizing problems, whereas substance use was not accounted for by genetic factors. The reasons for the discrepancies between the findings from these studies are not clear. However, although the precise nature of which genetic or environmental factors contribute to distinct developmental outcomes is not clear from the research to date, it is apparent that genetic and environmental contributions both shape whether individuals will eventually divorce and, if they do, how their children may adjust to the divorce.

Divorce Laws and Policies

The questions of whether family structure per se affects children's adjustment and, if so, why and how it does so are important in informing policy because one can adjust policy to influence different proximal mechanisms that may affect children's adjustment. At one level, answers to questions related to whether and how divorce affects children's adjustment also influence how hard it should be for parents to divorce in the first place (e.g., determining if it is better to stay in a conflicted marriage for the sake of the children). States differ in terms of requirements related to waiting periods, counseling, the length of separation needed prior to divorce, and other factors that affect how hard it is to get a divorce in a given state. Despite shifts in rates immediately after a new policy is implemented, the difficulty of divorcing and rates of divorce are for the most part unrelated after this initial phase (Wolfers, 2003), so policies are unlikely to influence how many parents divorce over the long run.

At another level, understanding children's adjustment following divorce is important for implementing policies that can help children once their parents have decided to divorce. For example, if divorce increases children's risk for externalizing behaviors because it results in more limited financial resources available to children and, in turn, the risks of dangerous neighborhoods associated with lower SES, then a reasonable policy response would be to make noncustodial parents more responsible for child-support payments. Similarly, state policies may minimize or exacerbate interparental conflict, with implications for children's adjustment. Key policy issues related to children's adjustment involve the divorce process (e.g., grounds for divorce), custody decisions, and financial support of children. Each category of policies is reviewed below.

Grounds for Divorce

The primary distinction of importance related to grounds for divorce involves whether fault is considered in the divorce proceedings. If fault is considered, then divorce is granted only if one spouse is determined to be "guilty" (of adultery, physically or sexually abusing the spouse or a child, abandoning the home for at least a year, or other serious offenses) and the other spouse is determined to be "innocent" (Nakonezny, Shull, & Rodgers, 1995). The consent of the "innocent" spouse is needed to grant the divorce, and divorce is not granted if both spouses are "guilty." In theory, the innocent spouse is awarded alimony, child support, and property in a fault-based divorce. If fault is not considered, both spouses do not need to provide consent, and alimony, child support, and property are no longer awarded according to fault but according to needs and the ability to pay.

No-fault grounds for divorce were enacted in all 50 states between the 1950s and 1980s, and all 50 states now allow no-fault divorces. However, only 15 states have entirely eliminated fault-based divorces (Grounds for Divorce, n.d.). In the other 35 states, one may choose between a no-fault divorce and a fault-based divorce. The most common reasons for selecting a fault-based divorce are to avoid a longer waiting period often required for a no-fault divorce or to obtain a larger share of the marital assets or more alimony. A main concern related to children's adjustment is that proving guilt and innocence in a fault-based divorce tends to perpetuate acrimony and conflict between the parents, which may lead to worse outcomes for their children.

Child Custody Policies

Child custody policies include several guidelines that determine with whom the child lives following divorce, how time is divided in joint custody situations, and visitation rights. The most frequently applied custody guideline is the "best interests of the child" standard, which takes into account the parents' preferences, the child's preferences, the interactions between parents and children, children's adjustment, and all family members' mental and physical health (see Kelly, 1994). Recently, the approximation rule has been proposed as an alternative to the best interests of the child standard because of concerns that the latter does not provide enough concrete guidance and leaves too many factors to be evaluated at the discretion of individual judges (American Law Institute, 2002). The approximation rule holds that custody should be awarded to each parent to approximate the amount of time each spent in providing care for the children during the marriage. Opinions range from support of the approximation rule as an improvement over the best interests of the child standard (Emery, Otto, & O'Donohue, 2005) to criticisms that the approximation rule would lead to biases against fathers and be less sensitive to the needs of individual families than is the best interests of the child standard (Warshak, 2007). Regardless of the custody standard applied, custody disputes that are handled through mediation rather than litigation have been found to be related to more involvement of the non-residential parent in the child's life, without increasing interparental conflict (Emery, Laumann-Billings, Waldron, Sbarra, & Dillon, 2001; Emery, Sbarra, & Grover, 2005).

A distinction is made between legal custody, which involves making decisions regarding the child, and physical custody, which involves daily living arrangements. The most common arrangement following divorce is for parents to share joint legal custody but for mothers to have sole physical custody. Several studies have investigated whether children's adjustment is related to custody arrangements following their parents' divorce. Using data from a large national sample, Downey and Powell (1995) found few differences between the adjustment of children whose fathers had custody following divorce and those whose mothers had custody. For the few outcomes in which differences did emerge, children appeared somewhat better adjusted in paternal custody families if income was left uncontrolled, but after controlling for income, children appeared somewhat better adjusted in maternal custody families (Downey & Powell, 1995).

Major benefits of joint custody include the access to financial resources and other resources that a second parent can provide and the more frequent and meaningful contact that is possible between both parents and the child (Bender, 1994). The major concerns raised with respect to joint custody are that it may prolong children's exposure to conflict between parents with acrimonious relationships and reduce stability that is needed for children's positive adjustment (Johnston, 1995; Twaite & Luchow, 1996). In a meta-analysis of 33 studies comparing joint physical or legal custody with sole maternal custody, Bauserman

(2002) concluded that children in joint custody (either physical or legal) had fewer externalizing and internalizing problems and better academic achievement and social relationships than did children in sole maternal custody. Parents with joint custody reported having less past and current conflict than did parents with sole custody, but the findings regarding better adjustment of children in joint custody held after controlling for interparental conflict. Nevertheless, caution is warranted, because there are a wide array of factors affecting the selection of joint versus sole custody that can plausibly explain differences in adjustment for children in these different custody situations. An additional methodological concern is that only 11 of the 33 studies included in Bauserman's meta-analysis were published—21 were unpublished dissertations, and 1 was another unpublished manuscript. Therefore, the majority of the studies included in the meta-analyses have not passed the rigor of peer review. The finding that joint physical and joint legal custody were equally associated with better child adjustment is consistent with the finding from Amato and Gilbreth's (1999) meta-analysis that there was little relation between children's adjustment and the frequency with which they had contact with their father. Amato and Gilbreth (1999) found that the quality of children's relationship with their father is a more important predictor of children's adjustment than is frequency of contact. If joint physical or legal custody promotes more positive father–child relationships, this might account for the more positive adjustment of children in joint custody reported by Bauserman (2002).

Child-Support Policies and Enforcement

Child-support policies involve a diverse set of factors related to ensuring that noncustodial parents provide financial support for their children. States vary in their statutory criteria for child support: whether the state can take a percentage of the noncustodial parent's wages, formulas for child support, discretion to have payment made directly to the court, and long-arm statutes. Historically, public assistance played an important role in the economic status of divorced mothers and children (see Garfinkel, Melli, & Robertson, 1994, for a review). Guidelines of "reasonableness" were used by states to determine noncustodial parents' responsibility to pay child support. Local judges used budgets submitted by custodial parents in conjunction with the ability of the noncustodial parent to pay (based on income and other factors), but awards differed considerably from court to court, and the child-support awards were generally too small to pay for a fair share of rearing the children (Garfinkel et al., 1994).

Federal legislation in 1984, 1988, and 1996 provided numerical formulas to guide decisions about child-support

awards, authorized states to withhold the noncustodial parent's wages to make child-support payments, and implemented other changes to make it easier for custodial parents to obtain a support award and for courts to enforce those awards (see Roberts, 1994). For example, some states will not issue driver's licenses, vehicle registrations, or state-issued permits to individuals who are behind in child-support payments. Nevertheless, only 57% of custodial parents have a child-support award, and only 47% of those receive full payments (Grall, 2007). Whether custodial parents receive payments is still highly dependent on noncustodial parents' motivation and ability to pay (Thomas & Sawhill, 2005).

In addition to policies specifically focused on child-support payments, policies related to alimony and distribution and maintenance of property also affect the financial resources available to children following divorce. Long-term alimony is no longer as common as it was in the past, except in situations with extenuating circumstances (e.g., a spouse has health problems that prohibit work; Katz, 1994). More common is short-term alimony or rehabilitative alimony, which is provided for a limited period of time during which the spouse receiving alimony (usually the wife) goes to school or gains other skills to enable her to return to the workforce (Katz, 1994). In determining how property is divided following divorce, both monetary and nonmonetary factors are typically considered. Over time, the nonmonetary contributions of parents who stay home with children and the economic needs of children have been given greater consideration in changing statutory laws affecting the distribution of assets following divorce. To the extent that they affect the financial resources available to children, policies involving child support, alimony, and distribution of property following divorce can be important for children's postdivorce adjustment.

Summary

In contrast to the necessity of correlational studies on effects of divorce itself, it is possible to collect experimental data to examine the effects of policies related to divorce. This will be an important direction for future research. Some data could come from natural experiments (e.g., comparing children in states with a particular policy of interest to children in states with a different policy). Other data could come from true experiments in which some children are randomly assigned to interventions being evaluated and other children are randomly assigned to the state's status quo (evaluations along these lines have been conducted in relation to different methods of determining child-support payments, such as in New York's Child Assistance Program; Hamilton, Burstein, & Long, 1998). Policy evaluations have the potential to lead to recommendations for a set of standards that could improve children's adjustment following their parents' divorce by making the divorce process less acrimonious and the decisions regarding finances and custody as conducive to children's well-being as possible.

Summary and Conclusions

In this article, I reviewed the research literature on links between parental divorce and children's adjustment. First, I considered evidence regarding how divorce is related to children's externalizing behaviors, internalizing problems, academic achievement, and social relationships. Research suggests that children whose parents have divorced have higher levels of externalizing behaviors and internalizing problems, lower academic achievement, and more problems in social relationships than do children whose parents have not divorced. However, even though children whose parents divorce have worse adjustment on average than do children whose parents do not divorce, most children whose parents divorce do not have long-term negative outcomes.

Second, I examined children's age at the time of the divorce, age at the time of the study, length of time since the divorce, demographic characteristics, children's adjustment prior to the divorce, and stigmatization as moderators of the links between divorce and children's adjustment. There is evidence that, for behavioral outcomes, children who are younger at the time of their parents' divorce may be more at risk than are children who are older at the time of the divorce, but for academic outcomes and social relationships (particularly with romantic partners), adolescents whose parents divorce may be at greater risk than are younger children. The evidence is inconclusive regarding whether girls or boys are more affected by divorce, but there is some evidence that European American children are more negatively affected by divorce than are African American children. Children who have adjustment difficulties prior to divorce are more negatively affected by divorce than are children who are functioning well before the divorce. In cultural and historical contexts in which divorce is stigmatized, children may show worse adjustment following divorce than they do in contexts where divorce is not stigmatized.

Third, I examined income, interparental conflict, parenting, and parents' well-being, as mediators of relations between divorce and children's adjustment. All four of these mediators attenuate the link between parental divorce and children's adjustment difficulties. Interparental conflict has received the most empirical support as an important mediator.

Fourth, I noted the caveats of the research literature. This review focused on the relation between divorce and children's adjustment, but stepfamily formation and subsequent divorces are often part of the experience of children whose biological parents divorce. Recent work using adoption and twin designs demonstrates the importance of both genetics and environments (and their interaction) in predicting the likelihood of divorce and children's adjustment following parental divorce.

Fifth, I considered notable policies related to grounds for divorce, child custody, and child support in light of how they might affect children's adjustment to their parents' divorce. Policies that reduce interparental conflict and provide economic security to children have the potential to benefit children's adjustment. Evaluating whether particular policies are related to children's adjustment following their parents' divorce has the potential to inform future policymaking.

It is important to end this review by emphasizing that not all children experience similar trajectories before or after experiencing their parents' divorce. Thus, trajectories of adjustment that may be typical of many children may not be exhibited by an individual child. Furthermore, what initially appear to be effects of divorce are likely to be a complex combination of parent, child, and contextual factors that precede and follow the divorce in conjunction with the divorce itself.

References

Allison, P.D., & Furstenberg, F.F., Jr. (1989). How marital dissolution affects children: Variations by age and sex. *Developmental Psychology, 25,* 540–549.

Amato, P.R. (1986). Marital conflict, the parent–child relationship, and child self-esteem. *Family Relations, 35,* 403–410.

Amato, P.R. (1993). Children's adjustment to divorce: Theories, hypotheses, and empirical support. *Journal of Marriage and the Family, 55,* 23–38.

Amato, P.R. (1996). Explaining the intergenerational transmission of divorce. *Journal of Marriage and the Family, 58,* 628–640.

Amato, P.R. (2001). Children of divorce in the 1990s: An update of the Amato and Keith (1991) meta-analysis. *Journal of Family Psychology, 15,* 355–370.

Amato, P.R. (2003). Reconciling divergent perspectives: Judith Wallerstein, quantitative family research, and children of divorce. *Family Relations, 52,* 332–339.

Amato, P.R., & Afifi, T.D. (2006). Feeling caught between parents: Adult children's relations with parents and subjective well-being. *Journal of Marriage and the Family, 68,* 222–235.

Amato, P.R., & Booth, A. (1996). A prospective study of divorce and parent–child relationships. *Journal of Marriage and the Family, 58,* 356–365.

Amato, P.R., & Cheadle, J. (2005). The long reach of divorce: Divorce and child well-being across three generations. *Journal of Marriage and the Family, 67,* 191–206.

Amato, P.R., & DeBoer, D.D. (2001). The transmission of marital instability across generations: Relationship skills or commitment to marriage? *Journal of Marriage and the Family, 63,* 1038–1051.

Amato, P.R., & Gilbreth, J.G. (1999). Nonresident fathers and children's well-being: A meta-analysis. *Journal of Marriage and the Family, 61,* 557–573.

Amato, P.R., & Keith, B. (1991a). Parental divorce and adult well-being: A meta-analysis. *Journal of Marriage and the Family, 53,* 43–58.

Amato, P.R., & Keith, B. (1991b). Parental divorce and the well-being of children: A meta-analysis. *Psychological Bulletin, 110,* 26–46.

Amato, P.R., Loomis, L.S., & Booth, A. (1995). Parental divorce, marital conflict, and offspring well-being during early adulthood. *Social Forces, 73,* 895–915.

American Law Institute. (2002). *Principles of the law of family dissolution: Analysis and recommendations.* Newark, NJ: Matthew Bender.

Bauserman, R. (2002). Child adjustment in joint-custody versus sole-custody arrangements: A meta-analytic review. *Journal of Family Psychology, 16,* 91–102.

Bender, W.N. (1994). Joint custody: The option of choice. *Journal of Divorce and Remarriage, 21,* 115–131.

Booth, A., & Amato, P.R. (1994). Parental marital quality, parental divorce, and relations with parents. *Journal of Marriage and the Family, 56,* 21–34.

Booth, A., & Amato, P.R. (2001). Parental predivorce relations and offspring postdivorce well-being. *Journal of Marriage and the Family, 63,* 197–212.

Buchanan, C.M., Maccoby, E.E., & Dornbusch, S.M. (1996). *Adolescents after divorce.* Cambridge, MA: Harvard University Press.

Buehler, C., Krishnakumar, A., Stone, G., Anthony, C., Pemberton, S., Gerard, J., & Barber, B.K. (1998). Interparental conflict styles and youth problem behaviors: A two-sample replication study. *Journal of Marriage and the Family, 60,* 119–132.

Chase-Lansdale, P.L., Cherlin, A.J., & Kiernan, K.K. (1995). The long-term effects of parental divorce on the mental health of young adults: A developmental perspective. *Child Development, 66,* 1614–1634.

Chase-Lansdale, P.L., & Hetherington, E.M. (1990). The impact of divorce on life-span development: Short and long term effects. In P.B. Baltes, D.L. Featherman, & R.M. Lerner (Eds.), *Life-span development and behavior* (pp. 105–150). Hillsdale, NJ: Erlbaum.

Cherlin, A.J. (1998). Marriage and marital dissolution among Black Americans. *Journal of Comparative Family Studies, 29,* 147–158.

Cherlin, A.J. (1999). Going to extremes: Family structure, children's well-being, and social science. *Demography, 36,* 421–428.

Cherlin, A.J., Chase-Lansdale, P.L., & McRae, C. (1998). Effects of parental divorce on mental health throughout the life course. *American Sociological Review, 63,* 239–249.

Cherlin, A.J., Furstenberg, F.F., Chase-Lansdale, P.L., Kiernan, K.E., Robins, P.K., Morrison, D.R., & Teitler, J.O. (1991). Longitudinal studies of effects of divorce on children in Great Britain and the United States. *Science, 252,* 1386–1389.

Coontz, S. (1992). *The way we never were: American families and the nostalgia trap.* New York: Basic Books.

Davies, P.T., & Cummings, E.M. (1994). Marital conflict and child adjustment: An emotional security hypothesis. *Psychological Bulletin, 116,* 387–411.

Doherty, W.J., & Needle, R.H. (1991). Psychological adjustment and substance use among adolescents before and after parental divorce. *Child Development, 62,* 328–337.

D'Onofrio, B.M., Turkheimer, E., Emery, R.E., Maes, H.H., Silberg, J., & Eaves, L.J. (2007). A children of twins study of parental divorce and offspring psychopathology. *Journal of Child Psychology and Psychiatry, 48,* 667–675.

D'Onofrio, B.M., Turkheimer, E., Emery, R.E., Slutske, W.S., Heath, A.C., Madden, P.A., & Martin, N.G. (2005). A genetically informed study of marital instability and its association with offspring psychopathology. *Journal of Abnormal Psychology, 114,* 570–586.

D'Onofrio, B.M., Turkheimer, E., Emery, R.E., Slutske, W.S., Heath, A.C., Madden, P.A., & Martin, N.G. (2006). A genetically informed study of the processes underlying the association between parental marital instability and offspring adjustment. *Developmental Psychology, 42,* 486–499.

Downey, D., & Powell, B. (1995). Do children in single-parent households fare better living with same-sex parents? *Journal of Marriage and the Family, 55,* 55–71.

Dunn, J. (2002). The adjustment of children in stepfamilies: Lessons from community studies. *Child and Adolescent Mental Health, 7,* 154–161.

Dunn, J., Deater-Deckard, K., Pickering, K., & O'Connor, T.G. (1998). Children's adjustment and prosocial behaviour in step-, single-parent, and non-stepfamily settings: Findings from a community study. *Journal of Child Psychology and Psychiatry, 39,* 1083–1095.

Emery, R.E., Laumann-Billings, L., Waldron, M.C., Sbarra, D.A., & Dillon, P. (2001). Child custody mediation and litigation: Custody, contact, and coparenting 12 years after initial dispute resolution. *Journal of Consulting and Clinical Psychology, 69,* 323–332.

Emery, R.E., Otto, R.K., & O'Donohue, W.T. (2005). A critical assessment of child custody evaluations: Limited science and a flawed system. *Psychological Science in the Public Interest, 6,* 1–29.

Emery, R.E., Sbarra, D., & Grover, T. (2005). Divorce mediation: Research and reflections. *Family Court Review, 43,* 22–37.

Emery, R.E., Waldron, M., Kitzmann, K.M., & Aaron, J. (1999). Delinquent behavior, future divorce or nonmarital childbearing, and externalizing behavior among offspring: A 14-year prospective study. *Journal of Family Psychology, 13,* 568–579.

Forehand, R., Thomas, A.M., Wierson, M., & Brody, G. (1990). Role of maternal functioning and parenting skills in adolescent functioning following parental divorce. *Journal of Abnormal Psychology, 99,* 278–283.

Garfinkel, I., Melli, M.S., & Robertson, J.G. (1994). Child support orders: A perspective on reform. *Future of Children, 4,* 84–100.

Glenn, N. (2001). Is the current concern about American marriage warranted? *Virginia Journal of Social Policy and the Law, 5,* 47.

Grall, T.S. (2007). *Custodial mothers and fathers and their child support: 2005.* Washington, DC: U.S. Bureau of the Census.

Grounds for Divorce. (n.d.). Retrieved March 1, 2008, from www.divorcelawinfo.com/Pages/grounds.html

Grych, J.H., & Fincham, F.D. (1990). Marital conflict and children's adjustment: A cognitive-contextual framework. *Psychological Bulletin, 108,* 267–290.

Guidubaldi, J., Cleminshaw, H.K., Perry, J.D., & McLoughlin, C.S. (1983). The impact of parental divorce on children: Report of the nationwide NASP study. *School Psychology Review, 12,* 300–323.

Hamilton, W.L., Burstein, N.R., & Long, D. (1998). *Using incentives in welfare reform: The New York State Child Assistance Program.* Cambridge, MA: Abt Associates.

Harris, J.R. (1998). *The nurture assumption: Why children turn out the way they do.* New York: Free Press.

Hetherington, E.M. (1989). Coping with family transitions: Winners, losers, and survivors. *Child Development, 60,* 1–14.

Hetherington, E.M., Bridges, M., & Insabella, G.M. (1998). What matters? What does not? Five perspectives on the association between marital transitions and children's adjustment. *American Psychologist, 53,* 167–184.

Hetherington, E.M., & Clingempeel, W.G. (1992). Coping with marital transitions: A family systems perspective. *Monographs of the Society for Research in Child Development, 57* (2–3, Serial No. 227).

Hetherington, E.M., Cox, M., & Cox, R. (1979). Stress and coping in divorce: A focus on women. In J.E. Gullahorn (Ed.), *Psychology and women: In transition* (pp. 95–128). Washington, DC: V. H. Winston & Sons.

Hetherington, E.M., Cox, M., & Cox, R. (1985). Long-term effects of divorce and remarriage on the adjustment of children. *Journal of the American Academy of Child Psychiatry, 24,* 518–530.

Hetherington, E.M., & Elmore, A.M. (2004). The intergenerational transmission of couple instability. In P.L. Chase-Lansdale, K. Kiernan, & R.J. Friedman (Eds.), *Human development across lives and generations: The potential for change* (pp. 171–203). New York: Cambridge University Press.

Hetherington, E.M., Henderson, S.H., Reiss, D., Anderson, E.R., Bridges, M., Chan, R.W., et al. (1999). Adolescent siblings in stepfamilies: Family functioning and adolescent adjustment. *Monographs of the Society for Research in Child Development, 64* (4).

Hetherington, E.M., & Kelly, J. (2002). *For better or worse.* New York: Norton.

Hetherington, E.M., & Stanley-Hagan, M. (1999). The adjustment of children with divorced parents: A risk and resiliency perspective. *Journal of Child Psychology and Psychiatry, 40,* 129–140.

Hetherington, E.M., Stanley-Hagan, M., & Anderson, E.R. (1989). Marital transitions: A child's perspective. *American Psychologist, 44,* 303–312.

Jeynes, W. (2002). *Divorce, family structure, and the academic success of children.* New York: Haworth Press.

Jocklin, V., McGue, M., & Lykken, D.T. (1996). Personality and divorce: A genetic analysis. *Journal of Personality and Social Psychology, 71,* 288–299.

Johnston, J.R. (1995). Research update: Children's adjustment in sole custody compared to joint custody families and principles for custody decision making. *Family and Conciliation Courts Review, 33,* 415–425.

Kasen, S., Cohen, P., Brook, J.S., & Hartmark, C. (1996). A multiple-risk interaction model: Effects of temperament and divorce on psychiatric disorders in children. *Journal of Abnormal Child Psychology, 24,* 121–150.

Katz, S.N. (1994). Historical perspective and current trends in the legal process of divorce. *Future of Children, 4,* 44–62.

Kelly, J.B. (1994). The determination of child custody. *Future of Children, 4,* 121–142.

Lansford, J.E., Ceballo, R., Abbey, A., & Stewart, A.J. (2001). Does family structure matter? A comparison of adoptive, two parent biological, single mother, stepfather, and stepmother households. *Journal of Marriage and the Family, 63,* 840–851.

Lansford, J.E., Malone, P.S., Castellino, D.R., Dodge, K.A., Pettit, G.S., & Bates, J.E. (2006). Trajectories of internalizing, externalizing, and grades for children who have and have not experienced their parents' divorce. *Journal of Family Psychology, 20,* 292–301.

Laosa, L.M. (1988). Ethnicity and single parenting in the United States. In E.M. Hetherington & J.D. Arasteh (Eds.), *Impact of divorce, single parenting, and stepparenting on children* (pp. 23–49). Hillsdale, NJ: Erlbaum.

Laumann-Billings, L., & Emery, R.E. (2000). Distress among young adults from divorced families. *Journal of Family Psychology, 14,* 671–687.

Lye, D.N. (1996). Adult child–parent relationships. *Annual Review of Sociology, 22,* 79–102.

Lykken, D.T. (2002). How relationships begin and end: A genetic perspective. In A.L. Vangelisti, H.T. Reis, & M.A. Fitzpatrick (Eds.), *Stability and change in relationships* (pp. 83–102). New York: Cambridge University Press.

Maes, H.H.M., Neale, M.C., Kendler, K.S., Hewitt, J.K., Silberg, J.L., Foley, D.L., et al. (1998). Assortative mating for major psychiatric diagnoses in two population-based samples. *Psychological Medicine, 28,* 1389–1401.

Malone, P.S., Lansford, J.E., Castellino, D.R., Berlin, L.J., Dodge, K.A., Bates, J.E., & Pettit, G.S. (2004). Divorce and child behavior problems: Applying latent change score models to life event data. *Structural Equation Modeling, 11,* 401–423.

Martinez, C.R., Jr., & Forgatch, M.S. (2002). Adjusting to change: Linking family structure transitions with parenting and boys' adjustment. *Journal of Family Psychology, 16,* 107–117.

McGue, M., & Lykken, D.T. (1992). Genetic influence on risk of divorce. *Psychological Science, 3,* 368–373.

McLanahan, S.S. (1999). Father absence and the welfare of children. In E.M. Hetherington (Ed.), *Coping with divorce, single parenting, and remarriage: A risk and resiliency perspective* (pp. 117–145). Hillsdale, NJ: Erlbaum.

McLanahan, S., & Sandefur, G. (1994). *Growing up with a single parent.* Cambridge, MA: Harvard University Press.

Mechanic, D., & Hansell, S. (1989). Divorce, family conflict, and adolescents' well-being. *Journal of Health and Social Behavior, 30,* 105–116.

Merikangas, K.R. (1984). Divorce and assortative mating among depressed patients. *American Journal of Psychiatry, 141,* 74–76.

Morrison, D.R., & Cherlin, A.J. (1995). The divorce process and young children's well-being: A prospective analysis. *Journal of Marriage and the Family, 57,* 800–812.

Nakonezny, P.A., Shull, R.D., & Rodgers, J.L. (1995). The effect of no-fault divorce law on the divorce rate across the 50 states and its relation to income, education, and religiosity. *Journal of Marriage and the Family, 57,* 477–488.

National Center for Health Statistics. (2008). Marriage and divorce. Retrieved March 3, 2008, from www.cdc.gov/nchs/fastats/divorce.htm

Neiderhiser, J.M., Reiss, D., & Hetherington, E.M. (2007). The nonshared environment in adolescent development (NEAD) project: A longitudinal family study of twins and siblings from adolescence to young adulthood. *Twin Research and Human Genetics, 10,* 74–83.

O'Connor, T.G., Caspi, A., DeFries, J.C., & Plomin, R. (2000). Are associations between parental divorce and children's adjustment genetically mediated? An adoption study. *Developmental Psychology, 36,* 429–437.

Orbuch, T.L., Thornton, A., & Cancio, J. (2000). The impact of marital quality, divorce, and remarriage on the relationships between parents and their children. *Marriage and Family Review, 29*, 221–246.

Popenoe, D. (1993). American family decline, 1960–1990: A review and appraisal. *Journal of Marriage and the Family, 55*, 527–542.

Popenoe, D. (2003). Can the nuclear family be revived? In M. Coleman & L. Ganong (Eds.), *Points and counterpoints: Controversial relationship and family issues in the 21st century* (pp. 218–221). Los Angeles: Roxbury Publishing.

Reifman, A., Villa, L.C., Amans, J.A., Rethinam, V., & Telesca, T.Y. (2001). Children of divorce in the 1990s: A meta-analysis. *Journal of Divorce and Remarriage, 36*, 27–36.

Roberts, P.G. (1994). Child support orders: Problems with enforcement. *Future of Children, 4*, 101–120.

Ruschena, E., Prior, M., Sanson, A., & Smart, D. (2005). A longitudinal study of adolescent adjustment following family transitions. *Journal of Child Psychology and Psychiatry, 46*, 353–363.

Shaw, D.S., Emery, R.E., & Tuer, M.D. (1993). Parental functioning and children's adjustment in families of divorce: A prospective study. *Journal of Abnormal Child Psychology, 21*, 119–134.

Short, J.L. (2002). The effects of parental divorce during childhood on college students. *Journal of Divorce and Remarriage, 38*, 143–156.

Simons, R.L., Whitbeck, L.B., Beaman, J., & Conger, R.D. (1994). The impact of mothers' parenting, involvement by nonresidential fathers, and parental conflict on the adjustment of adolescent children. *Journal of Marriage and the Family, 56*, 356–374.

Sun, Y., & Li, Y. (2001). Marital disruption, parental investment, and children's academic achievement: A prospective analysis. *Journal of Family Issues, 22*, 27–62.

Sun, Y., & Li, Y. (2002). Children's well-being during parents' marital disruption process: A pooled time-series analysis. *Journal of Marriage and the Family, 64*, 472–488.

Thomas, A., & Sawhill, I. (2005). For love and money? The impact of family structure on family income. *Future of Children, 15*, 57–74.

Tschann, J.M., Johnson, J.R., & Wallerstein, J.S. (1989). Family processes and children's functioning during divorce. *Journal of Marriage and the Family, 51*, 431–444.

Twaite, J.A., & Luchow, A.K. (1996). Custodial arrangements and parental conflict following divorce: The impact on children's adjustment. *Journal of Psychiatry and Law, 24*, 53–75.

U.S. Census Bureau. (2004). Detailed tables: Number, timing and duration of marriages and divorces, 2004. Washington, DC: Author. Retrieved March 3, 2008, from www.census.gov/population/www/socdemo/marr-div/2004detailed_tables.html

Vandewater, E.A., & Lansford, J.E. (1998). Influences of family structure and parental conflict on children's well-being. *Family Relations, 47*, 323–330.

Videon, T.M. (2002). The effects of parent-adolescent relationships and parental separation on adolescent well-being. *Journal of Marriage and the Family, 64*, 489–503.

Wallerstein, J.S., Lewis, J.M., & Blakeslee, S. (2000). *The unexpected legacy of divorce: A 25 year landmark study.* New York: Hyperion.

Warshak, R.A. (2007). The approximation rule, child development research, and children's best interests after divorce. *Child Development Perspectives, 1*, 119–125.

Wolfers, J. (2003). Did unilateral divorce laws raise divorce rates? A reconciliation and new results. National Bureau of Economic Research Working Paper No. 10014. Retrieved March 1, 2008, from www.nber.org/papers/w10014

Within-Family Differences in Parent–Child Relations across the Life Course

J. JILL SUITOR ET AL.

Despite a powerful social norm that parents should treat offspring equally, beginning in early childhood and continuing through adulthood, parents often differentiate among their children in such domains as closeness, support, and control. We review research on how parent–child relationships differ within families, focusing on issues of parental favoritism and differential treatment of children. We begin by examining within-family differences in childhood and adolescence and then explore differentiation by older parents among adult children. Overall, we find considerable similarities across the life course in the prevalence, predictors, and consequences of parents' differentiation among their offspring.

Literature and history abound with stories of parental favoritism, beginning with the Biblical story of Israel favoring his last-born son Joseph and continuing to Pat Conroy's novel *Beach Music*. In the early 20th century, both Sigmund Freud, who was his mother's favorite, and Alfred Adler, who was not, noted the potential consequences of such favoritism for children's development. Despite the attention that these two eminent psychoanalysts gave to this issue, scholars showed little interest in the topic until the early 1980s. In fact, according to Harris and Howard (1983), who published one of the earliest pieces on differential treatment, neither *Psychological Abstracts* nor the *Psychoanalytic Study of the Child* contained any references to parental favoritism in the preceding 20 years.

Since that time, within-family differentiation among offspring has gained widespread attention across a range of disciplines including evolutionary biology, psychology, sociology, and economics. Although much of this work has emphasized the ways in which birth order affects characteristics such as intelligence, personality, and social attitudes, an increasing focus has been on within-family differences in parent–child relationships. In this article, we explore the patterns and consequences of such differentiation in parents' relationships with their offspring across the life course, drawing upon a review of more than 120 articles and books.

We examined literature on both "parental favoritism" and "parental differential treatment" (PDT), given that the study of within-family differences encompasses these closely related areas of research. The primary distinction between these two phenomena is that favoritism generally refers to parents' differential affect and preferences among their children, whereas PDT typically describes ways in which parents differentiate among their children behaviorally, such as displays of affection, discipline, and the distribution of other interpersonal and instrumental resources. The literature on the early stages of the life course has included studies of both favoritism and PDT, whereas scholarship on within-family differences after children have entered adulthood has focused primarily on favoritism.

Within-Family Differences in Childhood and Adolescence

Parents are commonly exhorted not to favor some of their children over others, yet beginning in early childhood they often differentiate in terms of closeness, support, and control. Although the exact figures vary widely across studies, reports suggest that, in one third to two thirds of families, parents favor one or more of their children in at least one domain (Shebloski, Conger, & Widaman, 2005; Volling & Elins, 1998).

There is obviously considerable variation in reporting of PDT. One of the most important sources of this variation can be attributed to the diversity of methodologies.

For example, studies of families with preschoolers often include some combination of in-person interviews with the parents, videotaping of interactions between family members, and parents' completion of written questionnaires. In studies in which offspring are of school age or older, interviews are frequently conducted with the children.

Researchers have also examined whether reports of parental differentiation vary by the structural position of the family member responding. For instance, children tend to report favoritism more frequently than do their parents (Feinberg, Neiderhiser, Howe, & Hetherington, 2000), consistent with Bengtson's (Bengtson & Kuypers, 1971) argument that parents have a greater stake than children in portraying their intergenerational relations as harmonious. Although there is often overlap between parents' and children's perceptions, there is also substantial incongruence, highlighting the importance of collecting data from multiple family members. For example, in one recent investigation (Kowal, Krull, & Kramer, 2006), only about 60% of parents' and children's reports agreed about whether parents differentiated regarding affection.

Even across studies using subjects in the same structural position in the family and the same mode of data collection (e.g., interview), the measurement of PDT varies considerably. Few studies ask parents directly to differentiate among their children, instead typically asking the same questions about each child and using those data to create difference scores. No single measure of parents' reports of PDT has become standard, although a large number of investigations have used the Parent–Child Relationship Survey (Hetherington & Clingempeel, 1992). When studying children's perceptions of PDT, scholars have increasingly used the Sibling Inventory of Differential Experience (Daniels & Plomin, 1985), which asks subjects to compare their experiences directly to those of one of their siblings.

Explaining Differentiation: The Role of Family and Individual Characteristics

The literature provides a rich body of findings regarding which children are most often favored, the forms that favoritism takes, and the conditions under which particular patterns occur. We provide an overview of those findings that are the most uniform across studies.

One factor that predicts families in which parents differentiate is high levels of stress, particularly in the lives of parents. For example, favoritism is more common when parents experience marital problems and when children have serious health problems (Singer & Weinstein, 2000).

A second set of factors associated with PDT involves family structure and composition. Birth order is one of the structural factors that has received substantial attention in the study of PDT. The preponderance of evidence regarding comparisons of first- and last-borns suggests that youngest children are advantaged in terms of parental affection (Tucker, McHale, & Crouter, 2003), supporting theories that last-borns develop more sensitive social skills in an attempt to create a special position in families (Sulloway, 1996). However, the findings of other first-versus last-born comparisons are less consistent. In contrast, the literature is quite uniform regarding middle children, who are much less likely to be favored than are their eldest and youngest siblings across multiple domains (Hertwig, Davis, & Sulloway, 2002). Another important family-composition factor is the presence of both biological and nonbiological children, particularly in blended families (O'Conner, Dunn, Jenkins, & Rasbash, 2006). Parents in such families, especially mothers, tend to favor their biological children.

Finally, studies show that parents' differential responses reflect variations in the children's behaviors and personalities. In particular, mothers and fathers have been found to direct more control and discipline toward children whose behaviors are disruptive or aggressive, and express more warmth toward children who show greater positive affect toward their parents (Tucker et al., 2003). Perhaps because of the tendency for boys to display more aggression and for girls to show more warmth, studies have often found greater differential treatment in families with mixed offspring than in families with single-gender offspring (O'Conner et al., 2006; McHale, Updegraff, Tucker, & Crouter, 2000), particularly regarding affection and time spent with children. In some studies, this gender difference has been reduced by controlling for children's aggression and affection (Tucker et al., 2003).

Consequences of Within-Family Differentiation in Childhood and Adolescence

From the review we have presented, it is clear that parents often favor one or more of their children in childhood and adolescence—but does such differentiation have any consequences? Research has shown that least-favored children experience lower levels of self-esteem, self-worth, and sense of social responsibility, and higher levels of aggression, depression, and externalizing behaviors (Feinberg et al., 2000; Singer & Weinstein, 2000).

The evidence for effects of being most favored is less clear than for the effects of being unfavored. Although being favored has been shown to produce positive outcomes under particular sets of circumstances (McHale, Crouter, McGuire, & Updegraff, 1995; McHale et al., 2000), in most cases, it appears that regardless of which child is favored, PDT is problematic for the well-being of all off-spring in the family (Singer & Weinstein, 2000). Findings regarding the effects of PDT on the quality of siblings' relationships are among the most consistent in this body of research. With few exceptions, the literature indicates that siblings express less warmth and greater hostility toward one another when parents show favoritism (McHale et al., 1995).

One important line of inquiry involves the role of children's perceptions of fairness. The evidence suggests that perceptions of fairness moderate the relationship between PDT and both well-being and sibling relations. In some cases, perceptions of fairness have positive consequences. For example, children express less hostility toward siblings who receive more attention if they believe the other children are needier. However, perceptions of fairness can have detrimental consequences as well, such as when these perceptions lead unfavored children to feel that they deserve less affection from their parents than do their siblings (McHale et al., 2000).

It might be tempting to interpret these findings as evidence that difficult children increase parents' differentiation and sibling tensions, rather than differentiation affecting children's outcomes. Although it is clear that children's behaviors and temperaments affect these patterns (Tucker et al., 2003), our review leads us to believe that offspring characteristics alone cannot adequately account for the association between PDT and children's outcomes. First, as noted above, the literature demonstrates that PDT, regardless of the form it takes, typically increases hostility among siblings (McHale et al., 1995). Second, the findings of longitudinal investigations suggest that, over time, being unfavored by parents produces behavior problems in children (Richmond, Stocker, & Rienks, 2005).

Within-Family Differences in Adulthood

There is a vast literature on the quality of relationships between parents and their adult children; however, with few exceptions, this work is based on studies using between-family designs. In this review, we restrict our discussion to findings from studies that have used within-family designs and are therefore comparable to investigations of PDT in earlier life-course stages. Unlike research on children and adolescents, there are fewer than 20 articles on within-family differences in adult child–parent relations, about half of which are based upon only one study; thus, it is impossible to answer questions about PDT in adulthood as fully as those about earlier stages of the life course.

Do Parents Continue to Differentiate among Adult Children?

Studies of the middle and later stages of the life course have shown that parents are more likely to differentiate among their offspring in adulthood than in childhood. For example, in a recent study of 556 families, more than three quarters of mothers named a particular child whom they would choose as a confidant, nearly three quarters named a child whom they would prefer provide them assistance when ill or disabled, and nearly two thirds named a child to whom they were most emotionally close (Suitor & Pillemer, 2007). Fathers' reports closely mirrored those of the mothers. The majority of mothers also differentiated among their adult children regarding providing emotional and instrumental support (Suitor, Pillemer, & Sechrist, 2006). Studies using smaller and less representative samples (Aldous, Klaus, & Klein, 1985) have shown similar patterns. Such high levels of favoritism are particularly striking given that, in these studies, parents were asked directly to differentiate among their children.

Reports from offspring reveal that adult children often believe that their parents favor some children (Bedford, 1992; Suitor, Sechrist, Steinhour, & Pillemer, 2006). Suitor and colleagues found that 66% of children accurately reported that their mothers differentiated regarding closeness, but only 44% were correct about *which* offspring were favored (Suitor et al., 2006); most children reported themselves as the favorite.

Explaining Differentiation in Adulthood

Intergenerational relationships change as children move into adulthood, bringing with them the history from childhood onto which is superimposed a new set of expectations. Despite this different context, the factors that best explain within-family differences in parent–adult-child relations are related, conceptually, to those from earlier stages of the life course. These are (a) similarity between parents and children, (b) developmental histories, (c) equity and exchange, and (d) family structure and composition. Specifically, parents are more likely to favor daughters, children who share their values, children who have achieved normative adult statuses and avoided deviant behaviors, children who have provided parents with support, and children who are more geographically proximate (Aldous et al., 1985; Suitor et al., 2006). Mothers are also closest to last-borns and least close to middle-borns (Suitor & Pillemer, 2007). Further, these patterns are similar for Blacks and Whites. Thus, these patterns mirror those in childhood in terms of normative societal and parental expectations, positive affect, gender, and birth order.

Consequences of Within-Family Differentiation in Adulthood

There has been less attention to the effects of PDT in adulthood than to its effects in childhood. However, the few studies that have examined this issue reveal patterns similar to those of earlier stages of the life course. For example, adults who perceive that they have been unfavored in childhood or adulthood have less close relations with their parents (Bedford, 1992; Boll, Ferring, & Filipp, 2003). Being slightly favored improves adult children's relations with their parents; however, being highly favored also reduces relationship quality.

Consistent with earlier stages, sibling relations are most positive when adult children are treated equally (Boll et al., 2003). Also similar to studies in childhood, perceptions of fairness moderate the relationship between PDT and relations with parents and siblings (Boll et al., 2003). Whether PDT in adulthood has consequences for well-being remains to be investigated.

Future Directions

There is clear evidence that many parents differentiate among their offspring from the earliest stages of childhood through adulthood. Further, several factors explain PDT across the life course, such as children's behaviors, birth order, and gender. Because data do not yet exist to examine whether consistency in differentiation occurs within the same families across several decades, we can only speculate about this possibility. Some patterns we might expect would change over time; for example, comparisons across studies of families with preschoolers, adolescents, and adult children suggest that parents may differentiate more as their children mature. However, several of the factors that play important roles in PDT remain stable within families throughout the life course, perhaps leading some families to be more prone to continued favoritism. Thus, we would expect continued favoritism in families with more than two children, with children of both genders, and with children who engage in deviant behaviors in both adolescence and adulthood.

Another important research question that has yet to be answered is how PDT is moderated by socioeconomic status and race. Only a handful of investigations at any point in the life course have included minorities, and studies of the early life course have relied almost exclusively on middle-class families.

Finally, future research may show that PDT and parental favoritism have long-term effects on outcomes affecting both parents and adult children. An important dynamic in parent–child relations in later life revolves around both the anticipation of and actual provision of care for older parents. Further, most parents have strong preferences regarding which children will provide care to them in the later years (Suitor & Pillemer, 2007). It is possible that such expectations will affect both parents' and children's well being. For example, it is possible that greater caregiver stress and burden may result if circumstances require a nonpreferred child to become the primary caregiver. Thus the match between parental preference for caregiving and actual outcomes for both parties is likely to be a fruitful topic for research.

In sum, we know a great deal about the existence and predictors of parental favoritism across the life course and about the consequences of these patterns in childhood. We hope that future research will help us to better understand the ways in which these patterns change across time, are moderated by social factors, and have effects on children's and parents' well-being across the life course.

Recommended Reading

Downey, D.B. (1995). When bigger is not better: Family size, parental resources, and children's educational performance. *American Sociological Review, 60,* 746–761. A theoretically driven study demonstrating the role of family composition on children's outcomes.

Shanahan, L., McHale, S.M., Crouter, A.C., & Osgood, D.W. (2007). Warmth with mothers and fathers from middle childhood to late adolescence: Within- and between-families comparisons. *Developmental Psychology, 43,* 551–563. A representative study that provides further detail regarding changes in parental differential treatment from childhood through adolescence.

Steelman, L.C., Powell, B., Werum, R. & Carter, S. (2002). Reconsidering the effect of sibling configuration: Recent advances and challenges. *Annual Review of Sociology, 28,* 243–269. A clearly-written comprehensive review of the consequences of sibling composition.

Sulloway, F.J. (1996). (See References). A highly accessible overview of history, theory, and research on birth order.

References

Aldous, J., Klaus, E., & Klein, D.M. (1985). The understanding heart: Aging parents and their favorite children. *Child Development, 56,* 303–316.

Bedford, V.H. (1992). Memories of parental favoritism and the quality of parent–child ties in adulthood. *Journal of Gerontology: Social Sciences, 47,* S149–S155.

Bengtson, V.L., & Kuypers, J.A. (1971). Generational differences and the developmental stake. *Aging and Human Development, 2,* 249–260.

Boll, T., Ferring, D., & Filipp, S.H. (2003). Perceived parental differential treatment in middle adulthood: Curvilinear relations with individuals' experienced relationship quality to sibling and parents. *Journal of Family Psychology, 17,* 472–487.

Daniels, D., & Plomin, R. (1985). Differential experience of siblings in the same family. *Developmental Psychology, 21,* 747–760.

Feinberg, M.E., Neiderhiser, J.M., Howe, G., & Hetherington, E.M. (2000). Adolescent, parent, and observer perceptions of parenting: Genetic and environmental influences on shared and distinct perceptions. *Child Development, 72,* 1266–1284.

Harris, I.D., & Howard, K.I. (1983). Correlates of perceived parental favoritism. *Journal of Genetic Psychology, 1461,* 45–56.

Hertwig, R., Davis, J.N., & Sulloway, F.J. (2002). Parental investment: How an equity motive can produce inequality. *Psychological Bulletin, 128,* 728–745.

Hetherington, E.M., & Clingempeel, W.G. (1992). Coping with marital transitions: A family systems perspective. *Monographs of the Society for Research in Child Development, 57*(2–3, Serial No. 227).

Kowal, A.K., Krull, J.L., & Kramer, L. (2006). Shared understanding of parental differential treatment in families. *Social Development, 15,* 277–295.

McHale, S.M., Crouter, A.C., McGuire, S.A., & Updegraff, K.A. (1995). Congruence between mothers' and fathers' differential treatment of siblings: Links with family relations and children's well-being. *Child Development, 66,* 116–128.

McHale, S.M., Updegraff, K.A., Tucker, C.J., & Crouter, A.C. (2000). When does parents' differential treatment have negative implications for siblings? *Social Development, 9,* 149–172.

O'Conner, T.G., Dunn, J., Jenkins, J.M., & Rasbash, J. (2006). Predictors of between-family and within-family variation in parent-child relationships. *Journal of Child Psychology and Psychiatry, 47,* 498–510.

Richmond, M.K., Stocker, C.M., & Rienks, S.L. (2005). Longitudinal associations between sibling relationship quality, parental differential treatment, and children's adjustment. *Journal of Family Psychology, 19,* 550–559.

Shebloski, B., Conger, K.J., & Widaman, K.F. (2005). Reciprocal links among differential parenting, perceived partiality, and self-worth: A three-wave longitudinal study. *Journal of Family Psychology, 19,* 633–642.

Singer, A.T., & Weinstein, R. (2000). Differential parental treatment predicts achievements and self-perceptions in two cultural contexts. *Journal of Family Psychology, 14,* 491–509.

Suitor, J.J., & Pillemer, K. (2007). Mothers' favoritism in later life: The role of children's birth order. *Research on Aging, 29,* 32–55.

Suitor, J.J., Pillemer, K., & Sechrist, J. (2006). Within-family differences in mothers' support to adult children. *Journal of Gerontology: Social Science, 61,* S10–S17.

Suitor, J.J., Sechrist, J., Steinhour, M., & Pillemer, K. (2006). 'I'm sure she chose me!' Consistency in intergenerational reports of mothers' favoritism in later-life families. *Family Relations, 55,* 526–538.

Sulloway, F.J. 1996. *Born To Rebel.* New York: Pantheon Books.

Tucker, C.J., McHale, S.M., & Crouter, A.C. (2003). Dimensions of mothers' and fathers' differential treatment of siblings: Links with adolescents' sex-typed personal qualities. *Family Relations, 52,* 82–89.

Volling, B.L., & Elins, J.L. (1998). Family relationships and children's emotional adjustment as correlates of maternal and paternal differential treatment: A replication with toddler and preschool siblings. *Child Development, 69,* 1640–1656.

Address correspondence to **J. JILL SUITOR,** Department of Sociology and Anthropology, Purdue University, 700 Stone Hall, Purdue University, West Lafayette, IN 47907; e-mail: jsuitor@purdue.edu.

From *Current Directions in Psychological Science,* May 2008, pp. 334–338. Copyright © 2008 by the Association for Psychological Science. Reprinted by permission of Wiley-Blackwell.

The Messy Room Dilemma
When to Ignore Behavior, When to Change It

ALAN E. KAZDIN AND CARLO ROTELLA

Thanks to more than 50 years of research, we know how to change children's behavior. In brief, you identify the unwanted behavior, define its *positive opposite* (the desirable behavior you want to replace it with), and then make sure that your child engages in a lot of *reinforced practice* of the new behavior until it replaces the unwanted one. Reinforced practice means that you pay as much attention as possible to the positive opposite so that your child falls into a pattern: Do the right behavior, get a reward (praise or a token); do the behavior, get a reward. Real life is never as mechanically predictable as that formula makes it sound, and many other factors will bear on your success—including your relationship with your child, what behaviors you model in your home, and what influences your child is exposed to in other relationships—but, still, we know that reinforced practice usually works. If you handle the details properly, in most cases a relatively brief period of intense attention to the problem, lasting perhaps a few weeks, should be enough to work a permanent change in behavior.

So, yes, you can change your child's behavior, but that doesn't mean you always should. When faced with an unwanted behavior, first ask yourself, *Can I let this go?* Sometimes the answer is *Hell, no!* If your kid likes to spend hours at his window in full-body camo and a Sad Clown mask, tracking the neighbors in the sights of his BB gun, you'll probably want to put a stop to that right now. But a lot of behaviors fall into the lesser category of annoying but not necessarily worth addressing. Ask yourself if changing a behavior will really make a worthwhile difference in your child's life and your own.

Many unwanted behaviors, including some that disturb parents, tend to drop out on their own, especially if you don't overreact to them and reinforce them with a great deal of excited attention. Take thumb sucking, which is quite common up to age 5. At that point it drops off sharply and continues to decline. Unless the dentist tells you that you need to do something about it right now, you can probably let thumb sucking go. The same principle applies for most stuttering. Approximately 5 percent of all children stutter, usually at some point between ages 2 and 5. Parents get understandably nervous when their children stutter, but the vast majority of these children (approximately 80 percent) stop stuttering on their own by age 6. If stuttering persists past that point or lasts for a period extending more than six months, then it's time to do something about it.

There are a lot more behaviors, running the range from annoying to unacceptable, in this category. Approximately 60 percent of 4- and 5-year-old boys can't sit still as long as adults want them to, and approximately 50 percent of 4- and 5-year-old boys and girls whine to the extent that their parents consider it a significant problem. Both fidgeting and whining tend to decrease on their own with age, especially if you don't reinforce these annoying behaviors by showing your child that they're a surefire way to get your (exasperated) attention. Thirty to 40 percent of 10- and 11-year-old boys and girls lie in a way that their parents identify as a significant problem, but this age seems to be the peak, and the rate of problem lying tends to plummet thereafter and cease to be an issue. By adolescence, more than 50 percent of males and 20 percent to 35 percent of females have engaged in one delinquent behavior—typically theft or vandalism. For most children, it does not turn into a continuing problem.

Now, we're not saying that you should ignore lying or stealing or some other potentially serious misbehavior just because it will probably drop out on its own in good time. There's an important distinction to be made here between managing behavior and other parental motives and duties. Parents punish for several reasons—to teach right and wrong, to satisfy the demands of justice, to establish their authority—that have little to do with changing behavior. You can't just let vandalism go without consequences, and it's reasonable to refuse to put up with even a lesser offense such as undue whining, but don't confuse punishing misbehavior with taking effective steps to eliminate it. Punishment on its own (that is, not supplemented by reinforced practice of the positive opposite) has been proven again and again to be a fairly weak method for changing behavior. The misbehaviors in question, minor or serious, are more likely to drop out on their own than they are to be eliminated through punishment.

Especially as your child gets older, more independent, and more capable of holding her own in a household struggle over behavior, you will need to practice parenting triage—asking, *Is it worth drawing the line* here? Be especially wary of slippery slopes, falling dominoes, and other common but not necessarily relevant rationales for intervening in your child's behavior.

Consider, for example, an adolescent's fantastically messy room, a typical flash point for household conflicts about things that really matter to kids and parents, like autonomy and respect and the rights of the individual in relation to the family. Messiness is a habit, a set of behaviors, so it would not be difficult to define a positive opposite of mess-making, set up a system of rewards for cleaning up, and replace a bad habit with a better one. But let's first ask a basic question: *Why focus on the messiness of your child's room?* There may be good reasons to. It may be that your child never has presentable clothes to wear because they pile up dirty on her floor. Or her room could present a real sanitation problem, if there are dirty dishes or discarded food in there. Maybe there aren't enough clean forks in the house because they're all on her floor, in empty TV dinner trays.

These are significant matters that would need to be addressed right away, but what if the problem is not presentable clothing or sanitation or the household fork supply but just sloppiness? You could fix it, probably, but is it really that big a deal?

When you ask yourself, *Why focus on it?*, you may decide that it's not worth addressing the problem. Or asking *Why focus on it?* may help you to narrow down the problem to those elements that really do need to be addressed. Some aspects of a sloppy room may really be nonnegotiable: candles and incense near flammable material or rotting food or some other potential biohazard. If the mess is dangerous, if there are consequences for other people in the household, then it's certainly worth addressing. And, guided by your own answer to *Why focus on it?*, be prepared to trade an inessential for an essential. Let her keep her clothes on the floor if she does her own laundry and cleans up food mess as soon as she makes it.

Parents frequently respond to *Why focus on it?* by expressing a worry that if they let their child be sloppy in her room she will be sloppy everywhere: in her personal appearance, in her schoolwork, in her career. They have fantasies about her getting fired in middle age for having a messy office. But when it comes to messiness, the slippery-slope argument is a fallacy. Having a messy room is an identifiable stage that tends to appear in adolescence and then go away. After the messy interlude of the preteen and teen years, most people return to or rise to some basic standard of neatness—a standard very likely resembling the one you have modeled in your own housekeeping.

So if your adolescent child keeps herself reasonably clean and presentable, and if the problem's not so severe that it's causing other problems, consider letting slide the messiness of her room as a stage she's going through. Yes, every parent will always have a story of an adult who's a genuine slob to back up the claim that not everybody recovers from adolescent messiness, but those cases are exceptions. Really, how many adults do you know who have rooms like your kid's? Not many. They grew out of it. So why move heaven and earth—and increase the amount of conflict in the house, and use up energy and goodwill perhaps better reserved for more significant matters—to correct a problem that will almost certainly self-correct?

Of course, parents can have their own real reasons to object to even a little messiness in a child's room. It could be that you're a very tidy person, and you just can't abide it. That's a legitimate complaint, but recognize that it's not about any abnormal behavior on the part of your child. Be straight about it with her. Tell her that you can't live with such a mess in the house, and that, together, you're going to have to compromise on some middle ground between your standard (*no mess ever, anywhere*) and hers (*let the clothes fall where they may*). As you work out the compromise, consider that, especially if the rest of your house is neat, your child's messy room is an expression of autonomy and independence, normal for her stage of development. And try to remember that clutter, however much it offends you, may not belong in the same category of urgency as things that can lead to permanent consequences—like those candles right under the curtains.

What if you just ignore an unwanted behavior but don't reinforce its positive opposite? *Extinction*—eliminating an unwanted behavior just by ignoring it—does have the virtue of not reinforcing the unwanted behavior by attending to it, but it's not a very effective way to change behavior. The research shows that extinction on its own is likely to fail. And even if extinction works in the long run, the unwanted behavior you're ignoring often gets worse before it starts its slow decline, so you'll need to be disciplined and patient.

When the unwanted behavior does get worse before it begins to go away—a recognized effect called "extinction burst"—parents often become prematurely convinced that ignoring has failed and switch over to attending to the behavior again, explaining why it's bad, punishing it, yelling, and so on. This attention to the extinction burst unwittingly makes the behavior worse in two ways. First, the parent attended to a more extreme example of the behavior than usual—so, for instance, if you're trying to eliminate tantrums, you've now reinforced tantrums that register on the Richter scale. Second, the parent attended to the behavior after a period of ignoring it, which is called intermittent reinforcement and helps to maintain it. Yes, you can get back on track, but you have now made your task more difficult, and ignoring is more likely than ever to fail.

Let's say you have exercised yogic self-discipline and have successfully ignored an annoying behavior to the point that it begins to go away. As you continue to ignore the behavior and it declines (very slowly), one final nasty surprise lies in wait: Just when you think success is assured, the behavior may return out of the blue, almost as bad as ever. This temporary return, a predictable late spike, makes most parents who get this far decide that they have failed and go back to attending to the behavior, returning them to square one. But the final spontaneous return of the behavior, a last gasp before it disappears for good, would be short-lived if you could tie yourself to the mast and ignore it. In some especially frustrating cases, a forewarned parent does find the strength to ignore even this last onslaught, only to be undermined by a grandparent, spouse, or someone else in the house who feeds the futility by declaring defeat and jumping in to attend to the behavior.

That leaves a further question we'll take up in a subsequent article: When do you get serious about actively dealing with a child's misbehavior? Getting serious usually means first taking steps on your own, but sometimes it means seeking professional help. Even if you're inclined to let a behavior drop out on its own, and even if it's likely to, you're not always in a position to wait for nature to take its course. Yes, sure, if your 4-year-old tries to steal a candy bar from a store under your nose, you might just make him put it back, and you see it as a phase he'll grow out of. But what if your 11-year-old steals a candy bar when he's in a store without you, and the cashier grabs him and calls the police, and your enterprising heir takes a poke at the cop and makes a break for it? It may still be a phase, a statistically predictable dalliance with stealing that's likely to end on its own, but you're going to feel a much more urgent need to do something about it. And you may even decide that you need the help of an expert. In a follow-up article, we'll offer some guidelines for making such decisions.

The Role of Parental Control in Children's Development in Western and East Asian Countries

Eva M. Pomerantz and Qian Wang

There is a wealth of evidence from Western countries, such as the United States, that when parents exert control over children by intruding, pressuring, or dominating them in terms of their thoughts, feelings, and behavior, children suffer psychologically (for a review, see Pomerantz & Thompson, 2008). In contrast, when parents support children's autonomy by allowing them freedom of choice, supporting their initiative, and adopting their perspective, children in the West benefit. Initially, the assumption was that such effects are universal. However, beginning in the 1990s, it was suggested that several aspects of the culture in East Asian countries, such as China, make children more accepting of parental control so that the negative effects are not as strong as they are in Western countries (e.g., Chao, 1994; Iyengar & Lepper, 1999). Because control is considered one of the most influential dimensions of parenting (Maccoby & Martin, 1983), there has been much debate over the effects of parental control in East Asian (vs. Western) countries. As a consequence, there is now a sizable body of research, conducted mainly in the United States and China, from which it is possible to gain significant insights about similarities and differences in the effects of parental control in Western and East Asian countries.

Parental Control

In theory and research on parenting, the term "control" is often used to refer to parental intrusiveness, pressure, or domination, with the inverse being parental support of autonomy (Grolnick & Pomerantz, 2009). The focus of much research has been psychological control, or parents' regulation of children's feelings and thoughts (e.g., Barber, Stolz, & Olsen, 2005). Psychological control is frequently contrasted with behavioral control, defined as parents' regulation of what children do. Behavioral control commonly includes parental guidance, monitoring, and rule setting. As such, it does not necessarily entail intrusiveness, pressure, or domination; indeed, behavioral control has positive, rather than negative, effects on children's psychological development (Grolnick & Pomerantz, 2009). The debate about the effects of parental control in the West and East Asia has centered on control in the intrusive sense, with little attention to distinguishing between its targets—that is, whether parents are attempting to regulate children's psychology or behavior (Wang, Pomerantz, & Chen, 2007). We follow suit here, by focusing on parental control that is intruding, pressuring, or dominating, regardless of whether parents are attempting to regulate children's psychology or behavior.

Universalist Perspectives

Much of the research so far has been guided by the idea that parental control undermines children's sense of autonomy, thereby interfering with their psychological development (e.g., Barber et al., 2005). In the context of self-determination theory, Deci and Ryan (1985) argue that there is a universal need for autonomy and that satisfaction of this need is essential to optimal psychological functioning. These investigators make the case that controlling environments detract from feelings of autonomy, regardless of culture. Thus, when parents exert control over children, for instance by making decisions for them about personal issues (e.g., who to be friends with), children suffer, as they feel they do not have control over their lives. Such a universalist perspective is also evident in parental acceptance–rejection theory, which holds that parental control may negatively influence children by conveying rejection—for example, when parents withdraw love because children have not met their expectations, children may feel that parents no longer care about them. Parental acceptance–rejection theory postulates that children's feelings of being rejected (vs. accepted) by parents play a role in their development regardless of culture, because relatedness is universally important (e.g., Rohner, Khaleque, & Cournoyer, 2004).

Culture-Specific Perspectives

The major principle behind culture-specific perspectives is that Western and East Asian countries have distinct cultures that shape the effects of parental control on children's development leading the effects to be less negative in East Asian contexts. Iyengar and Lepper (1999), for instance, contend that when East Asian parents exert control over children by making decisions for them about personal issues, it does not have detrimental effects; taking on their parents' decisions as their own provides children with an opportunity to harmonize with parents, something that in East Asia is prioritized over autonomy, given the heightened cultural orientation toward interdependence. In a somewhat different vein, because East Asian notions about parents' role in children's development—such as the Chinese concept of *guan*, which means to govern as well as to care for—involve parental control with the ultimate aim of supporting children, parental control may not be experienced as rejecting by children (Chao, 1994). As parental control is more common in East Asia than in the West (e.g., Wang et al., 2007), it has also been suggested that East Asian parents may exert control more deliberately and calmly, with less negative affect, because control does not violate, and is even part of, "good parenting" (e.g., Grusec, Rudy, & Martini, 1997).

Empirical Evidence

The culture-specific perspectives arose in part in response to a series of findings from the 1990s showing that authoritarian (vs. authoritative) parenting has a greater negative effect on American children of European heritage than it does on American children of Asian heritage in terms of academic functioning (e.g., grades) but not necessarily in terms of emotional functioning (e.g., depressive symptoms; e.g., Steinberg, Lamborn, Darling, Mounts, & Dornbusch, 1994). Unfortunately, conclusions about the dissimilarity of the effects of parental control in Western and East Asian countries cannot be made from such data, because authoritarian parenting is an amalgamation of multiple dimensions of parenting including control, structure, and acceptance. Thus, it is unclear if it is parental control that drives the difference (or absence of difference) in the effects of authoritarian parenting; it could be one of the other dimensions or the interaction between two or more of the dimensions.

The research on the effects of authoritarian parenting on children of European and Asian heritage in the United States was followed by research on the effects specifically of parental control in Western and East Asian countries. Hasebe, Nucci, and Nucci (2004) found that parents making decisions for children about personal issues was associated with dampened emotional functioning among American and Japanese high-school children. Similarly, Barber et al. (2005) documented positive associations between parental psychological control and adolescents' depression and delinquency in a variety of countries including the United States, Germany, China, and India. Because these studies used concurrent designs in which parental control and children's psychological functioning were examined at a single point in time, the findings cannot provide insight into whether parental control precedes dampened psychological functioning among children similarly in Western and East Asian contexts; determining whether it does is critical in drawing conclusions about the role of parental control in children's psychological development in the two regions.

Research following children over time in the United States and China sheds light on this issue. The more parents make decisions for children about personal issues as children enter adolescence, the more children's emotional functioning suffers 2 years later, adjusting for their earlier functioning; notably, the size of the effects in the United States and China do not differ (Qin, Pomerantz, & Wang, 2009). A comparable pattern is evident for psychological control (Wang et al., 2007): During early adolescence, such control predicts children's dampened emotional functioning 6 months later, taking into account children's earlier emotional functioning, similarly in the United States and China. Conversely, parental support of children's autonomy (e.g., encouraging them to express their opinions) predicts better subsequent emotional functioning among children in both countries, albeit with a stronger effect for positive, but not negative, emotional functioning in the United States. Parental support of children's autonomy also predicts children's enhanced grades over time similarly in the two countries, but its effect on children's motivation (e.g., investment in school) is stronger in the United States.

Moderating Contexts

Although parental control appears to interfere with children's psychological functioning similarly in the West and East Asia, there may be some contexts in which it may do so to a greater extent in Western countries. Because the identification of such contexts represents a second step in elucidating whether the effects of parental control differ in the two regions, there is limited evidence on this issue. However, the existing evidence is suggestive of several circumstances under which the effects of parental control are stronger in the West. First, almost all of the research has been conducted in areas that are in or near urban centers. Given that such areas in East Asia have been increasingly exposed to Western values in the past few decades, it is unclear to what extent the findings are generalizable to rural areas. Indeed, parental control may play a stronger undermining role in urban areas than in rural areas, given that children, particularly boys, in urban China feel less of a sense of obligation to parents (Fuligni & Zhang, 2004) and are also more averse to conflict with parents than are their counterparts in rural areas (Zhang & Fuligni, 2006). Stronger effects of parental control in urban (versus rural) areas may also exist in the

West, however, given cultural variability by geographical area in the West (e.g., Plaut, Markus, & Lachman, 2002).

Second, differences in the strength of the effects of parental control in Western and East Asian countries may exist, as reflected in the extent to which parents decrease their control as children mature. Perhaps because of the West's heightened orientation toward independence and its less hierarchical structure (Triandis, 1994), American parents decrease their control (i.e., refraining from making decisions for their children about personal issues) more than do Chinese parents as children progress through the early adolescent years (Qin et al., 2009). As Western children expect this decrease in parental control more than East Asian children do (Feldman & Rosenthal, 1991), their psychological functioning may be influenced more by the extent to which their parents "loosen the reins" during these years. As shown in Figure 1, when American parents relinquish control by making fewer decisions for children about personal issues as children enter adolescence, children have better emotional functioning; although such a trend is also evident in China, it is substantially weaker (Qin et al., 2009). It is possible that Chinese children benefit more from a decline in parental control in later adolescence, when it may be more normative. Unfortunately, similarities and differences in how Western and East Asian children move through development have not been comprehensively documented.

Third, the effects of parental control over children's academic learning may be stronger in the West than in East Asia. In Confucian teaching, which is central in East Asian culture, learning is viewed as a moral endeavor in which individuals take on the lifelong task of constantly improving themselves (Li, 2005). Access to education is also more limited, but has greater financial impact, in East Asia (Pomerantz, Ng, & Wang, 2008). Given the moral and practical importance of children's learning, East Asian children may be particularly accepting of parental control when it comes to academics. Although the effects of parental control in the academic area have not been compared to the effects in other areas, there is some suggestive evidence. When European American children believe their mothers have made decisions for them about an academic task, they spend less time and perform more poorly on the task than they do when they make the decisions themselves; however, the reverse is true of Asian American children (Iyengar & Lepper, 1999). Research conducted in China, however, suggests this is the case only when children feel they have positive relationships with their mothers (Bao & Lam, 2008); it may be that children's sense of connectedness to their parents allows children to internalize parents' goals.

Fourth, parental control may take many forms, but the major focus of the comparative research has been on parents making decisions for children about personal issues and their exertion of psychological control over children. These forms of control may be at the extreme end of the continuum. It is possible that less extreme forms, such as

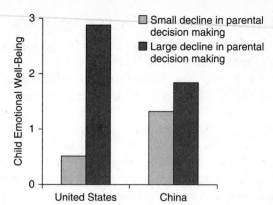

Figure 1 The effects of change over time in parental decision making on child emotional well-being during early adolescence in the United States and China (adapted from Qin, Pomerantz, & Wang, 2009). In the United States, the larger the decline in parental (vs. child) decision making about personal issues as children progressed through the seventh and eighth grades (adjusting for such decision making at the beginning of seventh grade), the better children's emotional well-being at the end of eighth grade (adjusting for such well-being at the beginning of seventh grade). In China, there was a similar pattern, but it was significantly smaller.

providing assistance when children do not request it or hovering over children as they work on something, are more open to interpretation by children in terms of the extent to which they are seen to violate their autonomy or convey rejection. Consequently, culture may play a greater part in how such forms of control are interpreted, leading Western children to hold more negative views of less extreme forms of control than do East Asian children and thus to suffer more when their parents use them. For example, because the West is oriented more toward independence than is East Asia, Western children may see parents' hovering as children complete their homework as more of a violation of their autonomy than might their East Asian counterparts, who may instead interpret such behavior as an expression of parents' love.

Underlying Mechanisms

Fully elucidating the effects of parental control in Western and East Asian countries involves identifying not only the circumstances that may lead to differences in the strength of effects but also the mechanisms underlying the effects. It is necessary to consider the possibility that similar effects reflect different processes. Given different cultural orientations toward independence and interdependence, for example, dampened feelings of autonomy may account for the negative effects of parental control to a greater extent among children in the West, whereas heightened feelings of rejection may account for them to a greater extent among children in East Asia. Under circumstances when there are differences in the effects, the differences need to be unpacked: For example, do they reflect differences in children's interpretation of parental control? In this vein, Chao's (1994) suggestion that parental control has less negative effects among East Asian (vs. Western) children because they view parents' attempts to regulate them as an act of love should be examined. And if differences in how children interpret parental control underlie differences in its effects, is this due, at least in part, to differences in how parents exert control—for instance, in the extent to which parents accompany control with negative affect, as suggested by Grusec et al. (1997)?

Conclusions

In line with universalist perspectives, when parents exert control over children by intruding, pressuring, or dominating them, children suffer, whether they live in the West or East Asia. This undermining role, however, may not be uniform; its strength may differ in the two regions in some contexts. The negative effects of parental control are stronger in the West than in East Asia when parents fail to decrease it as children enter adolescence; parental control may also have stronger effects in the West when it is exerted over academics than in other areas of children's lives. These potential contextual forces, as well as others such as the extremity of control, need more direct investigation—something that may be accomplished as the focus moves away from asking *whether* the effects of parental control are stronger in the West than in East Asia to asking *when* they may be stronger, and *why*. Despite these lingering issues, the findings to date are consistent with self-determination theory's (Deci & Ryan, 1985) notion that there is a universal need for autonomy whose fulfillment may be undermined by controlling environments. Hence, recommendations that parents limit their intrusiveness in children's lives are likely to be useful both in the West and in East Asia.

Recommended Readings

Chao, R.K. (1994). (See References). One of the first papers to suggest why parental control may not have as negative effects in East Asia as it does in the West.

Greenfield, P.M., Keller, H., Fuligni, A.J., & Maynard, A. (2003). Cultural pathways through universal development. *Annual Review of Psychology, 54,* 461–490. This paper provides a full discussion of issues of culture in children's development, including that of the differential effects of parental control.

Grolnick, W.S. (2003). *The psychology of parental control: How well-meant parenting backfires.* Mahwah, NJ: Erlbaum. A clearly written, user-friendly, and relatively comprehensive review for readers who wish to expand their knowledge of the effects of parental control.

Lansford, J.E., Chang, L., Dodge, K.A., Malone, P.A., Oburu, P., Palmerus, K., et al. (2005). Physical discipline and children's adjustment: Cultural normativeness as a moderator. *Child Development, 76,* 1234–1246. An innovative study that illustrates original research about the differential effects of parents' physical discipline in multiple countries.

Wang, Q., Pomerantz, E.M., & Chen, H. (2007). (See References). A representative study that illustrates original research about the differential effects of parental control in the United States and China.

References

Bao, X.-H., & Lam, S.-F. (2008). Who makes the choice? Rethinking the role of autonomy and relatedness in Chinese children's motivation. *Child Development, 79,* 269–283.

Barber, B.K., Stolz, H.E., & Olsen, J.A. (2005). *Parental support, psychological control, and behavioral control: Assessing relevance across time, culture, and method* (Monographs of the Society for Research in Child Development, Serial No. 282, Vol. 70, No. 2). Boston: Blackwell.

Chao, R.K. (1994). Beyond parental control and authoritarian parenting style: Understanding Chinese parenting through the cultural notion of training. *Child Development, 65,* 1111–1119.

Deci, E.L., & Ryan, R.M. (1985). *Intrinsic motivation and self-determination in human behavior.* New York: Plenum.

Feldman, S.S., & Rosenthal, D.A. (1991). Age expectations of behavioural autonomy in Hong Kong, Australian and American Youth: The influence of family variables and adolescents' values. *International Journal of Psychology, 26,* 1–23.

Fuligni, A.J., & Zhang, W. (2004). Attitudes toward family obligation among adolescents in contemporary urban and rural China. *Child Development, 75,* 180–192.

Grolnick, W.S., & Pomerantz, E.M. (2009). Issues and challenges in studying parental control: Toward a new conceptualization. *Child Development Perspectives, 2,* 165–171.

Grusec, J.E., Rudy, D., & Martini, T. (1997). Parenting cognitions and child outcomes: An overview and implications for children's internalization of values. In J.E. Grusec & L. Kuczynski (Eds.), *Parenting and children's internalization of values: A handbook of contemporary theory* (pp. 259–282). Hoboken, NJ: Wiley.

Hasebe, Y., Nucci, L., & Nucci, M.S. (2004). Parental control of the personal domain and adolescent symptoms of psychopathology: A cross-national study in the United States and Japan. *Child Development, 75,* 815–828.

Iyengar, S.S., & Lepper, M.R. (1999). Rethinking the value of choice: A cultural perspective on intrinsic motivation. *Journal of Personality and Social Psychology, 76,* 349–366.

Li, J. (2005). Mind or virtue: Western and Chinese beliefs about learning. *Current Directions in Psychological Science, 14,* 190–194.

Maccoby, E.E., & Martin, J. (1983). Socialization in the context of the family: Parent child interaction. In E.M. Hetherington (Ed.), *Handbook of child psychology: Vol. 4. Socialization, personality, and social development* (4th ed., pp. 1–101). New York: Wiley.

Plaut, V.C., Markus, H.R., & Lachman, M.E. (2002). Place matters: Consensual features and regional variation in American well-being and self. *Journal of Personality and Social Psychology, 83,* 160–184.

Pomerantz, E.M., Ng, F.F., & Wang, Q. (2008). Culture, parenting, and motivation: The case of East Asia and the United States. In M.L. Maehr, S.A. Karabenick, & T.C. Urdan (Eds.), *Advances in motivation and achievement: Social psychological perspectives* (Vol. 15, pp. 209–240). Bingley, England: Emerald Group Publishing.

Pomerantz, E.M., & Thompson, R.A. (2008). Parents' role in children's personality development: The psychological resource principle. In O.P. John, R.W. Robins, & L.A. Pervin (Eds.), *Handbook of personality: Theory and research* (Vol. 3, pp. 351–374). New York: Guilford.

Qin, L., Pomerantz, E.M., & Wang, Q. (2009). Are gains in decision-making autonomy during early adolescence beneficial for emotional functioning? The case of the United States and China. *Child Development, 80,* 1705–1721.

Rohner, R.P., Khaleque, A., & Cournoyer, D.E. (2004). Cross-national perspectives on parental acceptance-rejection theory. *Marriage and Family Review, 35,* 85–105.

Steinberg, L., Lamborn, S.D., Darling, N., Mounts, N.S., & Dornbusch, S. (1994). Over-time changes in adjustment and competence among adolescents from authoritative, authoritarian, indulgent, and neglectful homes. *Child Development, 65,* 754–770.

Triandis, H.C. (1994). *Culture and social behavior.* New York: McGraw-Hill.

Wang, Q., Pomerantz, E.M., & Chen, H. (2007). The role of parents' control in early adolescents' psychological functioning: A longitudinal investigation in the United States and China. *Child Development, 78,* 1592–1610.

Zhang, W., & Fuligni, A.J. (2006). Authority, autonomy, and family relationships among adolescents in urban and rural China. *Journal of Research on Adolescence, 16,* 527–537.

Address correspondence to EVA M. POMERANTZ, Department of Psychology, University of Illinois at Urbana-Champaign, 603 East Daniel Street, Champaign, IL 61820; e-mail: pomerntz@illinois.edu.

Acknowledgments—Writing of this article was supported by National Institute of Mental Health Grant R01 MH57505. We are grateful for the constructive comments on an earlier version of this article provided by Duane Kimme, Peggy Miller, Florrie Fei-Yin Ng, and members of the Center for Parent-Child Studies at the University of Illinois, Urbana-Champaign.

Fatal Distraction: Forgetting a Child in the Backseat of a Car Is a Horrifying Mistake. Is It a Crime?

Every year, at least a dozen children die in overheated cars in the U.S. because parents forgot they were there. Don't assume, says *The Washington Post*'s Gene Weingarten, that it couldn't happen to you.

GENE WEINGARTEN

The defendant was an immense man, well over 300 pounds, but in the gravity of his sorrow and shame he seemed larger still. He hunched forward in his wooden chair, sobbing softly into tissue after tissue, a leg bouncing nervously under the table. The room was a sepulcher. Witnesses spoke softly of events so painful that many lost their composure. When a hospital emergency room nurse described how the defendant had behaved after the police first brought him in, she wept. He was virtually catatonic, she remembered, his eyes shut tight, rocking back and forth, locked away in some unfathomable private torment. He would not speak at all for the longest time, not until the nurse sank down beside him and held his hand. It was only then that the patient began to open up, and what he said was that he didn't want any sedation, that he didn't deserve a respite from pain, that he wanted to feel it all, and then to die.

The charge in the courtroom was manslaughter, brought by the Commonwealth of Virginia. No significant facts were in dispute. Miles Harrison, 49, had been a diligent businessman and a doting, conscientious father until the day last summer—beset by problems at work, making call after call on his cell phone—he forgot to drop his son, Chase, at day care. The toddler slowly sweltered to death, strapped into a car seat for nearly nine hours in an office parking lot in the blistering heat of July.

It was an inexplicable, inexcusable mistake, but was it a crime? That was the question for a judge to decide.

"Death by hyperthermia" is the official designation. When it happens to young children, the facts are often the same: An otherwise attentive parent one day gets busy, or distracted, or confused by a change in his or her daily routine, and just . . . forgets a child is in the car. It happens that way somewhere in the United States 15 to 25 times a year, parceled out through the spring, summer, and early fall. The season is almost upon us.

Two decades ago, this was relatively rare. But in the early 1990s, car-safety experts declared that passenger-side front airbags could kill children, and they recommended that child seats be moved to the back of the car; then, for even more safety for the very young, that the baby seats be pivoted to face the rear. If few foresaw the tragic consequence of the lessened visibility of the child . . . well, who can blame them? What kind of person forgets a baby?

The wealthy do, it turns out. And the poor, and the middle class. Parents of all ages and ethnicities do it. Mothers are just as likely to do it as fathers. It happens to the chronically absent-minded and to the fanatically organized, to the college-educated and to the marginally literate. Last year it happened three times in one day, the worst day so far in the worst year so far in a phenomenon that gives no sign of abating.

The facts in each case differ a little, but always there is the terrible moment when the parent realizes what he or she has done, often through a phone call from a spouse or caregiver. This is followed by a frantic sprint to the car. What awaits there is the worst thing in the world.

In Miles Harrison's case, the judge ultimately decided there was no crime because there was no intent. Prosecutors, judges, and juries reach similar conclusions in many of these cases. But if Harrison's failing is not manslaughter, what is it? An accident?

"That's an imperfect word."

This is Mark Warschauer, an expert in language learning. "The word 'accident' makes it sound like it can't be prevented, but 'incident' makes it sound trivial. And it is not trivial."

Warschauer is a professor at the University of California at Irvine. In the summer of 2003, he returned to his office from lunch to find a crowd surrounding a car in the parking lot. Police had smashed the window open with a crowbar. Only as he got closer did Warschauer realize it was his car. That was his first clue that he'd forgotten to drop his 10-month-old son, Mikey, at day care that morning. Mikey was dead.

Warschauer wasn't charged with a crime, but for months afterward he contemplated suicide. Gradually, he says, the urge subsided, if not the grief and guilt.

"We lack a term for what this is," Warschauer says. And also, he says, we need an understanding of why it happens to the people it happens to.

D avid Diamond is picking at his breakfast at a Washington, D.C., hotel, trying to explain.

"Memory is a machine," he says, "and it is not flawless. If you're capable of forgetting your cell phone, you are potentially capable of forgetting your child."

Diamond is a professor of molecular physiology at the University of South Florida. He's in D.C. to give a conference speech about his research, which involves the intersection of emotion, stress, and memory. What he's found is that under some circumstances, the most sophisticated part of our thought-processing center can be held hostage to a competing memory system, a primitive portion of the brain that is—by a design as old as the dinosaur's—pigheaded, nonanalytical, stupid.

Diamond recently forgot, while driving to a mall, that his infant granddaughter was asleep in the back of his car. He remembered, he said, only because his wife mentioned the baby. So he understands what could have happened had he been alone with the child. Almost worse, he understands exactly why.

The human brain, he says, is a jury-rigged device in which newer and more sophisticated structures sit atop a junk heap of prototype brains still used by lower species. At the top are the most nimble parts: the prefrontal cortex, which thinks and analyzes, and the hippocampus, which makes and holds on to our immediate memories. At the bottom is the basal ganglia, nearly identical to the brains of lizards, controlling voluntary but barely conscious actions.

Diamond says that in situations involving familiar, routine motor skills, the human animal presses the basal ganglia into service as a sort of autopilot. When our prefrontal cortex and hippocampus are planning our day on the way to work, the ignorant basal ganglia is operating the car; that's why you'll sometimes find yourself having driven from point A to point B without a clear recollection of the route you took, the turns you made, or the scenery you saw.

Ordinarily, says Diamond, this delegation of duty "works beautifully, like a symphony." But sudden or chronic stress can weaken the brain's higher-functioning centers, making them more susceptible to bullying from the basal ganglia. He's seen that pattern in cases he's followed involving infant deaths in cars.

"The quality of prior parental care seems to be irrelevant," he said. "The important factors that keep showing up involve a combination of stress, emotion, lack of sleep, and change in routine, where the basal ganglia is trying to do what it's supposed to do, and the conscious mind is too weakened to resist. What happens is that the memory circuits in a vulnerable hippocampus literally get overwritten, like with a computer program. Unless the memory circuit is rebooted—such as if the child cries, or, you know, if the wife mentions the child in the back—it can entirely disappear."

Diamond stops. "There is a case in Virginia where this is exactly what happened, the whole set of stress factors. I was consulted on it a couple of years ago. It was a woman named, ah . . ."

He puts down his fork and shakes his head. He's been stressing over his conference speech, he says, and his memory retrieval is shot. He can't summon the name.

Lyn Balfour?

"Yeah, Lyn Balfour! The perfect storm."

R aelyn Balfour is what is commonly called a type-A personality. The 37-year-old Army reservist is the first to admit that her inclination to take on multiple challenges at once contributed to the death of her son, Bryce, two years ago. It happened on March 30, 2007, the day she accidentally left the 9-month-old in the parking lot of the Charlottesville, Va., judge advocate general's office, where she worked as a transportation administrator. The temperature that day was only in the 60s, but heat builds quickly in a closed vehicle in the sun. The temperature inside Balfour's car that day topped 110 degrees.

Circumstances had conspired against Balfour. She had been up much of the night, first baby-sitting for a friend with a pet emergency, then caring for Bryce, who was cranky with a cold. Because the baby was still tired, he uncharacteristically dozed in the car, so he made no noise. Because Balfour was planning to bring Bryce's usual car seat to the fire station to be professionally installed, Bryce was positioned in a different car seat that day, directly behind the driver, and thus less visible. Because of a phone conversation with a young relative in trouble, and another with her boss about a crisis at work, Balfour spent most of the trip on her cell, stressed, solving other people's problems.

One more thing: Because the baby sitter had a new phone, it didn't yet contain Balfour's office phone number, only her cell number—so when the sitter phoned to wonder why Balfour hadn't dropped Bryce off that morning, it rang unheard in Balfour's pocketbook.

Balfour was charged with second-degree murder in Bryce's death but was eventually acquitted. The key moment in her trial was when the defense attorney played for the jury a recording of a 911 call made by a passer-by in the first few seconds after Balfour discovered Bryce's body. That tape is unendurable. Mostly, you hear the passer-by's voice, tense but precise, explaining to a police dispatcher what she is seeing. Initially, there's nothing in the background. Then Balfour howls at the top of her lungs, "OH, MY GOD, NOOOO!"

For a few seconds, there's nothing. Then another deafening shriek: "NO, NO, PLEASE, NO!!!"

Unlike most parents who have suffered similar tragedies, Balfour now is willing to talk to the media, anytime. She works with a group called Kids and Cars, telling her story repeatedly. In public, she seldom seems in particular anguish. No one sees her cry. She has, she says, consciously crafted the face she shows. "People say I'm a strong woman, but I'm not. I would like to disappear, to move someplace where no one knows who I am and what I did. But I can't. I'm the lady who killed her child, and I have to be that lady because I promised Bryce."

Balfour has kept her promise in a way suited to her personality: She has become a modern, maternal version of the Ancient Mariner. When speaking to the media, her consistent message is that cars need safety devices to prevent similar tragedies. From time to time, though, she will simply belly up to strangers in, say, a Sam's Club, and start a conversation about children, so she can tell them what she did to one of hers. Her message: *This can happen to anyone.*

Siblings Play Formative, Influential Role as 'Agents of Socialization'

What we learn from our siblings when we grow up has—for better or for worse—a considerable influence on our social and emotional development as adults, according to an expert in sibling, parent-child and peer relationships at the University of Illinois.

Laurie Kramer, a professor of applied family studies in the department of human and community development at Illinois, says that although a parent's influence on a child's development shouldn't be underestimated, neither should a sibling's.

"What we learn from our parents may overlap quite a bit with what we learn from our siblings, but there may be some areas in which they differ significantly," Kramer said.

Parents are better at teaching the social niceties of more formal settings—how to act in public, how not to embarrass oneself at the dinner table, for example. But siblings are better role models of the more informal behaviors—how to act at school or on the street, or, most important, how to act cool around friends—that constitute the bulk of a child's everyday experiences.

"Siblings are closer to the social environments that children find themselves in during the majority of their day, which is why it's important not to overlook the contributions that they make on who we end up being," Kramer said.

Kramer, who along with Katherine J. Conger, of the University of California at Davis, co-edited a volume on this topic for a recent issue of the journal *New Directions for Child and Adolescent Development,* says a clearer understanding of how siblings function as "agents of socialization" will help answer critical societal questions such as why some children pursue antisocial behavior.

"We know that having a positive relationship with siblings is related to a whole host of better outcomes for teenagers and adults," Kramer said. "A lot of current research looks at how children learn undesirable behaviors like smoking, drinking and other delinquent acts, from exposure to an older sibling's antisocial behaviors as well as that of their sibling's friends. For example, a female teen is at higher risk for getting pregnant if her older sister was a teenage mother. Developing a better understanding of sibling influences can help us design effective strategies for protecting younger children in families."

According to Kramer, in order to maximize an older sibling's positive influence, one of the most important things

parents can do is to help foster a supportive relationship between the siblings from the very beginning. "We know from longitudinal studies that if kids start off their relationship with a sibling on a positive note, it's more likely to continue positively over time," she said.

Variables such as gender and age difference don't make much of a difference between siblings. "It's not all that important whether you're spaced closer together or farther apart, or if you have a brother or a sister," Kramer said. "What's really much more important are the social behaviors that children learn in their early years that they can use to develop a positive relationship with a sibling. That's why it's important for parents to encourage siblings to be engaged with one another and develop a relationship where there is mutual respect, cooperation and the ability to manage problems."

Kramer said children who grow up as an only child are not necessarily less socially competent than children who grow up with siblings, but they are more likely to have developed social skills through friends as opposed to brothers and sisters.

"Growing up just with parents is a different environment for young people," she said. "Parents of only children might want to think about how they can help their child have social experiences with other children, whether that's through childcare, preschool or play dates."

Do single children establish surrogate siblings with cousins and friends? "They may be encouraged by parents to develop deeper relationships, and that's a good thing because it provides them an opportunity to develop some of these social competencies that they probably won't acquire if they're limited to interacting with their parents and teachers," Kramer said. Parents who have children who are spaced closely together in age may not see much of a need to have children over to the house once a week because their children are already having significant social experiences within the family unit, Kramer said.

But children whose siblings are spaced further apart in age are most likely to have different sets of friends and different social experiences because they may be in distinct school contexts or involved in unique activities. "It's possible that siblings who are spaced further apart are very connected within the home, but their social experiences outside the family may be pretty different," Kramer said.

And, Kramer notes, having Wally Cleaver for an older brother doesn't necessarily mean the younger sibling will turn out like Wally—they may end up like Beaver.

"We know that not all younger children turn out like their older siblings," Kramer said. "There are many cases where younger siblings work very hard to carve out their own unique path and be different from their brothers and sisters, a process researchers refer to as 'de-identification.'

They may choose a different path in which to excel or make their mark to base their own identity on. That child may choose to focus on sports, the arts or being the social one. It relieves them from the pressure to be seen or compared to their elder sibling, particularly if they're afraid that they won't be able to measure up.

"So they out who they are, what they believe in and what's important to them, in reaction to how they perceive their siblings."

Kramer cautions that while we don't know all of the implications of sibling influence, "we do know that growing up in a family where there is another child makes it a very different environment socially, cognitively and emotionally," Kramer said.

"Children learn things through growing up with other children in the house, just as they learn things growing up in a more adult-oriented environment if they're a single child. We need to understand that better so that we can form a more realistic understanding of child and family development."

Funding for this research was provided by the U.S. Department of Agriculture.

UNIT 5

Cultural and Societal Influences

Unit Selections

Key Points to Consider

- Have you noticed the trend in product marketing, the media, and the music and entertainment industries to sexualize younger and younger girls? How do you feel about this increasing trend? What is the fallout for this pop culture depiction on the development of young girls and how can we more effectively counter these negative effects? Similarly, how do you feel about aggressive marketing and consumerism targeting young children (e.g., child specific toys, videos, food products)?

- Do you know anyone with autism? Describe his or her patterns of behavior and the severity level of autism. How did the parents and family cope with their child? What treatments or programs of support did this child get and did the programs help? What would you do if you had a child with autism?

- What can be done to help safeguard children both in our country and on other shores from the ravages of terrorism, war, violence, hunger, malnutrition, disease, and poor medical care? For example, do you remember where you were when 9/11 occurred? What were the reactions of children to the nonstop media? How did you in your role as an adult, teacher, relative, friend, or parent deal with children's reactions in the aftermath of this terrorist attack to help them cope with and understand this tragic event?

- At no other time in all of human history have we seen such an explosion and epidemic of child obesity particularly in the United States. Worse yet, it appears we are losing the battle. Why has there been such an enormous surge in childhood obesity? What factors have changed in our culture in the last 30 years that have played a large role in childhood obesity? How have our grocery stores, fast-food restaurants, television and marketing venues, family time, and work/lifestyle schedules changed? What can parents, schools, and society do help children and adults adopt healthier dietary and exercise lifestyles?

Student Website

www.mhhe.com/cls

Internet References

Association to Benefit Children (ABC)
www.a-b-c.org

Children's Defense Fund
www.childrensdefense.org

Children Now
www.childrennow.org

Council for Exceptional Children
www.cec.sped.org

Prevent Child Abuse America
www.preventchildabuse.org

Social scientists and developmental psychologists have come to realize that children are influenced by a multitude of complex social forces. In this unit we present articles to illuminate how children and adolescents are influenced by broad factors such as economics, culture, politics, and the media. These influences also affect the family, which is a major context of child development, and many children are now faced with more family challenges than ever. In addition, analysis of exceptional or atypical children gives the reader a more comprehensive account of child development.

Thus, articles are presented on special challenges of development, such as the effects of autism, prenatal drug exposure, wartime violence, terrorism, and other traumatic circumstances.

Other external societal factors that influence children's development include the powerful influence of the media and advertising shaping children's young minds. The authors of "Goodbye to Girlhood" decry merchandisers who are encouraging younger and younger girls to see themselves in sexualized terms. This aggressive, targeted marketing fills our stores with inappropriately sexualized clothing for younger and younger girls, putting an unhealthy emphasis on appearance and beauty.

Our fast-paced, convenience-fueled lifestyles have forever changed America's palate and eating habits and in many ways have contributed to an epidemic of child obesity. In the past, experts have advocated for parents to help restrict their obese children's diets in order to see a drop in weight. Unfortunately, these efforts generally do not produce enduring and sustained weight loss in children. Instead, today experts are calling for parents, families, schools, and society to shift the focus from weight loss to making lifestyle changes for children that include integrating exercise into a daily routine and reconnecting children with nature and outdoor activity. The authors of two articles describe some of these efforts in "How to Win the Weight Battle" and "Getting Back to the Great Outdoors."

Some children must cope with special psychological, emotional, and cognitive challenges such as autism or prenatal cocaine exposure. Such children are often misunderstood and mistreated and pose special challenges. The authors of the articles "Three Reasons Not to Believe in an Autism Epidemic" and "The Epidemic That Wasn't" describe the research and evidence to better inform us of some of the myths and truths about the incidence, potential causes, and interventions for various disorders.

The article "The Positives of Caregiving: Mothers' Experiences Caregiving for a Child with Autism" addresses resilience exhibited by mothers providing care to an autistic child. Mothers identify experiences that are appraised in a positive, even joyous, light. Practical ideas are included in this article.

Still other children both here and abroad face terrible conditions related to international poverty, malnutrition, and coping

© Fancy/Veer

with terrible situations such as the horrors of enslaving child soldiers for wartime violence and coping with posttraumatic stress due to natural disasters and terrorism. The articles "Childhood's End" and "Treatment and Prevention of Posttraumatic Stress Reactions in Children and Adolescents Exposed to Disasters and Terrorism: What Is the Evidence?" address these challenges. Although these articles are sometimes difficult to read, as future parents, teachers, and professionals it is important for us to learn more about these difficult and challenging situations in order to find ways to improve and solve future problems for children and their families.

Goodbye to Girlhood

As pop culture targets ever younger girls, psychologists worry about a premature focus on sex and appearance.

Stacy Weiner

Ten-year-old girls can slide their low-cut jeans over "eye-candy" panties. French maid costumes, garter belt included, are available in preteen sizes. Barbie now comes in a "bling-bling" style, replete with halter top and go-go boots. And it's not unusual for girls under 12 to sing, "Don't cha wish your girlfriend was hot like me?"

American girls, say experts, are increasingly being fed a cultural catnip of products and images that promote looking and acting sexy.

"Throughout U.S. culture, and particularly in mainstream media, women and girls are depicted in a sexualizing manner," declares the American Psychological Association's Task Force on the Sexualization of Girls, in a report issued Monday. The report authors, who reviewed dozens of studies, say such images are found in virtually every medium, from TV shows to magazines and from music videos to the Internet.

While little research to date has documented the effect of sexualized images specifically on *young* girls, the APA authors argue it is reasonable to infer harm similar to that shown for those 18 and older; for them, sexualization has been linked to "three of the most common mental health problems of girls and women: eating disorders, low self-esteem and depression."

Said report contributor and psychologist Sharon Lamb: "I don't think because we don't have the research yet on the younger girls that we can ignore that [sexualization is] of harm to them. Common sense would say that, and part of the reason we wrote the report is so we can get funding to prove that."

Boys, too, face sexualization, the authors acknowledge. Pubescent-looking males have posed provocatively in Calvin Klein ads, for example, and boys with impossibly sculpted abs hawk teen fashion lines. But the authors say they focused on girls because females are objectified more often. According to a 1997 study in the journal Sexual Abuse, 85 percent of ads that sexualized children depicted girls.

Even influences that are less explicitly erotic often tell girls who they are equals how they look and that beauty commands power and attention, contends Lamb, co-author of "Packaging Girlhood: Rescuing Our Daughters from Marketers' Schemes" (St. Martin's, 2006). One indicator that these influences are reaching girls earlier, she and others say: The average age for adoring the impossibly proportioned Barbie has slid from preteen to preschool.

When do little girls start wanting to look good for others? "A few years ago, it was 6 or 7," says Deborah Roffman, a Baltimore-based sex educator. "I think it begins by 4 now."

While some might argue that today's belly-baring tops are no more risque than hip huggers were in the '70s, Roffman disagrees. "Kids have always emulated adult things," she says. "But [years ago] it was, 'That's who I'm supposed to be as an adult.' It's very different today. The message to children is, 'You're already like an adult. It's okay for you to be interested in sex. It's okay for you to dress and act sexy, right now.' That's an entirely different frame of reference."

It's not just kids' exposure to sexuality that worries some experts; it's the kind of sexuality they're seeing. "The issue is that the way marketers and media present sexuality is in a very narrow way," says Lamb. "Being a sexual person isn't about being a pole dancer," she chides. "This is a sort of sex education girls are getting, and it's a misleading one."

Clothes Encounters

Liz Guay says she has trouble finding clothes she considers appropriate for her daughter Tanya, age 8. Often, they're too body-hugging. Or too low-cut. Or too short. Or too spangly.

Then there are the shoes: Guay says last time she visited six stores before finding a practical, basic flat. And don't get her started on earrings.

"Tanya would love to wear dangly earrings. She sees them on TV, she sees other girls at school wearing them, she sees them in the stores all the time. . . . I just say, 'You're too young.'"

"It's not so much a feminist thing," explains Guay, a Gaithersburg medical transcriptionist. "It's more that I want her to be comfortable with who she is and to make decisions based on what's right for her, not what everybody else is doing. I want her to develop the strength that when she gets to a point where kids are offering her alcohol or drugs, that she's got enough self-esteem to say, 'I don't want that.'"

Some stats back up Guay's sense of fashion's shrinking modesty. For example, in 2003, tweens—that highly coveted marketing segment ranging from 7 to 12—spent $1.6 million on thong underwear, *Time* magazine reported. But even more-innocent-seeming togs, toys and activities—like tiny "Beauty Queen" T-shirts, Hello Kitty press-on nails or preteen make-overs at Club Libby Lu—can be problematic, claim psychologists. The reason: They may lure young girls into an unhealthy focus on appearance.

Studies suggest that female college students distracted by concerns about their appearance score less well on tests than do others. Plus, some experts say, "looking good" is almost culturally inseparable for girls from looking sexy: Once a girl's bought in, she's hopped onto a consumer conveyor belt in which marketers move females from pastel tiaras to hot-pink push-up bras.

Where did this girly-girl consumerism start? Diane Levin, an education professor at Wheelock College in Boston who is writing an upcoming book, "So Sexy So Soon," traces much of it to the deregulation of children's television in the mid-1980s. With the rules loosened, kids' shows suddenly could feature characters who moonlighted as products (think Power Rangers, Care Bears, My Little Pony). "There became a real awareness," says Levin, "of how to use gender and appearance and, increasingly, sex to market to children."

Kids are more vulnerable than adults to such messages, she argues.

The APA report echoes Levin's concern. It points to a 2004 study of adolescent girls in rural Fiji, linking their budding concerns about body image and weight control to the introduction of television there.

In the United States, TV's influence is incontestable. According to the Kaiser Family Foundation, for example, nearly half of American kids age 4 to 6 have a TV in their bedroom. Nearly a quarter of teens say televised sexual content affects their own behavior.

And that content is growing: In 2005, 77 percent of prime-time shows on the major broadcast networks included sexual material, according to Kaiser, up from 67 percent in 1998. In a separate Kaiser study of shows popular with teenage girls, women and girls were twice as likely as men and boys to have their appearance discussed. They also were three times more likely to appear in sleepwear or underwear than their male counterparts.

Preteen Preening

It can be tough for a parent to stanch the flood of media influences.

Ellen Goldstein calls her daughter Maya, a Rockville fifth-grader, a teen-mag maniac. "She has a year's worth" of *Girls' Life* magazine, says Goldstein. "When her friends come over, they pore over this magazine." What's Maya reading? There's "Get Gorgeous Skin by Tonight," "Crush Confidential: Seal the Deal with the Guy You Dig," and one of her mom's least faves: "Get a Fierce Body Fast."

"Why do you want to tell a kid to get a fierce body fast when they're 10? They're just developing," complains Goldstein. She also bemoans the magazines' photos, which Maya has plastered on her ceiling.

"These are very glamorous-looking teenagers. They're wearing lots of makeup. They all have very glossy lips," she says. "They're generally wearing very slinky outfits. . . . I don't think those are the best role models," Goldstein says. "When so much emphasis is placed on the outside, it minimizes the importance of the person inside."

So why not just say no?

"She loves fashion," explains Goldstein. "I don't want to take away her joy from these magazines. It enhances her creative spirit. [Fashion] comes naturally to her. I want her to feel good about that. We just have to find a balance."

Experts say her concern is warranted. Pre-adolescents' propensity to try on different identities can make them particularly susceptible to media messages, notes the APA report. And for some girls, thinking about how one's body stacks up can be a real downer.

In a 2002 study, for example, seventh-grade girls who viewed idealized magazine images of women reported a drop in body satisfaction and a rise in depression.

Such results are disturbing, say observers, since eating disorders seem to strike younger today. A decade ago, new eating disorder patients at Children's National Medical Center tended to be around age 15, says Adelaide Robb, director of inpatient psychiatry. Today kids come in as young as 5 or 6.

Mirror Images

Not everyone is convinced of the uglier side of beauty messages.

Eight-year-old Maya Williams owns four bracelets, eight necklaces, about 20 pairs of earrings and six rings, an assortment of which she sprinkles on every day. "Sometimes, she'll stand in front of the mirror and ask, "Are these pretty, Mommy?"

Her mom, Gaithersburg tutor Leah Haworth, is fine with Maya's budding interest in beauty. In fact, when Maya "wasn't sure" about getting her ears pierced, says Haworth, "I talked her into it by showing her all the pretty earrings she could wear."

What about all these sexualization allegations? "I don't equate looking good with attracting the opposite sex," Haworth says. Besides, "Maya knows her worth is based on her personality. She knows we love her for who she is."

"Looking good just shows that you care about yourself, care about how you present yourself to the world. People are judged by their appearance. People get better service and are treated better when they look better. That's just the way it is," she says. "I think discouraging children from paying attention to their appearance does them a disservice."

Magazine editor Karen Bokram also adheres to the beauty school of thought. "Research has shown that having skin issues at [her readers'] age is traumatic for girls' self-esteem," says Bokram, founder of *Girls' Life*. "Do we think girls need to be gorgeous in order to be worthy? No. Do we think girls' feeling good about how they look has positive effects in other areas of their lives, meaning that they make positive choices academically, socially and in romantic relationships? Absolutely."

Some skeptics of the sexualization notion also argue that kids today are hardier and savvier than critics think. Isaac Larian, whose company makes the large-eyed, pouty-lipped Bratz dolls, says, "Kids are very smart and know right from wrong." What's more, his testing indicates that girls want Bratz "because they are fun, beautiful and inspirational," he wrote in an e-mail. "Not once have we ever heard one of our consumers call Bratz 'sexy.'" Some adults "have a twisted sense of what they see in the product," Larian says.

"It is the parents' responsibility to educate their children," he adds. "If you don't like something, don't buy it."

But Genevieve McGahey, 16, isn't buying marketers' messages. The National Cathedral School junior recalls that her first real focus on appearance began in fourth grade. That's when classmates taught her: To be cool, you needed ribbons. To be cool, you needed lip gloss.

Starting around sixth grade, though, "it took on a more sinister character," she says. "People would start wearing really short skirts and lower tops and putting on more makeup. There's a strong pressure to grow up at this point."

"It's a little scary being a young girl," McGahey says. "The image of sexuality has been a lot more trumpeted in this era. . . . If you're not interested in [sexuality] in middle school, it seems a little intimidating." And unrealistic body ideals pile on extra pressure, McGahey says. At a time when their bodies and their body images are still developing, "girls are not really seeing people [in the media] who are beautiful but aren't stick-thin," she notes. "That really has an effect."

Today, though, McGahey feels good about her body and her style.

For this, she credits her mom, who is "very secure with herself and with being smart and being a woman." She also points to a wellness course at school that made her conscious of how women were depicted. "Seeing a culture of degrading women really influenced me to look at things in a new way and to think how we as high school girls react to that," she says.

"A lot of girls still hold onto that media ideal. I think I've gotten past it. As I've gotten more comfortable with myself and my body, I'm happy not to be trashy," McGahey says. "But most girls are still not completely or even semi-comfortable with themselves physically. You definitely still feel the pressure of those images."

STACY WEINER writes frequently for *Health* about families and relationships. Comments: health@washpost.com.

Trials for Parents Who Chose Faith over Medicine

Dirk Johnson

Weston, Wis.—Kara Neumann, 11, had grown so weak that she could not walk or speak. Her parents, who believe that God alone has the ability to heal the sick, prayed for her recovery but did not take her to a doctor.

After an aunt from California called the sheriff's department here, frantically pleading that the sick child be rescued, an ambulance arrived at the Neumann's rural home on the outskirts of Wausau and rushed Kara to the hospital. She was pronounced dead on arrival.

The county coroner ruled that she had died from diabetic ketoacidosis resulting from undiagnosed and untreated juvenile diabetes. The condition occurs when the body fails to produce insulin, which leads to severe dehydration and impairment of muscle, lung and heart function.

"Basically everything stops," said Dr. Louis Philipson, who directs the diabetes center at the University of Chicago Medical Center, explaining what occurs in patients who do not know or "are in denial that they have diabetes."

About a month after Kara's death last March, the Marathon County state attorney, Jill Falstad, brought charges of reckless endangerment against her parents, Dale and Leilani Neumann. Despite the Neumanns' claim that the charges violated their constitutional right to religious freedom, Judge Vincent Howard of Marathon County Circuit Court ordered Ms. Neumann to stand trial on May 14, and Mr. Neumann on June 23. If convicted, each faces up to 25 years in prison.

"The free exercise clause of the First Amendment protects religious belief," the judge wrote in his ruling, "but not necessarily conduct."

Wisconsin law, he noted, exempts a parent or guardian who treats a child with only prayer from being criminally charged with neglecting child welfare laws, but only "as long as a condition is not life threatening." Kara's parents, Judge Howard wrote, "were very well aware of her deteriorating medical condition."

About 300 children have died in the United States in the last 25 years after medical care was withheld on religious grounds, said Rita Swan, executive director of Children's Health Care Is a Legal Duty, a group based in Iowa that advocates punishment for parents who do not seek medical help when their children need it. Criminal codes in 30 states, including Wisconsin, provide some form of protection for practitioners of faith healing in cases of child neglect and other matters, protection that Ms. Swan's group opposes.

Shawn Peters, the author of three books on religion and the law, including *When Prayer Fails: Faith Healing, Children and the Law* (Oxford, 2007), said the outcome of the Neumann case was likely to set an important precedent.

"The laws around the country are pretty unsettled," said Mr. Peters, who teaches religion at the University of Wisconsin Oshkosh and has been consulted by prosecutors and defense lawyers in the case.

In the last year, two other sets of parents, both in Oregon, were criminally charged because they had not sought medical care for their children on the ground that to do so would have violated their belief in faith healing. One couple were charged with manslaughter in the death of their 15-month-old daughter, who died of pneumonia last March. The other couple were charged with criminally negligent homicide in the death of their 16-year-old son, who died from complications of a urinary tract infection that was severely painful and easily treatable.

"Many types of abuses of children are motivated by rigid belief systems," including severe corporal punishment, said Ms. Swan, a former Christian Scientist whose 16-month-old son, Matthew, died after she postponed taking him to a hospital for treatment of what proved to be meningitis. "We learned the hard way."

All states give social service authorities the right to go into homes and petition for the removal of children, Ms. Swan said, but cases involving medical care often go unnoticed until too late. Parents who believe in faith healing, she said, may feel threatened by religious authorities who oppose medical treatment. Recalling her own experience, she said, "we knew that once we went to the doctor, we'd be cut off from God."

The crux of the Neumanns' case, Mr. Peters said, will be whether the parents could have known the seriousness of their daughter's condition.

Investigators said the Neumanns last took Kara to a doctor when she was 3. According to a police report, the girl had lost the strength to speak the day before she died. "Kara laid down and was unable to move her mouth," the report said, "and merely made moaning noises and moved her eyes back and forth."

The courts have ordered regular medical checks for the couple's other three children, ages 13 to 16, and Judge Howard ordered all the parties in the case not to speak to members of the news media. Neither Ms. Falstad nor the defense lawyers, Gene Linehan and Jay Kronenwetter, would agree to be interviewed.

The Neumanns, who had operated a coffee shop, Monkey Mo's, in this middle-class suburb in the North Woods, are known locally as followers of an online faith outreach group called Unleavened Bread Ministries, run by a preacher, David Eells. The site shares stories of faith healing and talks about the end of the world.

An essay on the site signed Pastor Bob states that the Bible calls for healing by faith alone. "Jesus never sent anyone to a doctor or a hospital," the essay says. "Jesus offered healing by one means only! Healing was by faith."

A link from the site, helptheneumanns.com, asserts that the couple is being persecuted and "charged with the crime of praying." The site also allows people to contribute to a legal fund for the Neumanns.

In the small town of Weston, many people shake their heads with dismay when Kara Neumann is mentioned. Tammy Klemp, 41, who works behind the counter at a convenience store here, said she disagreed with the Neumanns' passive response to their daughter's illness but said she was not sure they should go to prison.

"I've got mixed feelings," Ms. Klemp said. "It's just such a terribly sad case."

Chris Goebel, 30, a shipping department worker for a window maker, said many people in the area felt strongly that the parents should be punished.

"That little girl wasn't old enough to make the decision about going to a doctor," Mr. Goebel said. "And now, because some religious extremists went too far, she's gone."

Childhood's End

For 19 years, Joseph Kony has been enslaving, torturing, raping, and murdering Ugandan children, many of whom have become soldiers for his "Lord's Resistance Army," going on to torture, rape, and kill other children. The author exposes the vicious insanity—and cynical politics—behind one of Africa's greatest nightmares.

CHRISTOPHER HITCHENS

In William Faulkner's story "Raid," set in Alabama and Mississippi in the closing years of the Civil War, a white family becomes aware of a sudden, vast, nighttime migration through the scorched countryside. They can hear it and even smell it before they can see it; it's the black population voting with its feet and heading, so it fervently believes, for the River Jordan: "We couldn't see them and they did not see us; maybe they didn't even look, just walking fast in the dark with that panting, hurrying murmuring, going on . . ."

Northern Uganda is centered on the headstreams of the Nile rather than the Jordan, and is a strange place for me to find myself put in mind of Faulkner, but every evening at dusk the main town of Gulu starts to be inundated by a mass of frightened humanity, panting, hurrying, and murmuring as it moves urgently through the crepuscular hours. Most of the "night commuters," as they are known locally, are children. They leave their outlying villages and walk as many as eight kilometers to huddle for safety in the towns. And then, in the morning, often without breakfast and often without shoes, they walk all the way back again to get to their schools and their families. That's if the former have not been burned and the latter have not been butchered. These children are not running toward Jordan and the Lord; they are running for their lives from the "Lord's Resistance Army" (L.R.A.). This grotesque, zombie-like militia, which has abducted, enslaved, and brainwashed more than 20,000 children, is a kind of Christian Khmer Rouge and has for the past 19 years set a standard of cruelty and ruthlessness that—even in a region with a living memory of Idi Amin—has the power to strike the most vivid terror right into the heart and the other viscera.

Here's what happens to the children who can't run fast enough, or who take the risk of sleeping in their huts in the bush. I am sitting in a rehab center, talking to young James, who is 11 and looks about 9. When he actually was nine and sleeping at home with his four brothers, the L.R.A. stormed his village and took the boys away. They were roped at the waist and menaced with bayonets to persuade them to confess what they could not know—the whereabouts of the Ugandan Army's soldiers. On the subsequent forced march, James underwent the twin forms of initiation practiced by the L.R.A. He was first savagely flogged with a wire lash and then made to take part in the murder of those children who had become too exhausted to walk any farther. "First we had to watch," he says. "Then we had to join in the beatings until they died." He was spared from having to do this to a member of his family, which is the L.R.A.'s preferred method of what it calls "registration." And he was spared from being made into a concubine or a sex slave, because the L.R.A. doesn't tolerate that kind of thing for boys. It is, after all, "faith-based." Excuse me, but it does have its standards.

Talking to James about the unimaginable ruin of his childhood, I notice that when I am speaking he stays stock-still, with something a bit dead behind his eyes. But when it comes his turn to tell his story, he immediately starts twisting about in his chair, rubbing his eyes and making waving gestures with his arms. The leader of the L.R.A., a former Catholic acolyte in his 40s named Joseph Kony, who now claims to be a spirit medium with a special mission to impose the Ten Commandments, knows what old Fagin knew: that little boys are nimble and malleable if you catch them young enough, and that they make good thieves and runners. Little James was marched all the way to Sudan, whose Muslim-extremist government offers shelter and aid—such an ecumenical spirit!—to the Christian fanatics. There he was put to work stealing food from neighboring villages, and digging and grinding cassava roots. Soon enough, he was given a submachine gun almost as big as himself. Had he not escaped during an ambush, he would have gotten big enough to be given a girl as well, to do with what he liked.

I drove out of Gulu—whose approach roads can be used only in the daytime—to a refugee camp nearer the Sudanese border. A few Ugandan shillings and a few packets of cigarettes procured me a Ugandan Army escort, who sat heavily armed in the back of the pickup truck. As I buckled my seat belt, the driver told me to unbuckle it in spite of the parlous condition of the road. "If you have to jump out," he said, "you will have to jump out very fast." That didn't make me feel much safer, but only days after I left, two Ugandan aid workers were murdered in daylight on these pitted, dusty highways. We bounced along until we hit Pabbo, where a collection of huts and shanties huddle together as if for protection. In this place are packed about 59,000 of the estimated 1.5 million "internally displaced persons" (I.D.P.'s) who have sought protection from the savagery of the L.R.A. Here, I had the slightly more awkward task of interviewing the female survivors of Joseph Kony's rolling Jonestown: a campaign of horror and superstition and indoctrination.

The women of Uganda are naturally modest and reserved, and it obviously involved an effort for them to tell their stories to a male European stranger. But they stood up as straight as spears and looked me right in the eye. Forced to carry heavy loads through the bush and viciously caned—up to 250 strokes—if they dropped anything. Given as gifts or prizes to men two or three times their age and compelled to bear children. Made to watch, and to join in, sessions of hideous punishment for those who tried to escape. Rose Atim, a young woman of bronze Nubian Nefertiti beauty, politely started her story by specifying her primary-school grade (grade five) at the time of her abduction. Her nostrils still flared with indignation when she spoke, whereas one of her fellow refugees, Jane Akello, a young lady with almost anthracite skin, was dull and dead-eyed and monotonous in her delivery. I was beginning to be able to distinguish symptoms. I felt a strong sense of indecency during these interviews, but this was mere squeamish self-indulgence on my part, since the women were anxious to relate the stories of their stolen and maimed childhoods. It was as if they had emerged from some harrowing voyage on the Underground Railroad.

Kony appointed himself the Lord's anointed prophet in 1987.

Very few people, apart from his victims, have ever met or even seen the enslaving and child-stealing Joseph Kony, and the few pictures and films of him are amateur and indistinct. This very imprecision probably helps him to maintain his version of charisma. Here is what we know and (with the help of former captives and a Scotland Yard criminal profiler) what we speculate. Kony grew up in a Gulu Province village called Odek. He appointed himself the Lord's anointed prophet for the Acholi people of northern Uganda in 1987, and by the mid-90s was receiving arms and cash from Sudan. He probably suffers from multiple-personality disorder, and he takes his dreams for prophecies. He goes into trances in which he speaks into a tape recorder and plays back the resulting

words as commands. He has helped himself to about 50 captives as "wives," claiming Old Testament authority for this (King Solomon had 700 spouses), often insisting—partly for biblical reasons and partly for the more banal reason of AIDS dread—that they be virgins. He used to anoint his followers with a holy oil mashed from indigenous shea-butter nuts, and now uses "holy water," which he tells his little disciples will make them invulnerable to bullets. He has claimed to be able to turn stones into hand grenades, and many of his devotees say that they have seen him do it. He warns any child tempted to run away that the baptismal fluids are visible to him forever and thus they can always be found again. (He can also identify many of his "children" by the pattern of lashes that they earned while under his tender care.) Signs of his disapproval include the cutting off of lips, noses, and breasts in the villages he raids and, to deter informers, a padlock driven through the upper and lower lips. This is the sort of deranged gang—flagellant, hysterical, fanatical, lethal, underage—that an unfortunate traveler might have encountered on the roads of Europe during the Thirty Years' War or the last Crusade. "Yes," says Michael Oruni, director of the Gulu Children of War Rehabilitation Center, who works on deprogramming these feral kids, "children who have known pain know how to inflict it." We were sitting in a yard that contained, as well as some unreformed youngsters, four random babies crawling about in the dust. These had been found lying next to their panga-slashed mothers or else left behind when their mothers were marched away.

Children who have known pain know how to inflict it.

In October, the Lord of the Flies was hit, in his medieval redoubt, by a message from the 21st century. Joseph Kony and four other leaders of the L.R.A. were named in the first arrest warrants ever issued by the new International Criminal Court (I.C.C.). If that sounds like progress to you, then consider this. The whereabouts of Kony are already known: he openly uses a satellite phone from a base across the Ugandan border in southern Sudan. Like the United States, Sudan is not a signatory to the treaty that set up the I.C.C. And it has sponsored the L.R.A. because the Ugandan government—which *is* an I.C.C. signatory—has helped the people of southern Sudan fight against the theocracy in Khartoum, the same theocracy that has been sponsoring the genocide against Muslim black Africans in Darfur. Arrest warrants look pretty flimsy when set against ruthless cynicism of this depth and intensity. Kony has evidently made some kind of peace with his Sudanese Islamist patrons: in addition to his proclamation of the Ten Commandments, he once banned alcohol and announced that all pigs were unclean and that those who farm them, let alone eat them, were subject to death. So, unless he has undergone a conversion to Judaism in the wilderness, we can probably assume that he is repaying his murderous armorers and protectors.

I had a faintly nerve-racking drink with Francis Ongom, one of Kony's ex-officers, who defected only recently and who would not agree to be questioned about his own past crimes. "Kony has refused Sudan's request that he allow his soldiers to convert to Islam," said this hardened-looking man as he imbibed a Red Bull through a straw, "but he has found Bible justifications for killing witches, for killing pigs because of the story of the Gadarene swine, and for killing people because God did the same with Noah's flood and Sodom and Gomorrah." Nice to know that he is immersed in the Good Book.

The terrifying thing about such violence and cruelty is that only a few dedicated practitioners are required in order to paralyze everyone else with fear. I had a long meeting with Betty Bigombe, one of those staunch and beautiful women—it is so often the women—who have helped restore Uganda's pulse after decades of war and famine and tyranny and Ebola and West Nile fever and AIDS. She has been yelled at by Joseph Kony, humiliated by corrupt and hypocritical Sudanese "intermediaries," dissed by the Ugandan political elite, and shamefully ignored by the international "human rights" community. She still believes that an amnesty for Kony's unindicted commanders is possible, which will bring the L.R.A. children back from the bush, but she and thousands like her can always be outvoted by one brutalized schoolboy with a machete. We are being forced to watch yet another Darfur, in which the time supposedly set aside for negotiations is used by the killers and cleansers to complete their work.

The Acholi people are the chief sufferers in all this.

The Acholi people of northern Uganda, who are the chief sufferers in all this, have to suffer everything twice. Their children are murdered or abducted and enslaved and then come back to murder and abduct and enslave even more children. Yet if the Ugandan Army were allowed to use extreme measures to destroy the L.R.A., the victims would be . . . Acholi children again. It must be nightmarish to know that any feral-child terrorist who is shot could be one of your own. "I and the public know," wrote W. H. Auden in perhaps his greatest poem, "September 1, 1939":

> *What all schoolchildren learn,*
> *Those to whom evil is done*
> *Do evil in return.*

And that's what makes it so affecting and so upsetting to watch the "night commuter" children when they come scuttling and scampering into town as the sun departs from the sky. These schoolchildren have not yet had evil done to them, nor are they ready to inflict any evil. It's not too late for them, in other words.

I sat in the deepening gloom for a while with one small boy, Jimmy Opioh, whose age was 14. He spoke with an appalling gravity and realism about his mother's inability to pay school fees for himself and his brother both, about the fatigue and time-wasting of being constantly afraid and famished and continually on the run. In that absurd way that one does, I asked him what he wanted to be when he grew up. His unhesitating answer was that he wanted to be a politician—he had his party, the Forum for Democratic Change, all picked out as well. I shamefacedly arranged, along with the admirable John Prendergast of the International Crisis Group, to get him the meager sum that would pay for his schooling, tried not to notice the hundreds of other eyes that were hungrily turned toward me in the darkness, wondered what the hell the actual politicians, here or there, were doing about his plight, and managed to get out of the night encampment just before the equatorial rains hit and washed most of the tents and groundsheets away.

How to Win the Weight Battle

DEBORAH KOTZ

Families now stuffing backpacks and greeting the children's new teachers face a crisis that makes falling test scores and rising college costs dull by comparison. Ten years and billions of dollars into the fight against childhood fat, it's clear that the campaign has been a losing battle. According to a report released last week by the research group Trust for America's Health, one third of kids nationwide are overweight now; other stats show that the percentage of children who are obese has more than tripled since the 1970s. Now, experts are worrying about the collateral damage, too: A 2006 University of Minnesota study found that 57 percent of girls and 33 percent of boys used cigarettes, fasting, or skipping meals to control their weight and that diet-pill intake by teenage girls had nearly doubled in five years. Last year, nearly 5,000 teens opted for liposuction, according to the American Society of Plastic Surgeons—more than three times the number in 1998, when experts first warned of a "childhood obesity epidemic."

"We've taken the approach that if we make children feel bad about being fat or scare them half to death, they'll be motivated to lose excess weight," says Joanne Ikeda, nutritionist emeritus at the University of California-Berkeley, who studies pediatric obesity prevention. "It hasn't worked in adults, so what makes us think it will work in kids?" Many experts now believe that an emphasis on dropping weight rather than adding healthful nutrients and exercise is doing more harm than good.

Failure to end—or even slow—the epidemic has public-health experts, educators, and politicians in a near panic. All told, some 17 percent of kids are now obese, which means they're at or above the 95th percentile for weight in relation to height for their age; an additional 17 percent are overweight, or at or over the 85th percentile. This is despite massive government-funded education campaigns in schools, in libraries, and on TV to alert parents and kids to the dangers. "In the early 1980s, I used to see one or two kids a year with type 2 diabetes, and now I see one or two a month," says Alan Lake, an associate professor of pediatrics at the Johns Hopkins University School of Medicine. "Evidence now suggests that this type 2 diabetes progresses more rapidly in kids, which means we could be soon seeing 20-year-olds developing severe heart disease." Already, high blood pressure affects more than 2 million youngsters.

Long haul. Obesity is hard to outgrow, so about 50 percent of elementary-school kids and 80 percent of teens who are obese will battle the scales—and the greatly increased risk of disease—for the rest of their lives. A number of authorities have warned that today's youth could be the first ever to have a shorter life span than their parents.

What explains both the problem and the elusiveness of a solution? Blame the American "toxic environment." Cinnamon buns and candy are far cheaper and easier to sell at the local mall than, say, a fresh fruit cup or a packet of sliced almonds. Half of kids walked or biked to school a generation ago; today, only about 10 percent do—then they come home and plop down in front of their various screens. As if the inactivity weren't bad enough, preteens absorb more than 7,600 commercials a year for candy, sugary cereal, and fast food, according to the Kaiser Family Foundation. "They're surrounded by circumstances where the default behavior is one that encourages obesity," says Marlene Schwartz, deputy director of the Rudd Center for Food Policy and Obesity at Yale University. Busy parents contribute by stocking pantries with quick energy—sugary cereal, Fruit Roll-Ups, and Oreos—while bringing home Kentucky Fried Chicken for dinner.

Schools have taken a stab at introducing the basics of good nutrition and the four food groups. But such efforts pale beside a cutback of gym time in favor of academics and vending machines stocked with high-calorie (and high-profit-margin) snack foods. More than 90 percent of elementary schools don't provide daily physical education, according to the Robert Wood Johnson Foundation, and the share of high school students participating in daily gym has dropped from 42 percent in 1991 to 33 percent in 2005. Some states have reconsidered and passed laws to increase phys ed, but plenty of schools have yet to figure out how to comply; in California, more than half the school districts have failed to implement the 20 minutes a day of physical activity that the state law now requires, according to the California Center for Public Health Advocacy.

While eating too much and exercising too little clearly put children's health in jeopardy, so might the methods used to change their behavior. As with any losing war, this one lacks a battle plan that everyone agrees upon. Robert Jeffery, director of the Obesity Prevention Center at the University of Minnesota School of Public Health, is one of many who believe that the solution lies in focusing more attention on body weight by screening kids at school and educating them about the dangers of obesity. One Minnesota high school last year showed the documentary *Super Size Me,* for example, to illustrate the ill effects that greasy burgers and fries have on the body. And proactive states like Florida and Pennsylvania mandate that schools weigh students yearly and send letters home warning parents if their child's body mass index, a number that relates weight to height, is too high. Down the hall and around the corner from Jeffery, meanwhile, Minnesota's Dianne Neumark-Sztainer, who studies adolescent eating behaviors, argues that such "overzealous efforts" may push teens to seek a quick and unhealthful weight-loss remedy. "Overweight teens are far more likely to turn to these risky behaviors instead of incorporating exercise or a more nutritious diet," she says.

Jillian Croll, a nutritionist who treats eating disorders at the Anna Westin House, a private facility in Chaska, Minn., has seen the evidence. "We find ourselves unteaching" girls raised to believe that their self-worth is measured by how much they weigh, she says. On a June afternoon tour of the suburban house filled with handmade quilts and stuffed teddy bears, the mood is tense as the eight residents sit down to sloppy Joes and buttered broccoli.

50% of obese elementary-school kids and 80% of obese teens are apt to battle the scales for the rest of their lives.

No joke. The path to an eating disorder is often paved with the good intentions of parents and educators who presume that warning and cajoling or joking will motivate children to lose weight. Neumark-Sztainer's findings suggest just the opposite in a study of 130 previously overweight teens. About 65 percent of the teens reported being teased about their body weight, and they were more likely to engage in binge eating, which leads to weight gain over time. And when parents harp on children's body weight, kids are also likely to become preoccupied with achieving thinness, says Neumark-Sztainer. Her research found that approaches that may be effective weight-loss strategies in adults, like daily weigh-ins and attempting a restricted diet, may trigger diet-pill use and purging in teens.

Shaming kids is prevalent in schools as well, and it's just as counterproductive there. A review paper published in the July issue of the journal *Psychological Bulletin* found that teachers perceive obese people to be sloppy and less likely to succeed than thinner people. Gym teachers usually have higher expectations for normal-weight kids, which means they might let heavier kids languish on the sidelines. "When kids are made to feel ashamed of themselves for being fat, they will cope by finding ways to make themselves feel better, often turning to food," says Schwartz. Studies have shown they're more likely to be depressed and dissatisfied with their bodies and develop other health problems like high blood pressure and eating disorders. "Yet I still hear educators and health professionals at conferences saying that weight bias serves a purpose."

School weight screenings, now performed in 16 states, have yielded mixed reviews. Though the report cards sent home with kids who have high body mass indexes work to inform parents about the problem, they don't provide effective solutions. "Many parents assume they should put their child on a diet," says Berkeley's Ikeda.

Preteens absorb over 7,600 commercials a year for candy, and fast food.

What's worse, the reports may be inaccurate. A government analysis found that 17 percent of kids who have a BMI that nudges them into the overweight category actually have a normal percentage of body fat but are large boned or have a greater muscle mass. Nine-year-old Ben Baturka, an avid swimmer who does up to 2 miles of laps while training for his swim meets, was put in the BMI "at risk" zone last year by Hillcrest Elementary School in Drexel Hill, Pa. "He's always been a big boy, but he's a healthy eater and as fit as he can be, so I'm going to ignore the school letter," says Ben's mother, Angie. The American Medical Association recently recommended that doctors perform BMI screenings during annual physicals, looking for weight-related health risks like hypertension or high cholesterol, too.

Some families go too far by turning healthful eating into a new religion. "Anorexia often starts with healthy eating behaviors, like cutting down on bread and other starches, that evolve to become too restrictive," says pediatrician Tania Heller, director of the Washington Center for Eating Disorders and Adolescent Obesity in Bethesda, Md. "My mom was always into organic food, so she didn't notice when I got on a health kick, running more miles and avoiding all fat in my diet," says Marina Leith, 17, who was treated by Heller for anorexia after dropping 30 pounds in less than two months four years ago. She's now a high school senior, back to a normal weight.

Think positive. How to get a child to a healthy weight in the healthiest possible way? Most experts now favor a positive approach—showing, for example, ways that exercise strengthens the body and refreshes the mind and how certain nutrients in foods help cells, organs, and bones grow properly. Hundreds of schools are now trying out Planet Health, a curriculum developed by Harvard University researchers that disguises obesity prevention by integrating healthful messages about the power of food and exercise into various subjects. Students in math class, for example, come to appreciate the importance of reducing TV viewing by calculating the hours they've spent over their lifetime in front of the set. A 2005 study published in the *Archives of Pediatrics & Adolescent Medicine* found that middle school girls who had Planet Health in their schools were half as likely to purge or use diet pills as those in schools without it.

Half of kids walked or biked to school a generation ago; today, some 10% do.

A second program adopted by 7,000 elementary schools nationwide, the Coordinated Approach to Child Health, similarly puts the focus on good health habits instead of weight. In class, students use a traffic-light system to identify "go," "slow," and "whoa" foods and take breaks to do jumping jacks. In the cafeteria, fruits, vegetables, low-fat milk, and whole-grain starches are labeled with green-light tags, and pizza gets a yellow light. Gym activities are designed to keep students constantly moving. "Every kid gets a ball to dribble or a hula hoop; there's no lining up and waiting to take a turn," says Philip Nader, professor of pediatrics emeritus at the University of California-San Diego, who helped develop CATCH. One study found that the program succeeded at preventing the growth in number of overweight students that normally occurs from grade 3 to grade 5. CATCH schools in El Paso, Texas (with one of the highest obesity rates in the nation), held the line between those grades; elsewhere in the city, the share of overweight girls increased from 26 percent to 40 percent and of overweight boys from 39 percent to 49 percent.

Five Comments Parents Should Never Make

Teens Who Overcame Anorexia Consider How They Might Have Avoided It

Even gentle and well-meant comments about your kids' weight can have an unintended downside: an increased likelihood that they'll turn to dangerous dieting behaviors. U.S. News recently sat down with five teens who were treated for anorexia at the Emily Program, a private eating disorders facility in Minneapolis-St. Paul, to find out what sent their weight plunging. Their moms sat in, too. Here are some of the comments the girls wish they'd never heard.

1. You're Big Boned Compared to Your Sister

Even offhand comparisons can cause a harmful overreaction. "I'd overhear my mom saying to her friends, 'Katie's the bigger one,'" recalls Katie Million, a 19-year-old from Lino Lakes, Minn., whose shame contributed to her weight falling below 95 pounds during her sophomore year of high school. Although there's no way to protect children from every hurtful comment, parents can certainly avoid remarking on a child's weight—and insist that siblings do, too. Research has shown that kids who are teased are more prone to binge eating and other eating disorders.

2. Maybe This New Diet Will Help

"I'm always hearing about how bad food is," says Leah Schumacher, 18, of St. Paul. "I would have liked to have learned about the positives of food, like why I need some fat to build cells and what fruits and vegetables do for my body." Million recently had a roommate whose mother sent her diet products and then complained on visits that her daughter hadn't lost enough weight. "I couldn't stick around for those conversations," she says.

3. I Hated My Body, Too, When I Was Your Age

With the best of intentions, Natalie Durbin shared the insecurities she'd had as a teen with her daughter Hannah, now 16, when Hannah was going through puberty. "I told her that I'd always been really thin but then started hating my body when I developed curves. I wanted to be really open about it in case she was feeling the same way," Durbin explains. Hannah, though, took it as a cue for how she should feel about her own developing body—especially since her mother was still uncomfortable with her weight. "She would tell me not to focus on my body image, but then she'd talk about how she hated her body all the time," says Hannah. "Now I think it's best if my mom never talks about these things with me."

4. You're Such a Talented Athlete; Let's Crank It up a Notch

One Emily mom who recognized running talent in her daughter encouraged her to join the track team and began to run with her to help her train. "I praised her, thinking I was building up her self-esteem, but never realized she hated [running] and was only doing it for me," says the mother, who prefers not to be identified. When the girl began adding extra miles and rapidly shedding weight, her mother was shocked to discover the response was a statement of how much her daughter hated the pressure of the track meets. Some kids have a natural drive to excel in sports, but if parents are doing the pushing, they may need to stop and reassess.

5. You Look Great! Have You Lost Weight?

Nearly all the teens said they got praise from family and friends when they began restricting their food intake and dropping pounds. "You can put up with how painfully cold you are all the time," says 18-year-old Edie Kuss from Minneapolis, "and that you're so weak you can't stand up. What you crave is the praise—and that's what you remember even when it stops because you've gotten too thin."

—D.K.

Grass-roots efforts can make a difference, too. Hillcrest Elementary School nurse Kim Glielmi implemented a voluntary walking program last year in which 200 students, parents, and teachers put in 1 mile a day around the neighborhood to reach a grand total for the group. "Our goal had been to walk enough miles to get to California by the end of the year," she says, "but we actually got as far as Hawaii." A community garden project in New York City's Harlem section has increased inner-city kids' appreciation of fresh fruits and vegetables. A program to build bike paths and sidewalks in Marin County, Calif., is prompting more kids to transport themselves to school.

At home. Parents, of course, will have the biggest impact. In her book "I'm, Like, So Fat!" Neumark-Sztainer says the most important thing parents can do is to model healthful behaviors—not preach them—by avoiding fad diets, skipped meals, and too much junk food and by hitting the gym and planning active family outings on a regular basis. A slew of studies have shown that teens who regularly eat home-cooked family dinners enjoy healthier weights, higher grades, lower rates of smoking, less depression, and a lower risk of developing an eating disorder.

The home environment should be conducive to good habits: a fruit bowl on the kitchen counter, cut-up vegetables in the fridge, jump-ropes in the garage, a basketball hoop in the driveway. Lake advises introducing healthful foods again and again even if a child refuses to eat them, since research shows it may take 10 to 12 sightings before a picky eater lifts fork to mouth. And he recommends against enforcing a clean-plate rule, pointing out that toddlers up to age 4 naturally and wisely regulate their own intake and that older kids eat out of habit, even if they're feeling full. "Parents should choose when to eat and what to eat, while a child should choose when to stop," says Lake.

How to Succeed at Losing

It's Tough, but Kids Can Get to—and Stay at—a Healthy Weight

A focus on body weight may be necessary when a seriously overweight child's well-being is at stake. But parents need to be respectful and supportive, since pressuring kids—especially teens—to lose weight could cause them to overeat more or develop an eating disorder. After seeing her 18-year-old son, Wes, shave 65 pounds off his 270-pound frame, registered dietitian Anne Fletcher set out to discover the secret of other teens' success. In her recent book *Weight Loss Confidential,* she studies how 104 seriously overweight preteens and teens, 41 boys and 63 girls, got to a healthier weight and stayed there for two years or longer. The kids on average lost 58 pounds each, and one quarter lost 75 pounds or more. Here's how they did it:

They Took the Initiative

Readiness is everything, says Fletcher, and the teens she studied decided on their own when and how they were going to lose the weight. They were motivated by wanting to improve their health, look better, feel better about themselves, and improve their performance at sports and other activities.

They Got Active

Exercise was by far the most popular slimming strategy, with 83 percent of the teens reporting that they upped their calorie-burning efforts to lose and then to maintain. Running, walking, and lifting weights were the most common choices. Nearly two thirds of the kids continued to exercise three to five times a week.

They Got Real about Portions

These teens know that a proper portion of meat is the size of a deck of cards and that a cup of pasta is the size of their fist. Using smaller plates and cups helped them impose limits, as did avoiding eating directly out of a bag.

They Drew on Support from Their Parents

Never underestimate the power of a cheering section. Encouraging parents who stocked the kitchen with nutritious low-calorie fare and exercised with their kids were a key to these teens' success.

They Discovered What Worked Best for Them

Some of the teens went to nutritionists for one-on-one counseling or attended summer weight camps that emphasized the importance of a healthful lifestyle. Others created their own structure, by cutting portions or giving up certain foods like french fries or soda. Fletcher's son counted calories. "Wes had always been able to eat a huge amount of food without feeling full, so this really made him start paying attention to portion sizes," she says.

They Connected

Some teens discovered the power of bonding with peers in support groups like Take Off Pounds Sensibly. One girl went to meetings with her mother, and they both lost weight together.

They Gave Themselves Time

Some of the teens lost the weight over many months or, in some cases, years. Gradual weight loss, explains Fletcher, doesn't demand the kind of deprivation required for quick results.

They Didn't Use the Scale as Their Only Measure of Success

Although they were certainly motivated by drops in clothing sizes, the successful losers were also encouraged by feeling less winded when they climbed a flight of stairs, by improvements in their blood pressure, and by closer relationships with friends and relatives and greater self-confidence. Most realized that they were never going to reach society's thin ideal. So they chose to appreciate their assets and aimed for good health instead.

—D.K

Experts also emphasize the importance of fostering a positive body image since, according to the Minnesota data, 46 percent of teenage girls and 26 percent of boys are dissatisfied with the way they look. Parents should both avoid making negative comments about their own bodies and put a stop to any teasing (box, Page 136). They should also discuss healthful behaviors without focusing too much on size or body fat. Liza Miller, a lean and sprightly 10-year-old, shows the level of understanding that parents might wish to achieve. (Her father, Dirk Miller, heads the Emily Program, a private eating disorders organization that runs the Anna Westin House.) She has trained herself to say no at slumber parties to bowls of potato chips and ice cream. And she has made a firm decision not to use celebrities as role models. Witness the sign posted on her bedroom door: "I won't allow people like Nicole Richie to make me feel fat."

Note

"How to Win the Weight Battle" [September 10] stated that 17 percent of kids are now obese, which means they're at or above the 95th percentile for weight in relation to height. The reason that a greater percentage of kids now fall into the "top 5 percent" category is that the standard measurement charts that define obesity were created using data from the 1960s and '70s, when kids weighed less than they do now.

The Epidemic That Wasn't

SUSAN OKIE

Baltimore—One sister is 14; the other is 9. They are a vibrant pair: the older girl is high-spirited but responsible, a solid student and a devoted helper at home; her sister loves to read and watch cooking shows, and she recently scored well above average on citywide standardized tests.

There would be nothing remarkable about these two happy, normal girls if it were not for their mother's history. Yvette H., now 38, admits that she used cocaine (along with heroin and alcohol) while she was pregnant with each girl. "A drug addict," she now says ruefully, "isn't really concerned about the baby she's carrying."

When the use of crack cocaine became a nationwide epidemic in the 1980s and '90s, there were widespread fears that prenatal exposure to the drug would produce a generation of severely damaged children. Newspapers carried headlines like "Cocaine: A Vicious Assault on a Child," "Crack's Toll Among Babies: A Joyless View" and "Studies: Future Bleak for Crack Babies."

But now researchers are systematically following children who were exposed to cocaine before birth, and their findings suggest that the encouraging stories of Ms. H.'s daughters are anything but unusual. So far, these scientists say, the long-term effects of such exposure on children's brain development and behavior appear relatively small.

"Are there differences? Yes," said Barry M. Lester, a professor of psychiatry at Brown University who directs the Maternal Lifestyle Study, a large federally financed study of children exposed to cocaine in the womb. "Are they reliable and persistent? Yes. Are they big? No."

Cocaine is undoubtedly bad for the fetus. But experts say its effects are less severe than those of alcohol and are comparable to those of tobacco—two legal substances that are used much more often by pregnant women, despite health warnings.

Surveys by the Department of Health and Human Services in 2006 and 2007 found that 5.2 percent of pregnant women reported using any illicit drug, compared with 11.6 percent for alcohol and 16.4 percent for tobacco.

"The argument is not that it's O.K. to use cocaine in pregnancy, any more than it's O.K. to smoke cigarettes in pregnancy," said Dr. Deborah A. Frank, a pediatrician at Boston University. "Neither drug is good for anybody."

But cocaine use in pregnancy has been treated as a moral issue rather than a health problem, Dr. Frank said. Pregnant women who use illegal drugs commonly lose custody of their children, and during the 1990s many were prosecuted and jailed.

Cocaine slows fetal growth, and exposed infants tend to be born smaller than unexposed ones, with smaller heads. But as these children grow, brain and body size catch up.

At a scientific conference in November, Dr. Lester presented an analysis of a pool of studies of 14 groups of cocaine-exposed children—4,419 in all, ranging in age from 4 to 13. The analysis failed to show a statistically significant effect on I.Q. or language development. In the largest of the studies, I.Q. scores of exposed children averaged about 4 points lower at age 7 than those of unexposed children.

In tests that measure specific brain functions, there is evidence that cocaine-exposed children are more likely than others to have difficulty with tasks that require visual attention and "executive function"—the brain's ability to set priorities and pay selective attention, enabling the child to focus on the task at hand.

Cocaine exposure may also increase the frequency of defiant behavior and poor conduct, according to Dr. Lester's analysis. There is also some evidence that boys may be more vulnerable than girls to behavior problems.

But experts say these findings are quite subtle and hard to generalize. "Just because it is statistically significant doesn't mean that it is a huge public health impact," said Dr. Harolyn M. Belcher, a neurodevelopmental pediatrician who is director of research at the Kennedy Krieger Institute's Family Center in Baltimore.

And Michael Lewis, a professor of pediatrics and psychiatry at the Robert Wood Johnson Medical School in New Brunswick, N.J., said that in a doctor's office or a classroom, "you cannot tell" which children were exposed to cocaine before birth.

He added that factors like poor parenting, poverty and stresses like exposure to violence were far more likely to damage a child's intellectual and emotional development—and by the same token, growing up in a stable household, with parents who do not abuse alcohol or drugs, can do much to ease any harmful effects of prenatal drug exposure.

Possession of crack cocaine, the form of the drug that was widely sold in inner-city, predominantly black neighborhoods, has long been punished with tougher sentences than possession of powdered cocaine, although both forms are identically metabolized by the body and have the same pharmacological effects.

Dr. Frank, the pediatrician in Boston, says cocaine-exposed children are often teased or stigmatized if others are aware of their exposure. If they develop physical symptoms or behavioral problems, doctors or teachers are sometimes too quick to blame the drug exposure and miss the real cause, like illness or abuse.

"Society's expectations of the children," she said, "and reaction to the mothers are completely guided not by the toxicity, but by the social meaning" of the drug.

Research on the health effects of illegal drugs, especially on unborn children, is politically loaded. Researchers studying children exposed to cocaine say they struggle to interpret their findings for the public without exaggerating their significance—or minimizing it, either.

Dr. Lester, the leader of the Maternal Lifestyle Study, noted that the evidence for behavioral problems strengthened as the children in his study and others approached adolescence. Researchers in the study are collecting data on 14-year-olds, he said, adding: "Absolutely, we need to continue to follow these kids. For the M.L.S., the main thing we're interested in is whether or not prenatal cocaine exposure predisposes you to early-onset drug use in adolescence" or other mental health problems.

Researchers have long theorized that prenatal exposure to a drug may make it more likely that the child will go on to use it. But so far, such a link has been scientifically reported only in the case of tobacco exposure.

Teasing out the effects of cocaine exposure is complicated by the fact that like Yvette H., almost all of the women in the studies who used cocaine while pregnant were also using other substances.

Moreover, most of the children in the studies are poor, and many have other risk factors known to affect cognitive development and behavior—inadequate health care, substandard schools, unstable family situations and exposure to high levels of lead. Dr. Lester said his group's study was large enough to take such factors into account.

Ms. H., who agreed to be interviewed only on the condition that her last name and her children's first names not be used, said she entered a drug and alcohol treatment program about six years ago, after losing custody of her children.

Another daughter, born after Ms. H. recovered from drug and alcohol abuse, is thriving now at 3. Her oldest, a 17-year-old boy, is the only one with developmental problems: he is autistic. But Ms. H. said she did not use cocaine, alcohol or other substances while pregnant with him.

After 15 months without using drugs or alcohol, Ms. H. regained custody and moved into Dayspring House, a residential program in Baltimore for women recovering from drug abuse, and their children.

There she received psychological counseling, parenting classes, job training and coaching on how to manage her finances. Her youngest attended Head Start, the older children went to local schools and were assigned household chores, and the family learned how to talk about their problems.

Now Ms. H. works at a local grocery, has paid off her debts, has her own house and is actively involved in her children's schooling and health care. She said regaining her children's trust took a long time. "It's something you have to constantly keep working on," she said.

Dr. Belcher, who is president of Dayspring's board of directors, said such programs offered evidence-based interventions for the children of drug abusers that can help minimize the chances of harm from past exposure to cocaine or other drugs.

"I think we can say this is an at-risk group," Dr. Belcher said. "But they have great potential to do well if we can mobilize resources around the family."

The Positives of Caregiving: Mothers' Experiences Caregiving for a Child with Autism

MICHAEL K. CORMAN

The documentation and representation of the experiences of caregivers of children with autism and other developmental disabilities has been one dimensional at best, with a pervasive focus on the stresses, burdens, and parental coping associated with caregiving (Grant, Ramcharan, McGrath, Nolan, & Keady, 1998). Much of this focus is warranted. For example, sources of stress (stressors) for caregivers of these children are numerous and might include the autistic traits themselves (DeMyer, 1979; Tomanik, Harris, & Hawkins, 2004), social stigmas from the general public and health practitioners (Gray, 1998, 2002a, 2002b), and the social support system that is intended to alleviate stress (Corman, 2007a; DeMyer, 1979; Gray, 1998).

This multitude of stressors can have an immense effect on individuals in the family, including parents and siblings (DeMyer, 1979; Kaminsky & Dewey, 2001; Schopler & Mesibov, 1994), extended family members (Gray, 1998) and, depending on how caregivers cope, the possible life gains that the individual with autism can make (Schopler & Mesibov, 1994). For example, parents often experience a combination of emotional problems (such as depression, isolation, and feelings of being a failure as a parent), physical problems (fatigue, ulcers, headaches, fluctuation in weight, dermatitis, and other physical health conditions), career problems (limited or no employment—specifically for mothers and career changes), and negative effects on the marriage (marital discord often ending in divorce; Gray, 1998, 2002a). Parents also report feelings of guilt, isolation, doubts of their ability to care for their child, anger toward the symptoms of autism, increased physical and psychological tensions, frustrations, lack of life satisfaction, and feelings of exhaustion and old age (DeMyer, 1979; Gray, 2002b). Last, because of the unique and often complex symptomatology associated with autism, such as a lack of verbal communication, variant cognitive functioning, and severe behaviors, comparative studies have reported that the burden of caregiving for children with autism is greater than that of parenting a child with other disabilities (Weiss, 2002), such

as mental retardation, Down's syndrome, cystic fibrosis, and chronic and fatal physical illness.

Caregiving for a child with autism is stressful! But what about the positive side of caregiving? The narrow focus on the stressful and negative aspects of the caregiving experience offers only partial insights into the experiences of caregiving for children with chronic conditions. There is a need for research to examine the other side of the spectrum, the positive and often joyous side of parenting children with disabilities. The purpose of this article is to provide insight into that positive side by exploring the experiences of mothers of children with autism through in-depth interviews. Although these mothers portrayed an experience that was often stressful, they also discussed many joys of caregiving. This article attempts to strike a balance with the majority of research that focuses on the negatives of caregiving; it will show that caregiving for children with autism is not solely stressful. These findings have theoretical and practical implications. First, this article provides a brief overview of the literature on the positives of caregiving for individuals with chronic conditions.

Literature Review

Most caregiving research focuses solely on the negative aspects of the experience (Chappell, Gee, McDonald, & Stones, 2003), which may be indebted to the pathological models of stress that guide such inquiries. For instance, Pearlin, Lieberman, Menaghan, and Mullan's (1981) framework of the stress process focuses on the stressors (antecedents to stress) associated with caregiving and pays specific attention to the many related relationships, and the developing and changing nature of these relationships over time, that eventually lead to stress (see also Pearlin, Mullan, Semple, & Skaff, 1990). Lazarus and Folkman (1984) offered a framework that focuses on the more individual and psychological components of what they called the *stress-coping process*. They suggested that it is how stressors are appraised, in addition to individual resources, that determines whether or not an event is stressful (Lazarus & Folkman, 1984). Although these conceptualizations are useful for exploring the stressful aspects of caregiving and how individuals cope, they are limited in that they fail to address any positives of caregiving in a systematic way; positives have been left by the wayside (Kelso, French, & Fernandez, 2005). As Grant et al. (1998) suggested, such a singular view fails to account for other important dimensions.

Research on caregiving has only recently considered gratification and the role of positives in the caregiving experience. For example, in Susan Folkman's (1997) seminal study of caregiving for men with HIV/AIDS, she discussed how positive states of mind can co-occur with negative states. She reported that "despite high levels of distress, people also experience positive psychological states during caregiving and bereavement" (p. 1207). Folkman described four psychological states associated with coping: (a) positive reappraisal, (b) goal-directed problem-focused coping, (c) spiritual beliefs and practices, and (d) the infusion of ordinary events with positive meaning. All four states have an underlying characteristic, that is, the appraisal of positive meanings occurring within a stressful event, which she referred to as *meaning-based coping*.

Grant et al. (1998) explored the positives of caregiving by interviewing 120 caregivers of individuals with intellectual disabilities. They described rewards and caregiver gratification as emerging from three sources: (a) the relationship between caregiver and care receiver, (b) intrapersonal characteristics of the caregiver, and (c) the desire for positive outcomes or the avoidance of negative affect. They also found that many of the gratifications expressed by caregivers were related to, or a product of, successful coping strategies, supporting Folkman's (1997) findings.

More recently, Chaya Schwartz (2003) defined caregiver gratification as "fulfilling parental duties, a better idea of 'what's important in life', learning about inner strengths, aware of personal limitations, learning to do new things, satisfaction from doing what's right, personal growth, [and] becoming more self-confident" (p. 580). In her study of 167 primary caregivers of individuals with mental, developmental, or physical disabilities, she found that caregivers who were younger, unemployed, and had poor health were more likely to experience caregiver gratification. In addition, she found the only characteristics of the child that factored into experiencing gratification were the age of the child (younger children) and the type of disability (having a physical rather than a mental disability). Last, subjective (perceived stress) rather than objective burden (the level of care required) was associated with less caregiver gratification (Schwartz, 2003). Schwartz speculated that the gratification parents experienced might be a product of how they perceived or created meaning in their caregiving role.

In the field of autism, research has only provided marginal insights into the more rewarding aspects of caregiving. For instance, in a study about narratives published on the Internet by parents, Amos Fleischmann (2004) found that in addition to the demanding aspects of caregiving, a majority of websites focused on the positive essence of individuals with autism and the caregiving experience, with an emphasis on parents' positive relationship with their child and joyous experiences derived from caregiving. Fleischmann's study is supported by other research on the contributions people with disabilities make to their families: families might benefit in terms of strengthened family ties, compassion and fulfillment, and happiness (Pruchno, 2003).

Despite the shortcomings of Pearlin et al. (1981, 1990) and Lazarus and Folkman's (1984) models, they allow for a scope that looks beyond adjustment and toward positives (Kelso et al., 2005). This is apparent in Folkman's (1997) work on caregiving for individuals with HIV/AIDS (see also Folkman & Moskowitz, 2000a, 2000b). Using these insights, the positives of caregiving are defined in this article as experiences or events that caregivers appraise as positive and sometimes joyous. It is important to note that if this definition seems ambiguous, it is because the positives of caregiving remain relatively uncharted, lacking conceptual clarification (Grant et al., 1998). Based on mothers' reflections, this article explores the positives of caregiving for a child with autism. In doing so, a more complete understanding of these parents' lived experiences emerges, with important contributions to the broader constellation of caregivers of children with chronic conditions.

Method
Participants

Results reported in the next section were drawn from a larger study that explored mothers' experiences of caregiving for a child with autism, before and after their child was placed outside of the home (either in foster care, a group home setting, or a treatment-care facility, hereafter referred to as *placed* or *placement*). Interviews occurred between November 2005 and February 2006. Nine mothers participated in total; 6 lived in British Columbia, and 3 lived in Alberta, Canada. The average age of mothers was 46, with a range between 35 and 62 years old. For 7 out of the 9 mothers, family income ranged between $30,000 and more than $100,000. One mother responded "middle class," and another chose not to answer. As of the first interview, the children with autism were between the ages of 8 and 18, with the average being 14 years old. The age of these children at the time of placement was 6–15, with an average of 11 years old. Mothers were purposively chosen because they are usually the primary caregivers (Gray, 2003) and are therefore more likely to be involved in the day-to-day ups and downs of caregiving. Furthermore, a unique sample of mothers was chosen; their experiences were so stressful that their child was ultimately placed outside of the home (see Corman, 2007a). Although this study did not aim to be generalizable, it was assumed that if this sample experienced positives, caregivers in less stressful circumstances (e.g., caregivers of a child with less severe autistic characteristics and other disabilities) would also experience them. Therefore, these findings are potentially transferable to other constellations of caregivers.

A diagnosis of autism was reported by 7 out of the 9 mothers during the initial contact, with the remaining 2 mothers reporting a diagnosis of pervasive developmental disorder (PDD) and PDD not otherwise specific (PDD-NOS). Mothers also reported co-occurring conditions, including Landau-Kleffner syndrome, obsessive compulsive disorder, mental handicap, epilepsy (for three children), and Down's syndrome. Two of the mothers had a female child, and 7 had a male child. Although I refer to a generalized *autism,* it is important to note that there is no all-or-nothing form of autism but rather a continuum of severity, known as autism spectrum disorders (Wing, 1988). Based on mothers' descriptions, these children would most likely fall within the moderate to severe end of the spectrum.

Research Design

In-depth, semistructured interviews were conducted based on transcendental phenomenology (Moustakas, 1994), a qualitative research strategy and philosophy that allows researchers to identify the essence of experience as it relates to certain phenomena as described and understood by participants of a study (Creswell, 2002). Mothers were interviewed at their homes and asked to retrospectively talk about their caregiving experiences. Questions were geared toward exploring the positives and joys of caregiving, the demands of caregiving, and how mothers coped, focusing on the times before and after out-of-home placement. The portion of the interviews reported in the analysis below are based on the questions that explored the positives during the early years prior to placement (approximately 0–8 years of age, depending when the placement process was activated) and after their child left home. Interviews lasted on average 2.24 hours with a range of 1.5–3 hours. The interviews and the numbers of mothers interviewed continued until sufficiency and saturation of information were reached.

Interviews were transcribed in their entirety and analyzed based on a modified approach offered by Moustakas (1994), specifically intended for the analysis of qualitative data. Eight steps were followed: (1) identifying patterns in the data based on the lived experiences of participants, (2) reducing the data by identifying unique aspects of experience, (3) organizing the data into core themes that represent the experience of participants, (4) validating step 3 by reviewing the complete transcript of participants, (5) constructing an individual textural description of the experience presented by each participant, (6) based on step 5, constructing a clear account of the dynamics of the experience, (7) combining steps 5 and 6 to create a textural-structural description of each participant that incorporated the experiences of participants, and (8) combining individual textual descriptions of each participant into one that represents the experience presented by the group as a whole.

To assist in the process just described, insights offered by Moerer-Urdahl and Creswell (2004) were followed. Initially, significant statements within each participant's transcripts were identified, with a primary focus on understanding how individuals viewed different aspects of their experiences as they related to the positives and joys of caregiving. The goal here was to ground or contextualize the positives of caregiving to gain a better understanding of the distinct character of positives as described by mothers. The data were then broken down into themes based on the experiences of mothers. Once

themes were developed, a detailed description of the experience of each mother as it related to the themes that emerged was provided. Conclusions were then drawn in accordance with the lived experiences expressed by participants. The product of this process was the grouping of statements into the themes discussed in the next section.

Results
Pockets of Child Development

All parents expressed the positives during the early years of their child's development as "pockets" because they were "kind of few and far between." Positives discussed by mothers included their child developing, seeing their child happy, times devoid of negative autistic traits or maladaptive behaviors (as perceived by the mother) that are often associated with autism, spending time with their child, unique and/or positive personality traits of their child, and knowing or discovering what was wrong with their child. I discuss each in the following paragraphs.

Developmental gains. With a diagnosis on the autism spectrum, parents are often left in ambiguity because of the nature of the disability; they do not know how much their child will develop in the years to come. As a result, mothers described feelings of joy when their child started to make developmental gains. For example, one mother discussed how she was "very pleased" when her child progressed in developmental areas, such as "when he started to speak." Another mother commented on her child's success in learning new tasks; "Oh yeah, his success still makes me feel good, no matter what. Like I remember when he learned how to wave good-bye. That made me cry that day [laugh]." Another mentioned the "little milestones that parents take for granted, I think are tremendous."

Another mother discussed how watching her child was "hugely satisfying . . . it makes it all worth it when you start to see a little bit of language or a behavior, or a skill emerge." For some mothers, this gave them hope for their child's future. One mother explained, "I think . . . a little bit of joy with a child that's seriously handicapped goes a long way. It gives you a lot of hope."

Child being happy. All mothers experienced positives derived from seeing their child happy. Although this might seem like a common experience of all parents, it is important to contextualize this side of caregiving in that many mothers viewed their child as being chronically unhappy. One mother put it best, "just to see him happy, because all through his life he's lived either withdrawn or anxious, or afraid of doing things." When mothers saw their child happy, they were especially happy. For example, joy arose for one mother when she watched her child enjoy his favorite activity. She explained:

You see this bright-eyed little boy at the top of the slide, that was his favorite activity was going down the slides. So when you see him at the top of the slide with this big grin on his face, those kinds of times were really exciting for me. . . . I just knew that he enjoyed that.

Seeing her child happy made her feel "really good . . . That is sort of what we hope our kids are going to feel." Another mother described, "when he's happy and having a really good time, then I'm happy. It's like I'm just a normal parent."

Times devoid of negative autistic traits or maladaptive behaviors. Mothers also talked about times devoid of negative behaviors (negative autistic traits), which they thought of as "normal" times. For instance, one mother described how when her child "didn't throw his food . . . [or] didn't have any feces smearing in the bathroom," these were more positive times. Others experienced positives when their child "hadn't pinched another child or hit another child." One mother went on to explain, "So any time he was cooperating . . . times that he was being and not bothering anybody. . . . If I heard that he sat for five minutes in his desk, or he sat in circle time without poking the next person." During these times, some mothers expressed being "really happy."

Spending time with your child. Despite many of the difficulties, all mothers described the positives of spending time with their child. For instance, one mother discussed how she and her child would go swimming together and go down to the beach to spend time together. Her child "loved it" and always "liked hanging off me." She described how there were so many "nice times" that they spent together. Another mother described how she felt "just connected" to her child because of the times they spent together, specifically "the caregiving part . . . being hands on, physically connected." She talked about how she "really enjoyed" the connection she had with her child: "We're connected on a different level." This mother concluded:

> I guess having a child with autism, you connect with them on a completely different level than I think you would with other children because you don't have language. He's also mostly nonverbal, so physical connections are really important; it's the way you communicate that's beyond words I guess, so I think that's part of it.

For this mother, what might be viewed as a demanding aspect of caregiving was in fact very joyous for her.

Unique and/or positive personality traits of their child. Individuals with autism often have a variety of challenges, including maladaptive behaviors, difficulty in communicating with others, difficulty listening and following directions, and other co-occurring medical conditions. However, individuals who have autism are heterogeneous; the severities of impairments vary from person to person (Gray, 2003; Seltzer, Shattuck, Abbeduto, & Greenberg, 2004). Nonetheless, the positive side of this uniqueness often goes unrecognized. All mothers in this study recognized the uniqueness of their child. In doing so, they expressed many positives derived from the unique personality traits of their child.

For example, mothers discussed how their child was "real sweet" and showed affection. Another mother talked about her child being a "very warm individual. . . . We were blessed that way, I guess; very cuddly, quite attached to your close family members." Other personality traits included being "very funny, like she's got a good sense [of humor] . . . she's quite a little monkey," and being "a very good-natured kid . . . he still has a happy disposition." Despite the negative traits mothers dealt with throughout their caregiving experience, which sometimes worsen or change as their child ages into adulthood (Gray, 2002a), mothers described the many unique personality traits of their child as a positive side of caregiving.

Knowing or discovering what was wrong with their child. Common perceptions of receiving a diagnosis on the autism spectrum suggest that the experience is devastating, and often it is (Mansell & Morris, 2004). In fact, for many of the mothers in this study, the autism diagnosis represented the loss of the child that was or could have been. One mother explained how "the day that I found out [I was floored] because there's nothing like that in my family, and we've always been high achievers . . . and I don't know where that [diagnosis] came from."

Although some mothers described receiving the diagnosis of autism as very burdensome—"it was sad, it's pretty devastating, to have a child who's not typical"—for others, the receipt of the diagnosis was not a stressful experience but a positive one. With a diagnosis, mothers were relieved to finally know what was wrong with their child after having entered into multiple systems of care in search for answers and supports. For example, after receiving a diagnosis, one mother described how "all of a sudden you know . . . because up until this point everybody's been asking me 'Why is he doing this? What's he doing?' And I'd be going 'I don't know; I don't know'. I really had no answers for anybody." With a diagnosis, answers started "coming out." With these answers, mothers described a positive experience derived from knowing and understanding.

Furthermore, the receipt of a diagnosis allowed the mother to gain access to specialized services and supports for her child, such as intervention therapy, and herself, such as respite, and set out a pathway of care for her child.[1] The ability to take action was positive, and often a relief, because now the mother was able to help her child. One mother expanded upon this point:

> I'm very much a doer, and so when you have a diagnosis, then you can look at putting the pieces together to move forward and do something; especially I hear so much about early development and early intervention. It was right around the time that the money was being made available for early intervention, and I didn't want to waste a minute, especially knowing that that money would dissolve when he was 6.

The Impacts of Positives

Parents did not just describe the positive side of caregiving, they also discussed how the positives interacted with negative and stressful experiences (i.e., their stress-coping process). For example, the positives associated with their child developing gave mothers hope. One mother, like many parents of children with autism, worried about her child's future (Ivey, 2004).

When her child started to make developmental milestones, she began to have a more positive outlook for her child's future. This hope impacted the concerns and worries she had for her child's future. She went on to explain how the positives "are the things that keep you going . . . a little bit of joyful experience gives you . . . the ability to go on."

On a more general note, one mother described how the positives of caregiving had an impact on her stress-coping process.

Well they (the positives) kept me going . . . it wasn't all negative. It kind of gave me hope to continue on, like every day is a new day kind of thing. . . . It gave me a reason to get up in the morning so I wouldn't be waking up going "oh no, I have to deal with another day" sort of thing . . . any time you have any kind of joy or positive feelings then that . . . just gives you a really good feeling that you can continue over the next period of time.

Another mother explained:

[The positives] just keep you going. Without the moments of comic relief, without the joys, without those moments of connection where he catches your eye directly for 1 minute and you actually have his gaze directly, without those things, you'd go stir crazy. Those are the things that feed you. I get a huge amount of strength from the tiniest little things.

Despite the demands of caregiving, mothers experienced a multitude of positives during their caregiving years, many of which brought joy to their lives.

Positive Reflections on Their Overall Caregiving Experience

All mothers spoke about personal transformation as a result of their caregiving years. This transformation included learning from their experience and growing as a person. It is important to note that these positive reflections are not linked to any specific event but were a product of their caregiving experience as a whole. Furthermore, it is important to contextualize this positive side of caregiving: All mothers eventually placed their child with autism due to a number of factors, including their child's maladaptive behaviors increasing drastically, "getting more intense" and more difficult to deal with over time, a failure in the support system that was intended to alleviate stress, and a general inability to cope with the demands of caregiving, leading to mothers experiencing severe distress and feeling that they "couldn't go on" (Corman, 2007a). However, despite this experience of severe distress, all mothers ultimately reflected positively on their caregiving experience as a whole.

For example, one mother explained the learning involved in caregiving where she not only "learned a lot about autism, but I learned a lot about people, and I would have missed that . . . it was a really wonderful thing." Another explained how "the biggest positive is just the learning that came out of that for us as a family, but for me in particular as a person. But I think it's shaped all of us, it certainly has shaped [my husband and daughter] as well as me."

Others described caregiving as making them stronger as a person. One mother mentioned how she "became a fighter, just kind of like an advocate for the family but also for [my child with autism] . . . So, yeah, definitely it makes you stronger. And it makes you tougher in a way." Her experience also made her realize what is "important . . . So, you realize what's really important and don't sweat the small stuff." Another mother described her child with autism as being one of her greatest teachers in life:

I mean, I don't even know who I would be if I hadn't had May . . . it's kind of a weird thing, but in my life, she's been kind of one of my key teachers. She's kind of forced me to kind of examine parts of myself that I don't know if I ever would have got to if I didn't have her. And, she forced [my husband] and I to kind of deal with issues that might have taken us years . . . It's been a struggle, and sometimes I've hated her for it, [but] nobody has taught me so much.

Mothers also discussed how the caregiving experience made them more empathetic:

My husband and I were asked one time about the biggest thing that we got from Sam. I think it was the gift of patience 'cause I have patience unlimited, you know . . . 'cause once somebody's dumping milk out in your front yard [laugh], it's amazing how much patience you have.

Discussion and Conclusion

Despite the demanding aspects of caregiving for children with autism, and it is often very demanding, caregivers experience many positives and joys from their role as caregivers. However, the majority of research focuses on the negative and more stressful aspects of the caregiving experience. Breaking away from this preponderance of research in the field of autism, this article highlights some of the positives of caregiving that mothers experienced during the early years of their child's development and overall reflections on their caregiving experience after their child left home. When asked to discuss the positives of caregiving, all mothers expressed a multitude of positives directly related to their caregiving role (Chappell et al., 2003; Folkman, 1997; Grant et al., 1998; Schwartz, 2003). Others derived positives from finding the "positive essence" in their child (Fleischmann, 2004) and achievements of their child (Grant et al., 1998). More unique positives included discovering what was wrong with their child in the face of not knowing.

Implications for Practice

Many practical implications arise from this study. Although caregiving for children with autism is demanding, this article suggests that the positives and joys that emerge from this role are not only important but also have a specific function. Whereas current research describes the positives of caregiving as a *product* of successful coping—the adaptational function of positives (see Folkman, 1997; Grant et al., 1998)—parents in this study discussed how positives had an impact *on* their stress-coping process, rather than being simply a product of it. In other words, positives also occur outside of the stress-coping process, and interact with it, affecting how mothers experience stressors and negative outcomes, potentially impacting their ability to cope at different times. This finding expands on the function of positives within the caregiving experience; they go beyond adaptational function to being a core aspect of caregivers' experiences.

Furthermore, the importance and function of the positives and joys of caregiving is most apparent when they are not present. In the larger study that contributed to this article, all mothers described severe distress and solely negative outcomes during the time leading up to and immediately following the placement of their child, a time devoid of any positives or joys of caregiving. One mother described it best: "When the stresses got to be too much, the joy of everything started to disappear." Does a lack of positives impact caregiver well-being and a caregiver's ability to cope? Cummins (2001) explained that most caregivers are able to describe positives derived from their caregiving role; when they are unable to do so, the demands of their role are likely to be intolerable. Grant et al. (1998) further explained that without the positives of caregiving, it may not be possible for caregivers to feel as if they are able to continue encountering the stressful circumstances corollary to their role. As such, it might be concluded that the positives of caregiving are an integral part of parents' ability to cope, to the point that when they are not present, parents may not be able to continue caregiving. Policy and practice implications directly follow from these findings in that a lack of positives might be an indicator of the current state of a caregiver's well-being or lack of well-being. It might be an indicator for professional services and supports that additional supports are needed to proactively assist those in crisis or on the brink of crisis. Furthermore, policies need to be developed that are proactively geared toward preventing a crisis or assisting those on the brink of a crisis rather than solely intervening once the crisis emerges. Of equal importance, this examination of positives provides future families of children with autism and other disabilities a better understanding of the experience of caregiving as a whole—an experience that is very demanding at times but also has many positives.

How families cope with the demands associated with caring for a child with autism not only influences the well-being of the family but also possible life gains that an individual with autism can make (Schopler & Mesibov, 1994). Current research on caregiving for children with autism attempts to promote the use of successful coping strategies and resources to improve the quality of life of the caregiver and care receiver (Dunn, Burbine, Bowers, & Tantleff-Dunn, 2001; Gray, 1994, 1998). One practical implication that might inform research, policy, and practice on successful coping is the need to promote and draw attention to the positives of caregiving both within service agencies and for those caregiving for children with autism and other disabilities. If services and supports are able to enhance the positive aspects of caregiving by drawing

attention to them, parents might be able to cope more successfully with the difficulties of caregiving. In addition, it might be beneficial for services and supports to facilitate the joys of caregiving by drawing attention to the strengths of the caregiver and the positive contribution their child with a disability makes to their family (Pierpont, 2004). The strengths-based perspective and active interviewing are two resources that service providers might draw upon to help facilitate and draw attention to the positives of caregiving.

The strengths-based perspective is one orientation that might assist those whose work intersects with individuals with disabilities and their families in drawing attention to and facilitating the identification of the positive and joyous aspects of caregiving. This perspective shifts away from pathological conceptions of persons with disabilities and the experiences of caregiving to more qualitative and holistic understandings, aligned with the positives of caregiving discussed earlier. By focusing on strengths (see Cohen, 1999; Early, 2001), this perspective has the potential to assist service providers in gaining a more complete understanding of the caregiving experience and perceiving their experiences in a more positive light, which has the potential to increase caregivers' quality of life and the quality of care they provide (Berg-Weger, Rubio, & Tebb, 2001).

In addition to the strengths-based perspective, and complementary to it, insights offered by the reflexive and linguistic turns in sociology could be of use to service providers and researchers alike as a resource or tool to draw upon to explore the positives of caregiving and draw attention to them. One approach aligned with this shift is "the active interview," which is a methodological and analytical approach to interviewing that conceptualizes the interview as an active meaning-making process between interviewee and interviewer, who both participate in the coproduction of knowledge. The interviewer (i.e., service provider), in the context of exploring the positives of caregiving, might invite or "incite" the interviewee (i.e., caregiver) to talk about and reflect on the positives of caregiving. Traditionally, this approach might be viewed as leading the respondent, resulting in a social desirability bias (Esterberg, 2002; see also Cummins, 2001). However, the active interview suggests that interviewers are inevitably embedded and implicated in the meaning-making processes of respondents. Holstein and Gubrium (2002) explained:

> This is not to say that active interviewers merely coax their respondents into preferred answers to their questions. Rather, they converse with respondents in such a way that alternate considerations are brought into play . . . encouraging respondents to develop topics in ways relevant to their own everyday lives . . . to provide an environment conducive to the production of the range and complexity of meanings that address relevant issues. (pp. 120–121).

Furthermore, in the context of the positives of caregiving, the active interview is not solely concerned about the positives; it suggests that there is usefulness in inviting individuals to think about the positives and honor participants in the meaning-making process. As such, I suggest that this approach can provide a more fruitful examination of the caregiving experience as a whole by assisting researchers and service providers in exploring and gaining a better understanding and appreciation of the positives of caregiving. This process might also facilitate families and caregivers in talking about and reflecting upon their experiences in a more positive and joyous light (Berg-Weger et al., 2001).

Directions for Future Research

The findings from this study suggest that future research should focus on the factors that lead to positives of caregiving, which might identify and assist in the development of services, supports, and specific interventions that will potentially facilitate improved outcomes for individual caregivers, care receivers, and the family as a whole. As such, there is a need to explore links among positives, social supports, coping, and appraisal processes of caregivers of children with autism and other chronic conditions. Furthermore, future research should investigate these links to determine how the facilitation of positives might affect caregivers' lived experiences. Also, as mentioned earlier, it is important to examine positives and joys not only in relation to stressors but also as a significant factor throughout the entire stress-coping process.

Last, this study focused on the retrospective experience of mothers whose children were under 18 years old. However, for the first time in history, large numbers of people with autism are reaching old age (National Advisory Council on Aging, 2004; Seltzer et al., 2004). As a result, parents now "face a lifetime of caregiving responsibilities" (Kim, Greenberg, Seltzer, & Krauss, 2003, p. 313). However, very little is known about this constellation of caregivers and care receivers. There is need to explore the experiences of individuals with autism, their caregivers, and families as they age over the life course.

Note

1. In British Columbia and Alberta, for instance, institutional services and supports are attached to a diagnosis of autism (see Corman, 2007b).

References

Berg-Weger, M., Rubio, D., & Tebb, S. (2001). Strengths-based practice with family caregivers of the chronically ill: Qualitative insights. *Families in Society: The Journal of Contemporary Human Services, 82*(3), 263–272.

Chappell, N., Gee, E., McDonald, L., & Stones, M. (2003). *Aging in contemporary Canada.* Toronto, Canada: Pearson Educational Publishers/Prentice Hall.

Cohen, B. (1999). Intervention and supervision in strengths-based social work practice. *Families in Society: The Journal of Contemporary Human Services, 80*(5), 460–466.

Corman, M. K. (2007a). *Primary caregivers of children with autism spectrum disorders—An exploration of the stressors, joys, and parental coping before and after out-of-home placement.* (Masters Thesis, University of Victoria, Canada, 2007). Available from the Electronic Theses and Dissertations website: http://hdl.handle.net/1828/1227

Corman, M. K. (2007b, August). *Panning for gold—An institutional ethnography of health relations in the process of diagnosing autism in British Columbia.* Paper presented at the meeting of The Society for the Study of Social Problems, New York.

Creswell, J. (2002). *Research design: Qualitative, quantitative, and mixed methods approaches* (2nd ed.). Thousand Oaks, CA: Sage Publications.

Cummins, R. (2001). The subjective well-being of people caring for a family member with a severe disability at home: A review. *Journal of Intellectual & Development Disability, 26*(1), 83–100.

DeMyer, M. (1979). *Parents and children in autism.* Washington, DC: V. H. Winston & Sons.

Dunn, M., Burbine, T., Bowers, C., & Tantleff-Dunn, S. (2001). Moderators of stress in parents of children with autism. *Community Mental Health Journal, 37*(1), 39–52.

Early, T. (2001). Measures for practice with families from a strengths perspective. *Families in Society: The Journal of Contemporary Human Services, 82*(2), 225–232.

Esterberg, K. G. (2002). *Qualitative methods in social research.* Boston: McGraw-Hill.

Fleischmann, A. (2004). Narratives published on the Internet by parents of children with autism: What do they reveal and why is it important? *Focus on Autism and Other Developmental Disabilities, 19*(1), 35–43.

Folkman, S. (1997). Positive psychological states and coping with severe stress. *Social Science & Medicine, 45*(8), 1207–1221.

Folkman, S., & Moskowitz, J. T. (2000a). Positive affect and the other side of coping. *American Psychologist, 55*(6), 647–654.

Folkman, S., & Moskowitz, J. T. (2000b). Stress, positive emotion, and coping. *Current Directions in Psychological Science, 9*(4), 115–118.

Grant, G., Ramcharan, P., McGrath, M., Nolan, M., & Keady, J. (1998). Rewards and gratifications among family caregivers: Towards a refined model of caring and coping. *Journal of Intellectual Disability Research, 42*(1), 58–71.

Gray, D. (1994). Coping with autism: Stresses and strategies. *Sociology of Health & Illness, 16*(3), 275–300.

Gray, D. (1998). *Autism and the family: Problems, prospects, and coping with the disorder.* Springfield, IL: Charles C. Thomas Publisher.

Gray, D. (2002a). Ten years on: A longitudinal study of families of children with autism. *Journal of Intellectual & Development Disability, 27*(3), 215–222.

Gray, D. (2002b). 'Everybody just freezes. Everybody is just embarrassed': Felt and enacted stigma among parents of children with high functioning autism. *Sociology of Health & Illness, 24*(6), 734–749.

Gray, D. (2003). Gender and coping: The parents of children with high functioning autism. *Social Sciences & Medicine, 56,* 631–642.

Holstein, J. A., & Gubrium, J. F. (2002). Active interviewing. In D. Weinberg (Ed.), *Qualitative research methods* (pp. 112–126). Oxford, UK: Blackwell.

Ivey, J. (2004). What do parents expect? A study of likelihood and importance issues for children with autism spectrum disorders. *Focus on Autism and Other Developmental Disabilities, 19*(1), 27–33.

Kaminsky, L., & Dewey, D. (2001). Sibling relationships of children with autism. *Journal of Autism and Developmental Disorders, 31*(4), 399–410.

Kelso, T., French, D., & Fernandez, M. (2005). Stress and coping in primary caregivers of children with a disability: A qualitative study using the Lazarus and Folkman process model of coping. *Journal of Research in Special Educational Needs, 5*(1), 3–10.

Kim, W., Greenberg, S., Seltzer, M., & Krauss, W. (2003). The role of coping in maintaining the psychological well-being of mothers of adults with intellectual disability and mental illness. *Journal of Intellectual Disability Research, 47*(4–5), 313–327.

Lazarus, R., & Folkman, S. (1984). *Stress, appraisal, and coping.* New York: Springer Publishing.

Mansell, W., & Morris, K. (2004). A survey of parents' reactions to the diagnosis of an autistic spectrum disorder by a local service: Access to information and use of services. *Autism, 8*(4), 387–407.

Moustakas, C. (1994). *Phenomenological research methods.* Thousand Oaks, California: Sage Publications.

Moerer-Urdahl, T., & Creswell, J. (2004). Using transcendental phenomenology to explore the "ripple effect" in a leadership mentoring program. *International Journal of Qualitative Methods, 3*(2), 1–28.

National Advisory Council on Aging. (2004). *Seniors on the margins: Aging with a developmental disability.* Canada: Minister of Public Works and Government Services Canada.

Pearlin, L., Lieberman, M., Menaghan, E., & Mullan, J. (1981). The stress process. *Journal of Health and Social Behavior, 22*(4), 337–356.

Pearlin, L., Mullan, J., Semple, S., & Skaff, M. (1990). Caregiving and the stress process: An overview of concepts and their measures. *The Gerontologist, 30*(5), 583–594.

Pierpont, J. (2004). Emphasizing caregiver strengths to avoid out-of-home placement of children with severe emotional and behavioral disturbances. *Journal of Human Behavior in the Social Environment, 9*(1/2), 5–17.

Pruchno, R. (2003). Enmeshed lives: Adult children with developmental disabilities and their aging mothers. *Psychology and Aging, 18*(4), 851–857.

Schopler, E., & Mesibov, G. (1994). *Behavioral issues in autism.* New York: Plenum Press.

Schwartz, C. (2003). Parents of children with chronic disabilities: The gratification of caregiving. *Families in Society: The Journal of Contemporary Human Services, 84*(4), 576–584.

Seltzer, M., Shattuck, P., Abbeduto, L., & Greenberg, J. (2004). The trajectory of development in adolescents and adults with autism. *Mental Retardation and Developmental Disabilities Research Reviews, 10*(4), 234–247.

Tomanik, S., Harris, G., & Hawkins, J. (2004). The relationship between behaviours exhibited by children with autism and maternal stress. *Journal of Intellectual & Developmental Disability, 29*(1), 16–26.

Weiss, M. (2002). Hardiness and social support as predictors of stress in mothers of typical children, children with autism, and children with mental retardation. *Autism, 6*(1), 115–130.

Wing, L. (1988). The continuum of autistic characteristics. In E. Schopler & G. Mesibov (Eds.), *Diagnosis and assessment in autism* (pp. 91–110). New York: Plenum Press.

MICHAEL K. CORMAN, MA, is a doctoral student in the Department of Sociology at the University of Calgary and a part-time faculty member in the Department of Sociology & Anthropology at Mount Royal College in Calgary, Alberta. His research and teaching interests include the sociology of health and illness, aging, institutional ethnography, caregiving and autism spectrum disorders, health care work, and critical research strategies. Correspondence regarding this article can be sent to the author at mkcorman@ucalgary.ca or University of Calgary, Department of Sociology, Social Sciences 913, 2500 University Drive NW, Calgary, AB, T2N IN4 Canada.

Author's note—I would like to thank Dr. Neena L. Chappell for her continued support throughout the larger study that contributed to this article and the preparation of this manuscript.

Three Reasons Not to Believe in an Autism Epidemic

According to some lay groups, the nation is experiencing an autism epidemic—a rapid escalation in the prevalence of autism for unknown reasons. However, no sound scientific evidence indicates that the increasing number of diagnosed cases of autism arises from anything other than purposely broadened diagnostic criteria, coupled with deliberately greater public awareness and intentionally improved case finding. Why is the public perception so disconnected from the scientific evidence? In this article we review three primary sources of misunderstanding: lack of awareness about the changing diagnostic criteria, uncritical acceptance of a conclusion illogically drawn in a California-based study, and inattention to a crucial feature of the "child count" data reported annually by the U.S. Department of Education.

MORTON ANN GERNSBACHER, MICHELLE DAWSON, AND H. HILL GOLDSMITH

If you have learned anything about autism lately from the popular media, you most likely have learned—erroneously—that there is "a mysterious upsurge" in the prevalence of autism (*New York Times,* October 20, 2002, Section 4, p. 10), creating a "baffling . . . outbreak" (CBSnews.com, October 18, 2002), in which new cases are "exploding in number" (*Time,* May 6, 2002, p. 48), and "no one knows why" (*USA Today,* May 17, 2004, p. 8D). At least a handful of U.S. Congress members decree on their .gov websites that the nation is facing an autism epidemic. Several national media have erroneously concluded that a set of data from California "confirms the autism epidemic," and the largest autism-advocacy organization in the world has expressed alarm over astronomical percentage increases in the number of autistic children served in the public schools since 1992. However, no sound scientific evidence indicates that the increase in the number of diagnosed cases of autism arises from anything other than intentionally broadened diagnostic criteria, coupled with deliberately greater public awareness and conscientiously improved case finding. How did public perception become so misaligned from scientific evidence? In this article, we review three major sources of misunderstanding.

The Changing Diagnosis of Autism

The phenomenon of autism has existed most likely since the origins of human society. In retrospect, numerous historical figures—for instance, the 18th-century "wild boy of Aveyron"—fit autism diagnostic criteria but were not so diagnosed in their day (Frith, 1989). Only in the 1940s did a constellation of differences in social interaction, communication, and focused interests come to be categorized by Leo Kanner as "autism." However, another 40 years would elapse before American psychiatric practice incorporated criteria for autism into what was by then the third edition of its *Diagnostic and Statistical Manual of Mental Disorders* (*DSM-III;* American Psychiatric Association, APA, 1980). Thus, estimates of the prevalence of autism prior to 1980 were based on individual clinicians' (e.g., Kanner & Eisenberg, 1956) or specific researchers' (e.g., Rutter, 1978) conceptions—and fluctuated because of factors that continue to introduce variation into current-day estimates (e.g., variation in the size of the population sampled and the manner of identification).

Autism has remained in the *DSM* (under the title, Pervasive Developmental Disorders), but not without modification through subsequent editions. Whereas the 1980 *DSM-III* entry required satisfying six mandatory criteria, the more recent 1994 *DSM-IV* (APA, 1994) offers 16 optional criteria—only half of which need to be met. Moreover, the severe phrasing of the 1980 mandatory criteria contrasts with the more inclusive phrasing of the 1994 optional criteria. For instance, to qualify for a diagnosis according to the 1980 criteria an individual needed to exhibit "*a pervasive lack of responsiveness* to other people" (emphasis added; APA, 1980, p. 89); in contrast, according to 1994 criteria an individual must demonstrate only "a lack of spontaneous seeking to share . . . achievements with other people" (APA, 1994, p. 70) and peer relationships less sophisticated than would be predicted by the individual's developmental level. The 1980

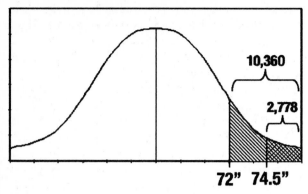

Figure 1 Distribution of male height in McClennan county, Texas. Shaded areas represent segments of the population defined as "tall" according to two standards: men over 74.5 in. (2,778) versus men over 72 in. (10,360).

mandatory criteria of *"gross deficits* in language development" (emphasis added; APA, 1980, p. 89) and "if speech is present, peculiar speech patterns such as immediate and delayed echolalia, metaphorical language, pronominal reversal" (APA, 1980, p. 89) were replaced by the 1994 options of difficulty "sustain[ing] a conversation" (APA, 1994, p. 70) or "lack of varied . . . social imitative play" (p. 70). *"Bizarre responses* to various aspects of the environment" (emphasis added; APA, 1980, p. 90) became "persistent preoccupation with parts of objects" (APA, 1994, p. 71).

Furthermore, whereas the earlier 1980 (*DSM-III*) entry comprised only two diagnostic categories (infantile autism and childhood onset pervasive developmental disorder), the more recent 1994 (*DSM-IV*) entry comprises five. Three of those five categories connote what is commonly called autism: Autistic Disorder, Pervasive Developmental Disorder Not Otherwise Specified (PDDNOS), and Asperger's Disorder. Autistic Disorder requires meeting half of the 16 criteria, but Asperger's Disorder, which did not enter the *DSM* until 1994, involves only two thirds of that half, and PDDNOS, which entered the *DSM* in 1987, is defined by subthreshold symptoms. Therefore, Asperger's Disorder and PDDNOS are often considered "milder variants." These milder variants can account for nearly three fourths of current autism diagnoses (Chakrabarti & Fombonne, 2001). Consider also the recent practice of codiagnosing autism alongside known medical and genetic conditions (e.g., Down syndrome, Tourette's syndrome, and cerebral palsy; Gillberg & Coleman, 2000); the contemporary recognition that autism can exist among people at every level of measured intelligence (Baird et al., 2000), the deliberate efforts to identify autism in younger and younger children (Filipek et al., 2000), and the speculation that many individuals who would meet present-day criteria were previously mis- or undiagnosed (Wing & Potter, 2002), including some of the most accomplished, albeit idiosyncratic, historical figures such as Isaac Newton, Lewis Carroll, W.B. Yeats, Thomas Jefferson, and Bill Gates (Fitzgerald, 2004).

The California Data

In California, persons diagnosed with autism (and other developmental disabilities) qualify for services administered by the statewide Department of Developmental Services (DDS). In 1999, the California DDS reported that from 1987 to 1998 the number of individuals served under the category of "autism" had increased by 273% (California DDS, 1999). Alarmed by this 273% increase, the California legislature commissioned the University of California Medical Investigation of Neurodevelopmental Disorders (M.I.N.D.) Institute to determine whether the increase could be explained by changes in diagnostic criteria. The M.I.N.D. Institute (2002) concluded, on the basis of data we describe next, that there was "no evidence that a loosening in the diagnostic criteria has contributed to the increased number of autism clients served by the [California DDS] Regional Centers" (p. 5). Although this unrefereed conclusion made national headlines and continues to be articulated on innumerable websites, it is unwarranted.

The study involved two samples of children who had been served under the California DDS category of "autism": One sample was born between 1983 and 1985 (the earlier cohort); the other sample was born between 1993 and 1995 (the more recent cohort). Both cohorts were assessed with the same autism diagnostic instrument (an interview conducted with care providers). However, the autism diagnostic instrument was based on *DSM-IV* criteria—criteria that were not even published until 1994. When the same percentage of children in the earlier and the more recent cohort met the more recent *DSM-IV* criteria, the researchers imprudently concluded that the "observed increase in autism cases cannot be explained by a loosening in the criteria used to make the diagnosis" (M.I.N.D. Institute, 2002, p. 7).

To understand the fallacy of the conclusion, consider the following analogy, based on male height and graphically illustrated in Figure 1. Suppose the criterion for "tall" was 74.5 in. and taller in the mid-1980s, but the criterion was loosened to 72 in. and taller in the mid-1990s. A diagnostic instrument based on the looser, more recent criterion of 72 in. would identify males who met the 74.5-in. criterion as well as those who met the 72-in. criterion.[1] Although a perfectly reliable diagnostic instrument based on a looser criterion would identify 100% of the individuals who meet the looser criterion along with 100% of the individuals who meet the more restricted criterion, a highly reliable instrument might identify about 90% of each group; this is the percentage of each cohort in the California study who met the more recent autism criteria.

Most crucially, broadening the criterion will result in a dramatic increase in diagnosed cases. For instance, census data allow us to estimate that 2,778 males in McClennan County, Texas would be called tall by the more restricted 74.5-in. criterion, and 10,360 males would be called tall by the broader 72-in. criterion; if those two criteria had been applied a decade apart, a 273% increase in the number of males called tall would have emerged—without any real increase in Texans' height. In the same way, the 273% increase from 2,778 versus 10,360

California children who received services for "autism" in 1987 versus 1998 could well be a function of broadened criteria.

As we have already detailed, the commonly applied diagnostic criteria for autism broadened nationally from the 1980s to the 1990s; thus, it would be unusual if the criteria used for eligibility in California had not also broadened during this time. Two further aspects of the California data suggest that the criteria must have broadened. First, children in the more recent cohort were dramatically less likely to have intellectual impairment: Whereas 61% of the children in the earlier cohort were identified as having intellectual impairments, only 27% of the children in the more recent cohort were so identified. The lower rate of intellectual impairment in the more recent cohort matches recent epidemiological data, and the difference between the two rates suggests a major difference between the two cohorts (e.g., that the more recent cohort was drawn from a less cognitively impaired population).

Second, on two of the three dimensions measured by the autism diagnostic instrument, the children in the more recent cohort were, on average, less symptomatic than the children from the earlier cohort. The researchers stated that although these differences were statistically significant (i.e., they exceeded the criterion of a statistical test), they were likely not clinically significant (i.e., they were likely not of significance to the clinical presentation); therefore, the researchers suggested that these differences should not be taken as evidence that the diagnostic criteria had broadened. However, refer again to the tallness analogy: Comparing two cohorts of males in McClennan County diagnosed according to our more restricted (74.5-in.) versus our broader (72-in.) criterion would probably result in a statistically significant difference between the two cohorts' average height—but the difference would be just about an inch (i.e., most likely not a clinically significant difference).

The "Child Count" Data

The purpose of the federal Individuals With Disabilities Education Act (IDEA), passed in 1991, is to ensure that all children with disabilities are provided a free, appropriate, public education including an individually designed program. Schools comply with the IDEA by reporting to the federal Department of Education an annual "child count" of the number of children with disabilities served. It is the data from these annual child counts that have been the most egregiously misused in arguments for an autism epidemic.

For example, in October 2003, the Autism Society of America sent its 20,000 members the following electronic message: "Figures from the most recent U.S. Department of Education's 2002 Report to Congress on IDEA reveal that the number of students with autism [ages 6 to 21] in America's schools *jumped an alarming 1,354% in the eight-year period from the school year 1991–92 to 2000–01*" (emphasis added). What the Autism Society failed to note is the following fact (available in the *Report to Congress,* immediately under the autism data entries): Prior to the 1991–1992 school year, there was no child count of students with autism; autism did not even exist as an IDEA reporting category. Moreover, in 1991–1992, use of the autism reporting category was optional (it was required only in subsequent years).

Whenever a new category is introduced, if it is viable, increases in its usage will ensue. Consider another IDEA reporting category introduced along with autism in 1991–1992: "traumatic brain injury." From 1991–1992 to 2000–2001, this category soared an astronomical 5,059%. Likewise, the reporting category "developmental delay," which was introduced only in 1997–1998, grew 663% in only 3 years.

After the initial year, the number of children reported under the IDEA category of autism has increased by approximately 23% annually. Why the continuing annual increase? As is the case with new options in the marketplace, like cellular phones and high-speed Internet, new reporting categories in the annual child count are not capitalized upon instantaneously; they require incrementally magnified awareness and augmentation or reallocation of resources. Currently no state reports the number of children with autism that would be expected based on the results of three recent, large-scale epidemiological studies, which identified 5.8 to 6.7 children per 1,000 for the broader autism spectrum (Baird et al., 2000; Bertrand et al., 2001; Chakrabarti & Fombonne, 2001). In 2002–2003, front-runners Oregon and Minnesota reported 4.3 and 3.5 children with autism per 1,000, respectively, while Colorado, Mississippi, and New Mexico reported only 0.8, 0.7, and 0.7 children with autism per 1,000. Thus, most likely IDEA child counts will continue to increase until the number reported by each state approaches the number of children identified in the epidemiological studies.

Why do states vary so widely in the number of children reported (or served)? Each state's department of education specifies its own diagnostic criteria, and states differ (as do school districts within states, and individual schools within school districts) in the value given to a diagnosis in terms of services received. States also vary from year to year in the number of children served and reported. For instance, Massachusetts historically reported the lowest percentage of children with autism: only 0.4 or 0.5 per 1,000 from 1992 through 2001. Then, in 2002, Massachusetts reported a 400% increase in one year, when it began using student-level data (i.e., actually counting the students) rather than applying a ratio, which was calculated in 1992, based on the proportion of students in each disability classification as reported in 1992. In their 2002 IDEA report to Congress, Massachusetts state officials warned that the increase will continue for several years as "districts better understand how to submit their data at the student level" (IDEA, 2002, p. 4) and "all districts comply completely with the new reporting methods" (IDEA, 2002, p. 4).

Other Reasons Not to Believe in an Autism Epidemic

In this article we have detailed three reasons why some laypersons mistakenly believe that there is an autism epidemic. They are unaware of the purposeful broadening of diagnostic criteria, coupled with deliberately greater public awareness; they accept the unwarranted conclusions of the M.I.N.D. Institute study; and they fail to realize that autism was not even an IDEA reporting category until the early 1990s and incremental increases will most likely continue until the schools are identifying and serving the number of children identified in epidemiological studies. Apart from a desire to be aligned with scientific reasoning, there are other reasons not to believe in an autism epidemic.

Epidemics solicit causes; false epidemics solicit false causes. Google *autism* and *epidemic* to witness the range of suspected causes of the mythical autism epidemic. Epidemics also connote danger. What message do we send autistic children and adults when we call their increasing number an epidemic? A pandemic? A scourge? Realizing that the increasing prevalence rates are most likely due to noncatastrophic mechanisms, such as purposely broader diagnostic criteria and greater public awareness, should not, however, diminish societal responsibility to support the increasing numbers of individuals being diagnosed with autism. Neither should enthusiasm for scientific inquiry into the variety and extent of human behavioral, neuroanatomical, and genotypic diversity in our population be dampened.

Note

1. Wing and Potter (2002) provide a similar illustration. The same percentage of children who met Kanner's earlier, more restricted criteria met *DSM-IV*'s more recent, broadened criteria; if the child was autistic according to Kanner's restricted criteria, the child was autistic according to *DSM-IV*'s broadened criteria. Of course, the reverse was not true. Only 33 to 45% of the children who met more recent *DSM-IV* criteria met earlier Kanner criteria.

References

American Psychiatric Association. (1980). *Diagnostic and statistical manual of mental disorders* (3rd ed.). Washington, DC: Author.

American Psychiatric Association. (1994). *Diagnostic and statistical manual of mental disorders* (4th ed.). Washington, DC: Author.

Baird, G., Charman, T., Baron-Cohen, S., Cox, A., Swettenham, J., Wheelwright, S., & Drew, A. (2000). A screening instrument for autism at 18 months of age: A 6 year follow-up study. *Journal of the American Academy of Child and Adolescent Psychiatry, 39,* 694–702.

Bertrand, J., Mars, A., Boyle, C., Bove, F., Yeargin-Allsopp, M., & Decoufle, P. (2001). Prevalence of autism in a United States population: The Brick Township, New Jersey, investigation. *Pediatrics, 108,* 1155–1161.

California Department of Developmental Services. (1999). *Changes in the population with autism and pervasive developmental disorders in California's developmental services system: 1987–1998.* A report to the legislature. Sacramento, CA: California Health and Human Services Agency.

Chakrabarti, S., & Fombonne, E. (2001). Pervasive developmental disorders in preschool children. *Journal of the American Medical Association, 285,* 3093–3099.

Filipek, P.A., Accardo, P.J., Ashwal, S., Baranek, G.T., Cook, E.H. Jr., Dawson, G., Gordon, B., Gravel, J.S., Johnson, C.P., Kallen, R.J., Levy, S.E., Minshew, N.J., Ozonoff, S., Prizant, B.M., Rapin, I., Rogers, S.J., Stone, W.L., Teplin, S.W., Tuchman, R.F., & Volkmar, F.R. (2000). Practice parameter: Screening and diagnosis of autism: Report of the Quality Standards Subcommittee of the American Academy of Neurology and the Child Neurology Society. *Neurology, 55,* 468–479.

Fitzgerald, M. (2004). *Autism and creativity: Is there a link between autism in men and exceptional ability?* London: Brunner-Routledge.

Frith, U. (1989). *Autism: Explaining the enigma.* Oxford, England: Blackwell.

Gillberg, C., & Coleman, M. (2000). *The biology of the autistic syndromes* (3rd ed.). London: MacKeith Press.

IDEA. (2002). *Data Notes for IDEA, Part B.* Retrieved April 22, 2005, from IDEAdata website: www.ideadata.org/docs/bdatanotes2002.doc

Kanner, L., & Eisenberg, J. (1956). Early infantile autism 1943–1955. *American Journal of Orthopsychiatry, 26,* 55–65.

M.I.N.D. Institute. (2002). *Report to the Legislature on the principal findings from The Epidemiology of Autism in California: A Comprehensive Pilot Study.* Davis: University of California-Davis.

Rutter, M. (1978). Diagnosis and definition. In M. Rutter & E. Schopler (Eds.), *Autism: A reappraisal of concepts and treatments* (pp. 1–25). New York: Plenum Press.

U.S. Department of Education. (2002). *Twenty-fourth annual report to Congress on the implementation of the Individuals With Disabilities Education Act.* Washington, DC: Author.

Wing, L., & Potter, D. (2002). The epidemiology of autistic spectrum disorders: Is the prevalence rising? *Mental Retardation and Developmental Disabilities Research Reviews, 8,* 151–162.

Morton Ann Gernsbacher: University of Wisconsin-Madison; **Michelle Dawson:** University of Montreal, Montreal, Quebec, Canada; **H. Hill Goldsmith:** University of Wisconsin-Madison

Address correspondence to Morton Ann Gernsbacher, Department of Psychology, University of Wisconsin-Madison, 1202 W. Johnson St., Madison, WI 53706; e-mail: MAGernsb@wisc.edu.

From *Current Directions in Psychological Science,* vol. 14, no. 2, February 2005. Copyright © 2005 by the Association for Psychological Science. Reprinted by permission of Blackwell Publishing, Ltd.

Getting Back to the Great Outdoors

With children spending less time in nature than ever before, the biggest victim may be Mother Earth. Psychologists are helping kids connect.

AMY NOVOTNEY

Martha Erickson, PhD, always believed that her frequent nature outings with her children, and her encouragement of their independent play and exploration outdoors, helped them mature into well-rounded adults. These days, she's getting confirmation of that fact.

"As many young people were spending increasing amounts of time watching television or playing video games, my kids were much more likely to head off on their bikes, canoe down the creek that flows through our city or rally some friends to create an outdoor adventure," she says. "Now, as young adults, they are fit, creative, adventurous and striving to protect the environment."

Increasing evidence demonstrates the many benefits of nature on children's psychological and physical well-being, including reduced stress, greater physical health, more creativity and improved concentration.

"The basic finding seems to be yes, nature does seem to be really good for kids," says Frances Kuo, PhD, founder of the Landscape and Human Health Laboratory at the University of Illinois at Urbana-Champaign.

Beyond the health and cognitive benefits children may gain from free and unstructured play outdoors, nature also provides them with a sense of wonder and a deeper understanding of our responsibility to take care of the Earth, says Richard Louv, author of "Last Child in the Woods: Saving Our Children from Nature Deficit-Disorder" (Algonquin Books, 2005). Yet increasingly, nature is the last place you'll find children, research shows.

Many factors have come together to push children indoors, he says, including land development and more people living in cities, additional demands on children's time—such as more homework and structured activities—video games and the Internet, and parental fear, particularly of strangers. In today's society of indoor children, personal connections with nature seem hard to come by, which threatens to lessen future generations' concerns about the environment, Louv says.

"Last time I checked, it was pretty tough to have a sense of wonder when you're playing 'Grand Theft Auto,'" Louv says.

"If we're raising a generation of children under protective house arrest, where does that lead us in terms of our connection to the natural world?"

As experts in child development and learning, psychologists are helping children reconnect with nature by conducting research, incorporating the outdoors into clinical interventions and educating parents, says Erickson, a director of early childhood mental health training programs at the University of Minnesota in Minneapolis.

"People often listen to what psychologists have to say when it comes to kids' learning and development," she says. "We really need to work as advocates and in our practices to think about the potential of nature to improve the health and well-being of children."

Green Is Good

Psychologists have actively studied the role nature plays in children's mental health since the early 1980s, when Harvard University biologist Edward O. Wilson, PhD, introduced his theory of "biophilia," which argues that humans have an innate affinity for the natural world. Now, a host of studies are showing just how essential outdoor activities are for the developing mind.

One of the most influential longitudinal studies, led by Cornell University environmental psychologist Nancy M. Wells, PhD, found that children who experienced the biggest increase in green space near their home after moving improved their cognitive functioning more than those who moved to areas with fewer natural resources nearby (*Environment and Behavior* (Vol. 32, No. 6). Similarly, in a study of 337 school-age children in rural upstate New York, Wells found that the presence of nearby nature bolsters a child's resilience against stress and adversity, particularly among those children who experience a high level of stress (*Environment and Behavior*, Vol. 35, No. 3).

But while such studies support the notion that nature is good for children, psychologists may need to act fast to get children back outside. A study by University of Maryland sociologist

Sandra Hofferth, PhD, shows that between 1997 and 2003, the amount of time children ages 9 to 12 spent participating in outdoor activities such as hiking, horseback riding, fishing, camping and gardening declined by 50 percent.

What are children doing instead? Playing video games, watching TV and spending time on the computer, Hofferth found.

Such activities are, of course, linked with the rise in childhood obesity. A 2004 National Health and Nutrition Examination Survey found that one-third of children and teens, ages 2 to 19, were overweight or at risk of becoming overweight. By 2010, about half of school-age children in North and South America will be overweight or obese, predicts an article in the *International Journal of Pediatric Obesity* (Vol. 1, No. 1).

Without building a connection to the natural world when they're young, it seems unlikely that children will possess much of an affiliation with Mother Earth as adults, says Wells. In fact, a 2006 study—led by Wells and published in *Children, Youth and Environments* (Vol. 16, No. 1)—suggests that childhood participation with nature may set individuals on a trajectory toward adult environmentalism.

"Kids are already hearing that polar bears don't have anywhere to rest. If we don't have them outside thinking that squirrels are fascinating, they may get overwhelmed and close down completely."

Meg Houlihan
Charlotte, N.C.

"This study shows that there really may be a connection between kids' experiences in nature and their later life attitudes and behaviors," Wells says.

Erickson agrees. "It's a principle of human nature that you care for what you know and what you love," says Erickson. "Learning about climate change just by studying it on the Internet or reading about it in books is one thing, but to come to know and love the natural world firsthand from an early age just gives you a different kind of motive [for preserving it]."

Reinventing Children of Nature

Practitioners can use this research as strong evidence for incorporating nature into their client interventions, says Erickson.

"Making time to get outside to play, run and explore could be a really important part of a treatment plan," she says.

Psychologists can also encourage school administrators to get children outside during the school day, by working with their state psychological associations to develop briefing papers for local school boards, contacting local news media to encourage coverage of the benefits of nature to children or leading volunteer efforts to plant gardens at a local schools, Erickson

recommends. Creative exploration and firsthand experience discovering nature appear to be the best ways for children to learn about a host of subjects—particularly, Erickson says. More recess time and greener playgrounds might also enable children to learn more effectively and improve a child's ability to concentrate in the classroom, says Kuo. In a study published in the September 2004 issue of the *American Journal of Public Health* (Vol. 94, No. 9), Kuo and her colleague, Andrea Faber Taylor, PhD, found that green outdoor activities reduced attention-deficit hyperactivity disorder symptoms significantly more than activities in built outdoor and indoor settings.

"If we had kids moving around and burning off energy, I think we would have much less difficulty with kids having trouble paying attention in the classroom," Erickson says.

Wells says research by psychologists and others may help determine whether there may be a "critical period" for children's exposure to the natural environment, and if so, when that might be.

Perhaps most importantly, psychologists are among those helping to educate the public—particularly parents—on the importance of getting children outside. In April, Erickson will help kick off a statewide children and nature awareness campaign in Minnesota, which will include television and radio coverage and public events—such as moonlight walks at a Minneapolis-area nature center—focused on specific steps parents and other caregivers can take to help renew children's interest in the natural world. Similar public outreach initiatives are also under way in New Hampshire, Massachusetts and California, among other states, according to the Children and Nature Network (www.cnaturenet.org), a national organization that Louv and Erickson help lead, dedicated to reconnecting children with nature.

Often, parents aren't aware of nature's benefits to their children, or they aren't sure how to tear their children away from the computer or television screen, says Meg Houlihan, PhD, a private practitioner in Charlotte, N.C., who speaks locally to parents and teachers about overcoming barriers to getting kids outside. She emphasizes gradual change: taking children out on the front lawn for an hour, for example.

"It's important to give the message to parents that it doesn't have to be a huge trip to Yellowstone to be nature," says Houlihan.

She tells parents to pick up a handful of paint chips from the hardware store and have their children find things in the backyard that match those colors, or to host a neighborhood scavenger hunt in the park. These types of activities help children build a love for nature through everyday interactions—with birds, trees and community gardens, for example. Only then will they be able to fully appreciate—and hopefully take action against—issues such as climate change, Houlihan says.

"Kids are already hearing that polar bears don't have anywhere to rest," she says. "If we don't have them outside thinking that squirrels are fascinating, they may get overwhelmed and close down completely."

Treatment and Prevention of Posttraumatic Stress Reactions in Children and Adolescents Exposed to Disasters and Terrorism: What Is the Evidence?

ANNETTE M. LA GRECA AND WENDY K. SILVERMAN

I n the United States and abroad, research has documented high levels of posttraumatic stress disorder (PTSD) and post-traumatic stress (PTS) reactions in children and adolescents exposed to catastrophic natural disasters (hurricanes, earthquakes, tsunamis, and floods; e.g., Goenjian et al., 2005; La Greca, Silverman, Vernberg, & Prinstein, 1996; Weems et al., 2007) and terrorist attacks (Hoven et al., 2005; Lengua, Long, Smith, & Meltzoff, 2005; see reviews by Comer & Kendall, 2007; Gurwitch, Sitterle, Young, & Pfefferbaum, 2002). The development of interventions for youths' reactions to natural disasters and acts of terrorism to prevent serious youth adjustment problems is of considerable public health significance (Vernberg, 2002).

This article summarizes existing evidence on the prevention and treatment of PTS reactions in youth exposed to natural disasters and terrorism, with an eye toward highlighting gaps in current knowledge and directions for future research. (For information on the prevalence and course of PTS and other reactions in children following disasters and terrorism, see the American Academy of Child and Adolescent Psychiatry, 1998; Gurwitch et al., 2002; Vogel & Vernberg, 1993; Yule, Udwin, & Bolton, 2002; for studies of risk factors of PTS reactions, see Comer & Kendall, 2007; Silverman & La Greca, 2002.)

Evidence-Based Interventions for PTS Reactions

A useful way to conceptualize postdisaster interventions is whether they were designed for the *immediate* aftermath of the event, the *short-term* recovery and rebuilding phase, or the *long-term* recovery phase (Vernberg, 2002); there has also been recent interest in predisaster efforts to prevent PTS reactions. Treatment goals depend on the time frame and context in which interventions are delivered.

Immediate Postimpact Phase (The Event through the First Few Weeks Postdisaster)

After a devastating natural disaster or act of terrorism, victims' concerns about personal safety and physical needs (such as food and shelter) are paramount (Vogel & Vernberg, 1993). Youth exposed to such events may also experience sudden loss and bereavement (Gurwitch et al., 2002). Psychological interventions provided during this period are *brief and present focused;* their main goal is to *reduce or prevent long-term psychological difficulties* (La Greca, 2008).

Critical Incident Stress Debriefing (CISD)

CISD was designed to relieve trauma-related distress by providing opportunities for victims to express their feelings, to understand that their responses are normal reactions to trauma, and to learn about common disaster reactions in a supportive context (Chemtob, Tomas, Law, & Cremniter, 1997). Mental health workers and disaster responders typically deliver CISD in field settings, such as community shelters.

There is currently no empirical support for CISD's effectiveness (Gibson, 2006; Rose, Bisson, & Wessely, 2003). In the only controlled study of youth that we are aware of, Stallard et al. (2006) compared a single session of CISD to a single-session "neutral discussion" control condition with 158 youth (7–18 years) who survived motor vehicle accidents. Significant improvements in PTS levels and reduction in anxiety and depression symptoms were evident in both the CISD and the control condition. Because both conditions produced improvement, it appears premature to recommend CISD. In addition, although Stallard et al reported no inadvertent negative effects from the intervention, concerns about using CISD include the possibility that recipients may be "retraumatized";

that the intervention may be insufficient to address the multiple, complex stressors resulting from disasters and terrorism; and that it may reduce further help-seeking behaviors because individuals may believe they have received sufficient care (La Greca, 2008; Ruzek et al., 2007).

Psychological First Aid (PFA)

PFA, which can be implemented in field settings such as schools and community crisis centers (Amaya-Jackson & March, 1995), was developed by disaster mental health experts from the National Child Traumatic Stress Network. It is an "evidence-informed" approach that is culturally informed and appropriate for developmental levels across the life span and can be flexibly delivered (Brymer et al., 2008; Vernberg et al., 2008).

PFA's key elements include promoting a sense of safety, "calming," self and community efficacy, connectedness, and hope (Brymer et al., 2008). It provides children with an opportunity to express their feelings through drawings and storytelling, to clarify areas of confusion, and to identify areas of need (Amaya-Jackson & March, 1995). PFA also allows mental health professionals and disaster responders to identify youth who are experiencing severe postdisaster reactions so that these youth may receive further assistance.

PFA appears promising as part of a comprehensive, post-disaster intervention strategy. However, controlled evaluations of PFA are scant (Brymer et al., 2008; Ruzek et al., 2007), probably because of the challenges of conducting postdisaster treatment research. Further, PFA requires trained personnel to administer, and many disaster and terrorism youth victims may not be present in the field settings, such as shelters, where PFA typically is delivered (La Greca, 2008).

Psychoeducational Materials

Relief (such as the American Red Cross and the Federal Emergency Management Agency) and mental health organizations (including the American Psychological Association, National Institute of Mental Health [NIMH], and the American Academy of Child and Adolescent Psychiatry) have developed psychoeducational brochures and fact sheets that provide useful information about children's coping; children's fears, worries, and security concerns; and how to encourage children to resume roles and routines following disasters (Prinstein, La Greca, Vernberg, & Silverman, 1996). Similar to CISD and PFA, however, no evidence is available on these materials' effectiveness, and some sophistication may be needed to adapt the materials to the specific disaster or event. Further, however, useful psychoeducational information alone is unlikely to be sufficient to alleviate severe PTS reactions in youth.

Summary

At present, there is no evidence that psychological interventions delivered in the immediate aftermath of disasters and terrorist events are effective for reducing short or long-term distress (Gibson, 2006; La Greca, 2008). Although PFA and well-designed psychoeducational materials are promising for certain purposes, we still need controlled evaluations of these materials. Moreover, it is unclear whether interventions should be implemented directly with children (as are PFA or CISD) or whether it would be more beneficial to target parents, teachers, or school counselors, who in turn can help children. The latter strategy may be more practical for reaching a large number of youth affected by disasters. On the other hand, "early detection" for further referral and treatment of youth with severe, acute responses might be as beneficial as universal interventions. We need further investigation of whether and how to deliver services in the aftermath of disasters.

Undoubtedly, the lack of evidence about the effectiveness of postdisaster interventions is directly related to the numerous challenges of conducting controlled research in the aftermath of disasters or terrorist events (such as ethical concerns regarding withholding treatment and difficulties obtaining Institutional Review Board [IRB] approval or funding). Interested readers should review *Methods for Disaster Mental Health Research* (Norris, Galea, Friedman, & Watson, 2006) and consult the Research Education in Disaster Mental Health [REDMH] website (www.redmh.org).

Until then, however, our "best practices" suggestions for this phase would be for caring adults (parents, teachers, and health professionals) to reassure children; to encourage (but not press) them to express their feelings; to provide information and "normalize" disaster reactions; to address their fears, worries, and security concerns as they arise; and to help them resume normal roles and routines. It is also important to help parents and teachers identify acute stress responses.

Short-Term Recovery Phase (First Few Weeks Postdisaster through the 1st Year)

Although most youth will recover during this period, as many as one third report severe or very severe levels of PTS reactions 3 months postdisaster, about 18% report severe or very severe levels 7 months postdisaster, and about 13% report such levels close to 1 year after the disaster event (e.g., La Greca et al., 1996). This highlights the need to expend efforts to reduce or prevent long-term youth psychological difficulties and promote positive adaptation. "High-risk" youth or those with high PTS reactions may require intensive psychological interventions.

To date, no controlled outcome studies are available for the interventions developed for this short-term recovery phase. These interventions typically provide psychoeducation, often in combination with cognitive behavioral therapy (CBT). In one of the few studies, Wolmer, Laor, Dedeoglu, Siev, and Yazgan (2005) conducted a classroom-based "School Reactivation Program" 4–5 months after a major 1999 earthquake in Turkey. In the program, which was led by teachers over a 4-week period, in eight 2-hr meetings ($N = 202$; 9–17 years), PTSD rates were reduced from 32% to 17% among treated youth. At 3-year follow-up, 33% of the treated youth were compared to 220 untreated control youth who reported similar levels of PTS symptoms and disaster exposure. Although PTS symptoms in both groups declined, almost 50% in both groups reported moderate to severe levels of PTS symptoms. More positively, however, teacher ratings of youth adaptive functioning were higher for treated than for untreated youth.

Several "empirically informed" psychoeducational manuals were developed to help youth cope with large-scale disasters, including *The Bushfire and Me: A Story of What Happened to Me and My Family* (Storm, McDermott, & Finlayson, 1994), *Helping Children Prepare for and Cope With Natural Disasters* (La Greca, Vernberg, Silverman, Vogel, & Prinstein, 1994), *After the Storm* (La Greca, Sevin, & Sevin, 2005), and *StArT: Strength*

After Trauma (Saltzman, 2007). Manuals focusing on coping with terrorism include *Healing After Trauma Skills* (Gurwitch & Messenbaugh, 1998) and *Helping America Cope: A Guide to Help Parents and Children Cope With the September 11th Terrorist Attacks* (La Greca, Sevin, & Sevin, 2001). Several intervention manuals, each focusing on specific youth symptom clusters (including PTS), were also developed after the September 11th attacks for "Project Liberty."

Overall, these "evidence-informed" manuals cover strategies for helping children and adolescents "process" the traumatic events in a supportive manner, developing effective coping strategies for dealing with feelings of distress and with ongoing stressors that result from the trauma, maintaining regular roles and routines, increasing social support, and preparing for future events. The manuals also contain "lessons" that teachers, parents, and mental health providers can use with children and provide information to help identify children with severe reactions. The Project Liberty PTSD manuals also provide information on developing trauma-focused narratives and prescribing graded in vivo or imaginal exposure tasks to therapeutically reactivate youth's traumatic disaster memories.

Many of the above materials require Internet connections (for downloads) or substantial funding to print the large number of copies needed after major disasters. The manuals typically require an eighth-grade reading level and may need adaptation to fit new disasters or to be used effectively by different adults (such as parent vs. teacher vs. counselor). Ongoing, open trial investigations for several of the manuals are assessing feasibility, counselor adherence, and preliminary evidence for effectiveness. Such efforts may set the stage for future randomized controlled trials.

Long-Term Recovery Phase (1 Year or More Postdisaster)

Most children recover within 1 year or more of devastating, traumatic events. However, a significant minority experience persistent, chronic stress reactions (Gurwitch et al., 2002; La Greca & Prinstein, 2002; Yule et al., 2002), which may be complicated by secondary stressors (including relocation and loss of family members). Current interventions typically target persistent or chronic youth PTSD reactions.

Cognitive-Behavioral Therapy

Exposure-based CBT is thought to promote habituation by targeting stimulus-response associations and correcting distorted cognitions (see Foa & Rothbaum, 1998), although determining exactly how this works requires further empirical verification. Prolonged exposure involves psychoeducation, breathing retraining, imaginal exposure to the trauma memory, and in vivo exposure to trauma reminders. Despite the scarcity of disaster-related studies, well-controlled studies with sexual abuse victims provide relatively strong evidence that CBT may reduce PTS in youth (e.g., Cohen, Deblinger, Mannarino, & Steer, 2004; Cohen, Mannarino, & Knudsen, 2005; Deblinger, Stauffer, & Steer, 2001), although follow-up data have been reported in only a few studies (e.g., Deblinger, Mannarino, Cohen, & Steer, 2006). A positive feature of this literature is that most of these studies have compared CBT to an active credible control comparison condition (such as client-centered therapy). Importantly, reductions in youth PTS (as well

as in depression and externalizing problem behaviors) have been significantly greater for CBT than for other comparison control conditions.

In the absence of any alternative intervention with supportive empirical evidence for traumatized youth, we recommend that CBT be used with children and adolescents traumatized by disasters and terrorism. Below, we summarize the open trials researchers have conducted in this area.

Multimodality Trauma Treatment

March, Amaya-Jackson, Murray, and Schulte (1998) evaluated an 18-week exposure-based CBT with 17 youth (10–15 years of age; average duration of PTSD was 1.5–2.5 years) who displayed PTSD after a single-stressor trauma (such as car accidents or shootings), including disasters (severe storms and fires). Multimodality trauma treatment focused on (a) habituating conditioned anxiety through narrative exposures, (b) modifying maladaptive trauma-related cognitions through positive self-talk and cognitive restructuring, (c) teaching adaptive coping strategies for disturbing feelings and physiological reactions, and (d) reducing co-occurring symptoms through problem-solving and self-management strategies. Several sessions included imaginal exposures, and in vivo exposures were assigned out of session.

March et al. (1998) used a single-case multiple-baseline design, and their findings revealed significant improvements in clinician-rated PTSD, which were maintained at 6-month follow-up. They also observed improvements in child ratings of depression, anxiety, and anger. Of the 14 treatment completers, 8 (57%) no longer met PTSD criteria at posttreatment and 12 (86%) no longer met criteria at 6-month follow-up. These findings provide initial evidence for the effectiveness of exposure-based CBT, although further randomized controlled studies using larger samples of children are needed.

Brief Trauma-/Grief-Focused Psychotherapy

Goenjian et al. (1997) evaluated a school-based brief trauma-/grief-focused intervention that contained treatment components similar to exposure-based CBT with 64 adolescents (median age = 13.2 years) who experienced a devastating earthquake in Armenia and displayed high levels of PTS and depressive reactions 1.5 years later. Because of limited resources, schools and students were not randomly assigned; 35 youth participated in the treatment and 29 were not treated. The intervention included two individual and four classroom sessions over 3 weeks that addressed reconstructing and reprocessing traumatic experiences and associated thoughts and feelings, identifying trauma reminders and cues and improving tolerance for and reactivity to these reminders and cues, enhancing social support-seeking behaviors, enhancing coping strategies, dealing with grief and bereavement, and identifying missed developmental opportunities and promoting positive development.

Treated adolescents had significantly lower rates of PTSD (28%) than untreated adolescents (69%) at 18 months posttreatment (i.e., 3 years postearthquake). Estimated rates of depression symptoms did not change from pretreatment (46%) to follow-up (46%) for the treated adolescents but increased significantly (from 35% to 75%) for the untreated adolescents. In a second follow-up, 5 years postdisaster (Goenjian et al., 2005), reductions in youth PTS symptoms were 3 times greater for the treated group than for the untreated comparison group. Untreated adolescents also showed significant increases in depression. This nonrandomized trial suggests the importance of intervening with youth in the aftermath of natural disasters because PTS symptoms did not necessarily remit spontaneously.

School-Based Psychosocial Interventions

Chemtob, Nakashima, and Hamada (2002) screened children enrolled in all of the public elementary schools in Kauai, HI (Grades 2–6; $n = 3,864$) for high levels of PTS symptoms 2 years after Hurricane Iniki. The 248 children (6.4%) with high PTSD scores (above the 94th percentile) were randomly assigned to consecutively treated cohorts (i.e., children (6.4%) with high PTSD scores (above the 94th percentile) were randomly assigned to consecutively treated cohorts (i.e., children awaiting treatment served as wait-list controls). Within each cohort, children were randomly assigned to individual or group treatment. Four weekly sessions focused on helping children (a) restore a sense of safety, (b) grieve losses and renew attachments, (c) express disaster-related anger, and (d) achieve closure about the disaster. Treated children reported significant reductions in PTS symptoms and maintained these reductions at 12-month follow-up. Although the group and individual treatment approaches did not differ significantly, more children completed group treatment (95%) than individual treatment (85%).

This study is important because it demonstrates the feasibility of screening a large population of disaster-affected children 2 years postdisaster, as well as the feasibility and efficacy of a brief school-based psychosocial intervention. Future studies would benefit from incorporating measures of clinically significant change and evaluating potential moderators of treatment outcome (Kazdin, 2002).

Eye Movement Desensitization Processing (EMDR)

EMDR aims to reduce distress associated with traumatic memories by engaging clients' attention to an external stimulus (such as by tracking a therapist's finger movements back and forth with one's eye movements) while clients are concurrently focusing on the distressing memories (i.e., engaged in imaginal exposures; Shapiro, 1989). Eye movements are most often used as the external stimulus to which clients are asked to attend, but other stimuli such as hand tapping and auditory stimulation can also be used (Shapiro, 1989). Chemtob, Nakashima, and Carlson (2002) reported the results of EMDR among 32 children (median age = 8.4 years) who were nonresponders at 1-year follow-up of a prior intervention for disaster-related PTS. Using an ABA design plus follow-up, Group 1 was assessed at pretreatment, provided treatment (three weekly sessions), and reassessed at posttreatment. Group 2 consisted of wait-listed children who were assessed at baseline; then, following treatment for Group 1, they were reassessed at pretreatment, provided treatment, and assessed at posttreatment. Both groups were assessed 6 months posttreatment. EMDR involved the identification of distressing memories and images, cognitive restructuring, and inducing sets of eye movements by having the child track the therapist's hand movements back and forth while concentrating on the traumatic memories and images.

On child-rated symptoms of PTS, anxiety, and depression, both the immediate and the delayed treatment groups showed significant declines from pre- to posttreatment that were maintained at 6-month follow-up. Although the study demonstrated positive effects, the design did not include an active comparison control condition. Moreover, because EMDR contains many of the same components as exposure-based CBT, it is possible that CBT elements, rather than eye movements, contributed to the positive effects.

Predisaster Preventive Interventions

Because it is difficult to conduct controlled investigations after unexpected disasters or terrorist attacks, efforts are under way to examine ways of screening children *even before a disaster strikes* to identify those who may be vulnerable to experiencing severe reactions and to develop predisaster "resilience" programs. Along with Claudio Ortiz, and with support from the Terrorism and Disaster Branch of the National Center for Child Traumatic Stress (led by Dr. Pfefferbaum), we have developed and gathered preliminary data on a "Resilience Building Screen" designed to identify children who are at risk for showing impairing, negative reactions to the cues, and signals of disasters prior to personal experience with a hurricane or natural disaster (Silverman, La Greca, & Ortiz, 2004).

The Screen is based on empirical research showing that the most consistent predictors of enduring PTS reactions to hurricanes are (a) aspects of traumatic exposure, (b) lack of a social support network, and (c) psychopathology before the traumatic event (e.g., La Greca, Silverman, & Wasserstein, 1998; Lengua et al., 2005; Weems et al., 2007; for a review, see Silverman & La Greca, 2002). Other predictors, less consistently found in the literature, include children's coping strategies and parental reactions. Items for the Screen map onto each of these predictors or variables. Analyses for this project are ongoing; our primary objective is to develop a screening measure to identify children who might benefit from a predisaster "Resilience Building Training" program. Such a program would focus on targeting and enhancing those variables the Screen shows to be deficient (such as children's coping strategies) so that youth might be better prepared for a disaster. On a related note, we are revising *After the Storm* (La Greca et al., 2005) to help youth in the aftermath of hurricanes; a *Before the Storm* version will include lessons on preparing for storms and coping with hurricane-related stressors (e.g., disruption of normal routines). This program could then be implemented in hurricane-prone areas, and its effectiveness evaluated when a disaster or near-disaster strikes.

Conclusions

Remarkably, few evidence-based interventions are available for children and adolescents exposed to natural disasters and acts of terrorism. The few well-controlled studies have focused on children with persistent PTSD, occurring a year or more after the disaster or event and suggest that exposure-based CBT interventions are promising. We know considerably less about interventions designed for the immediate aftermath of a disaster or during the short-term recovery phase. Until further studies have been conducted, mental health professionals are advised to draw on "evidence-informed" psychoeducational materials and CBT procedures for helping children and adolescents cope with the aftermath of disasters and acts of terrorism.

Although the limited amount of evidence on interventions for children following disasters and acts of terrorism is disheartening, this reflects the challenges of conducting controlled outcome research following such events, especially in their immediate aftermath (La Greca, 2006; La Greca, Silverman, Vernberg, & Roberts, 2002). These challenges include numerous ethical and practical constraints, including ethical concerns regarding withholding treatment and difficulties obtaining IRB approval or funding. Schools, for example, are often in chaos after destructive communitywide disasters and have more pressing priorities than conducting research (La Greca, 2006). Moreover, significant adults in children's lives also are affected by the disaster and may be unaware of children's distress. Nevertheless, continued research is important, and we recommend that interested readers review *Methods for Disaster Mental Health Research* (Norris et al., 2006) and consult the REDMH website: www.redmh.org.

We emphasize that children and adolescents exposed to disasters and acts of terrorism are likely to need *more than* interventions that focus exclusively on PTSD reactions because their reactions are often complex and multifaceted and may include other problems (such as grief, depression, and anxiety). Additional intervention components (dealing with grief and bereavement, handling anger, and promoting coping) are likely to be important adjuncts to PTSD-oriented interventions. Although further evidence is needed, children and adolescents with complex disaster reactions might profit from CBT treatments that focus on comorbid psychological reactions, in addition to PTSD reactions.

References

Amaya-Jackson, L., & March, J. S. (1995). Posttraumatic stress disorder. In J. S. March (Ed.), *Anxiety disorders in children and adolescents* (pp. 276–300). New York: Guilford.

American Academy of Child and Adolescent Psychiatry. (1998). Practice parameters for the assessment and treatment of children and adolescents with posttraumatic stress disorder. *Journal of the American Academy of Child and Adolescent Psychiatry, 37*(Suppl.), 4S–26S.

Brymer, M. J., Steinberg, A. M., Vernberg, E. M., Layne, C. M., Watson, P. J., Jacobs, A. K., et al. (2008). Acute interventions for children and adolescents exposed to trauma. In E. Foa, T. Keane, M. Friedman, & J. A. Cohen (Eds.), *Effective treatments for PTSD* (2nd ed., pp. 106–116). New York: Guilford.

Chemtob, C. M., Nakashima, J., & Carlson, J. G. (2002). Brief treatment for elementary school children with disaster-related posttraumatic stress disorder: A field study. *Journal of Clinical Psychology, 58,* 99–112.

Chemtob, C. M., Nakashima, J. P., & Hamada, R. S. (2002). Psychosocial intervention for postdisaster trauma symptoms in elementary school children: A controlled community field study. *Archives of Pediatric and Adolescent Medicine, 156,* 211–216.

Chemtob, C. M., Tomas, S., Law, W., & Cremniter, D. (1997). Postdisaster psychosocial intervention: A field study of the impact of debriefing on psychological distress. *American Journal of Psychiatry, 154,* 415–417.

Cohen, J. A., Deblinger, E., Mannarino, A. P., & Steer, R. A. (2004). A multisite randomized controlled study of sexually abused, multiply traumatized children with PTSD: Initial treatment outcome. *Journal of the American Academy of Child and Adolescent Psychiatry, 43,* 393–402.

Cohen, J. A., Mannarino, A. P., & Knudsen, K. (2005). Treating sexually abused children: 1 year follow-up of a randomized controlled trial. *Child Abuse and Neglect, 29,* 135–145.

Comer, J. S., & Kendall, P. C. (2007). Terrorism: The psychological impact on youth. *Clinical Psychology: Science and Practice, 14,* 179–214.

Deblinger, E., Mannarino, A. P., Cohen, J. A., & Steer, R. A. (2006). A follow-up study of a multisite, randomized, controlled trial for children with sexual abuse-related PTSD symptoms. *Journal of the American Academy of Child and Adolescent Psychiatry, 45,* 1474–1484.

Deblinger, E., Stauffer, L., & Steer, R. (2001). Comparative efficacies of supportive and cognitive behavioral group therapies for young children who have been sexually abused and their nonoffending mothers. *Child Maltreatment, 6,* 332–343.

Foa, E. B., & Rothbaum, B. O. (1998). *Treating the trauma of rape: Cognitive-behavioral therapy for PTSD.* New York: Guilford.

Gibson, L. E. (2006). *A review of the published empirical literature regarding early- and later-stage interventions for individuals exposed to traumatic stress.* Research Education Disaster Mental Health. Retrieved September 10, 2007, from http://redmh.org/research/general/treatmt.html

Goenjian, A. K., Karayan, I., Pynoos, R. S., Minassian, D., Najarian, L. M., Steinberg, A. M., et al. (1997). Outcome of psychotherapy among early adolescents after trauma. *American Journal of Psychiatry, 154,* 536–542.

Goenjian, A. K., Walling, D., Steinberg, A. M., Karayan, I., Najarian, L. M., & Pynoos, R. (2005). A prospective study of posttraumatic stress and depressive reactions among treated and untreated adolescents 5 years after a catastrophic disaster. *American Journal of Psychiatry, 162,* 2302–2308.

Gurwitch, R. H., & Messenbaugh, A. K. (1998). *Healing after trauma: Skills manual for helping children.* Oklahoma City, OK: Author.

Gurwitch, R. H., Sitterle, K. A., Young, B. H., & Pfefferbaum, B. (2002). The aftermath of terrorism. In A. M. La Greca, W. K. Silverman, E. M. Vernberg, & M. C. Roberts (Eds.), *Helping children cope with disasters and terrorism* (pp. 327–358). Washington, DC: American Psychological Association.

Hoven, C. W., Duarte, C. S., Lucas, C. P., Wu, P., Mandell, D. J., Goodwin, R. D., et al. (2005). Psychopathology among New York City public school children 6 months after September 11. *Archives of General Psychiatry, 62,* 545–552.

Kazdin, A. (2002). A school based psychosocial intervention was effective in children with persistent post-disaster trauma symptoms. *Evidence Based Mental Health, 5,* 76.

La Greca, A. M. (2006). School-based studies of children following disasters. In F. Norris, S. Galesto, D. Reissman, & P. Watson (Eds.), *Methods for disaster mental health research* (pp. 141–157). New York: Guilford.

La Greca, A. M. (2008). Interventions for posttraumatic stress in children and adolescents following natural disasters and acts of terrorism. In M. C. Roberts, D. Elkin, & R. Steele (Eds.), *Handbook of evidence based therapies for children and adolescents* (pp. 137–157). New York: Springer.

La Greca, A. M., & Prinstein, M. J. (2002). Hurricanes and tornadoes. In A. M. La Greca, W. K. Silverman, E. M. Vernberg, & M. C. Roberts (Eds.), *Helping children cope with disasters and terrorism* (pp. 107–138). Washington, DC: American Psychological Association.

La Greca, A. M., Sevin, S., & Sevin, E. (2001). *Helping America cope: A guide for parents and children in the aftermath of the September 11th national disaster.* Miami, FL: Sevendippity. Retrieved September 24, 2007, from www.7-dippity .com/index.html

La Greca, A. M., Sevin, S., & Sevin, E. (2005). *After the storm.* Miami, FL: Sevendippity. Retrieved September 24, 2007, from www.7-dippity.com/index.html

La Greca, A. M., Silverman, W. K., Vernberg, E. M., & Prinstein, M. (1996). Symptoms of posttraumatic stress after Hurricane Andrew: A prospective study. *Journal of Consulting and Clinical Psychology, 64,* 712–723.

La Greca, A. M., Silverman, W. K., Vernberg, E. M., & Roberts, M. C. (2002). Children and disasters: Future directions for research and public policy. In A. M. La Greca, W. K. Silverman, E. M. Vernberg, & M. C. Roberts (Eds.), *Helping children cope with disasters and terrorism* (pp. 405–423). Washington, DC: American Psychological Association.

La Greca, A. M., Silverman, W. K., & Wasserstein, S. B. (1998). Children's predisaster functioning as a predictor of posttraumatic stress following Hurricane Andrew. *Journal of Consulting and Clinical Psychology, 66,* 883–892.

La Greca, A. M., Vernberg, E. M., Silverman, W. K., Vogel, A., & Prinstein, M. (1994). *Helping children cope with natural disasters: A manual for school personnel.* Miami, FL: Author.

Lengua, L. J., Long, A. C., Smith, K. I., & Meltzoff, A. N. (2005). Preattack symptomatology and temperament as predictors of children's responses to the September 11th terrorist attacks. *Journal of Child Psychology and Psychiatry, 46,* 631–645.

March, J. S., Amaya-Jackson, L., Murray, M. C., & Schulte, A. (1998). Cognitive-behavioral psychotherapy for children and adolescents with posttraumatic stress disorder after a single-incident stressor. *Journal of the American Academy of Child and Adolescent Psychiatry, 37,* 585–593.

Norris, F. H., Galea, S., Friedman, M. J., & Watson, P. J. (Eds.). (2006). *Methods for disaster mental health research.* New York: Guilford.

Prinstein, M. J., La Greca, A. M., Vernberg, E. M., & Silverman, W. K. (1996). Children's coping assistance after a natural disaster. *Journal of Clinical Child Psychology, 25,* 463–475.

Rose, S., Bisson, J., & Wessely, S. (2003). A systematic review of single-session psychological interventions ("debriefing") following trauma. *Psychotherapy and Psychosomatics, 72,* 176–184.

Ruzek, J. I., Brymer, M. J., Jacobs, A. K., Layne, C. M., Vernberg, E. M., & Watson, P. J. (2007). Psychological first aid. *Journal of Mental Health Counseling, 29,* 17–49.

Saltzman, W. (2007). *StArT: Strength after trauma: A modular intervention for children and adolescents affected by hurricanes.* Los Angeles: Author.

Shapiro, F. (1989). Eye movement desensitization: A new treatment for post-traumatic stress disorder. *Journal of Behavior Therapy and Experimental Psychiatry, 20,* 211–217.

Silverman, W. K., & La Greca, A. M. (2002). Children experiencing disasters: Definitions, reactions, and predictors of outcomes. In A. M. La Greca, W. K. Silverman, E. M. Vernberg, & M. C. Roberts (Eds.), *Helping children cope with disasters and terrorism* (pp. 11–34). Washington, DC: American Psychological Association.

Silverman, W. K., La Greca, A. M., & Ortiz, C.D. (2004, July). Resilience building in children prior to traumatic exposure: Screening considerations. In R. H. Gurwitch (Chair), *Trauma risk factors and resilience: Making connections.* Symposium presented at the annual meeting of the American Psychological Association, Honolulu, HI.

Stallard, P., Velleman, R., Salter, E., Howse, I., Yule, W., & Taylor, G. (2006). A randomised controlled trial to determine the effectiveness of an early psychological intervention with children involved in road traffic accidents. *Journal of Child Psychology and Psychiatry, 47,* 127–134.

Storm, V., McDermott, B., & Finlayson, D. (1994). *The bushfire and me: A story of what happened to me and my family.* Newtown, Australia: VBD Publications.

Vernberg, E. M. (2002). Intervention approaches following disasters. In A. M. La Greca, W. K. Silverman, E. M. Vernberg, & M. C. Roberts (Eds.), *Helping children cope with disasters and terrorism* (pp. 55–72). Washington, DC: American Psychological Association.

Vernberg, E. M., Steinberg, A. M., Jacobs, A. K., Brymer, M. J., Watson, P. J., Osofsky, J. D., et al. (2008). Innovations in disaster mental health: Psychological first aid. *Professional Psychology: Research and Practice, 39,* 381–388.

Vogel, J., & Vernberg, E. M. (1993). Children's psychological responses to disaster. *Journal of Clinical Child Psychology, 22,* 464–484.

Weems, C., Pina, A. A., Costa, N. M., Watts, S. E., Taylor, L. K., & Cannon, M. F. (2007). Predisaster trait anxiety and negative affect predict posttraumatic stress in youths after Hurricane Katrina. *Journal of Consulting and Clinical Psychology, 75,* 154–159.

Wolmer, L., Laor, N., Dedeoglu, C., Siev, J., & Yazgan, Y. (2005). Teacher mediated intervention after disaster: A controlled three-year follow-up of children's functioning. *Journal of Child Psychology and Psychiatry, 46,* 1161–1168.

Yule, W., Udwin, O., & Bolton, D. (2002). Mass transportation disasters. In A. M. La Greca, W. K. Silverman, E. M. Vernberg, & M. C. Roberts (Eds.), *Helping children cope with disasters and terrorism* (pp. 223–240). Washington, DC: American Psychological Association.

Correspondence concerning this article should be addressed to **Annette M. La Greca,** Department of Psychology, University of Miami, PO Box 249229, Coral Gables, FL 33124; e-mail: alagreca@ miami.edu.

Test-Your-Knowledge Form

We encourage you to photocopy and use this page as a tool to assess how the articles in *Annual Editions* expand on the information in your textbook. By reflecting on the articles you will gain enhanced text information. You can also access this useful form on a product's book support website at www.mhhe.com/cls

NAME: DATE:

_____

TITLE AND NUMBER OF ARTICLE:

_____

BRIEFLY STATE THE MAIN IDEA OF THIS ARTICLE:

_____

LIST THREE IMPORTANT FACTS THAT THE AUTHOR USES TO SUPPORT THE MAIN IDEA:

_____

WHAT INFORMATION OR IDEAS DISCUSSED IN THIS ARTICLE ARE ALSO DISCUSSED IN YOUR TEXTBOOK OR OTHER READINGS THAT YOU HAVE DONE? LIST THE TEXTBOOK CHAPTERS AND PAGE NUMBERS:

_____

LIST ANY EXAMPLES OF BIAS OR FAULTY REASONING THAT YOU FOUND IN THE ARTICLE:

_____

LIST ANY NEW TERMS/CONCEPTS THAT WERE DISCUSSED IN THE ARTICLE, AND WRITE A SHORT DEFINITION:

We Want Your Advice

ANNUAL EDITIONS revisions depend on two major opinion sources: one is our Advisory Board, listed in the front of this volume, which works with us in scanning the thousands of articles published in the public press each year; the other is you—the person actually using the book. Please help us and the users of the next edition by completing the prepaid article rating form on this page and returning it to us. Thank you for your help!

ANNUAL EDITIONS: Child Growth and Development 11/12

ARTICLE RATING FORM

Here is an opportunity for you to have direct input into the next revision of this volume.
We would like you to rate each of the articles listed below, using the following scale:

1. **Excellent: should definitely be retained**
2. **Above average: should probably be retained**
3. **Below average: should probably be deleted**
4. **Poor: should definitely be deleted**

Your ratings will play a vital part in the next revision.
Please mail this prepaid form to us as soon as possible.
Thanks for your help!

RATING	ARTICLE	RATING	ARTICLE
	1. New Calculator Factors Chances for Very Premature Infants		22. A Profile of Bullying at School
	2. Genes in Context: Gene–Environment Interplay and the Origins of Individual Differences in Behavior		23. When Girls and Boys Play: What Research Tells Us
	3. Effects of Prenatal Social Stress on Offspring Development: Pathology or Adaptation?		24. Playtime in Peril
	4. Infants' Differential Processing of Female and Male Faces		25. The Role of Neurobiological Deficits in Childhood Antisocial Behavior
	5. The Other-Race Effect Develops during Infancy: Evidence of Perceptual Narrowing		26. Children of Lesbian and Gay Parents
	6. New Advances in Understanding Sensitive Periods in Brain Development		27. Evidence of Infants' Internal Working Models of Attachment
	7. Contributions of Neuroscience to Our Understanding of Cognitive Development		28. Parental Divorce and Children's Adjustment
	8. It's Fun, but Does It Make You Smarter?		29. Within-Family Differences in Parent–Child Relations across the Life Course
	9. Language and Children's Understanding of Mental States		30. The Messy Room Dilemma: When to Ignore Behavior, When to Change It
	10. Developmental Narratives of the Experiencing Child		31. The Role of Parental Control in Children's Development in Western and East Asian Countries
	11. Social Cognitive Development: A New Look		32. Fatal Distraction: Forgetting a Child in the Backseat of a Car Is a Horrifying Mistake. Is It a Crime?
	12. Future Thinking in Young Children		33. Siblings Play Formative, Influential Role as 'Agents of Socialization'
	13. Talking about Science in Museums		34. Goodbye to Girlhood
	14. When Should a Kid Start Kindergarten?		35. Trials for Parents Who Chose Faith over Medicine
	15. Should Learning Be Its Own Reward?		36. Childhood's End
	16. Social Awareness + Emotional Skills = Successful Kids		37. How to Win the Weight Battle
	17. A Neurobiological Perspective on Early Human Deprivation		38. The Epidemic That Wasn't
	18. Don't!: The Secret of Self-Control		39. The Positives of Caregiving: Mothers' Experiences Caregiving for a Child with Autism
	19. Children's Capacity to Develop Resiliency: How to Nurture It		40. Three Reasons Not to Believe in an Autism Epidemic
	20. Emotions and the Development of Childhood Depression: Bridging the Gap		41. Getting Back to the Great Outdoors
	21. Children's Social and Moral Reasoning about Exclusion		42. Treatment and Prevention of Posttraumatic Stress Reactions in Children and Adolescents Exposed to Disasters and Terrorism: What Is the Evidence?

ABOUT YOU

Name   Date

Are you a teacher? ☐ A student? ☐
Your school's name

Department

Address   City   State   Zip

School telephone #

YOUR COMMENTS ARE IMPORTANT TO US!

Please fill in the following information:
For which course did you use this book?

Did you use a text with this ANNUAL EDITION? ☐ yes ☐ no
What was the title of the text?

What are your general reactions to the Annual Editions concept?

Have you read any pertinent articles recently that you think should be included in the next edition? Explain.

Are there any articles that you feel should be replaced in the next edition? Why?

Are there any World Wide Websites that you feel should be included in the next edition? Please annotate.

May we contact you for editorial input? ☐ yes ☐ no
May we quote your comments? ☐ yes ☐ no

NOTES

NOTES

NOTES

NOTES